"Yarhouse and Tan's second edition of *Sexuality and Sex Therapy* is a must-read for clinicians and students alike. Their Christian and theological approach provides a strong foundation and lens for practical application. Each of the sexual disorders are thoroughly introduced with practical insight and tools for practice. This is a foundational text for both counselors and ministers, especially for those that have not received professional training, as they work with these personal and sensitive issues. I highly recommend this book as required reading for students, new counselors, and ministers."

Corey Gilbert, author of *I Can't Say That! Going Beyond the Talk* and *I Can't Say That! Parent Workbook*, professor of counseling psychology at Corban University, and founder of The HealingLives Center in Salem, Oregon

"This book delivers clarity in a comprehensive manner, the key to a great textbook. The authors again provide both students and practitioners alike a great survey of the topics that affect the sex therapy field and the field itself from a Christian perspective."

Kimberly Lee, licensed marriage and family therapist, certified sex therapist, and owner of the Center for Sexual and Relational Healing

"The essential textbook for Christian therapists is updated and revised to incorporate current research as well as developments in the broader culture. *Sexuality and Sex Therapy* is a critical read for any active clinician working with Christian clients. While this text began its life as a textbook specifically for sex therapists, it has now become a fundamental tool for all therapists, whether seeing couples, families, adults, or children. While issues of sexuality, gender identity, and sex therapy may have been a specialized niche in the 1990s, it is likely that every therapist will encounter these topics in general therapy. Not just recommended, this book is mandatory for any serious Christian therapist."

Joshua Matlack, psychologist and outpatient therapist at Pine Rest Christian Mental Health Services

"With culturally relevant and compassionate consideration of humanity's current social, spiritual, and political state, Yarhouse and Tan bring a fresh perspective and updated research on sexual dysfunctions, disorders, treatment, and other clinical considerations from a fundamental Christian worldview. This text offers a comprehensive understanding of human sexuality and encourages curiosity and dialogue around the theological and scriptural integration of redemption and transformation from sexual brokenness to intimacy with Christ and others."

Vanessa Snyder, professor at Richmont Graduate University with the Institute for Sexual Wholeness and licensed therapist and certified sex therapist at Resilience Source in Roswell, GA

"This resource is indispensable for professionals navigating the complexity between sexuality and faith. This edition integrates up-to-date research with Christian theology, addressing significant topics like non-normative sexualities, gender dysphoria, and societal trends, making it invaluable for clinicians, pastoral caregivers, and scholars. This comprehensive guide equips readers to handle diverse client needs while remaining true to their faith, demonstrating Yarhouse and Tan's commitment to merging scientific understanding and Christian values in sex therapy."

Danisa Suarez, certified sex therapist with CCI Counseling

"If you are wanting to become a Christian sex therapist or desire an understanding of sex therapy from a Christian perspective, this is an all-encompassing read. When I finished the book, I felt like I had taken a refresher course in sex therapy. Yarhouse and Tan have masterfully conveyed some of the difficult dynamics of approaching such sensitive and complex aspects of sexuality with Christlike compassion. The layout of the book is a helpful guide in challenging the reader to face honestly one's own comfort and struggles around sexuality and to process out ambivalence. Great resource!"

Deborah Wade, certified sex therapist, licensed marriage and family therapist, and founder of ACTSolutions at The Gathering Place

"Yarhouse and Tan's updated edition of *Sexuality and Sex Therapy* covers all of the key areas necessary to effectively work in the sphere of human sexuality and does so in a faithfully Christian way. This resource is holistic, thoughtful, and expansive in its treatment of so many considerations important to Christian clinicians at a time when the sexuality landscape is increasingly complex. It is an essential text for developing and seasoned clinicians alike and brilliantly attunes to the specific questions of those working and living at the intersection of faith and human sexuality."

Julia Sadusky, owner of Lux Counseling and Consulting and author of *Start Talking to Your Kids About Sex*

"The second edition of *Sexuality and Sex Therapy* advances us in responding to the current complexities of sexuality from a firm Christian foundation and scholarly research. Yarhouse and Tan make a strong case that because Christianity holds a high view of sexuality and sexual expression, a Christian worldview provides motivation for the study and practice of sex therapy. They also highlight that being a Christian is not a substitute for professional competence. Their updated work provides us with a much-needed resource with a value-added component that is a tremendous enhancement to what is offered in the field today."

C. Gary Barnes, professor of counseling at Dallas Theological Seminary and director of the Institute for Sexual Wholeness

"Yarhouse and Tan offer a groundbreaking and invaluable resource with *Sexuality and Sex Therapy*. This comprehensive guide uniquely bridges the gap between faith and practice, providing an insightful, in-depth review of sex therapy through a distinctly Christian lens. Whether you're a new therapist seeking a solid foundation or a seasoned clinician exploring the treatment of sexual difficulties, this book is a must-have for anyone looking to enhance their understanding and approach to sexuality and therapy. An essential read for every student and practitioner eager to deepen their expertise."

Josh Spurlock, founder of MyCounselor.Online and developer of Neuroscience Informed Christian Counseling (NICC)

MARK A. YARHOUSE
and ERICA S. N. TAN

SEXUALITY

AND SEX

THERAPY

SECOND EDITION

A COMPREHENSIVE
CHRISTIAN APPRAISAL

ivp
Academic
An imprint of InterVarsity Press
Downers Grove, Illinois

InterVarsity Press
P.O. Box 1400 | Downers Grove, IL 60515-1426
ivpress.com | email@ivpress.com

InterVarsity Press® is the publishing division of InterVarsity Christian Fellowship/USA®. For more information, visit intervarsity.org.

All Scripture quotations, unless otherwise indicated, are taken from The Holy Bible, New International Version®, NIV®. Copyright © 1973, 1978, 1984, 2011 by Biblica, Inc.™ Used by permission of Zondervan. All rights reserved worldwide. www.zondervan.com. The "NIV" and "New International Version" are trademarks registered in the United States Patent and Trademark Office by Biblica, Inc.™

While any stories in this book are true, some names and identifying information may have been changed to protect the privacy of individuals.

Figure 1. The Organs Of The Human Female Reproductive System. Encyclopaedia Britannica/Universal Images Group/ Getty Images. Used by permission.
Figure 2. The Organs Of The Human Male Reproductive System. Encyclopaedia Britannica/Universal Images Group/ Getty Images. Used by permission.

The publisher cannot verify the accuracy or functionality of website URLs used in this book beyond the date of publication.

Cover design: David Fassett
Interior design: Daniel van Loon
Image: © tomozina / iStock / Getty Images Plus

ISBN 978-1-5140-1097-6 (print) | ISBN 978-1-5140-1098-3 (digital)

Printed in the United States of America ∞

Library of Congress Cataloging-in-Publication Data
Names: Yarhouse, Mark A., 1968- author. | Tan, Erica Sok-Nyee, author.
Title: Sexuality and sex therapy : a comprehensive Christian appraisal /
    Mark A. Yarhouse and Erica S. N. Tan.
Description: Second edition. | Downers Grove, IL : InterVarsity Press,
    [2025] | Series: Christian association for psychological studies books |
    Includes bibliographical references and index.
Identifiers: LCCN 2024031442 (print) | LCCN 2024031443 (ebook) | ISBN
    9781514010976 (hardcover) | ISBN 9781514010983 (ebook)
Subjects: LCSH: Sex–Religious aspects–Christianity. | Sex therapy.
Classification: LCC HQ61 .Y37 2025 (print) | LCC HQ61 (ebook) | DDC
    261.8/357–dc23/eng/20240820
LC record available at https://lccn.loc.gov/2024031442
LC ebook record available at https://lccn.loc.gov/2024031443

32   31   30   29   28   27   26   25 | 13   12   11   10   9   8   7   6   5   4   3   2   1

CONTENTS

PREFACE

THE SECOND EDITION OF *Sexuality and Sex Therapy: A Comprehensive Christian Appraisal* updates key research findings in each of the chapters. We also updated societal trends in the areas of gender identity, non-normative sexualities, and other areas of interest in the field of sexuality and sex therapy.

Since the first edition of *Sexuality and Sex Therapy*, we have also contributed to an integration resource (Hathaway & Yarhouse, 2021) that organizes integration into various domains: worldview, theoretical, applied, personal, and role integration. Worldview integration attempts to reposition the field of psychology on a Christian worldview, so in the area of sexuality and sex therapy, when we are repositioning sex therapy on a Christian worldview, we are engaging in worldview integration. Theoretical integration engages the personality theories associated with dominant approaches to psychology, and when Christians look for commonalities and identify points of disagreement, we are engaging in theoretical integration; this occurs in the study of sex therapy as well. Applied integration has to do with the practical dimensions of our work. When clinicians meet with couples to address sexual concerns and draw on Christian protocols and related resources, they are engaging in applied integration, and this happens frequently in the area of sex therapy as Christians either develop explicitly integrative protocols or adapt existing protocols for their work with Christian couples. Personal integration has to do with the life of the Christian engaged in the study of sexuality and the practice of sex therapy. Role integration has to do with tensions that arise when Christians serve the public and the profession as licensed mental health professionals, in this case as sex therapists. The societally granted privilege of being a mental health professional can come with professional expectations that can at times reflect challenges for the Christian. We will reference these domains, as appropriate, throughout this second edition of *Sexuality and Sex Therapy*.

Many people in our field have shared that there is a need for a resource for Christians engaged in the study of sexuality and the clinical practice of therapy/counseling/ministry. We do see a number of quality texts on the integration of Christianity and sexuality, broadly understood, and we do see an emerging number of practical resources for applied integration for Christians who conduct sex therapy. However, what we did not see was more of an integration textbook that provides students with a primer in this important area. We both felt a desire to take on what became quite a challenging undertaking. You will see upon reading the book that rather than creating a radically new model of sex therapy or the final word on integration in this area, we draw attention to what theorists have gotten right (theoretical integration) and how their insights can be understood and acknowledged, while relying more on a Christian view of the person and of sexuality and sexual expression (worldview integration).

We do this through a couple of steps. First, we explore theological perspectives on sexuality from Christian tradition and Scripture. This is primarily worldview integration. Although we might be tempted to treat the Bible as a handbook for sex therapy or sexual functioning, we see Scripture as providing moral clarity in many areas, while also providing several principles that inform moral decision making. We learned that the Scriptures are not a sex therapy sourcebook. Rather, we can find in the Bible broad principles that contribute to our understanding of sexuality, sexual intimacy, and sex therapy. The next step was to look at some of the most influential models of professional services in the areas of sexual disorders as well as other clinical presentations, such as sexual and gender identity, sexual addiction, and the paraphilias. This is applied integration, as we wanted to look at the practical outworking of that engagement in key areas that affect people today.

The book is intended for a broad audience. We would like to see it as a helpful resource for students and clinicians in the mental health fields (e.g., psychology, counseling, social work, marriage and family therapy, and so on), pastoral care staff and local pastors, and youth ministry leaders.

OVERVIEW OF THE BOOK

The book is divided into four parts. In part one (chapters one through four), we set the stage for the discussion of sexuality by considering four perspectives: theological, sociocultural, biological, and clinical. Chapter one is a discussion of a theological perspective insofar as we consider a distinctively Christian perspective on sexuality and sexual behavior. Chapter two is a discussion of sociocultural perspective on how sexuality is understood in our culture today. In the second edition, we updated this chapter to reflect current cultural trends particularly related to social media as well as responses to purity culture. Chapter three considers a biological perspective, so that students are familiar with anatomy and sexual functioning. We added more material here on menopause. Chapter four introduces a clinical perspective, as we transition the reader into some of the applied dimensions that will be the focus of the next two parts of the book.

Part two of the book (chapters five through nine) devotes one chapter apiece to the various sexual disorders often addressed in traditional sex therapy (e.g., sexual pain disorders, erectile disorder). We explain the disorders in question—their prevalence, etiology, treatment, and prevention. These are all updated in the second edition, and we added information on experiences of gay and lesbian couples in each of the chapters on sexual disorders. We recognize that working with gay and lesbian couples may not be what most Christians offer in this area, but for those who do, we want to help the reader be familiar with some of the issues that arise in the care for that population. Then we focus on closing Christian reflection on the trends in that area of study and practice.

Part three (chapters ten through thirteen) extends the discussion by taking topics that are commonly addressed in the field and inviting Christians to interact with the relevant materials. We introduce the reader to the paraphilias, sexual addiction, sexual identity, and gender identity and then review the literature in each area, followed by Christian engagement in light of what we know at this time. We added a new chapter here for the second edition; it is a chapter on non-normative/alternative sexualities. In our experience, most Christians will not necessarily specialize with this population; at the same time, we want the Christian sex therapist to be familiar with the population and common presenting concerns.

Part four (chapter fourteen) reflects our desire to cast a vision for integrative Christian sex therapy/counseling/ministry. In particular, we discuss recent developments in training and competence in these different areas. Societal and cultural changes will have an impact on our work and the ways in which we think about and engage the topics covered in this book in ministry and service.

ACKNOWLEDGMENTS

We have been blessed by stimulating conversations with a number of people—probably far too many to acknowledge. Mark would like to thank those who taught him about sex therapy, particularly Stanton Jones and the team from the Institute for Sexual Wholeness: Debra Taylor, Michael Sytsma, and the late Douglas Rosenau. He would also like to thank Cliff and Joyce Penner, James and Cathryn Childerston, and the many students he has had over the years in Sexuality and Sex Therapy at Wheaton College and at Regent University, as well as students from the Basic Issues in Sex Therapy at the Institute for Sexual Wholeness. Mark would also like to thank the Fellows in the Sexual and Gender Identity Institute at Wheaton College: Janet Dean, Stephen P. Stratton, Julia Sadusky, and Olya Zaporozhets, as well as students who are a part of SGI. David O'Connor in particular helped locate countless articles, read chapters, and provided helpful feedback.

Erica would like to thank Mark for the opportunity and encouragement to join him in the process of assembling this resource, as well as Michael Sytsma, Debra Taylor, and the late Douglas Rosenau from the Sexual Wholeness Institute, who provided feedback on the first edition. She would also like to thank students who assisted by finding resources and articles because that task is monumental in itself! Erica would also like to thank those who encouraged her in this process—friends, family members, and clients whose lived experiences helped to broaden her perspective.

We would both like to acknowledge our formal reviewers who provided us with constructive feedback that helped us in the fine-tuning.

REFERENCES

Hathaway, W. L., & Yarhouse, M. A. (2021). *The Integration of Psychology and Christianity: A Domain-Based Approach.* IVP Academic.

PART ONE

FOUNDATIONAL

CONSIDERATIONS

ONE

SEXUALITY IN THEOLOGICAL PERSPECTIVE

WHAT IS INTERESTING ABOUT FLYING FISH is their ability to use their pectoral fins to get sufficient speed—as much as 35 mph or more—to break the surface of the water and elevate into the air. They can fly up to four feet into the air and glide along the surface of the water for over 600 feet. They can do this multiple times, touching the surface and extending their flight for sometimes as long as 1,300 feet.[1] While many fish are drawn to the light above the surface of the water, most fish do not have this level of exposure to the world above them. Fish live in the water, under the surface, breathing the water just as we breathe the air. Their blissful lack of awareness is sometimes used to illustrate something about people: we often are unaware of our beliefs, assumptions, and values—our broad worldview—much like fish (with the exception of flying fish, perhaps) are typically unaware of the water they live in.

We have seen something similar happen in training Christians in the fields of psychology and counseling broadly, as well as in sexuality and sex therapy more narrowly. That is, one of the dangers that comes with teaching in a Christian setting is that students can become so familiar with Christianity that they see it up close, sometimes taking it for granted, but often they are far less familiar with other worldviews or perspectives. Other worldviews and other religions can actually benefit from lack of familiarity because the curiosity that accompanies the lack of familiarity deepens the pursuit of knowledge and understanding. There is a risk in not taking the

---

[1]See "Flying Fish," National Geographic, www.nationalgeographic.com/animals/fish/facts/flying-fish.

time to study what another worldview says about a topic the way we have become familiar with a Christian perspective on a topic.

We would like to spend some time examining what other worldviews and perspectives say about human sexuality and sexual expression. Christianity has important things to say about human sexuality; however, being overly familiar with those claims may make it difficult to appreciate them for what they are, and a lack of familiarity with worldviews that offer competing claims makes us unaware of other views of human sexuality.

We have also been impressed by how often the subtle assumptions of competing worldviews enter into the ways Christians reflect on important issues. As we will see, assumptions from naturalism may keep the Christian from reflecting on transcendent reality, let alone the connections between transcendent reality and human sexuality and its expression. The mental health fields are deeply steeped in naturalism because of their reliance on scientific methodology. While we understand and value the scientific method, it is not the beginning and end of discussions on the study of persons, including the study of human sexuality, so we are challenged to critically evaluate naturalistic assumptions when they conflict with a Christian worldview. The same can be said for humanism, a worldview that has made an indelible mark on contemporary mental health. Yet many of the assumptions in humanism are at odds with a Christian view of the person (theological anthropology), and they must be understood to advance our critical engagement and integration discussions. Finally, pluralism has entered into contemporary discussions, particularly for the next generation of Christians, who are growing up in an age in which sincerity about one's beliefs is often considered trump in comparison to the veracity of one's claims. While we want to encourage sincerity, we need to think carefully about what is right and true—in terms of sexual ethics and morality—as well as what is felt strongly.

One of the best resources for exploring this topic of competing worldviews is the book *The Meaning of Sex* by Dennis Hollinger. He covers many different perspectives. For the purposes of this chapter and to begin to reposition sex therapy on a Christian worldview, we are going to review what we see as the three most influential perspectives in our culture today: naturalism, humanism, and pluralism.

COMPETING WORLDVIEWS

We begin with naturalism, a common worldview encountered within the field of contemporary psychology and the broader sciences in general.

Then we discuss humanism and pluralism, both competing worldviews that are reflected in our current cultural emphasis on human potential and diversity.

Naturalism. The basic premise of naturalism is that there is no reality apart from what exists in nature, as well as what is observable in nature. There is no supernatural or transcendent reality. The preference among naturalists is to value contemporary science, the scientific method, and scientific explanations for what we have confidence to believe in, to claim as constituting reality.

Naturalism can take a few different forms. Some (Goetz & Taliaferro, 2008) have distinguished between strict and broad forms of naturalism. The strict form of naturalism rejects reality apart from what exists in nature but also rejects consciousness. A broad form of naturalism recognizes consciousness but anticipates a future explanation of it. Both forms of naturalism reject the mind and the soul and any kind of true purpose to human experience.

When it comes to sexuality, sex is understood as a natural drive that has been imbued with significance within our sociocultural context. Sex is not in and of itself special or inherently meaningful; rather, it is a natural, biological drive. From a naturalist perspective, for example, self-stimulation or masturbation is "just a form of biological release." There is no emphasis on the effects of the behavior cognitively, emotionally, relationally, or spiritually. When people raise questions about behaviors such as masturbation, premarital sex, use of erotica, and so on, the questions are considered by the naturalist to be derived primarily from a sociocultural context of meaning imposed on the activity.

Morality and ethics derived from naturalism tend to look to the consequences of actions. So some sexual behavior might be viewed as "right" or "wrong" based on what results from the behavior rather than some other way of determining morality. For example, having multiple sex partners may not be beneficial because of an increased risk of sexually transmitted infections (STIs). Living in a sociocultural context in which people who have made commitments to fidelity do not practice fidelity might be detrimental to society; so fidelity could be valued and infidelity seen as wrong, but more with reference to the consequences rather than to anything particularly substantive about the nature of faithfulness.

Hollinger critiques naturalism's claims. For Christians, nature is from God, but it is not superior to God or even the primary reference point. It is certainly not all there is. We can learn from nature, but nature is also fallen. It is touched by original sin and is distorted. Thus, it cannot provide a reliable basis for morality, as nature itself is groaning and eager for its redemption (Rom 8:22). Indeed, one of the challenges naturalism presents, according to Hollinger, is that it tends to keep people from identifying the abnormal, as we tend to think of the normal as that which merely exists in nature. Of course, many behaviors exist in nature; the Christian argues that the existence of behavior in nature is not a basis for the morality of or participation in that behavior.

Humanism. The fundamental assertion in *humanism* is that human beings are of utmost significance. So humanism is concerned with the welfare of human beings, as they are deemed central to the narrative; they are the source of all purpose and morality (Hollinger, 2009). Humanists are often naturalists in their worldview. In other words, they too tend to see nature as all there is, but rather than see life as having no meaning, they are more likely to see genuine meaning and purpose in life, but they frame that purpose around the welfare and interests of humanity and what it means to be human.

The result of such an understanding of human beings as the pinnacle of existence is that humanity determines what is right or wrong. Human beings do not look outside themselves for moral guidance; they certainly do not turn to the divine or the sacred for answers to ethical or moral dilemmas or for answers on how to live one's life.

A consequence of the high view placed on human experience can be seen in the humanist's understanding of sexual ethics. Sexual ethics is based on human potential; it is based on human self-actualization (or what we have sometimes referred to as "sexual self-actualization") and flourishing (Hollinger, 2009). Such a view rejects any ethical or moral claims by God but would look only to human beings for guidance on one's ethical responsibilities. An example of a humanistic perspective of sexuality is that if the pursuit of happiness is the ultimate goal, it would not matter how someone becomes happy, even if the source of "happiness" were an extramarital affair.

A Christian critique of humanism is that God is the author of the human narrative. Indeed, God is the central figure in the person and work of Jesus Christ. While the humanistic worldview may uphold the perspective of human nature as fundamentally good, Christians may deem that view incomplete and distorted because the effects of the Fall and resultant sin are denied. Brokenness, including sexual brokenness, is a reflection of our fallen nature, and at the same time presents an opportunity for redemption.

In both humanism and naturalism we also see a tendency to find moral authority in the experience of the organism. This has been referred to as "organismic congruence" (APA, 2009, p. 18). This means that the organism has its own urges and drives that, when met, give a "sense of wholeness" (p. 18) to the organism that can quickly be translated as morally good behavior. A Christian alternative to organismic congruence is what has been referred to as "telic congruence" (p. 18). This refers to living in accordance with one's values or sense of transcendent purpose or ideals. In other words, the Christian has historically looked outside one's own impulses to determine whether those impulses are reliable moral guides for living. Telic congruence raises the question of transcendent purpose—do standards exist outside (apart from) the organism? Do these standards provide a moral compass for one's life? Christians have historically affirmed this position.

Pluralism. The third competing worldview we highlight is *pluralism*. This is the worldview that asserts that there are many diverse beliefs and values, including moral and ethical claims. None is better than the other; none has more of a claim to truth than the others. Pluralism is like going out to dinner at a buffet; there are a variety of food options at a buffet, and people gravitate to one option over another as a matter of personal preference or taste, not as a matter of which item is "better" in any meaningful sense of the word. When we apply this experience to ethical claims or moral values, the pluralist argues that the many diverse beliefs and worldviews that exist are all potentially legitimate and no one belief, value, or ethic stands above the others as true or right.

Pluralism is particularly popular today in Western cultures in which there is a great regard for diversity of thought and experience, where intentions and sincerity tend to be valued above absolute truth or values. As an example, we recently heard one woman say that she would never participate in "naked hot-tubbing" with strangers; however, she felt that if someone wanted to, it was "their business" and they could do "whatever because it's their preference." Her own view of right and wrong was for herself and did not speak to values that transcend her personal preferences. "Each to his (or her) own" is the motto of the pluralist.

What is offensive to the pluralist about a Christian worldview is the exclusive claim to truth presented within Christianity. Christianity stands in sharp contrast to pluralism insofar as Christians make claims about God and truth and ethics that are not just one good idea among many. Rather, a Christian understanding is that God has revealed his purposes and will for human beings for how we ought to relate to one another and to God.

When we extend the discussion to the area of sexuality, we see Christianity claims that in God's revealed will are principles for human sexuality and sexual expression. These biblical principles are not mere opinion but reflect God's will and character, as well as transcendent reality that we may not fully appreciate this side of eternity.

We also see today a culture that claims to value pluralism but has indeed merely the appearance of true pluralism. As Carson (2012) observes, "Genuine pluralism within the broader culture is facilitated when there is a strong Christian voice loyal to the Scriptures—as well as strong Muslim voices, skeptical voices, Buddhist voices, atheistic voices, and so forth" (p. 35).

Whereas we used to coexist with different truth claims (what Carson describes as the old kind of tolerance), we now live in a cultural setting in which there is great disdain for anyone who claims truth. As Carson points out,

> The media may present popes such as John Paul II and Benedict XVI in a positive light, provided these popes are restricting themselves to ceremony or world poverty, but if they show how their beliefs impinge on social issues such as premarital and extramarital sex, abortion, homosexuality, and euthanasia, then they must be bigoted, out of date, slightly bizarre, even dangerous, and certainly intolerant. (p. 35)

These important cultural changes affect several discussions tied to sexuality and sexual behavior, particularly in areas with differing normative moral claims and visions for the human person, including homosexuality, sexual identity, gender identity, premarital sex, extramarital sex, abortion, and so on.

In any case, we encourage students to reflect on the various worldviews that coexist with Christianity in our current cultural setting. In the spirit of engaging in worldview integration, it is important to understand different religious worldviews (e.g., Islam, Judaism, Buddhism), but it is just as important to recognize how competing worldviews found in naturalism, humanism, and pluralism shape our cultural discourse, particularly in the area of sexuality and sexual behavior.

We find that many Christian students have struggled to contrast their own basic Christian commitments with other worldviews. They are familiar with Christianity but not with alternative explanations for understanding human experience, morality, ethics, and sexuality. We should note too that Christianity has not always taught on sexuality with one voice or in a way that we recognize as correct today. We turn now to that discussion.

CHRISTIANITY

Christianity as a world religion and as a worldview stands in contrast to competing worldviews such as naturalism, humanism, and pluralism. But Christianity or the Christian tradition has its own unflattering history with sexuality and sexual ethics. There are many such instances we could highlight, but one is the medieval Christian view of sex, with its overvaluing of asceticism, which emphasized simplicity and abstinence from objects and activities that might induce feelings of pleasure. As Hollinger (2009) points out, Christian history records a time when asceticism was upheld as the preferred way to be a Christian (a "higher" way of living characterized by chastity, obedience, and poverty) rather than a "lower" way of marriage and sexual behavior in that relational context.

These two contrasting ways of being a Christian (the higher path of asceticism and the lower path of marriage) fueled the notion that contrasted sharply with the "historic Hebraic affirmation of body life and sexuality," and would be asserted in various forms by Justin Martyr, Origen, Tertullian, and other early church leaders in the West (Jones, 1999, p. 1107). Many Christians also viewed sex in marriage as tainted, a view held by Thomas Aquinas (Hollinger, 2009). This view obviously casts a shadow over a healthy and positive view of human sexuality and contrasts significantly with how Christians understand sexuality and sexual behavior today.

In historical perspective this medieval Christian view of sex reflected a low view of the creation, the human body, and our intended physical existence. It cast a vision of human sin as tied primarily to physical existence (rather than sinful self-centeredness) and suggested that the best response is asceticism (or strict obedience to a life of restraint) (Hollinger, 2009). It also fostered a rather narrow view of sexual behavior, as though it were solely for the purpose of procreation. This would have consequences, particularly much later in the twentieth century when advances in medical science in the area of contraception meant that sexual behavior was able to be routinely divorced from procreation. These advances had a number of consequences for how people (Christians included) approached sexuality and sexual behavior in terms of single sexuality, sexual practices among married couples, cohabitation, and the broader sexual revolution and consequent liberation movements associated with sexual minority communities (see Herdt, 1996).

Some Christians today undoubtedly retain remnants of what we see reflected in a medieval Christian asceticism in how they may approach the topic of sexuality and sexual behavior. But thankfully there is a sense of historical perspective on medieval asceticism as an extreme response to human sexuality, one that most Christians today would reject in favor of a more balanced view.

One of the most significant recent contributions to a Christian understanding of human sexuality is John Paul II's (1997) *Theology of the Body*. In fact, many commentaries on this dense treatise suggest that it will be many years before the church fully appreciates the theological reflections contained in this compilation (it is a series of 129 lectures given between 1979 and 1984). In his writing John Paul II lays a foundation around sex that is intended to provide freedom for the person to love properly. There are two halves to his work, each containing three cycles. The first three cycles examine who we are as human beings, which for the Christian is tied to creation (an embodied sexuality that existed prior to sin), the Fall (how our embodied sexuality is tainted by our fallen condition), and our destiny in glorification (what an embodied sexuality is in the context of the resurrection) (West, 2004).

This teaching is in some ways similar to what we will present here as we discuss our understanding of a theology of sex as tied to the four acts of the biblical drama: creation, the Fall, redemption, and glorification.

For John Paul II (1997), creation points to a state of innocence that teaches us about three experiences: solitude, unity, and nakedness. Solitude is found in the original state in which Adam "realizes that love is his origin, his vocation, and his destiny" (West, 2004, p. 22). The unity found in the creation story points to the covenant Adam and Eve are to have with one another as persons who are distinct from the rest of creation but are unified in a biological reality, as well as a spiritual and theological reality (West, 2004). The last original experience in the creation story is that of nakedness insofar as there is no shame for Adam and Even in relation to each other, freely giving the gift of love to each other.

John Paul II (1997) then discusses the fact that human beings are fallen and in the process of being redeemed, but the Fall affects our sexuality in profound ways. He examines lust and adultery in his discussion of our fallen condition. Lust (or adultery of the heart) is when we indulge the pull of lust in the violation of the dignity of another person (and our own dignity) (West, 2004). In our redemptive state, while we do not fully experience a renewed life until eternity, we can "begin to experience the redemption of our sexual desires, the gradual transformation of our hearts" (p. 34). Human beings have a tendency to question and deny God's good gift of sex, and it is only by and through God's grace that we are able to live (however incompletely) in the freedom of self and the gift of our sexuality and a life in the Spirit.

John Paul II (1997) goes on to reflect on a theology that touches on the resurrection of the body, celibacy and virginity, the sacrament of marriage, and contraception. Indeed, his is a fully orbed reflection on human sexuality that is tied to theological anthropology, and we would agree with several commentators that the full impact of his writing is likely yet to be understood.

Today evangelical Christians look to Scripture as a source of authority on matters of faith and living. It is given greater weight than other possible sources of authority, such as Christian history, reason, and personal experience. So while John Paul II's (1997) *Theology of the Body* is a tremendous reflection on theological anthropology for any thoughtful Christian interested in the study of sexuality, in matters of faith and practice, Scripture is the source of God's revelation about salvation, a redemptive plan centering on the person and work of Jesus. We turn now to a discussion of a biblical perspective on sexuality.

SCRIPTURE

Christians affirm that Scripture is a reliable guide for the believer, "fully truthful in all its teachings" (Erickson, 2001, p. 68). When it comes to how we ought to live, the Scriptures also provide believers with the broad principles for behavior and relationships, particularly in view of what it means to live in a way that reflects gratitude for God's provision in our lives and a desire to bring honor and glory to God.

> All Scripture is God-breathed and is useful for teaching, rebuking, correcting and training in righteousness, so that the servant of God may be thoroughly equipped for every good work. (2 Tim 3:16-17)

While we recognize that Scripture is an invaluable source of instruction for right living, we do not read Scripture as a handbook on sexual functioning. We cannot derive directly from Scripture a protocol for conducting sex therapy or for the treatment of the paraphilias or gender identity issues.

So we feel this tension between those who want to treat Scripture as a handbook on sexual functioning, as if there were protocols and manuals just waiting to be written, derived entirely from the Song of Solomon, and those who dismiss Scripture as though it were of no relevance to contemporary discussions of sexuality and sex counseling.

Our position is that in some cases Scripture provides us with clear teaching on questions of morality. In other cases we see indirect reference to topics that inform our moral reasoning (see Rosenau & Wilson, 2006, for a discussion of direct and indirect reference in Scripture, followed by a discussion of God's heart in an area of moral consideration). In other matters we look to broad principles for living, and these principles are relevant to sexuality and sexual behavior.

One way to think about it is that there are general instructions (in the form of principles) that can be derived from Scripture. Marva Dawn, in her book *Sexual Character*, shares a story about the value of looking for instructions on how to live as a sexual being.

> Before the personal computer era, I used an excellent typewriter to write books. It has a corrector ribbon that was especially helpful. . . . The corrector and typing ribbons had to be carefully positioned around certain sprockets and divider bars in order not to interfere with each other's functioning. . . . The most amazing thing always happened: I would get out the instruction book. A picture showed me how the ribbons were to be positioned, and written instructions guided me step by step through the process of threading them into place. Voila! I could successfully type and correct!
>
> Why would the instruction book solve my problem every time? It is because the company that built the typewriter wrote the instruction book. Those who know the design of the machine are the ones most able to teach me how the machine can be most effectively used and maintained. (Dawn, 1993, p. 21)

There are many Christians today who would see Scripture as providing meaningful information and instruction on sexuality and sexual behavior. But they might wrestle with whether they can equate the complexity of human sexuality and sexual expression with replacing a typewriter ribbon. After all, each model of typewriter manufactured by a specific company is going to be the same, but people are not all the same. As we enter into discussions of human sexuality, we quickly learn to appreciate the variety and complexity associated with human sexuality and sexual experience. So we want to strike an important balance moving forward in our analysis. While we do not see Scripture as a textbook on human sexuality or sexual behavior, we do see Scripture as providing important information about God's revealed will for sexuality and its expression. There are broad themes in Scripture that we do well to understand and apply in our own lives and in the life of the church.

We see the instruction about sexuality and sexual behavior, then, as less comparable to a manual with step-by-step instructions and more like a map with an overview of the land. It provides the Christian with important information about the landscape and about the terrain. This information is found in biblical principles that we believe can guide our thinking and decision making.

GENERAL THEMES AND PRINCIPLES

The goodness of creation. In this section we want to explore some of the general themes and principles from Scripture that are related to human sexuality and sexual expression.[2] To begin, the general tenor and the broad themes from the Old Testament introduce us to the goodness of our physical existence, including our sexuality, as well as our utter dependence on and separateness from God. We have only a brief glimpse into the story of creation and the experience of Adam and Eve as free from sin and shame in their physical existence and sexuality. They are revealed to us as having an embodied existence and are then given souls, suggesting a positive view of their inherent physicality, which we shall return to later.

The story of creation also reveals the creature in relation to a Creator. "Then God said, 'Let us make mankind in our image, in our likeness'" (Gen 1:26). It is notable that in the process of creation, God declared that

---

[2]Portions of this section are adapted from Jones & Yarhouse (2000) and Jones & Jones (2007).

everything he made prior to man was "good" (Gen 1:4, 12, 18, 21, 25); however, his declaration after creating man, in looking at all that he had made, was, "it was very good" (Gen 1:31). Human beings are a valued (by God) part of the created order, but they remain part of creation. As such, human beings are utterly dependent on God for their existence (Erickson, 2001), which is the case whether they recognize it or not. In other words, humans are part of the created order and dependent on God for their existence whether or not they see themselves in that way.

So, to be human is to be created by God and dependent on God for existence. To be human also means to be separate and distinct from God (Jones & Butman, 1991). Indeed, as we will see, our separateness from God is also reflected in our longing for completion in God, which is tied to our sexuality, as we will discuss later.

Christians have historically understood that God's intent at creation was to place human beings in a family by bringing man and woman together in monogamous union (Gen 2:21-24), where we also see gender complementarity. From this perspective, the distinctiveness of the person is also retained: in marriage two people become one but do not lose their personal identity.

The reality of the Fall. The Old Testament also introduces us to the Fall and how original sin has corrupted all of existence, including human sexuality and its expression. The consequences of the Fall are far reaching, but we get glimpses into the purpose of sexuality and its complementarity in what God chooses to relate about his relationship with Israel. Indeed, God reveals a very intimate relationship with his people by equating Israel to a wayward wife who prostitutes herself with others while God is a faithful husband.

How does the Fall affect sexuality? Here are a few of the potential effects. First, there is strife built into male-female relations (Gen 3:16). It may be difficult to understand the extent of this (Jones, 1999), but many Christian scholars have devoted time and energy into unpacking the meaning of this for male-female relationships, as we have seen numerous debates about complementarian and egalitarian views of marriage and so on. In our role as clinicians we do not take a position on which of those views most accurately reflects a Christian understanding of male-female relations. We note that the Fall led to strife between men and women that had not been there previously and that could take the form of struggle, animosity, competition, discord, contention, or disunity, particularly in the marital relationship.

In addition to the discord or strife in male-female relationships, there is now the possibility for short-term, selfish gratification (Prov 5:1-6) that can be seen in interpersonal relationships, including sexually intimate relationships. While this can take many forms, in contemporary culture we see it in exemplified in the "hook-up" culture, wherein sex is reduced to merely the exchange of fluids or a way to manage stress or meet felt needs. We see it too in the ubiquitous pornography industry, with easy online access and its "no strings attached" promises of sexual self-gratification. Related to this concern for selfish gratification and, in particular, the pornography industry, we should note that we are now able to fragment, objectify, and reduce others, to see and use parts and activities for our own interests and not for anything relational or meaningful in and of itself.

Consistent with this concern, the Christian stands against objectifying others or devaluing them. When we read that Adam "knew" Eve his wife (Gen 4:1 ESV), we understand that the Hebrew word for "sex," "perceive," and "knowledge" is the same. The word implies intimacy and fellowship. The Christian considers whether his or her actions or desires make another into an object rather than someone to delight in and to cherish. This is why fantasy can be treacherous: it can invite the opportunity to lose the personhood of the individual who is being fantasized about.

It is important, then, from a Christian perspective to see a person's value in their *essence* rather than *function*:

> The only question is whether I can see the whole person if I do not see him in his relationship to God and therefore as the bearer of an "alien dignity." If I am blind to this dimension then I can give the other person only a partial dignity insofar as I estimate his importance "for me"—even if this includes far more than his mere *functional* importance for me!—but not insofar as I see in him his importance "for God." (Thielicke, 1975, p. 26)

In other words, whenever people are valued not for their essence but rather for their functional value (what they can do for me), they become interchangeable and devalued (Thielicke, 1975). It is important that students studying sexuality and sex therapy recognize the many ways that our culture does this (valuing function over essence). As we are an increasingly sexualized culture (see chap. 2), partners (real and imagined) can readily be reduced to vehicles by which people accrue orgasms. While there are many potential consequences to the person and to society, one consequence of note is that the ease with which pleasures can be met obviates the discipline of self-restraint.

It should also be noted that the Fall was an act of rebellion that itself gave birth to rebellion as a motive in life. Rebellion can be expressed in many ways and often against authority, including God. There are times when rebellion is expressed in and through our sexuality and sexual behavior, as if we are essentially saying no to God's revealed will for human sexuality and its expression.

We can also ask whether another effect of the Fall is that shame is now a part of sexuality. A genuine sense of shame is introduced in the story of the Fall, as Adam and Eve responded to God by covering themselves and hiding from God's presence (Gen 3:8). So it can be argued that one possible effect of the Fall is introducing shame as a part of human sexuality, or at least the potential for shame to be experienced in our sexuality.

We see so far that Scripture affirms the goodness of creation and of our physical existence, including our sexuality. We also see the reality of the Fall and some of the possible effects of the Fall on sexuality. We turn now to how redemption breaks into human history, into the story of creation and the Fall, and what that may mean for human sexuality.

Redemptive elements. We turn, then, to redemption as discussed in Scripture. The Old Testament begins to point us toward a future redemption as found in the person and work of Christ Jesus. We do not have explicit instruction as to what that means for sexuality or sexual behavior, just that a Messiah is anticipated (Is 9:6-7; 11:10).

In the New Testament we see glimpses of redemption in areas of sexuality. Perhaps what comes most readily to mind is Jesus' encounter with those who brought the woman caught in the act of adultery to him (Jn 7:53–8:11). They approached Jesus, as many leaders of that time did, to trick Jesus with a difficult decision he would have to make publicly. They challenged Jesus with the idea that they should fulfill the law by stoning the woman caught in the act of adultery. As we know, Jesus never takes the bait, and he turns their accusation on its head by bringing to their awareness the gap existing between their private sin and their public position against sin. His words to the woman were an expression of grace and mercy, with instruction to make changes to live in faithful obedience to the very law that Jesus came to fulfill.

This tendency to speak to what is in a person's heart is also part of another teaching in which Jesus talks about impure, lustful thoughts that are the same in essence as having sex with another person (Mt 5:28). This cut to the core of the problem with some of the religious leaders of the day who thought that their behavior justified them before God. To those who understood Jesus' teachings, his response leveled that structure.

Much of what we have as biblical instruction dealing with sexuality and sexual behavior comes through the writings of Paul to the many churches under his care. In Paul's writing we see a preference for singleness that has been all but lost on evangelicals today (1 Cor 7:1-7). The Roman Catholic Church has a high view of being single, but evangelicals often relate to people in the church as though they have not quite arrived if they are not paired off. An example of this in the church is the frequency of sermons about marriage compared with those that address singleness, or where programming is more about couples and children than about a healthy and balanced view of singleness in midlife and beyond.

Paul also wrote about the importance of sex in marriage as primarily a protective measure, as a guard against temptation (1 Cor 7:8-9). He reiterated the teachings familiar to the Jews of that day that sex outside marriage is sin, as was sex with a partner of the same sex.

RELATED PRINCIPLES

To be human is to be relational. Christianity has historically affirmed, then, that from creation, God places people in relationships, in families (Gen 1–2). The families that people are born into, the nature of these relationships that is seen in creation and affirmed by Jesus, Paul, and others in the New Testament, are a lifelong commitment between husband and wife. This has been important in Christianity because it is in this context that God also places genital sex. When we talk about genital sex, we are talking about full sexual intimacy. Christianity affirms that sexuality in general and genital sexual expression in particular are good things, and that while all of us experience and express our sexuality in how we relate to one another, Christianity has historically taught that lifelong heterosexual relationships are God's revealed will for full genital sexual intimacy.

To be human is to be sexual. Christians understand sexuality to be a gift from God, an integral part of what it means to be human. Genital sexual activity is the means of procreation, which not only brings about life and reflects the divine act of creation but also is the basis for family life in all cultures throughout history. But sexuality is more than genital sexual activity, as we suggested earlier. A Christian understanding of human sexuality is that it reflects who we are as much as or more so than what we do, an observation made by Lewis Smedes in *Sex for Christians*. Our sexuality instructs us of our need for God as we experience in our sexuality a longing for completion in another (*eros*). The marriage relationship, we are told in Scripture, reflects the relationship between God and ancient Israel, and between Christ and the church, the bride of Christ. Interestingly, many of the references in the Old Testament compare the idolatry of Israel to adultery in relationship to God; God revealed how important idolatry is by drawing an analogy based on what humans know about marital intimacy (see Jer 3:8; Eph 5:15-32).

Sex as life uniting and reflective of transcendent reality. Christianity, then, affirms that sex in marriage is a "life-uniting act" that is a physical activity but also one that is tied to transcendent purposes (Smedes, 1994). As Smedes observes, sex has the potential to bring about new life and is the natural means by which a couple can procreate. Of course, not all sex in marriage brings about new life, whether by the intention of the couple or as a result of infertility (which Christianity would see as an expression of the Fall). Nevertheless, sexual intercourse is the means by which new life is formed, and the formation of new life occurs in a specific relationship: heterosexual marriage.

We can already see this in how Scripture points to marital relationships as instructive of the intimacy found in Christ's relationship with the church. Christine Colón and Bonnie Field (2009) note that while marriage instructs us about Christ's relationship to the church, it should not be used to idolize marriage or denigrate being single. In fact, singles also reflect important values regarding Christianity, including our primary loyalty and identity as followers of Christ, and a shift in understanding God's family as tied to salvation rather than lineage. This connection to transcendence can be contrasted with what we see as commonplace in our contemporary culture. Take, for example, the hook-up culture that exists on many college campuses today (Freitas, 2008, 2013). Christianity teaches that even hooking up is much more than just an exchange of bodily fluids, even if the two people engaged in the act insist otherwise. The act itself is tied to transcendent meaning that exists quite apart from the intentions of the people involved. Sex has a spiritual dimension to it such that any sex outside the context of a life union of a man and woman is a violation of the meaning and purpose of sex.

WHAT ARE THE IMPORTANT QUESTIONS?

In his thoughtful analysis of sexuality and sexual behavior from a Christian worldview, the late Lewis Smedes (1994) asked, What is the goal of studying sexuality? We have always appreciated his answer: "To catch a vision of the place and nature of sexuality in human life and to clarify as best we can the nature of Christian ethics in this area" (p. 24).

One of the first points of consideration for the Christian is that sex transcends genital sex or any specific sexual action or behavior. As Smedes says, sex is something we are, not something we do. Smedes removes the emphasis on behavior as though a discussion of actions would somehow encapsulate a full-orbed discussion of human sexuality. Rather, he prefers we view sex as an important aspect of what it means to be human.

To get at this point that our sexuality is an important aspect of what it means to be human, it may be helpful to distinguish between types of sexuality: *gender sexuality*, *erotic sexuality*, and *genital sexuality* (Jones, 1999).

Gender sexuality. Gender sexuality is the broadest of the three levels. It refers to being a person who is either male or female. Although we will discuss gender identity and related concerns in greater detail in chapter thirteen, Christians have historically understood there to be two biological sexes, and gender sexuality is a reflection of that distinction and complementarity seen in the creation narrative (Gen 2:21-24). By saying this, we are in no way meaning to diminish the experience of those who have an intersex condition or experience gender incongruence. Some would say such rare conditions or experiences are exceptions that perhaps prove the rule, that is, that there are two distinct and complimentary sexes, just as we see reflected in the story of creation.

According to Jones (1999), questions for reflection for the Christian include, Why did God create two sexes? What was God's purpose in so doing? What are the meaningful differences between men and women, if we can tease those out from our sociocultural context? And how does our gender permeate our lives as we live after the Fall and before glorification? How ought gender to permeate our lives?

Erotic sexuality. The next level of sexuality is erotic sexuality. This refers to the passionate desire and longing for completion in another. The longing for completion is experienced at all levels, including the physical. Erotic sexuality is related to gender sexuality for most people (Jones, 1999). The complementarity of male and female anatomy certainly reflects this, but same-sex partners can also experience a longing for completion in the other that reflects this level of erotic sexuality. The desire itself is instructive. As an example, Smedes reflects on the feeling of guilt that many individuals experience after masturbating. His opinion is that the sense of guilt is actually a sense of incompletion and longing for what is actually meant to be—the experience of pleasure in the context of sexual intimacy within marriage.

Questions that arise in the study of erotic sexuality have to do with the place of sexuality in our lives: What place does sexuality have in our lives? How central is it to who we are? What do we do with the desire and longing for completion in another if we are not presently married?

Genital sexuality. The third and final level of sexuality is the most specific. It is genital sexuality. Genital sexuality comprises and focuses on physical acts themselves (Jones, 1999). It is probably the focal point of most evangelical Christians when they discuss sex. We can quickly focus on list making: Which behaviors are acceptable and which are unacceptable? What is right and wrong in terms of sexual behavior? Too often the discussion begins and ends here, with list making. We want to recognize that these are important questions to ask, but a broader, fuller view of sexuality will inform a Christian understanding.

Helmut Thielicke (1975) offers the following observation about genital sexuality or specific sex acts in light of a broader Christian view of sexuality:

> He who seeks only the partial—only the body, only the function, and possibly only a part of this—remains unfulfilled even on the level of *eros*, because, having lost the wholeness of the other person, he also loses the other person's uniqueness. (p. 25)

We turn now to an important theological issue for our consideration. It has to do with a proper understanding of our physical nature, including our sexuality.

OUR PHYSICAL NATURE

One of the critical theological issues for evangelical Christians has to do with our physical nature: How central to our existence is our physical nature? We have witnessed a tendency among evangelicals to distance themselves from the natural world in favor of the spiritual world. This is popularly captured in the hymn by Albert E. Brumley "This World Is Not My Home" (1965).

There is often a tension between living in this world and anticipating the life beyond this world. There is also a sense in which the world we live in, our physical existence included, is "less than" what we are moving toward.

This tendency to devalue life in the present world often extends to our physical existence in discussions about sexuality. In the most extreme forms it can lead to expressions of gnosticism (see Ehrman, 2006; Pagels & King, 2008), in which matter and physical existence are devalued (and ultimately identified as the sources of evil) in favor of the life of the mind and spirit or a secret spark of divine light that is supposedly within us, which is at risk of being quenched by what has become orthodoxy.

However, this seems to contrast sharply with the broader witness of Scripture (and data on historical Christianity, which is beyond the scope of our discussion). Creation, the incarnation, and the resurrection all point in favor of a high view of our inherent and intended physicalness.

We discussed Genesis 1–2 earlier, but we can certainly see in these passages our embodied nature. The story itself reflects that human beings became souls.

The incarnation—the doctrine of God becoming flesh, taking on bodily existence—elevates our view of physical existence. In John 1:14 Scripture reads, "The Word became flesh and made his dwelling among us. We have seen his glory, the glory of the one and only Son, who came from the Father, full of grace and truth." Christ became flesh, and that would be impossible if physical existence were inherently bad.

Finally, the resurrection is understood as the unfolding event that precedes the glorification and consummation of the created order. We are told that there will be a bodily resurrection, although it is unclear the full ramifications of that understanding:

> But someone will ask, "How are the dead raised? With what kind of body will they come?" How foolish! What you sow does not come to life unless it dies. When you sow, you do not plant the body that will be, but just a seed, perhaps of wheat or of something else. But God gives it a body as he has determined, and to each kind of seed he gives its own body. Not all flesh is the same: People have one kind of flesh, animals have another, birds another and fish another. There are also heavenly bodies and there are earthly bodies; but the splendor of the heavenly bodies is one kind, and the splendor of the earthly bodies is another. The sun has one kind of

splendor, the moon another and the stars another; and star differs from star in splendor.

So will it be with the resurrection of the dead. The body that is sown is perishable, it is raised imperishable; it is sown in dishonor, it is raised in glory; it is sown in weakness, it is raised in power; it is sown a natural body, it is raised a spiritual body.

If there is a natural body, there is also a spiritual body. (1 Cor 15:35-44)

We are told our bodies will be transformed: "Our citizenship is in heaven. And we eagerly await a Savior from there, the Lord Jesus Christ, who, by the power that enables him to bring everything under his control, will transform our lowly bodies so that they will be like his glorious body" (Phil 3:20-21).

One of the tension points for some evangelicals is how to understand passages that appear to carry negative charges against our physical existence. One of the most widely cited (but misunderstood) passages dealing with "the flesh" is Galatians 5:19-21:

The acts of the flesh are obvious: sexual immorality, impurity and debauchery; idolatry and witchcraft; hatred, discord, jealousy, fits of rage, selfish ambition, dissensions, factions and envy; drunkenness, orgies, and the like. I warn you, as I did before, that those who live like this will not inherit the kingdom of God.

As we approach a biblical understanding of "the flesh" (*sarx*) in this context, there are many possible meanings of *flesh*. For example, *flesh* can refer to the aspect of the person that is frail or creaturely. *Flesh* can also refer to the physical aspect of personhood. It can refer to the union produced by marriage and can also refer to the outlook or orientation of the whole person—oriented toward self and in active rebellion against God.

When we look at the list of "acts of the flesh" listed in Galatians 5:19-21, we have to consider which meaning makes the most sense in light of the list given. While we may be tempted to say that Paul is critical of our physical existence in this passage, there are many acts listed that are not tied to physical existence per se (e.g., selfish ambition, hatred). Taken together, each act in the list commonly reflects an outlook or orientation toward oneself and in active rebellion against God. Indeed, that is the flesh that we are to reject. Not our physical existence but our sinful self-centeredness.

As we come into a more accurate understanding of sexuality and sexual behavior from a Christian perspective, we want to consider the purposes of sexuality. Let's turn to that topic.

PURPOSES OF SEXUALITY

Historically, there have been two primary purposes of sexuality discussed among Christians—procreative and unitive. Sex is the means by which human beings procreate. Male-female relationships have the potential for procreation. The other primary purpose is the unitive dimension of sexuality: two people are united in marriage and in and through sexual intimacy. Genesis 2:24 reads, "That is why a man leaves his father and mother and is united to his wife, and they become one flesh."

Paul then references this passage in his letter to the church in Corinth:

> Do you not know that your bodies are members of Christ himself? Shall I then take the members of Christ and unite them with a prostitute? Never! Do you not know that he who unites himself with a prostitute is one with her in body? For it is said, "The two will become one flesh." But whoever is united with the Lord is one with him in spirit.
>
> Flee from sexual immorality. All other sins a person commits are outside the body, but whoever sins sexually, sins against their own body. Do you not know that your bodies are temples of the Holy Spirit, who is in you, whom you have received from God? You are not your own; you were bought at a price. Therefore honor God with your bodies. (1 Cor 6:15-20)

So in addition to procreative purposes of sexuality, there are also unitive purposes (see also Mk 10:2-12). Furthermore, additional purposes might include the physical gratification or pleasure that is associated with sexual intimacy (Prov 5:15-19). The experience of pleasure with a loved one is an experience of increased emotional closeness as well.

Sex is also instructive, as we suggested earlier in the chapter when we discussed *eros* or the longing for completion in another. Sex instructs us about our relational nature and in so doing reflects God's nature as a relational being. This is seen in our longing for completion with another. As we experience that longing, we experience a desire that is only incompletely met in relationship with others, including those with whom we are sexually intimate.

Marva Dawn makes an interesting observation about the love that exists in marriage and the common phrase *to make love*:

> The common slang "to make love" does not accurately describe what happens in the sexual union of committed marriage partners. Love is made all the time in marriage—when together we clean up the kitchen, sing a hymn side by side in a worship service, ride our bicycles to the neighborhood park, talk on the porch swing

about the day's work, play a game, plan for the future, or remember the past. Love grows when, apart from each other, we speak lovingly about our spouse, work at our jobs with a sense of the other's support, or plan surprises. (Dawn, 1993, p. 55)

Another aspect of the instructive purpose of our sexuality is that sex instructs the world about the love of Christ for his bride, the church (Eph 5:22-24). Paul instructs husbands to love their wives in the same way that Christ sacrificed himself for the church. That love for one another, that willingness to put the other first, to make sacrifices on behalf of the other, is an important characteristic of love that is meant to be instructive to us and the culture we live in.

In addition to these important theological issues, we want to reflect on the tendency among evangelicals to focus almost exclusively on behavior over other considerations.

YOUR WORKING THEOLOGY OF SEX

As you begin a book on sexuality and sex therapy, it can be important to reflect on a working theology of sexuality. How would you outline your own theology of sexuality? What would you see as the most important considerations? How do specific passages from Scripture inform your theology? Or are there broader themes from Scripture that you see as particularly relevant to a practical theology?

In this chapter we focused on creation, the Fall, redemption, and glorification. Does this organization make sense to you—in terms of the four acts of the biblical drama? If so, how do themes from creation inform your theology of sexuality? In what ways do you see the Fall influencing a theology of sexuality? What is "fallen," exactly? How does redemption (or various "redemptive structures") fit into your emerging theology? As you consider glorification, what bearing does eternity have on how we think about sexuality this side of heaven?

In addition to the four acts of the biblical drama—creation, the Fall, redemption, and glorification—are there any specific principles that you derive from Scripture that inform your understanding of sexuality?

How would you compare and contrast your working theology of human sexuality from a Christian perspective with the various worldviews mentioned at the outset of this chapter, that is, naturalism, humanism, and pluralism? What are you identifying as true that would be in conflict with these various worldviews and their assumptions about sexuality, sexual expression, and morality?

BEYOND BEHAVIOR

There is an unfortunate stereotype about evangelical Christian circles and the tendency to make lists. We like to have lists of what we cannot do and can do. This is perhaps no more evident than when we turn to discussions about sexuality and morality.

Here is an excerpt from an email we received recently:

> Please forgive my out of the blue e-mail and questions, but I really am in need of some Christian perspective on something. I am a full time student, am employed full time and have been married eight years. A lot of married friends have been expressing their interest and involvement in sharing verbal fantasies (between husband and wife) in the bedroom. Needless to say this idea is extremely exciting. As a result, we have tried it and like it. My concern is: is this behavior healthy? Online articles and relationship books at Barnes and Noble all say yes. However, I cannot find the topic addressed by any Christian author. So my question to you is simple. Is this behavior OK? If so what are reasonable boundaries? Is there a book or article that addresses this issue from Christian perspective?

Is the behavior healthy? Is it OK? What are the boundaries? One problem with lists is that they often do not contain all of the behaviors we have questions about. And if they do create boundaries, context is often neglected and behaviors altogether become reduced to "right" and "wrong." For example, if a view is taken that "masturbation is wrong," would that apply in the case of a Navy couple where one partner is deployed and both husband and wife experience sexual tension in the absence of the other? Would it be wrong for them to masturbate while they are on the phone with each other, sharing fantasies in a moment of intimacy? The flip side may be that while it may not be wrong, their distance may be an opportunity to exercise discipline.

When we look at Scripture we see a short list of sexual behaviors that are expressly commanded or approved. The list includes marital intercourse and celibacy. Marital intercourse is commanded by Paul in his letter to the church in Corinth: "The husband should fulfill his marital duty to his wife, and likewise the wife to her husband" (1 Cor 7:3). Marriage itself is honored in several other passages; for example, Hebrews 13:4: "Marriage should be honored by all, and the marriage bed kept pure, for God will judge the adulterer and all the sexually immoral." Likewise, celibacy is affirmed in Scripture: "There are eunuchs who were born that way, and there are eunuchs who have been made eunuchs by others—and there are those who choose to live like eunuchs for the sake of the kingdom of heaven. The one who can accept this should accept it" (Mt 19:12; see also 1 Cor 6–7).

There is a much longer list of acts that are expressly condemned in Scripture. The word *porneia*, which originally and more narrowly meant "to prostitute" or "to sell," was translated in the KJV and NASB as "fornication" more broadly and in the ESV as sexual "immorality."[3] It can also be thought of as "illicit sex." It would include all sexual intercourse with someone who is not one's spouse. Other sexual behaviors that Christians have historically viewed as condemned include incest (Lev 18:6-18; 20:11-22), rape or forced sex (Deut 22), same-sex behavior (Lev 18:22; 20:13; Rom 1; 1 Cor 6:9), bestiality (Lev 20:15-16), cross-dressing (Deut 22:5), lust (Mt 5:28), and withholding sex in marriage (1 Cor 7).

That leaves a number of concerns for which we receive little guidance directly through Scripture, except through broad principles, not to mention some of the topics above that are being revisited or further contextualized. Concerns often raised today include questions about self-stimulation (masturbation), oral sex, petting, modesty and nudity, fetishism, and birth control. The email we received about fantasy in a marriage is another question raised that is not directly addressed in the context of Scripture.

When Christians do not have clear teachings on matters of morality, they are to look to broad principles to guide their understanding and practical application of what is affirmed and what is condemned in Scripture.

PRINCIPLES GUIDING ETHICAL DECISION MAKING

Which principles should guide ethical decision making? The list making that is common in evangelical circles focuses on acts. This is an important consideration, particularly when there is clear teaching about a behavior. Other principles consider the consequences of a behavior. Still other principles look at character.

It is not uncommon for Christians to fall into either extreme when deciding about gray areas. They either believe that everything not mentioned in Scripture is quite good and to be enjoyed, or they believe that everything that is not mentioned in Scripture directly is to be avoided.

---

[3]"Porneia Definition," Never Thirsty, www.neverthirsty.org/bible-qa/qa-archives/question/what -is-meaning-of-greek-word-porneia-in-bible.

Marva Dawn, in her book *Sexual Character*, reflects on the character of the Christian cited in Paul's letter to the church in Galatia. In that passage, Paul shares, "The fruit of the Spirit is love, joy, peace, forbearance, kindness, goodness, faithfulness, gentleness and self-control. Against such things there is no law" (Gal 5:22-23). In our sexuality, sexual intimacy, and sexual expression, Dawn discusses agape love, contrasting it with love often expressed in the Roman context.

> In the Greek/Roman milieu of Asia Minor, men typically loved (with *eros*, "passionate eroticism") their high-class prostitutes, cared for (with *storge* or "family love") their wives, and most highly esteemed (with *philia*, the bonds of common interest) their friends.

In contrast to the Greco-Roman setting, Christians were instructed to love with agape love:

> In great contrast, men in the Christian community were commanded to love their wives with an intelligent, purposeful love, directed toward their wives' needs (*agape*). Moreover, this love was to be a symbol for all the world to see of Christ's love for his Bride, the Church. Their love for their wives was to illustrate the profound love that led Christ to submit to death in order to purify the Church. (Dawn, 1993, p. 45)

Joy is also expressed in our sexuality. It reflects gladness and delight in God's design, wonderment at the experience of pleasure, and living by God's revealed will in our sexuality. Peace reflects a sense of satisfaction in our lives. Patience is a "steadfast commitment" to one another, while kindness is our being "beneficial to others."

Goodness is expressed in generous giving, while faithfulness is shown in fidelity. Gentleness is reflected in our courtesy and consideration for one another. The Christian demonstrates self-control by exercising restraint. In 1 Corinthians 6:12, Paul writes about not being brought under the power of any particular behavior: "'All things are lawful for me,' but not all things are helpful. 'All things are lawful for me,' but I will not be dominated by anything" (ESV).

These sexual character traits, we believe, can be anchored in some relevant biblical principles. For example, we see Scripture teaching an integrated, holistic view (1 Cor 6:16-18), intimacy (Gen 4:1), creation (Rom 1:27), and stewardship (1 Cor 6:19-20).

In terms of wholeness, Christians do not want to isolate what they do from who they are and the relationship that they are in. They do not want to isolate a bodily function (genital sex) from the emotions and relationships they have, nor from the transcendent reality of God and God's purposes and intentions for sexual expression and intimacy.

True sexual intimacy, then, is an expression of this holistic view.

> Do you not know that he who is joined to a harlot is one body *with her*? For "the two," He says, "shall become one flesh." But he who is joined to the Lord is one spirit *with Him*.
>
> Flee sexual immorality. Every sin that a man does is outside the body, but he who commits sexual immorality sins against his own body. Or do you not know that your body is the temple of the Holy Spirit *who is* in you, whom you have from God, and you are not your own? For you were bought at a price; therefore glorify God in your body and in your spirit, which are God's. (1 Cor 6:16-20 NKJV)

In terms of creation, Christians understand that there is a principle grounded in the created order that can itself be ignored. For example, in Romans 1:27, Paul writes, "In the same way the men also abandoned natural relations with women." This is not meant as an argument for the origins of same-sex sexuality; we will discuss that in chapter twelve. However, a relevant question for the believer is this: Has God created the body to function in this way naturally? That principle may also be helpful to the Christian who is reflecting on sexual ethics.

CLOSING REFLECTIONS

What makes it possible to foster these qualities and characteristics in and through our sexuality? While ultimately these are reflected in the work of the Holy Spirit in the life of the Christian, we do see an important principle in the concept of stewardship. Stewardship means seeing ourselves as being responsible for those things we either have been given in this life or otherwise experience in this life. The principle of stewardship can be found in a number of passages in the Bible, such as Matthew 25:21 (where the person faithful over a few things will be made faithful over more), 1 Corinthians 4:2 (where we are encouraged to be found faithful), 1 Corinthians 6:19-20 (where our body is a temple that we are to take care of), Romans 14:12 (where we are told we will one day give an account to God), and Luke 16:1-13 (the story of the wise steward).

In the church today most discussions about stewardship are limited to what it means to steward our finances, perhaps in the context of raising funds for a new building (often referred to as a stewardship campaign), and what it means to be good stewards of the environment. Younger readers may resonate more with our application of stewardship, as there has been a generational shift in how we have prioritized taking good care of the local and global environments, in addition to concerns regarding social justice and the distribution of material goods.

Our view is that it can been helpful to extend the discussion of stewardship to the area of human sexuality and sexual expression. In matters of sexuality and the desires and impulses we may feel, it will be important to steward what has been given to us (e.g., a partner in marriage) and what we experience in our desires and impulses (e.g., sexual desires toward people where acting on those desires would be wrong).

A key consideration is that stewardship is not state dependent. The message to single Christians is not "Steward your sexuality until you get married," as if stewardship were code for practicing abstinence. Rather, stewardship is for those who are single and those who are married. It is a concept that applies to those who are primarily attracted to the opposite sex and to those who are attracted to the same sex. In that sense the principle of stewardship cuts across all of these differences among people.

There are important differences, of course, in ways people find themselves in either the married or single state. Concerning singleness, for example, a twenty-year-old male sexual minority faces different issues from a single heterosexual who lost her spouse in her mid-forties—so we will want to recognize those differences and consider what pastoral care looks like in specific cases (see Rosenau & Wilson, 2006, pp. 68-70). But stewardship reflects a call for all of us to honor God with our sexuality, as our sexuality is not ours to begin with but rather is one of many aspects of human experience that is ultimately God's, and we can find ways to honor God through our sexuality and its expression.

Stewardship can also be related to our expanded capacity to trust God. When we seek to steward our sexuality, we can invite the Holy Spirit to expand our capacity to trust God as a good and loving Father whose plan for our sexuality is better than our own plan or the plans we will hear about from others and from the broader culture. Stewardship and trust go hand in hand.

STEWARDING YOUR SEXUALITY

What does it mean to you to steward sexuality? Take a sheet of paper and draw a line down the middle vertically. On the left-hand side, write the words Sexual Self-Actualization at the top of the page. On the right-hand side, write the words Steward-ship of Sexuality at the top of the page. Now look at the left-hand side of the page. How would you describe messages from culture and personal experiences that are part of a culture of sexual self-actualization? For example, if you heard "Do what you want" as a message about sex, you might identify where you first heard that message, how it was conveyed, and so on. You might also identify messages that have ridiculed a Christian sexual ethic in the media or popular culture. Again, identify that specific message (e.g., "Folks who wait until marriage to have sex are just pitiful!") and how it was communi-cated to you. Write these messages on the left-hand side of the page. Some people have written down TV shows or movies that have contributed to the message of sexual self-actualization. Others have added some of their own experiences that were based more on short-term interests than longer-term considerations.

Now look at the right-hand column. What messages from your community, close friends, and your own personal decisions seem to reflect what it means to steward your sexuality? Write these on the right-hand side of the page. These might include decisions to be transparent with close friends about difficult decisions you are facing, times when you have resisted temptation in an area that has been difficult for you, or saying no to one thing so you could say yes to something you saw as better for you so that you experienced delayed gratification in a meaningful way.

We close our discussion of a Christian perspective on sexuality and sexual behavior with a reminder about our first love. For Christians, our first love is God, and God is actually jealous for us. Jealousy is an unpleasant emotion that reflects concern or wariness that the intimacy shared with the one I love will be supplanted by another. It is the sentiment that goes with the statement "You can't have what is mine!" God is described as jealous, suggesting he does not want to lose the love we have for him to a rival. Indeed, God's name is Jealous (Ex 34:14), so it is more than just an adjective to describe God or an attribute of God; rather, it is who God is. God is jealous for our love and desire.

Although the focus of this chapter is on sexuality, obviously human love and desire can be directed toward many things that are not sexual: money and possessions are probably two of the top rivals for our interests. When we covet what other people have—money and possessions—we are allowing our desires to be directed away from God and toward our own self-interest (Jas 4:2-3). At the same time, sexuality does seem to hold a unique place in discussions of jealousy.

Sexuality becomes an area of concern insofar as we allow our sexual interests to reflect things that are not blessed by God, not part of God's intention for sexuality and sexual expression. We can then rightly be described as "adulterous" people when we seek intimacy in and through what the world offers rather than through who God is and what God provides for us (Jas 4:4). We are to be faithful to God, yet we can often drift away from God and his purposes and toward our own sinful self-centeredness. What God longs for is his own spirit that is within us (Jas 4:5). We do not know all of what this entails, but there is certainly a faithfulness to God that is reflected in how we live our lives, what posture we take toward our own sin (a posture of repentance as contrasted with a posture of defiance), and how we form our identity as sexual beings.

REFERENCES

American Psychological Association. (2009). *Report of the task force on appropriate therapeutic responses to sexual orientation.*

Carson, D. A. (2012). *The intolerance of tolerance.* Eerdmans.

Colón, C. A., & Field, B. E. (2009). *Singled out: Why celibacy must be reinvented in today's church.* Brazos.

Dawn, M. (1993). *Sexual character: Beyond technique to intimacy.* Eerdmans.

Ehrman, B. D. (2006). *The lost Gospel of Judas Iscariot: A new look at betrayer and betrayed.* Oxford University Press.

Erickson, M. J. (2001). *Introducing Christian doctrine* (2nd ed.). Baker.

Freitas, D. (2008). *Sex and the soul: Juggling sexuality, spirituality, romance, and religion on America's college campuses.* Oxford University Press.

Freitas, D. (2013). *The end of sex: How hookup culture is leaving a generation unhappy, sexually unfulfilled, and confused about intimacy.* Basic Books.

Goetz, S., & Taliaferro, C. (2008). *Naturalism.* Eerdmans.

Hathaway, W. L., & Yarhouse, M. A. (2021). *The Integration of psychology and Christianity: A domain-based approach.* InterVarsity Press.

Herdt, G. (1996). Developmental discontinuities and sexual orientation across cultures. In D. P. McWhirter, S. A. Sanders, & J. M. Reinisch (Eds.), *Homosexuality/ heterosexuality: Concepts of sexual orientation* (pp. 208-36). Oxford University Press.

Hollinger, D. P. (2009). *The meaning of sex.* Baker Academic.

John Paul II (1997). *The theology of the body: Human love in the divine plan.* Pauline Books & Media.

Jones, S. L. (1999). Sexuality. In D. G. Benner & P. C. Hill (Eds.), *Baker encyclopedia of psychology & counseling.* Baker.

Jones, S. L., & Butman, R. E. (1991). *Modern psychotherapies: A comprehensive Christian appraisal.* InterVarsity Press.

Jones, S. L., & Jones, B. (2007). *How and when to tell your kids about sex: A lifelong approach to shaping your child's sexual character.* NavPress.

Jones, S. L., & Yarhouse, M. A. (2000). *Homosexuality: The use of scientific research in the church's moral debate.* InterVarsity Press.

Pagels, E., & King, K. L. (2008). *Reading Judas: The Gospel of Judas and the shaping of Christianity.* Penguin.

Rosenau, D., & Wilson, M. T. (2006). *Soul virgins: Redefining single sexuality.* Baker.

Smedes, L. (1994). *Sex for Christians* (Rev. ed.). Eerdmans.

Thielicke, H. (1975). *The ethics of sex.* Baker.

West, C. (2004). *Theology of the body for beginners.* Ascension Press.

TWO

SEXUALITY IN SOCIOCULTURAL PERSPECTIVE

Sexuality is a big issue, but there are others—how much you commit to a relationship, to social obligation, to honesty and being honest with yourself.

ANG LEE

Sexuality is a private matter; some believe that broadcasting it destroys the very things that make it sacred.

LANCE LOUD

THE LEE AND LOUD QUOTES in this chapter's epigraphs suggest that there is variability regarding the issue of sexuality in terms of how it is viewed, how it may be approached as a topic of discussion, and how it may be presented from one individual to another. While some individuals may believe that sexuality is a matter of individual concern, others may believe that it is a significant cultural and communal experience. For example, in *Real Sex*, Lauren Winner posits that it is important to consider the communal nature of sexuality because it manifests in the presentation of gender, male versus female, and how we interact on the topic affects how we think and feel about it, and how we act on it.

An individual's sexuality is not developed in a vacuum apart from influences. Various aspects of one's sexuality are affected by the culture we grew up in. For example, the perception of gender, gender roles, values related to sexual behavior and sexual identity, communication from family members and peers about sexuality and sexual behaviors (both content and presentation), exposure to media, and education about sexuality may all weigh in on an individual's experience of his or her sexuality. This section examines several contributions to the development of sexuality from a sociocultural perspective.

In recognition of the complexity of sexuality, the following was described in a call to action to promote sexual health and responsible sexual behavior (Satcher, 2001):

> We must understand that sexuality encompasses more than sexual behavior, that the many aspects of sexuality include not only the physical, but the mental and spiritual as well, and that sexuality is a core component of personality. Sexuality is a fundamental part of human life. While the problems usually associated with sexual behavior are real and need to be addressed, human sexuality also has significant meaning and value in each individual's life. This call, and the discussion it is meant to generate, is not just intended for health care professionals or policy makers. It is intended for parents, teachers, clergy, social service professionals—all of us. (p. 2)

As such, sexuality is much more than just a biological thing. As humans, we interact daily out of our sexuality, whether it is conscious or not. Our sexuality manifests in our behaviors, thoughts, attitudes, values, and speech.

HOW DO SOCIETY AND CULTURE CONTRIBUTE TO VIEWS OF SEX?

Society's and culture's views of sex are generally derived from anthropological studies. Surveys are common methods of data collection that can elucidate differences from one culture to another. From a global perspective Laumann et al. (2006) conducted a global assessment of sexual satisfaction with a survey of 27,500 men and women between the ages of forty and eighty in twenty-nine countries. Citizens of Austria, Canada, France, Mexico, Sweden, and the United States reported the highest level of sexual satisfaction. Citizens in Brazil, Israel, Italy, and Turkey reported a medium level of satisfaction. Those who resided in Japan and Taiwan were found to report the lowest level of satisfaction.

Among those surveyed (Laumann et al., 2006), two-thirds of people in Western countries reported physical and emotional satisfaction regarding their sexual life. Half of the men and a third of the women stated that sex was extremely important in their lives. The portion of the population reporting this was smaller in the Middle East, where 50% of men and 38% of women stated their sex lives were satisfying. Sixty percent of men and 37% of women identified sex as being important in their lives. In East Asian countries, one-fourth of men and women reported satisfying sex lives. Twenty-eight percent of men and 12% of women reported sex as being important in their lives.

In spite of differences in culture and tradition, monogamy and commitment were reported as valued and cherished across the world. In all countries surveyed (Laumann et al., 2006), women had positive associations with foreplay. One in three women reported sexual problems affecting her happiness. As such, sexual well-being was correlated with happiness for both men and women.

In addition to positive emotions, Laumann et al. (2006) found that couples who resided in countries where men and women held equal status were more likely to report physically and emotionally satisfying sex lives. In more patriarchal countries, where men tend to be more dominant, older couples reported less satisfying sex, particularly in East Asia. As such, relationships that are based on equality are more likely to support interactions and behaviors where both partners' needs are met. Establishment of these patterns of interaction may be due to cultural scripts (McMinn, 2004), which are learned ways of relating that reinforce men and women for behaviors that are pertinent to their cultural context. As such, these scripts tend to vary between cultures and geographic locations, and from one time period in history to another.

SEXUAL ATTITUDES AND BEHAVIORS IN THE UNITED STATES

Every few years the Centers for Disease Control and Prevention (CDC) conducts the Youth Risk Behavior Surveillance Survey (YRBS) to capture trends among adolescents with respect to risky behaviors and physical health. Among high school students surveyed in 2021, the CDC continues to report a decline in sexual behavior among adolescents.

- 30% have had sexual intercourse
- 21% had had sexual intercourse during the previous three months, and of these 48% did not use a condom the last time they had sex; 67% did not use birth control pills or Depo-Provera to prevent pregnancy the last time they had sex

- 6% had had sex with four or more people during their life
- 3% of teens have had sex prior to the age of thirteen

It is encouraging to see a steady decline in sexual behavior among adolescents. Teens who are sexually active put themselves at risk for HIV infection, other sexually transmitted infections (STIs), and unintended pregnancy. According to the CDC (2023), "annual HIV infections dropped from 9,300 in 2017 to 6,100 in 2021 among 13- to 24-year-olds." Much of the decline is apparently due to reductions in infections among young gay and bisexual males, which is encouraging.

Although we see a reduction in teen sexual activity, it is still important to be familiar with factors that increase the likelihood of teen sexual activity (see Inanc et al., 2020). These include the following:

- early pubertal development
- being born to teen parents
- insecure attachment to parents
- history of abuse or neglect
- alcohol and drug use
- living in a single-parent household
- having an older, influential sibling
- perceiving that "everyone" is engaging in sexual activity
- impulsive personality
- deviant peer group

In spite of the consequences of teen sexual activity, which include STIs, pregnancy, and early parenting, teens report positive motivations for sex, such as pursuit of intimacy, sexual pleasure, and social status. Co-occurring issues that facilitate risky sexual behaviors include alcohol consumption and illicit drug use. According to the CDC, of the 30% of adolescents who reported they are currently sexually active, 21% reported having consumed alcohol or having taken some drug prior to their last sexual intercourse (CDC, 2021).

According to the Guttmacher Institute, "rates of adolescent pregnancies, births and abortions have all been plummeting for decades, mostly as the direct result of improved contraceptive use. Likewise, for the population overall, there is no evidence that sexual activity has increased—and pregnancy, birth and abortion rates have been declining" (Dreweke, 2019).

The data on sexuality and sexual behavior in the United States actually reflect a trend toward more conservative attitudes for older adolescents and young adults compared to the previous generation. Any movement toward sexual restraint is quite remarkable when we consider the sociocultural context of sexualization of young people that is so apparent in the media and entertainment.

In a study (Lastoria & Association for Christians in Student Development, 2011) of over 2,300 Christian college students, there was a negative relationship between religiosity and sexual permissiveness. The greater the religiosity, the less likely the student was to be sexually permissive. Indeed, scores on measures of sexual permissiveness fell as church attendance rose; as students reported more prayer, meditation, and reading of Scripture; or as the belief that religion influenced one's life increased (Lastoria & Association for Christians in Student Development, 2011, p. 11). Both males and females were generally opposed to casual sexual contact (hooking up), including sexual intercourse but also oral sex, mutual masturbation, dry sex ("bumping and grinding"), and fondling of genitals or breasts (see Freitas, 2008, 2013).

The attitudes and behaviors of these Christian college students contrast with other large-scale studies of the broader population of college-age students. In the spring 2023 *National College Health Assessment* (American College Health Association, 2023), for instance, males and females were in the minority if they reported no sexual partners (oral or vaginal intercourse) in the past twelve months, whereas most students (74%–75% for oral sex, 80%–84% for vaginal sex) in the Christian college study did not report this behavior in the past twelve months.

SEXUALIZATION

Societal influences on the development of sexuality are complex. Of particular interest is the phenomenon of sexualization, the process by which a culture or society may communicate values about sexuality to an individual. The American Psychological Association (APA) set up a task force to evaluate the sexualization of girls. After two years of data collection, the report was released in 2007 and is available to the public and widely cited. The results of the report identify media sources that sexualize girls as having a negative impact on girls' self-image and healthy development.

According to the APA task force, *sexualization* is defined as the value that a person receives from sexual behavior or appeal (excluding other characteristics), the objectification of a person in a sexual manner, the definition of *sexiness* as standard of physical attractiveness, and the inappropriate imposition of sexuality and values on another. This last point is particularly important with respect to children because they are usually not the ones to choose exposure or to be sexualized. Any one of these points needs to be fulfilled to meet criteria for "sexualization"—particularly objectification.

Examples of sexualization include the following (APA, 2007):

- a five-year-old girl wearing a T-shirt that says "Flirt"
- ads portraying grown women as young girls, who are dressed with pigtails in sexual poses
- the higher frequency of females portrayed sexually in an objectified manner compared with males

A subtler example may be hair removal under the arms, on the legs, even the bikini line, which recasts women's bodies as those of prepubescent girls. Problems arise when sexualized adolescent girls believe that they ought to look sexy but do not know or are not aware of what it means to be sexual, to have sexual desires, and to be responsible with respect to their sexuality.

In considering influences of sexualization, it is necessary to consider the importance of modeling—whether it is by family members, peers, representatives in the media, and so on. Explicit and implicit messages are being communicated to adolescents—boys and girls—about what is considered to be "sexy." All forms of media, such as ads, commercials, music, television programs, movies, websites, digital and social media, and other outlets not only cultivate values but also assist in the proliferation of present values that a particular culture may endorse about sexuality. At the same time it is also important to recognize that children, adolescents, and adults are not simply empty vessels that media is poured into; they are active in seeking these things out.

We have seen a rise in the use of social media, especially YouTube, Tik Tok, Instagram, and Snapchat. A 2022 Pew survey (Vogels, Gelles-Watnick, & Massarat, 2022) reported that

- 95% of teens have access to a smartphone, 90% to a desktop or laptop computer, and 80% to a gaming console
- 95% of teens use YouTube (19% "almost constantly" visiting the site)

- 67% of teens use Tik Tok (16% "almost constantly," and girls more likely than boys)
- 62% of teens use Instagram and 59% of teens use Snapchat
- over a third (36%) of teens say they spend too much time on social media

Sexualization is often conveyed via traditional visual communication such as television, movies, and magazines, where television programming, for instance, has been disproportionately male oriented, with the majority of comments objectifying women. This is particularly concerning because the majority of moviegoers are adolescents. Thus, it is notable that nudity is asymmetrical in its presentation (that is, more women than men are depicted nude or partially nude). In addition, the majority of characters in top-grossing movies are male. Sexual harassment is demonstrated in sexist comments (e.g., derogatory names), verbal sexual comments (e.g., "knockers," "jugs"), and body language (e.g., leering).

Cartoons are not absolved of responsibility from sexualization. As an example, as years have passed with the release of more animated features, female characters portrayed have more cleavage and less clothing, and are sexier than those in the past (e.g., Jasmine from *Aladdin* versus Cinderella). Other cartoons depict female characters as lovesick, interested in boys, and overly concerned with their appearance.

Compared to traditional visual communication, social media is today the more prominent source of messaging for adolescents (Papageorgiou, Cross, & Fisher, 2022). Social media "features an abundance of images portraying girls and women as sexually available and objectified that emphasize sexual attractiveness and physical appearance" (p. 433). Moreover, "when adolescent girls view sexualized images while using social media, they may internalize an observer's perspective as a primary view of themselves and their body as an object valued for its appearance" (p. 433).

Similarly, relationships are also a significant source of sexualization, such as peers, parents, teachers, coworkers, and institutions. Some relationships may proliferate sexualization by emphasizing that a certain physique needs to be maintained for attractiveness. For example, organizations, institutions, and employers may choose members or employees who cater to a particular look or presentation, such as Hooters.

While the majority of individuals may be exposed to more subtle forms of sexualization, some are forced to participate in more extreme forms, such as assault, abuse, and sex trafficking. In these instances the effects may include trauma and other significant concerns, such as mental health issues, impacted relationships, and problems with self-objectification.

This latter experience, self-objectification, is the process of sexualizing oneself by pursuing a particular image, treating oneself as an object, and reducing one's value to one's perception of one's sexuality. Although self-objectification is most obviously seen in extreme examples of sexual abuse and sex trafficking, it is also conveyed in more subtle messages associated with sexualization.

The negative effects of sexualization. With respect to cognitive and emotional consequences, sexualization and objectification can undermine a girl's self-confidence and comfort in her own body, resulting in emotional and self-image problems, such as shame and anxiety. This effect can also apply to boys, who may perceive that they need to be more muscular or strong. Self-objectification can also detract from attention that needs to be directed toward other things. In one study, students tried on swimsuits or sweaters. While they were waiting, they completed a math test. Performance was notably worse for females who tried on swimsuits (Fredrickson et al., 1998).

Sexualization is linked with the three most common disorders diagnosed in girls and women: eating disorders, low self-esteem, and depression. Sexualization also affects a girl's ability to maintain a healthy sexual self-image and healthy sexual behavior. Girls who demonstrate more self-objectification are less likely to engage in condom usage (Impett et al., 2006) and express less sexual assertiveness. Research has also found that females who consume more mainstream media are more likely to endorse stereotypes of sex roles and to place physical attractiveness at the core of a woman's value (Zurbriggen & Morgan, 2006).

The sexualization of girls also affects how boys view girls and interact within their own relationships. For example, sexualization can contribute to relational difficulties insofar as men have more difficulty finding "acceptable" female partners or otherwise make unreasonable comparisons to images and fantasy. Sexualization can also lead to increased sexism, increased sexual harassment, and increased child pornography (APA, 2007).

How can we help combat the effects of sexualization? Although sexualization is in some ways ubiquitous in our culture, and the effects of sexualization are profound, there are helpful, constructive ways to respond to and combat sexualization. One of the more promising responses is to foster personal resilience. Resilience is a skill set that can be taught. It is not just a trait that people have or don't have. It comprises multiple skills, attributes, and abilities that promote endurance of hardship, difficulties, and challenges. Although resilience is often discussed in the context of overcoming odds that seem stacked against a person—as in identifying resilient factors that distinguish children who might succeed despite an impoverished family life from those who do not succeed—it is also a concept that can be applied to the area of sexualization and how a person responds to a sexualizing sociocultural context as they develop a sense of self-worth.

Protective factors for resilience are internal and external. Internal factors include intelligence, social facility, and self-regulation. People vary in these areas, some of which can be developed or cultivated, such as being intentional about delaying gratification and learning how to regulate emotions and responses to felt needs.

External factors include competent parents, friendships, supportive social networks, and schools. Having supportive parents, healthy and supportive friendships, and extended social networks, as well as school systems that both challenge and provide support to young people, are all factors related to resilience.

In their description of resilience, Dent and Cameron (2003) note the following:

> Resilience is the concept that is used to describe the flexibility that allows certain children and young people who appear to be at risk to bounce back from adversity, to cope with and manage major difficulties and disadvantages in life, and even to thrive in the face of what appear to be overwhelming odds. Resilient individuals seem to be able to understand what has happened to them (insight), develop an understanding of what has happened to others (empathy) and experience a quality of life that is often denied to others (achievement). (p. 5)

Adverse factors hindering resilience include maternal depression, marital discord, domestic violence, abuse, neglect, and separation and loss through bereavement, divorce, or separation (Dent & Cameron, 2003). These factors tend to be beyond a child or adolescent's control; however, the benefit to developing resilience is that protective factors are well within the grasp of an individual and can be taught. These protective factors include proactive orientation, self-regulation, proactive parenting, having connections and attachments, school orientation, and participation in community.

Proactive orientation refers to the ability to take initiative in one's life, believing in one's effectiveness and having a realistic and positive sense of self. With a proactive orientation an individual believes he or she can influence the environment and is not passive. Hardships are seen as learning opportunities. With self-regulation, an individual maintains control over his or her emotions, behavior, and attention. Modulation of emotions and behavior are due to the use of self-soothing to calm oneself and can elicit positive attention from other people. Impulse control and delay of self-gratification are byproducts of self-regulation.

Interpersonal support is a vital part of resilience and takes the form of the other factors mentioned. The balance of warmth, support, and love with reasonable limits (i.e., an authoritative parenting style) is correlated with high levels of resilience. In addition, having secure attachment between a child and parent figures can help facilitate emotional regulation, as well as the development of trust and resilience. Securely attached children are more likely to participate in activities requiring exploration, thus extending beyond themselves and their present circumstances. Insecurely attached children are more likely to perceive ordinary stressors as intense threats and are more susceptible to bullying, accidents, delinquency, poor relationship development, eating disorders, drug abuse, early pregnancy, and other chronic health problems.

SEX AND THE iWORLD

Sociocultural changes have led to an age of individualism or what Kuehne (2009) describes as "iWorld." He contrasts the iWorld with the traditional world of the previous generation. That world "was constructed on relationships of obligation. Each person was born into a matrix of relationships in which there were mutual obligations and responsibilities" (p. 35). In contrast, the iWorld claims to be free from nature, authority, and want (at least in the West). It functions "like a mechanism that consistently attempts to determine and deliver the broadest possible extent of individual freedom" (p. 67). Sexuality in the iWorld is not constrained by normative claims about sexual morality, cultural expectations for gender, or even biological differences. Rather, the freedoms we claim give us access to unprecedented self-expression, identity, and behavior.

As Kuehne (2009) observes, it is unclear whether the iWorld can sustain itself:

Does the iWorld possess enough coherence to continue to hold itself together, or will its citizens, in their individual pursuits, find themselves diverging even further from any shared interests with their fellow citizens? Will the iWorld be able to avoid the social, societal, and political fragmentation that would lead to its disintegration? (p. 213)

What do you see as a way forward in response to the iWorld we currently live in? It is unlikely we will move back toward a world we once knew. If that is the case, what does moving ahead mean for the church? How do you see meaningful relationships and community playing a part of the future vision for the local church and the broader body of Christ? What challenges will Christians face? How might some of those challenges be addressed?

Outside the family, developing positive connections with others facilitates social competence and positive attention. Being achievement oriented in school can decrease the risk of antisocial behavior. Emphasizing areas of competence in children can help them experience a sense of achievement. IQ or intelligence is multifaceted and includes academic, athletic, relational, emotional, musical, bodily-kinesthetic, and artistic modalities. Last, participation in social organizations, religious organizations, and ethnic community groups is helpful for modeling various coping strategies, and the latter is especially important for fostering a secure identity and managing racism for ethnic minorities.

Fostering resilience has many implications (Dent & Cameron, 2003). It teaches discrimination of controllable from uncontrollable events, encourages emotional expression, provides opportunities for mastery, and promotes positive thinking. Being able to distinguish between controllable and uncontrollable events promotes problem solving and question generation to enhance alternative thinking. Accurate emotional expression requires the ability to tolerate both pleasant and unpleasant emotions. By being able to communicate emotions effectively, needs are more likely to be met. Positive thinking is a keystone in the development of optimism and varied perspectives. Teaching children to think that negative events are temporary versus permanent and "changing channels" through stopping of unpleasant thoughts and emotions facilitates positive thinking.

The principles of developing resilience are beneficial for countering the subtle and pervasive messages prescribed by sexualization, which negatively affect cognitive functioning, attitudes and beliefs, sexuality, emotional health, and physical health, especially for girls (APA, 2007). The ability to resist these messages can lead to critical thinking and selective consumption of media, empowerment, and education.

RESEARCH ACROSS THE LIFESPAN

Adolescents. Facts regarding the prevalence of adolescent sexuality were reported earlier. One notable factor contributing to sexual behavior, especially among adolescent girls, is the age of a girl's first sexual partner. In a study of 4,201 adolescent girls between eighth and twelfth grade, the researchers found that among teen girls who first had sex between thirteen and fifteen, the proportion who had partners who were much older was not significant. However, for those who had their first experience of sexual intercourse between the ages of eleven and twelve, 34% had partners who were much older (Leitenberg & Saltzman, 2000). It was observed that problem behaviors, such as more suicide attempts, increased alcohol and drug abuse, more truancy, and a greater likelihood of pregnancy, were correlated with a younger age of first sexual intercourse.

Summarizing the research found on school attendance as a correlate of reduced risky sexual behaviors, the Surgeon General's *Call to Action to Promote Sexual Health and Responsible Sexual Behavior* reports that around the world, as girls become more educated by completing elementary school, the frequency of births given by adolescents has diminished (Satcher, 2001, p. 9). In the United States adolescents who drop out of school are more likely to participate in sexual activity earlier, not use contraception, become pregnant, and give birth. Conversely, research has also found that participation in extracurricular activities, such as athletics, are especially helpful for reducing risky sexual behavior for girls.

Young adults. Young adulthood, particularly the transition between high school and college or university, is a significant time of change for many. Developmental shifts in values occur at this stage, which affect behaviors and attitudes, including sexual behaviors and values. What are the differences between those who participate in sexual activity and those who do not?

In a sample of college students, those who had high levels of parental and peer perceived awareness and caring (PAC) participated less frequently in sexual behaviors (Wetherill, Neal, & Fromme, 2010). Previous research has found that parental monitoring is an important factor in regulating teen risky behavior. Similarly, peer support and peer monitoring can help to decrease risky behaviors. Wetherill et al. (2010) propose that perceived awareness and caring is the synthesis of monitoring and support from peers and parents. Being aware of how others may perceive an individual's behavior may result in altered behaviors as a result of these perceptions. Higher levels of perceived awareness and caring from parents and peers was associated with fewer risky behaviors and sexual behaviors. They also found that having liberal sexual values in conjunction with high PAC from parents and peers was associated with a higher number of sexual partners and more frequent unsafe sexual behavior. Thus, PAC may not be a deterrent for individuals who hold more permissive views regarding sexual behavior. Students who had liberal sexual values, high PAC from parents, and low peer PAC tended to engage less frequently in unsafe sex. In this study an increase in the number of sexual partners was found for women but not men, suggesting that there may be more opportunities for freshman women to have sexual partners who are upperclassman compared with freshman men. The lack of increase in unsafe sex may be a result in the availability of contraceptives in college compared with high school. For individuals who endorsed more conservative sexual values, increased PAC from parents was associated with a slight decrease in sexual partners, whereas individuals who endorsed more liberal sexual values tended to increase their number of sexual partners.

Among students who initiated sexual activity compared with those who continued to abstain in their first six months of college, differences were found in motivation, which tended to occur prior to behavioral changes (Patrick & Lee, 2010). Specific motivations included intimacy and a sense of relational enhancement. Those who transitioned also reported that there were greater motivational changes in the six months preceding college, including decreases in values and not being ready for sex. At the end of six months those who had transitioned endorsed similar values to those who had been sexually active prior to college.

The definition of what it means to "have sex" may also play a role in motivations, attitudes, and sexual behaviors. A sample of young adults in college tended to define activities that included genital stimulation in their definition of "having sex," specifically penile-vaginal intercourse and penile-anal intercourse (Byers, Henderson, & Hobson, 2009). The definition of "sexual abstinence" was more variable in regards to sexual activities that included unidirectional genital stimulation (e.g., oral sex, genital fondling); however, more students tended to identify these behaviors as "abstinent" versus "having sex." Orgasm was often used as a hallmark to determine whether a behavior was considered abstinent. Religiously conservative students, males more than females, were likely to consider unidirectional genital activities as sexual abstinence, suggesting that they may be most at risk for sexually transmitted infections. These views appear to be fairly consistent across the Atlantic Ocean. In comparing the sexual attitudes of undergraduates in the United States with those in the United Kingdom, there appears to be consensus regarding the definition of "having sex" as it relates to the role of penile-vaginal penetration (Pitts & Rahman, 2001). The area of least consensus was oral-genital contact, as demonstrated by the fact that some who have had oral-genital contact in the absence of penile-vaginal penetration do not consider it to be sex. The majority (82%) of women who have experienced penile-anal intercourse considered it to be sex, whereas 30% of men who have had that experience did not consider it to be so.

There were 26 million new cases of STIs in 2018, and nearly half of those were among older adolescents and young adults (CDC, 2022). As such, it is important to discern what factors promote risky sexual behaviors, such as lack of condom usage. Oncale and King (2001) sampled undergraduate men and women regarding their attitudes toward condom usage. Fourteen percent of women and 17% of men reported they actively attempted to dissuade their sexual partners from using a condom. Thirty percent of men and 41% of women reported that their partners had made those attempts to dissuade them from use of a condom with verbal strategies including, "sex feels better without a condom," "won't get pregnant," "will not get a sexually transmitted disease," and "condoms presented a lack of spontaneity." Those who reported ten or more lifetime sexual partners were more likely to attempt to dissuade their partners from using condoms. In addition, these individuals were less likely to use condoms consistently.

In looking at the sexual practices of college students, females with both sex experience and males with both sex or only same-sex experiences reported having multiple recent sexual partners compared to their peers who reported only opposite-sex partners (Eisenberg, 2001). Consistent condom use was lower for men with only same-sex experience compared with those who reported only opposite-sex experience. In addition, nonwhite students and older male students reported a higher number of sexual partners within thirty days compared with those who were younger and lived on campus.

Developmental contexts have been found to predict risky sexual behaviors (Bailey et al., 2011). Participation in a romantic relationship was correlated with a lower probability of casual sex, yet inconsistent condom use was likely to be higher. Young adults who lived at home were also less likely to participate in high-risk sexual behavior, which is consistent with prior research regarding parental monitoring. Attendance in college was also correlated with a lower probability with high-risk sex; however, it did not diminish the probability of casual sex or inconsistent condom use. Young adults are more likely to continue patterns of behavior that were established in high school, without the influence of college.

Adults. Among adults, healthy sexuality is composed of physical, emotional, and mental health. It tends to foster intimacy, bonding, and shared pleasure. It is consensual and mutually respectful between partners. It is assumed that healthy sexuality can be the normative experience for many adults. What are factors that can hinder healthy sexuality?

Sexual health refers to the experience of protection against STIs (including HIV), a lack of sexual dysfunction or coercion, and the possibility of sexually pleasurable experiences. Kuyper and Vanwesenbeeck (2011) examined sexual health domains among heterosexual and LGB adults. Compared with their heterosexual peers, bisexual women and bisexual or gay men reported experiencing sexual coercion more frequently. Specifically, compared with heterosexual women, bisexual women reported a higher incidence of sexual coercion. In addition, they reported greater need for professional sexual health care. A similar pattern was reported for bisexual and gay men. Having a higher number of sexual partners was observed as a risk factor for sexual victimization in women. Bisexual women were observed to have a higher level of sexual victimization compared with lesbian or heterosexual women; however, this may be due to the greater number of sexual partners. Younger, more religious women and women with more sexual partners reported needing greater sexual health care compared with their peers. For men, those who were younger, single men with more sexual partners, and gay men reported requiring greater sexual health care. Sexual victimization was related to having more partners and more negative social reactions.

What about frequency of sex among married couples? In a more recent set of studies of marital couples (Feldhahn & Sytsma, 2023), 4% reported having sex daily, 29% of couples having sex one to two times per week, 28% reported one to three times per month, and 23% reported less than once a month (or not at all). Those who reported less frequent sex tended to be older (among those over 60, 36% reported less than monthly or not at all, while 27% of those age 41-60 reported less than monthly or not at all, and only 5% of those under age 40 reported the same). Reasons for less frequent sexual activity included age but also physical issues, while for some it was by choice or relational matters (Feldhahn & Sytsma, 2023).

Greater sexual satisfaction was reported for men and women who stated that they had a steady partner. For men in this study (Kuyper & Vanwesenbeeck, 2011), higher sexual satisfaction was also reported for those who also had a higher number of different sexual partners. Within the LGB subsample, sexual satisfaction with women was related to having a steady partner, being older, having lower internalized homonegativity, and experiencing fewer negative reactions from others as a result of same-sex attraction (SSA). Bisexual men and men with steady partners were reported to be most satisfied with their sex lives. Men who reported lower levels of sexual satisfaction tended to also report a negative opinion of their sexual orientation. High levels of internalized homonegativity were associated with more frequent sexual dysfunction. Sexual orientation did not predict any differences regarding sexual satisfaction or dysfunction between LGB and heterosexual groups. The results suggest that healthcare practitioners benefit from being aware that minority stress is a helpful factor to consider regarding sexual health. Specifically, internalized homonegativity was predictive of lower sexual satisfaction, increased dysfunction, and greater healthcare need.

Although there are some countries and cultures that practice non-monogamy and polygamy, monogamy tends to be valued in the United States. A study conducted by Henrich, Boyd, and Richerson (2012) found that monogamous relationships have tended to become the standard in developed nations because there is less crime, violence, poverty, and gender inequality in societies where monogamous marriages are the norm. In addition, monogamous marriages are also related to lower rates of child abuse and neglect, and accidental death and homicide.

In spite of the benefits associated with monogamous marriages, affairs still occur. Banfield and McCabe (2001) examined extra-relationship involvement (ERI) in women to assess the factors that contribute to sexual, emotional, or combined emotional and sexual ERIs. Positive influences on a woman's decision to participate in an ERI included social norms, planning, relationship satisfaction, and past behavior. Women who expressed commitment to their present relationship tended to diminish ERI intentions. Women who were more likely to participate in a combined (i.e., sexual and emotional) ERI tended to have more positive attitudes toward a combined

ERI, in addition to greater intentions for participating in one. The results suggest that women tend to base their decision on participation in an ERI on other people's opinions as opposed to their own beliefs. For the most part women who participated in emotional and combined ERIs did so because of the romantic feelings they had toward their ERI partner. As such, women tend to need an emotional connection in order to participate in an ERI.

Emotional well-being has been found to be a predictor of sexual distress, along with the quality of the emotional relationship partners experience during sexual activity (Bancroft, Loftus, & Long, 2003). In this sample, physical aspects of women's sexual response, such as arousal, vaginal lubrication, and orgasm, were not found to be reliable predictors of sexual distress. Those who "thought about sex with interest every day" tended to experience the most distress with respect to their relationship. Individuals who tend to think about sex with interest are more likely to be distressed if the relationship is not going well. A problematic sexual relationship may increase the likelihood of thinking and ruminating about sex. In addition, if a woman is not comfortable thinking about sex, she may subsequently be troubled by thoughts about sex. Although older women may experience more frequent problems with sex, younger women appear to be more likely to be troubled by it.

CULTURE AND ETHNICITY

It is well documented in research that ethnic and cultural experiences significantly affect sexuality and sexual expression. For example, even in the same country, ethnic heritage and the process of acculturation can mediate sexual behaviors and attitudes. Meston and Ahrold (2010) sought to examine general differences in normative sexual practices among Euro-American, Asian, and Hispanic individuals. Similar to previous studies, Asians were found to have more conservative sexual experiences, lower frequency of sexual behaviors, and fewer lifetime partners, and were older during their sexual debut compared with their Euro-American or Hispanic peers.

Hispanic participants reported similar sexual experiences in frequency and attitudes as the Euro-Americans. Among Asian women, there was a significant interaction between acculturation of mainstream and heritage experiences in predicting the number of lifetime sexual partners. The correlation between heritage acculturation and casual sexual behavior was stronger with lower mainstream acculturation. Among Hispanic men, higher levels of mainstream acculturation predicted more casual sexual behavior if heritage acculturation was low.

In this sample (Meston & Ahrold, 2010), Asian men reported the least amount of sexual experience. Asian men and women reported longer gaps in time between first sexual caress and sexual intercourse compared with Euro-American women, whose age at first intercourse and first sexual activity tended to converge. Among Asian women, differences in casual sexual behavior were predicted by assimilation, which is the process of giving up heritage culture in adoption of mainstream culture. Heritage acculturation tended to predict age of sexual debut for Asian men. These results suggest that in the development of sexual attitudes, acculturation to the mainstream may function as exposure to new perspectives regarding sexuality. This in turn may be affected by an individual's heritage acculturation because interpersonal sexuality tends to be influenced more by the environment.

In addition to cultural and ethnic influences, religiosity and spirituality have been documented as factors that mediate sexual behaviors. Generally, religiously conservative individuals are less likely to participate in risky sexual behaviors. How do culture and religiosity interact as factors in sexual attitudes? In a study examining sexual attitudes as influenced by acculturation and religiosity, 1,415 college students participated in a study assessing attitudes toward casual sex, extramarital sex, traditional gender roles, and homosexuality (Ahrold & Meston, 2010). Compared with their Hispanic and Euro-American peers, Asians tended to report the most conservative sexual attitudes. Hispanic and Euro-American participants reported attitudes similar to each other. Higher levels of acculturation yielded more similar sexual attitudes to Euro-Americans for the Hispanic and Asian participants.

Among Asian, Hispanic and Euro-American women, higher levels of spirituality predicted more conservative sexual attitudes and intrinsic religiosity. For the Euro-American and Asian participants, intrinsic religiosity and religious fundamentalism also predicted conservative sexual attitudes, which was not as pronounced among the Hispanic participants (Ahrold & Meston, 2010). The effects of ethnic differences in religiosity were found to be separate from the influences of acculturation. Higher levels of mainstream acculturation predicted greater conservativism of attitudes toward extramarital sexuality in Hispanic and Asian males because of shifts in cultural values. For Hispanic males, machismo has been found to be associated with multiple sexual partners in previous research. In more traditional Asian cultures, the expectation of conformity to gender roles suggested that fulfillment of duties to one's wife and family first may elicit condoning of extramarital sex. Thus, acculturation to mainstream values tended to elicit more conservative views of extramarital sex with Hispanic and Asian males in this sample.

Liberal sexual attitudes, with the exception of extramarital sex, were related to higher levels of mainstream acculturation for Hispanic participants. Among Asians, less heritage acculturation predicted more liberal sexual attitudes as they moved away from more traditional values consistent with their culture. As such, heritage acculturation may be a significant factor in Asian cultures with respect to development of sexuality. Heritage culture may be the lens through which Asians participate in mainstream culture. In this study (Ahrold & Meston, 2010), acculturation appeared to predict greater variability in sexual attitudes among Asians compared with Hispanics.

Since it is evident that sexual behaviors and attitudes are predicted by ethnic and cultural influences, the experience of sexual desire may also be affected. Woo, Brotto, and Gorzalka (2011) posited that sexual conservatism mediated the relationship between culture and sexual desire. The construct of sex guilt was explored as a link between culture and sexual desire. Previous research had documented that greater sex guilt is highly correlated with poorer sexual functioning. In comparison with Caucasian women, East Asian women more frequently report poorer sexual functioning. Compared with East Asian women, Caucasian women's report of sexual desire was significantly higher. In addition, sex guilt and sexual conservatism were significantly lower. Among this sample, women who endorsed sexual conservatism and reported higher sex guilt also stated that their level of sexual desire was lower. With the sample of East Asian women, sex guilt, but not sexual conservatism, was found to mediate the relationship between acculturation and sexual desire. Thus, greater sex guilt was related to lower sexual desire. The authors posited that cognitive constructs functioning as self-imposed sexual constraints may be especially detrimental in the role of sexual desire for East Asian women. For clinical purposes, sexual conservativism may be an important factor to assess and understand in light of sexual difficulties reported by clients.

MEDIA

Previously, we identified the effect of media as a contributor to sexualization. The proliferation of technology has made it much easier to consume media via cell phones, tablet computers, laptops, and desktops. With the increased availability of various forms of media, what are the effects on the experience of sexuality? Conversely, how does sexuality affect choice of media?

Stulhofer, Busko, and Landripet (2010) looked at the effects of sexually explicit materials (SEM) on sexual scripting. They used Gagnon and Simon's (1973) conceptualization of sexual socialization as a reference point for their study. Sexual socialization is thought to occur through the integration of interpersonal, intrapersonal, and sociocultural or environmental influences. Consequently, sexual scripts are formed, which are personalized ways of defining a person's sexual reality. As such, it influences decision-making processes. The authors suggested that SEM exposure may affect the scripting process by shaping the viewer's role, as well as their perception of their partner's role. Perceptions of what may be "good," in addition to scripting of what is attractive with respect to one's own body, may be influenced. Stulhofer et al. posit that early exposure to pornography affects intrapersonal sexual scripting, which then affects sexual and relationship experiences, finally eliciting an effect on sexual satisfaction. Sexual scripts direct sexual behaviors and reactions, and are also affected by the experience of reality. The purpose of the study was to look at the association between early SEM exposure and sexual satisfaction. A significant effect was found for paraphilic SEM, compared with other forms of SEM.

Although pornography is criticized for what is believed to be its contribution to the sexualization of women, proponents of pornography propose that it has the benefit of expanding sexual horizons and is built on established scripts. Weinberg et al. (2010) posit that the main purpose of pornography is to create or enhance sexual fantasy or arousal. They propose that sexually explicit images have the potential to have a positive effect on a person's sexuality: they can promote the transition from everyday life into an erotic reality and provide "the presentation of idealized bodies" performing an abundance of sexual acts (p. 1391). The process of normalization is proposed to be a part of the effects of pornography. In addition, they believe that it promotes a sense of empowerment in creating and altering sexual scripts, as well as acting on them. As such, pornography can enhance interest and confidence in trying sexual behaviors that were previously untried. In their study pornography usage was related to the appeal of having a third-party observer. Heterosexual men and women viewed use of a vibrator or sex toy as appealing. The appeal of anal sex appeared to increase for heterosexual and nonheterosexual men, and heterosexual women. Heterosexual women also reported that viewing pornography was helpful in increasing the appeal of oral sex. Increases in the frequency of heterosexual coitus as well as solo and partnered sex were associated with viewing pornography. Several female participants in this study reported a sense of empowerment. Pornography consumption was related to a greater number of partners with whom heterosexual women had oral and genital sex. However, these partners were deemed "significant others."

In terms of patterns of behavior associated with consumption of visually stimulating materials, there appears to be more variability among women compared with males. Previous research studies suggested that males tend to respond more to visual sexual stimulation in contrast with their female counterparts. However, Rupp and Wallen (2009) found that viewing times for sexually explicit material did not differ between male and female participants. Pictures of opposite-sex partners receiving oral sex were rated as least sexually attractive, whereas both males and females tended to spend the most time viewing pictures of sexual intercourse with the female body visible. According to the authors, the results were consistent with previous literature that women tend to prefer projection strategies, suggesting that they tend to identify with the female actor, whereas males tend to use objectification and projection strategies, as suggested by the lack of difference in viewing time based on the gaze of the female actor.

Previous research suggests that there appear to be personality correlates with the type of sexual media preferred. Bogaert's (2001) study of 160 undergraduate males found traits that seemed to predict an interest in sexually violent films included antisocial tendencies, low social desirability, lower intelligence, and interest in sexual variation. Sexual experience did not appear to predict sexual media preference.

LEVERAGING TECHNOLOGY

Our culture is steeped in technological advances that have dramatically shaped society. The internet, smartphones, social networks, and so many other advances have made an indelible mark on how many people think, behave, and relate to one another. Technology has also contributed to the sexualization of our culture through the ubiquitous exposure to titillating images, including pornography.

The question is, Can technology be harnessed to address the effects of sexualization of our culture? Perhaps a good place to begin is to think through the following questions: *How do you view technology in terms of its effects on culture? In what ways do technological advances shape culture toward greater sexualization? Can you think of ways technology can be leveraged to address sexualization? Can you think of practical ways technology can shape culture toward greater stewardship of our sexuality?*

PURITY CULTURE

Readers of this book may have noticed an increase in books, documentaries, articles, and social media posts since 2017 addressing "purity culture," the evangelical Christian phenomenon focusing on sexual abstinence as a result of fear regarding the dissolution of traditional Christian values. Part of the criticism of purity culture was in response to the #MeToo movement, which increased in popularity after Harvey Weinstein's sexual allegations. Sexual impropriety and abuse allegations were revealed in various settings and organizations, including churches, higher education, workplaces, and so on. This seemed to open the door for the discussion around the impact of purity culture on the sexual experiences of those who were introduced to practices, beliefs, teachings, and events in the early 1990s.

True Love Waits is an example of such a movement. It began in 1993 and was founded by Southern Baptists. The True Love Waits pledge states: "Believing that true love waits, I make a commitment to God, myself, my family, my friends, my future mate and my future children to be sexually abstinent from this day until the day I enter marriage" ("Abstinence Pledge," 2024). Total sexual purity (i.e., abstaining from anything sexual, such as thoughts, actions, use of pornography, or anything increasing sexual arousal) was expected.

On July 11, 2023, Joshua Harris, who had previously written *I Kissed Dating Goodbye: A New Attitude Toward Romance and Relationships* in 1997, which was heralded as the manifesto for the purity movement by abstaining from dating and any behaviors associated with dating, issued a statement apologizing for the harm caused by this book. He stated he came to an understanding of the harms caused and experienced by those who took his book as guidance for how to develop a "happy-ever ending—a great marriage, a great sex life—even though this is not promised by scripture."[1] As a repair for the harms caused by his books, he asked his publisher to cease further publication in 2018 after hearing firsthand accounts of how people, particularly women, were affected by the messages from purity culture.

Research on the impacts of purity culture are becoming more frequent, and several books have been written on the topic. Though the depth and breadth of the research and writings are beyond the scope of this chapter, we summarize a few studies that highlight key themes relevant for therapists working with individuals who have been harmed.

Some of the harms and effects from the purity culture movement include the cognitive association between beliefs associated with purity culture and acceptance of rape myths (e.g., "the woman asked for it by dressing in a suggestive manner"; Klement et al., 2022; Owens et al., 2021), problematic thoughts (e.g., obeying the high standards of purity culture will result in a perfect Christian marriage; Pate, 2022), feelings of guilt and shame (Pate, 2022; Estrada, 2022), disempowerment of young women and their bodies (Pate, 2022), the burden of responsibility for male sexual thoughts and behaviors (Pate, 2022), sexual dysfunction and dissatisfaction (Estrada, 2022), internalization of whiteness as the ideal (Natarajan et al., 2022), and interpersonal difficulties (Estrada, 2022).

It is imperative for therapists to be aware of how the influence of purity culture may affect the sexual functioning of clients who were raised with these beliefs. As Estrada (2022) summarizes in her article, shame invariably affects sexual experiences and other areas of functioning, such as emotional, spiritual, mental, and relational:

> The EPM (Evangelical Purity Movement) not only taught women a very narrow view of sex, but also informed them of their worth, value, and role according to the divine creator God. Additionally, these women have been taught to minimize their own experience and take responsibility for others' mistakes as an act of

---

[1]Joshua Harris (2023, July 11), "A statement on *I Kissed Dating Goodbye*," https://joshharris.com/a -statement-on. Harris would later leave the Christian faith, as discussed in Cosper's (2021) article, "I kissed Christianity goodbye," Christianity Today. www.christianitytoday.com/ct/podcasts/rise -and-fall-of-mars-hill/joshua-harris-mars-hill-podcast-kissed-christianity-goodbye.html

faithfulness. They've been raised to believe men are untrustworthy as are their own bodies. (p. 129)

Pate (2022) interviewed women affected by purity culture who self-reported themes of sexual shame and guilt, restricted sexual communication, and sexual suppression. Participants also expressed beliefs that "sex is dangerous," in addition to fear related to a potential loss of inherent value for engaging in sexual behaviors. These participants felt it was necessary to comply with and trust religious and parental authority. A few also expressed feeling responsible for men's sexual thoughts and behaviors and that having agency in their sexuality as females was wrong. As adults, the participants described how their sexuality was inhibited by teachings from purity culture and the shame and guilt they experienced.

In a study of 99 Christian men and women, endorsing purity culture was correlated with endorsement of rape myths and mislabeling both marital and acquaintance rape as consensual sex. Intrinsic religiosity was found to be a moderator, with individuals who had lower levels of intrinsic religiosity being more likely to endorse rape myths and purity culture beliefs. Owens et al. (2021) suggest that rather than teaching purity culture in Christian churches and schools, it would be more effective to teach biblical sexual ethics that do not victim-blame, in addition to nurturing internal religious motivation (see also Morgant, 2024). They also highlight the possibility that survivors of rape or sexual assault who experience intense self-blame, guilt, shame, and self-loathing may have exposure to purity culture. Klement et al. (2022) noted, "One disturbing implication . . . is that putting an emphasis on female purity could have the paradoxical effect of enhancing rape tendencies via increasing acceptance of rape myths" (p. 2098).

The discussion on purity culture also needs to include an awareness of intersectional identities and impacts. Natarajan et al. (2022) examined specific impacts of purity culture on a small sample of women of color. While they do not purport to generalize their findings to all women of color, significant themes were present, such as the internalization of white idealization, historical and contemporary manifestations of oppression, Black love and marriageability, and healing, liberation, and reconciliation. In particular, several women in the study expressed that the purity movement was connected to the historical oppression of Black and Brown women, particularly with respect to a lack of body or sexual autonomy. The participants also shared beliefs and experiences referred to as the "racial halo effect" regarding double standards for white women and women of color (e.g., Black women being perceived as overly sexual, Asian women being perceived as coy, soft, etc.). Of note, in this study, Black women described how purity culture affected their marriageablity, specifically as a result of the emotional toll regarding the unfulfilled purity prosperity gospel (i.e., if you remain pure until marriage, you'll be given the perfect partner) and its effect on finding a life partner. In addition, they also expressed feeling burdened with having to change societal views of the sexuality of Black women. The impact of the purity prosperity gospel was particularly notable for Black women in this study, whose unfulfilled desires could not be separated from broader systems of harm:

> The theology of evangelical purity rhetoric is rooted in the hegemonic notion of white marital norms and fails to consider how interlocking systems of oppression affect Black women's lives (e.g., racist criminal justice system, inequitable education system that disproportionately fast-tracks Black boys on to the school-to-prison pipeline vs. into college, etc.). (p. 325)

The study (Natarajan et al., 2022) highlighted the tendency to refer to white women as the ideal pure woman, which is problematic in that when examining the effects of purity culture, it is important to keep in mind the diversity of experiences for women as a result of race, religion, socioeconomic status, ethnicity, disability, and so on.

In response to the harms many have experienced within the context of the church and religious teachings, Nadia Bolz-Weber, a Lutheran pastor, writes:

> It doesn't feel very difficult to draw a direct line between the messages many of us received from the church and the harm we've experienced in our bodies and spirits as a result. So my argument in this book is this: we should not be more loyal to an idea, a doctrine, or an interpretation of a Bible verse than we are to *people*. If the teachings of the church are harming the bodies and spirits of people, we should rethink those teachings. (2019, p. 7)

Bolz-Weber's book *Shameless* is a missive for those of us who are sexual beings (i.e., all of us) to consider and reconsider different messages we have learned about our sexuality, what it means to be sexual, and what it means to be a creation of God. She writes, "Let us consider the harm that has been caused in God's name, but let's not be satisfied with stopping there. We must reach for a new Christian sexual ethic."

While this is not an exhaustive account of the literature and research regarding purity culture and the impact on individuals who were involved and exposed to it as adolescents and young adults, it is helpful to assess whether there were practices, messages, beliefs, and so on that affect your current clients with respect to their emotional health, sexual functioning, and interpersonal relationships (see Morgante, 2024).

CLOSING REFLECTIONS

Earlier, we presented research identifying the factors that facilitate resilience in children and adolescents against the effects of sexualization. Children who feel close to a parent and who experience academic confidence and success tend to avoid or delay sexual experimentation. Part of the human experience includes needs pertaining to relatedness and being significant, feeling loved and connected to others, and emotional closeness. While children may be most susceptible because of their immaturity and vulnerability, adolescents and adults must also be considered regarding the needs for relatedness and significance. As such, our values help us to navigate the decisions and choices toward having the needs of significance, relatedness, love, and closeness met. How we do so can help to buffer against the effects of sexualization.

How do we communicate value to ourselves and those around us? How do we communicate the value of our sexuality and the sexuality of others around us? Do we conceptualize sexuality as a set of behaviors that fall within categories of do and don't, acceptable and unacceptable, or bad or other dichotomous labels?

RITES OF PASSAGE

A few years ago Mark attended a rite of passage ceremony for a thirteen-year-old African American adolescent, the son of a friend from church. As Christians, his parents wanted him to have a rite of passage ceremony that drew on their religious and cultural history, so they set up the ceremony very intentionally to draw on those resources—some of which reflected elements of a bar mitzvah, while others were more from their heritage as African Americans. The ceremony included having their son carried in on a chair by four elders (older men), having him put on a suit and tie, passing a Bible from his grandparents to his parents to him, and saying prayers for him. Each aspect of the ceremony in some way emphasized his journey from childhood into adulthood.

> We see a remarkable absence of intentional, meaningful rites of passage from childhood to adulthood in our culture today. In our discussions with students who have shared from their own experiences growing up, few have experienced intentional rites of passage ceremonies. Rather, most identify largely unintentional events or activities that have served as rites of passage nonetheless. These have included significant birthdays (turning sixteen, eighteen, twenty-one), new purchases steeped in meaning (e.g., females going with their mother to buy a training bra), new skills (e.g., learning to drive), increased independence (e.g., getting married, being financially independent), and specific experiences (e.g., first sexual intercourse).
>
> As you think about your own development, what would you say have been the most meaningful rites of passage for you as you entered into adulthood? How did those rites of passage teach healthy roles, convey messages about masculinity or femininity, or teach you about expectations for behavior? What specifically made these experiences meaningful as rites of passage? How many of these experiences were intentional, and how many "just happened" without much thought or purpose as a rite of passage?
>
> As an exercise, consider designing a rite of passage for a thirteen-year-old boy or girl. What would you want to include and why?

In part because this book is a resource to enhance clinical practice, let's close with a thought exercise. Weinberg et al.'s (2010) study of the effects of pornography presented a position that is oftentimes inconsistent with that of the Christian community: that pornography may have positive effects with respect to the expansion of sexual scripts. As a Christian clinician, how would you respond to secular sex therapists who consider pornography an aid when working with clients who have limited sexual scripts? If you had a client who had a limited repertoire of sexual behaviors as a result of past sexual trauma and she expressed a desire to expand her perspective, how would you facilitate that for her?

What are values pertaining to sexual behaviors and attitudes that you may have grown up with that you may or may not possess presently? If they have changed, what are the reasons for doing so?

REFERENCES

Abstinence pledge. (2024, May 9). In *Wikipedia*. https://en.wikipedia.org/wiki/Abstinence_pledge

Ahrold, T., & Meston, C. M. (2010). Ethnic differences in sexual attitudes of U.S. college students: Gender, acculturation, and religiosity factors. *Archives of Sexual Behavior, 39*, 190-202.

American College Health Association. (2023). *National College Health Assessment: Spring 2023 Reference Group Data Report*. www.acha.org

American Psychological Association. (2007). *Report of the APA task force on the sexualization of girls*. American Psychological Association. www.apa.org/pi/women /programs/girls/report-full.pdf

Bailey, J. A., Haggerty, K. P., White, H. R., & Catalano, R. F. (2011). Associations between changing developmental contexts and risky sexual behavior in the two years following high school. *Archives of Sexual Behavior, 40*(5). https://doi.org/10.100 7/s10508-010-9633-0

Bancroft, J., Loftus, J., & Long, J. S. (2003). Distress about sex: A national survey of women in heterosexual relationships. *Archives of Sexual Behavior, 32*(3), 193-208.

Banfield, S., & McCabe, M. P. (2001). Extra relationship involvement among women: Are they different from men? *Archives of Sexual Behavior, 30*(2), 119-42.

Bogaert, A. F. (2001). Personality, individual differences, and preferences for the sexual media. *Archives of Sexual Behavior, 30*(1), 29-53.

Bolz-Weber, N. (2019). *Shameless*. Convergent Books.

Byers, E. S., Henderson, J., & Hobson, K. M. (2009). University students' definitions of sexual abstinence and having sex. *Archives of Sexual Behavior, 38*, 665-74.

Centers for Disease Control and Prevention (2021). Youth Risk Behavior Survey 2021. www .cdc.gov/healthyyouth/data/yrbs/index.htm

Centers for Disease Control and Prevention. (2022). *CDC fact sheet: Information for teens and young adults: Staying Healthy and Preventing STDs*. Retrieved April 12, 2022, from www.cdc.gov/std/life-stages-populations/stdfact-teens.htm# :~:text=There%20were%2026%20million%20new,biologically%20more%20prone %20to%20STDs

Centers for Disease Control and Prevention (2023, May 23). *HIV declines among young people and drives overall decrease in new HIV infections* [Press release]. www.cdc.gov /media/releases/2023/p0523-hiv-declines-among-young-people.html#:~:text =Estimated%20annual%20new%20HIV%20infections,among%20gay%20and%20 bisexual%20males

Dent, R. J., & Cameron, J. S. (2003). Developing resilience in children who are in public care: The educational psychology perspective. *Educational Psychology in Practice, 19*(1), 3-19.

Dreweke, J. (2019). Promiscuity propaganda: Access to information and services does not lead to increases in sexual activity. The Guttmacher Institute. *Guttmacher Policy Review, 22*. www.guttmacher.org/gpr/2019/06/promiscuity-propaganda-access -information-and-services-does-not-lead-increases-sexual

Eisenberg, M. (2001). Differences in sexual risk behaviors between college students with same-sex and opposite-sex experience: Results from a national survey. *Archives of Sexual Behavior, 30*(6), 575-89.

Estrada, L. L. (2022). Clinical considerations of the evangelical purity movement's impact on female sexuality. *Journal of Sex & Marital Therapy 48*(2), 121-32.

Feldhahn, S., & Sytsma, M. (2023). *Secrets of sex & marriage: 8 surprises that make all the difference*. Bethany House.

Fredrickson, B. L., Roberts, T. A., Noll, S. M., Quinn, D. M., & Twenge, J. M. (1998). That swimsuit becomes you: Sex differences in self-objectification, restrained eating, and math performance. *Journal of Personality Social Psychology, 75*(1), 269-84.

Freitas, D. (2008). *Sex and the soul: Juggling sexuality, spirituality, romance, and religion on America's college campuses.* Oxford University Press.

Freitas, D. (2013). *The end of sex: How hookup culture is leaving a generation unhappy, sexually unfulfilled, and confused about intimacy.* Basic Books.

Gagnon, J. H., & Simon, W. (1973). *Sexual conduct: The social sources of human sexuality.* Aldine.

Guttmacher Institute. (2013). Facts on American teens' sexual and reproductive health. Retrieved from www.guttmacher.org/sites/default/files/pdfs/pubs/fb_ATSRH.pdf

Henrich, J., Boyd, R., & Richerson, P. J. (2012). The puzzle of monogamous marriage. *Philosophical Transactions of the Royal Society, 367,* 657-69. http://rstb.royalsociety publishing.org/content/367/1589/657.full.pdf+html

Impett, E. A., Schooler, D., & Tolman, D. L. (2006). To be seen and not heard: Femininity ideology and adolescent girls' sexual health. *Archives of Sexual Behavior, 35*(2), 131-44.

Inanc, H., Meckstroth, A., Keating, B., Adamek, K., Zaveri, H., O'Neil, S., McDonald, K., & Ochoa, L. (2020). *Factors Influencing youth sexual activity: Conceptual models for sexual risk avoidance and cessation.* OPRE Research Brief #2020-153. Office of Planning, Research, and Evaluation, Administration for Children and Families, U.S. Department of Health and Human Services.

Klement, K., Sagarin, B. J., & Skowronski, J. J. (2022). The one ring model: Rape culture beliefs are linked to purity culture beliefs. *Sexuality & Culture, 26,* 2070-2106. https://doi.org/10.1007/s12119-022-09986-2

Kuehne, D. S. (2009). *Sex and the iWorld: Rethinking relationship beyond an age of individualism.* Baker Academic.

Kuyper, L., & Vanwesenbeeck, I. (2011). Examining sexual health differences between lesbian, gay, bisexual, and heterosexual adults: The role of sociodemographics, sexual behavior characteristics, and minority stress. *Journal of Sex Research, 48*(2/3), 263-74.

Lastoria, M., & Association for Christians in Student Development (Eds.). (2011). *Sexuality, religiosity, behaviors and attitudes: A look at religiosity, sexual attitudes, and sexual behaviors of Christian college students.* Association for Christians in Student Development.

Laumann, E. O., Paik, A., Glasser, D. B., Kang, J. H., Wang, T., Levinson, B., . . . Gingell, C. (2006). A cross-national study of subjective sexual well-being among older women and men: Findings from the global study of sexual attitudes and behaviors. *Archives of Sexual Behavior, 35*(2), 143-59.

Leitenberg, H., & Saltzman, H. (2000). A statewide survey of age at first intercourse for adolescent females and age of their male partners: Relation to other risk behaviors and statutory rape implications. *Archives of Sexual Behavior, 29*(3), 203-15.

Martino, S. C., Collins, R. L., Elliot, M. N., Strachman, A., Kanouse, D. E., & Berry, S. H. (2006). Exposure to degrading versus nondegrading music lyrics and sexual behavior among youth. *Pediatrics, 118,* 430-41.

McMinn, L. G. (2004). *Sexuality and holy longing: Embracing intimacy in a broken world.* San Francisco: Jossey-Bass.

Meston, C. M., & Ahrold, T. (2010). Ethnic, gender, and acculturation influences on sexual behaviors. *Archives of Sexual Behavior, 39,* 179-89.

Morgante, C. (2024). *Recovering from purity culture: Dismantle the myths, reject shame-based sexuality, and move forward in your faith.* Baker Books.

Natarajan, M., Wilkins-Yel, K. G., Sista, A., Anantharaman, A., & Seils, N. (2022). Decolonizing purity culture: Gendered racism and white idealization in evangelical Christianity. *Psychology of Women Quarterly, 46*(3), 316-36.

Oncale, R. M., & King, B. M. (2001). Comparison of men's and women's attempts to dissuade sexual partners from the couple using condoms. *Archives of Sexual Behavior, 30*(4), 379-91.

Owens, B. C., Lewis Hall, M. E., & Anderson, T. L. (2021). The relationship between purity culture and rape myth acceptance. *Journal of Psychology and Theology, 49*(4), 405-18.

Papageorgiou, A., Cross, D., & Fisher, C. (2022). Sexualized images on social media and adolescent girls' mental health: Qualitative insight from parents, school support service staff, and youth mental health service providers. *International Journal of Environmental Research and Public Health, 20*(1), 433-51.

Pate, M. D. (2022). *The felt sense of evangelical purity culture* [Doctoral dissertation, Sofia University].

Patrick, M. E., & Lee, C. M. (2010). Sexual motivations and engagement in sexual behavior during the transition to college. *Archives of Sexual Behavior, 39,* 674-81.

Pitts, M., & Rahman, Q. (2001). Which behaviors constitute "having sex" among university students in the UK? *Archives of Sexual Behavior, 30*(2), 169-76.

Rideout, V. J., Foehr, U. G., & Roberts, D. F. (2010). Generation M2: Media in the lives of 8- to 18-year-olds. Kaiser Family Foundation. Retrieved from www.kff.org/other/event/generation-m2-media-in-the-lives-of/

Rupp, H. A., & Wallen, K. (2009). Sex-specific content preferences for visual sexual stimuli. *Archives of Sexual Behavior, 38,* 417-26.

Satcher, D. (2001). *The surgeon general's call to action to promote sexual health and responsible sexual behavior.* Retrieved from www.ncbi.nlm.nih.gov/books/NBK44220/#:~:text=This%20Call%20to%20Action%20focuses,communities%20and%20in%20our%20homes

Stulhofer, A., Busko, V., & Landripet, I. (2010). Pornography, sexual socialization, and satisfaction among young men. *Archives of Sexual Behavior, 39,* 168-78.

Vogels, E. A., Gelles-Watnick, R., & Massarat, N. (2022, August 10). *Teens, social media, and technology 2022.* Pew Research Center Report. www.pewresearch.org/internet/2022/08/10/teens-social-media-and-technology-2022/

Weinberg, S. M., Williams, C. J., Kleiner, S., & Irizarry, Y. (2010). Pornography, normalization, and empowerment. *Archives of Sexual Behavior, 39,* 1389-1401.

Wetherill, R. R., Neal, D. J., & Fromme, K. (2010). Parents, peers, and sexual values influence sexual behavior during the transition to college. *Archives of Sexual Behavior, 39,* 682-94.

Woo, J. S. T., Brotto, L. A., & Gorzalka, B. B. (2011). The role of sex guilt in the relationship between culture and women's sexual desire. *Archives of Sexual Behavior, 40*, 385-94.

Zurbriggen, E. L., & Morgan, E. M. (2006). Who wants to marry a millionaire? Reality dating television programs, attitudes toward sex, and sexual behaviors. *Sex Roles, 54*, 1-17.

THREE

SEXUALITY IN BIOLOGICAL PERSPECTIVE

A FEW YEARS AGO Erica dropped by a friend's house just as she was about to bathe her sixteen-month-old son. She asked whether Erica would be able to help her as he was her first child and she was still mastering the basics of trying to get a fidgety baby clean while letting him play. While bathing him, Erica noticed that his little fingers seemed to automatically gravitate toward his genitals when his hands were not occupied by a bath toy or when they were not being washed. As soon as Erica's friend saw him pulling and tugging on his penis while looking around inquiringly, she redirected his hand by washing it or by placing it elsewhere. With the same stealth that she used in distracting him, his hand returned to pulling and tugging on his penis. It was interesting to observe that in spite of her sixteen-month-old son's lack of exposure to any sex education, pictures, or sexual material, it was his natural inclination to self-soothe by playing with his genitals.

UNDERSTANDING BIOLOGY AS A FOUNDATION TO LEARNING ABOUT SEXUALITY

The preceding vignette demonstrates both the complexity and simplicity of human sexuality. Here we have a sixteen-month-old boy who can utter telegraphic sentences and understands simple questions and statements directed by his parents. He does not have any vocabulary to describe his motivation for the behavior of touching his genitals, and yet it appears that he finds pleasure in this behavior. Interestingly, if this behavior were repeated at the age of ten, fifteen, twenty-five, or fifty, the motivation may be the same; however, the interpretation of his behavior may be different.

Understanding the biology of sexuality gives us a framework to comprehend the thoughts and behaviors that accompany our experiences. For example, the experiences of arousal and attraction are more than just feelings that a person has. When you encounter someone you are attracted to, your heart rate increases, and it may seem as though your heart skips a beat. At the same time, you may notice that you begin to experience sensations that you did not will your body to feel. Genital tension, caused by the increased blood flow to the genitals, may occur simultaneously as a tightening in your throat (and the two are not related!).

FEMALE REPRODUCTIVE SYSTEM

Structures. The female reproductive system is analogous to the male reproductive system; however, the functions of the female reproductive system are different. The female reproductive system produces female egg cells called "ova" or "oocytes" that are important for reproduction. In addition, this system enables the transportation of ova to the site of fertilization by sperm, which usually occurs within the fallopian tubes. After fertilization the egg or zygote implants in the walls of the uterus, which is the beginning of pregnancy. If pregnancy as a result of fertilization and implantation does not occur, menstruation, which is the regular shedding of the uterine lining, maintains the receptivity of the uterus. Last, the female reproductive system also produces female sex hormones.

The female reproductive system is composed of internal and external parts. The internal parts of the female reproductive system include the uterus or womb, vagina, ovaries and the fallopian tubes. The vagina is a muscular channel that connects the lower part of the uterus to the outside of the body. Compared with the outer third of the vagina, the inner two-thirds are not well supplied with nerve endings. The uterus or womb is a hollow, pear-shaped organ divided into two parts; the first is the cervix, which is the lower part that opens into the vagina. The larger, main body of the uterus is called the corpus, which can expand to accommodate a developing baby. The ovaries are small oval-shaped glands situated to either side of the uterus. The ovaries produce hormones (i.e., progesterone and estrogen) and a limited number of eggs. Finally, the fallopian tubes are attached to the upper part of the uterus and enable the ova (egg cells) to travel from the ovaries to the uterus.

The external part of the female reproductive system consists of several parts that are visible: mons pubis, labia majora, labia minora, the clitoris, the urethral opening, the vaginal opening, and the perineum. There are two functions of the external female reproductive system: to facilitate entrance of sperm into the female body for reproduction, and to protect the internal genital organs from infectious organisms. The mons pubis is a fleshy, rounded protuberance that protects the pubis bone. In adolescence, pubic hair begins to grow on the mons pubis with the secretion of sex hormones. The labia majora are larger, fleshy tissue bodies (i.e., large lips) that enclose and protect the other external reproductive organs. They are analogous to the scrotum in males, yet they secrete oil and sweat. The labia minora are the small lips that surround the openings to the vagina and urethra. The labia minora swell and darken during sexual arousal, and are made up of erectile, connective tissue. The clitoris is a bundle of nerve endings where the labia minora meet. It is comparable in some regards to the penis in males and is covered by a fold of skin, known as the prepuce. It is very sensitive to stimulation and can become erect when stimulated and engorged with blood. The urethral opening is located an inch or so below the clitoris above the vaginal opening. The perineum is the area of muscle and tissue between the anus and the labial opening of the vagina. In some women, a thin, fibrous tissue called the hymen partially closes the vaginal opening. It may remain intact until it is penetrated.

The menstrual cycle. Menses usually begins about two years after a girl's breasts begin to develop. The average age for girls beginning menses in the United States is twelve years. If a girl has not had her first period by age fifteen or if three years have passed since breast growth started, a doctor may need to be consulted.

In the event that an ovum is not fertilized, a girl or woman's uterus undergoes a monthly cycle whereby the lining of the uterus is sloughed off after having been built up in anticipation of protecting a fertilized ovum. The blood and tissue flow from the uterus through the cervix to the vagina and out of the body.

At the beginning of the menstrual cycle, levels of estrogen, which is referred to as the "female hormone," increase, causing the lining of the uterus to thicken and grow. By thickening, the walls of the uterus will be more capable of nourishing a fertilized ovum if one is implanted. While the walls of the uterus are thickening, an ovum is maturing in the ovaries. Around day fourteen of an average twenty-eight-day cycle, the ovum leaves the ovary, traveling through the fallopian tubes, which is the process of ovulation.

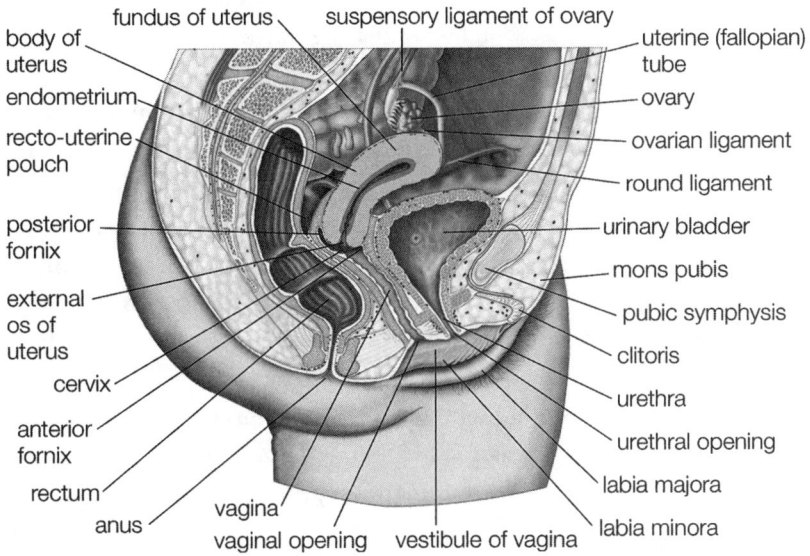

Figure 1

The first day of the menstrual cycle is the first day of the period, when the lining of the uterine wall is shedding, resulting in bleeding for about five days. The bleeding is initiated after a drop in hormone levels after ovulation if a sperm has not fertilized the ovum. The previously thickened walls of the uterus begin to break down, resulting in the shedding of tissues and the unfertilized egg as waste when the blood supply is cut off.

By day seven, bleeding has usually stopped. For the past few days, hormones have stimulated the development of follicles, which are fluid-filled pockets that each contain an ovum, on the ovaries. Between days seven and fourteen, one follicle will develop to maturity. The uterus walls thicken in anticipation of a fertilized egg for implantation, and as such are rich in blood and nutrients. Around day fourteen, the mature follicle bursts and releases an egg from the ovary, which is the process of ovulation. The ovum will travel down the fallopian tube for the next few days on the way to the uterus. Should it become fertilized with a sperm, it will attach to the lining of the uterus. If the egg is not fertilized, hormone levels will drop around day twenty-five, which signals the next menstrual cycle to begin. The egg will break apart and be shed within the next cycle.

Women will usually have their periods until menopause, which occurs between the ages of forty-five and fifty-five. In menopause, a woman ceases ovulation and is no longer able to get pregnant.

Hormonal phases of the menstrual cycle. The menstrual cycle is maintained by four hormones: follicle-stimulating hormone (FSH), luteinizing hormone (LH), estrogen, and progesterone.

The follicular phase or proliferative phase of the menstrual cycle begins on the last day of the menstrual cycle and tends to last between nine and ten days. In this phase the first layer of the uterus, the endometrium, develops as certain ovarian follicles mature in preparation for ovulation. Two hormones, FSH and LH are released from the brain into the bloodstream, traveling to the ovaries. FSH and LH stimulate the growth of approximately fifteen to twenty ova contained in their own follicles in the ovaries. FSH and LH also trigger an increased production of estrogen. As estrogen levels increase, FSH decreases production. The purpose of this balance in hormonal influences limits the number of follicles that mature for ovulation. One follicle in each ovary becomes dominant, suppressing other follicles and causing them to die. The dominant follicle maintains estrogen production.

The ovulatory phase is also known as ovulation, which begins fourteen days after the start of the follicular phase. This is the midpoint of the menstrual cycle. Ovulation is initiated when estrogen levels reach a critical peak. The hypothalamus senses the high level of estrogen and triggers the pituitary to release large amounts of FSH and LH. This surge in LH triggers ovulation, usually twelve to twenty-four hours after the level of LH peaks in the body. Consequently, the follicle releases its egg from the ovary. As the ovary releases the ovum, the fimbriae, or finger-like projections of the fallopian tube, sweep the ovum into the tube. During this phase, the amount of mucous produced by the cervix increases and is observed to have a thicker texture. The thicker mucous would make it easier for sperm to be captured and nourished as they are moved toward the egg for fertilization.

The luteal phase or secretory phase begins right after ovulation. Once the follicle has released the egg, it becomes a new structure called the corpus luteum, which secretes progesterone, preparing the uterus for the fertilized egg to implant. If implantation does not occur, the hypothalamus senses that the levels of progesterone are high and signals the pituitary gland to stop producing LH and FSH. Declining levels of LH and FSH cause the corpus luteum to decompose. If the egg has been fertilized, it will implant in the uterine walls after traveling through the fallopian tubes. Thus, the woman is now pregnant. If the ovum has not been fertilized it is shed along with the uterine walls.

The last phase is the menstrual phase, which is the sloughing off of the uterine lining (the endometrium) in menstrual flow. At this point the levels of estrogen and progesterone are so low that the uterine lining can no longer be sustained and the lining begins to disintegrate and is discharged from the body. Low estrogen levels lead the hypothalamus to secrete gonadotropin-releasing hormone (Gn-RH), which then stimulates the pituitary gland to release FSH. FSH then prompts the ovaries to secrete estrogen, and another proliferative phase begins.

Problems with the menstrual cycle. Amenorrhea is the lack of a menstrual period, which may be caused by a number of situations, including pregnancy, breastfeeding, extreme weight loss, eating disorders, excessive exercise, stress, and serious medical conditions requiring treatment.

Dysmenorrhea is the experience of painful periods and cramps. In most adolescent females the cause of dysmenorrhea is elevated levels of prostaglandin. In older women the painful cramps may be caused by uterine fibroids or endometriosis.

Endometriosis is a health disorder some women experience when the cells of the uterus grow elsewhere in the body (e.g., bladder, ovaries, bowel, rectum, and the lining of the pelvic area), causing pain, irregular bleeding, and possible pregnancy complications. These cell growths outside the uterus are called endometrial tissue implants.

Secondary sex characteristics. The breasts of women are secondary sex characteristics in the sense that although they are not directly involved in reproduction, they do distinguish females from males. Each breast has fifteen to twenty clusters of mammary glands that secrete milk through its own duct located at the nipple, which contains many nerve fibers and can become erect through stimulation.

Perimenopause. For females, this is the transitional phase prior to menopause. During this time, the menstrual cycle becomes much more unpredictable and variable, going from a 25- to 40-day cycle that typically lasts three to seven days to moments when the cycle may last for what seems like a very long time, or perhaps the opposite, when periods are missed.

During perimenopause, there is an imbalance of estrogen and progesterone, which is a function of eggs not being released from the ovaries regularly because the number of eggs declines prior to menopause. When the uterus is primed to thicken the uterus lining, estrogen increases; however, without releasing an egg, there is no progesterone. This predominance of estrogen can lead to various symptoms, such as mood swings, headaches, and so on. However, it is important to note that there is a lot of variability in the presentation of perimenopause as some women may experience both low progesterone and low estrogen.

Fluctuations and symptoms related to perimenopause may be experienced for up to ten years; however, they are most acute in the five years prior to the cessation of periods.

Menopause. Menopause begins when a woman has ceased having menstrual periods for a year. Though the average age for menopause is in the early fifties, some women may experience menopause in their forties, and others may experience it in their early sixties.

There are many symptoms associated with menopause, including hot flashes, weight gain, increased heaviness of periods, urinary incontinence, increased frequency of urination, burning sensations during urination, increased UTIs, fatigue, brain fog, irritability and anger, sleep disruptions, headaches and migraines, new and unexpected facial hair, muscle pain, joint pain, breast tenderness, increased bloating and gas, heart palpitations, hearing loss, mood changes, and changes in sensations (particularly extremities).[1]

A lack of awareness of the impact of menopause on the sexual functioning of women can significantly affect treatment in sex therapy. Presently, research on the impact of menopause is growing. The SWAN study (Study of Women's Health Across the Nation) began in 1994 and collected data from more than 3,000 women in a manner that is culturally sensitive, with representation of women proportional to the US population.

According to the SWAN study, more than 1 million women experience changes related to vaginal, urogenital, and sexual health during menopause. Key points highlighted by the SWAN study include the following:

- Vaginal dryness and sexual pain are related to decreasing estrogen levels.
- Urinary incontinence and other urinary symptoms are more likely due to the process of aging versus menopause.
- "A pivotal revelation is the myth-busting conclusion that reduced sexual activity does not inherently lead to sexual pain."

---

[1]"Sexual Problems at Midlife," The North American Menopause Society, 2024, www.menopause.org/for-women/sexual-health-menopause-online/sexual-problems-at-midlife.

- There are differences in sexual functioning and menopause between racial and ethnic groups.[2]

Most pertinent to sexual functioning are the symptoms of vaginal pain, low libido, vaginal dryness and thinning of vaginal walls, and pain or discomfort during intercourse. These experiences are known as "genitourinary syndrome of menopause" (GSM). The reduction in estrogen during menopause contributes to the thinning and drying of vaginal tissues, which affects the elasticity and lubrication of the vagina, resulting in pain during sexual activity and possibly discomfort during wiping after urination or activities such as cycling where there is pressure on the vulva.

To cope with this discomfort as a result of vaginal pain and the thinning of the vaginal walls, nonhormone lubricants and moisturizers may be used to help maintain moisture. Low-dose vaginal estrogens in the form of inserts, capsules, creams, or rings can help to change the atrophy and dryness without increasing systemic estrogen, which for some women may be a risk factor for breast cancer.

Some women may want to consider other nonhormone remedies, such as regular sexual stimulation to increase vaginal blood flow and secretions, various methods of engaging in sexual pleasure that are not limited to intercourse, vaginal dilators, and pelvic floor exercises that can reduce muscle imbalances in the pelvic floor and treat incontinence.

Postmenopause. As Stacy Sims and Selene Yeager (2022) put it, "Once . . . you've hit menopause, the rest of your life is called postmenopause. Hormonally speaking, this is your biological state for the rest of your life." After menopause, estrogen is still produced in the form of estrone, which is much weaker than estradiol, which is the predominant form of estrogen prior to menopause.

Estrone is stored in fat, which can in excess increase hot flashes, night sweats, and heart palpitations, as well as other vasomotor symptoms.

If clinicians are interested in becoming more acquainted with the effects of menopause, as well as strategies for helping their menopausal clients thrive, various trainings and resources are available, such as The North American Menopause Society (www.menopause.org) and the International Menopause Society (www.imsociety.org/ and www.menopauseinfo.org).

---

[2]See www.swanstudy.org/womens-health-info/gynecologic-sexual-health-during-the-menopause-transition.

MALE REPRODUCTIVE SYSTEM

Structures. The male reproductive system has several functions: sperm production, maintenance, and transportation, along with the protective fluid; dissemination of sperm to the female reproductive system during sexual intercourse; and production and secretion of male sex hormones that maintain the male reproductive system.

Unlike the female reproductive system, the majority of the male reproductive system is located outside the body and is composed of the penis, scrotum, and testicles.

The penis is the male organ that is used in sexual intercourse and has three parts. It is attached to the wall of the abdomen at the root. The body or shaft of the penis is cylindrical in shape and is made up of three chambers that are made up of sponge-like tissue. The larger cylinder is called the corpora cavernosa. When a man is sexually aroused, these chambers fill with blood, producing an erection of the shaft that enables penetration during sexual intercourse. The head of the penis is called the glans and is covered with a loose layer of skin called foreskin. Like the clitoris in the woman, the glans is extremely sensitive to touch because of the high number of nerve endings. The opening of the urethra, which enables transportation of semen and urine, is found at the tip of the penis. The glans has many sensitive nerve endings.

The scrotum is the loose sack of skin that hangs below the root of the penis. It contains the testicles (i.e., testes), and also has many nerve endings and blood vessels. The scrotum functions as a climate-control system for the testes, regulating temperature for normal sperm development. Depending on the environmental temperature, the scrotum's muscles may pull the testes closer if they need to be warmer, or these muscles may relax to move the testes farther from the body.

The testicles are oval-shaped organs that lie in the scrotum and are connected to the body by the spermatic cord. The testes are responsible for making testosterone and for generating sperm. Within the testes are coiled tubes called seminiferous tubules, which produce sperm cells. FSH regulates production of sperm, and LH stimulates testosterone secretion from the interstitial cells. When testosterone levels are low, the hypothalamus secretes LH-releasing hormone (LH-RH), which then causes the pituitary gland to secrete LH. The testes are then stimulated to release testosterone into the bloodstream. After a certain level of testosterone has been reached, the hypothalamus regulates androgen levels by directing the pituitary gland to stop secreting LH.

Inside the body there are internal accessory organs of the male reproductive system: the epididymis, vas deferens, ejaculatory ducts, urethra, seminal vesicles, prostate gland, and bulbourethral gland.

The epididymis is a long, coiled tube found on the backside of each testicle. It stores and transports sperm cells and helps sperm with maturation, because sperm from the testes are not able to help with fertilization. During sexual arousal, contractions of the epididymis force the sperm into the vas deferens.

The vas deferens is the long, muscular tube connecting the epididymis to the pelvic cavity behind the bladder. It helps to transport mature sperm to the urethra in preparation for ejaculation.

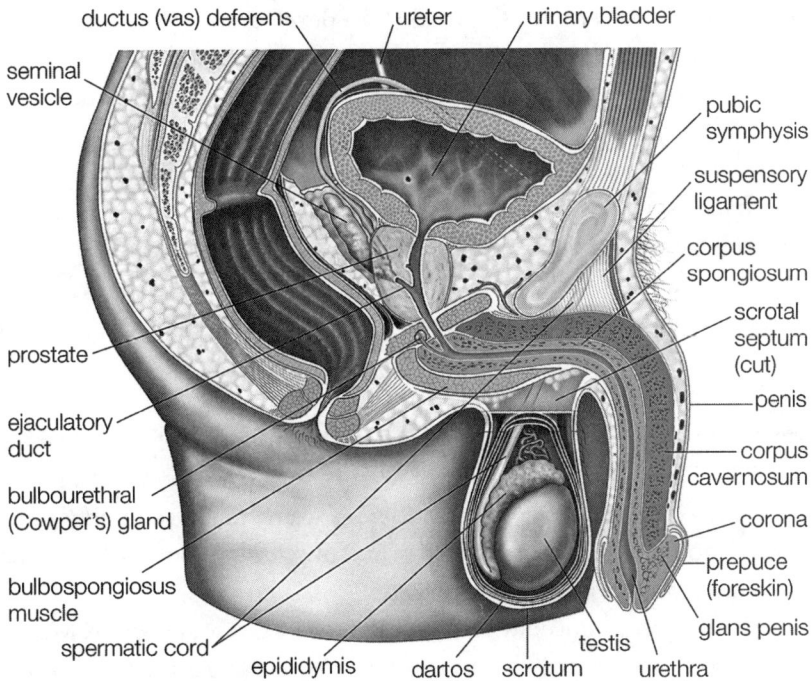

Figure 2

Seminal vesicles are the sack-like pouches that are attached to the vas deferens near the base of the bladder. They produce a sugar-rich fluid that facilitates movement for sperm because of the energy produced. The fluid from the seminal vesicles comprises most of the ejaculate.

The ejaculatory ducts are formed by the fusion of the vas deferens and the seminal vesicles. The ejaculatory ducts empty into the urethra.

The prostate gland is located below the bladder in front of the rectum and contributes additional fluid to the ejaculate. These fluids also assist in nourishing the sperm. The urethra runs through the center of the prostate gland.

The bulbourethral glands are also known as Cowper's glands. These are located on the sides of the urethra just below the prostate gland and produce a clear, slippery fluid that empties into the urethra, helping to lubricate and neutralize the urethra in the event that there are residual drops of urine.

The hormonal cycle of the male reproductive system. The male reproductive system is dependent on FSH, LH, and testosterone for the activities of different cells and organs. FSH is necessary for sperm production, whereas LH stimulates the production of testosterone, which is essential in generating sperm. Testosterone also prompts the development of male characteristics, including an increase in muscle mass and strength, fat distribution, increase in bone mass, facial hair growth, voice changes, and sex drive.

The distinction between primary and secondary sex characteristics is that the latter appear during puberty as a result of hormonal release. For males, these changes include an increase in muscle mass, broadened shoulders and chest, enlargement of the size of testicles, pubic hair growth (and hair on the chest for some males), deepening of the voice as a result of a larger larynx, and the development of facial hair above the lips and on the cheeks and chin.

PHYSIOLOGICAL EXPERIENCES

Sexual arousal, while it may be experienced as a moment of overwhelming intensity with little predictability, is actually very consistent in its presentation and experience, even though there is tremendous variability in the sexual response. What one person may find physically, emotionally, or mentally stimulating, another person may not.

There are several conceptualizations of the sexual response cycle. Masters and Johnson have a four-phase model, while Helen Singer Kaplan describes the experience with three stages. In any case, what is important to remember is that these stages of the sexual response cycle are not limited to penile-vaginal intercourse. A person is able to experience these stages regardless of the source of stimulation—masturbation, fantasy, and manual or oral stimulation. These stages are descriptions of the common experiences that people have when they are sexually stimulated and aroused; however, it is notable that the richness of sexual intimacy with one's partner is not adequately captured on paper, and that the comparison of that experience with a written description cheapens the encounter.

The sexual response cycle is dependent on two physiological processes that occur in both men and women: vasocongestion and myotonia. Penile erections, increased breast size, and lubrication of the vagina during sexual excitation are caused by vasocongestion, which is the swelling of body tissues when they are filled with blood, leading to increases in size. Other areas of the body that experience vasocongestion include the labia, clitoris, nipples, and testicles. The sense of genital tension that may occur during sexual arousal and stimulation is a result of myotonia, which is increased muscle tension, and consists of voluntary flexing and involuntary contractions. During orgasm in both males and females, myotonia causes the muscle contractions, as well as the clenching of toes or fingers and facial grimaces.

Masters and Johnson's four-phase model. In the Masters and Johnson model (Masters & Johnson, 1966), the first phase of the sexual response cycle is *excitement* and is variable in duration, lasting from minutes to hours. Commonly, increased heart rate and blood pressure are experienced in addition to myotonia, which lead to engorgement with blood in the penis, testes, clitoris, and breasts. The increased swelling with blood can lead to a deepening of color of the genitals in addition to what is known as a "sex flush," the pink or red rash that appears on the chest or breasts. For males, while their penises may become erect, there is variability in terms of its engorgement, depending on the state of arousal. In addition, the testes may also become engorged with blood and elevate, pulling in closer to the body. For females, the clitoral shaft increases in size by swelling and elongating, while the labia majora separate. The labia minora increase in size and darken as well. The uterus begins to elevate, and the inner one-third of the vagina begins to enlarge. Some women begin to produce large amounts of lubrication, whereas others produce a smaller amount.

The second phase is the *plateau*, which is of a shorter duration, lasting between a couple seconds and a few minutes. A clear demarcation between the excitement phase and the plateau phase is not noticeable since the experience of the previous phase becomes more pronounced. Heart rate and breathing rates increase, as does muscle tension, and a deepening in color of the genitals continues. In men the coronal ridge may increase in size

slightly, the penile glans becomes a deeper purplish hue, and the testes elevate farther in preparation for orgasm. In addition, the bulbourethral gland
increases in activity and begins to secrete fluid. For women the outer third
of the vagina forms the "orgasmic platform," because it is particularly engorged with blood. The inner portion of the vagina expands fully, the uterus
elevates, and the clitoris withdraws beneath the clitoral hood.

The shortest phase of Masters and Johnson's model is the *orgasm*, which
typically lasts several seconds. It is observed that males tend to experience
orgasm after the plateau phase; however, some women do not reach orgasm.
For males the experience of orgasm is correlated with the ejaculation;
however, ejaculation may not occur at the time of the orgasm. "Orgasmic
inevitability" is a sensation that the orgasm is going to happen and is caused
by the accumulation of seminal fluids in the ejaculatory ducts and the upper
urethra. Semen is ejected from the penis at the time of orgasm. The penis,
vas deferens, ejaculatory muscles, prostate, anus, and seminal vesicles all
contract. For women the experience of orgasm occurs when the uterus and
orgasmic platform (of the vagina) contract three to fifteen times. Wavelike
contractions of the uterus also occur.

The last phase of the model is *resolution*, which occurs immediately after
orgasm without additional stimulation. In this phase the body returns to the
state of prearousal. While females are able to experience orgasm even during
resolution and may experience multiple orgasms, males are unable to do so
during the *refractory period*, which is the time when a male is unable to
achieve excitement, plateau, or orgasm through any sexual stimulation. Depending on the male's age, frequency of sexual activity, and other factors, the
refractory period may last between minutes and days.

Kaplan's three-phase model. The three phases of Kaplan's (1995) model
are *desire*, *excitement* (or *arousal*), and *orgasm*. In working with individuals
who experienced sexual dysfunction, she believed that these three phases
facilitated classification of her clients' difficulties. Her model not only included physiological experiences (i.e., excitement and orgasm) but also considered psychological conflicts that could lead to disorder. For example,
desire disorders could occur as a result of more substantive, unresolved
psychological conflicts, whereas a concern such as premature ejaculation
reflected lack of control that would not necessarily point to a deeper psychological issue (Kaplan, 1995). Kaplan's model is not built on successive stages
per se, as each phase is considered to be somewhat independent.

Kaplan's model would shape how the *Diagnostic and Statistical Manual-III* (DSM-III) classified sexual disorders (along these three phases). It offered much more insight into possible origins of some sexual disorders, as prior to her contributions most sex therapists considered deficits in sexual functioning as physiological problems or problems associated with performance anxiety rather than any other meaningful intrapsychic or interpersonal (partner-related) conflict (Kaplan, 1995).

David Reed's erotic stimulus pathway. There are additional models of sexual arousal and interaction. We note two more. The first is David Reed's erotic stimulus pathway model (see Stayton, 1996). In this model Reed added desire to Masters and Johnson's model of sexual arousal and interaction, which the reader will recall was excitement, plateau, orgasm, and resolution. Desire was presumed to be in play for Masters and Johnson. Reed adds it to the model and then considers four stages of seduction, sensations, surrender, and reflection.

The first two phases are essentially psychosocial (rather than biological). Seduction refers to the behaviors and activities that draw a person to sexual intimacy. This can range from wearing perfume to cleaning up the kitchen, depending on the couple you meet! Sensations are essentially the use of the senses to move from initial seduction or appeal to greater excitement. The next two phases are surrender and reflection. Surrender is essentially the experience of orgasm, while reflection refers to a time to literally reflect on the time of sexual intimacy and to make meaning of the experience. The interpretation of the event as positive or negative can determine the desire for future experiences of sexual intimacy.

Basson's nonlinear female model. Rosemary Basson developed a nonlinear female model of arousal to describe more accurately the experiences of sexual arousal of many of her clients (Basson, 2002, 2007, 2012). The purpose of this model was to help validate the experiences of the women she worked with, who often reported that when their male partners expressed sexual desire and arousal, there was not a corresponding experience. Her model described "receptive desire," which is a responsive, subjective experience as opposed to merely describing arousal as being a physiological experience. Her model accounts for the possibility of having physiological arousal without subjective arousal and vice versa.

Basson's model begins with *sexual neutrality*, which refers to an ambivalent space that is neither antisex nor prosex. When women are distracted or busy, their minds tend to be here. After experiencing some *sexual stimuli*, women's bodies may begin to observe physiological arousal leading to the development of *sexual arousal*, often preceding *desire*, which may arise during sexual activity. After experiencing sexual intimacy, some women may have feelings of *emotional and physical satisfaction*, accompanied by *emotional intimacy* or, for some, sexual neutrality. However, some women may also observe that upon introduction of sexual stimuli, they have feelings of *spontaneous sexual desire or hunger* arise. She also observed that many women did not require orgasm to be a part of the process of sexual satisfaction.

Basson observed the more women thought about sex, the more desire they reported. As part of her treatment, she had her clients keep a journal documenting their thoughts and feelings about sex.

The lovemaking cycle. Another model we want to introduce is the "lovemaking cycle" discussed by McCluskey and McCluskey (2006). The four phases discussed in the cycle are *atmosphere, arousal, apex,* and *afterglow*. Atmosphere refers to a range of things that foster the kind of intimacy that a couple desires: making time for each other, creating anticipation for intimacy, having energy for each other, having privacy, and so on. Arousal refers to mutual exploration and a build-up of excitement by appealing to the senses. Apex refers to more than just climax, although it includes that. It also refers to increased build-up of pleasure and spiritual connection with each other, as well as surrender to each other and the experience. The final phase, afterglow, refers to a time of caressing, affirmation, and feedback following climax.

David Schnarch. In contrast to early models (or first-generation models) of sexual response that are grounded much more in physiology and drive, David Schnarch (1991, 2009, 2011) has proposed a focus on three elements of sexual desire that had been neglected. The first is sexual desire not to initiate sex solely but desire during times of sexual intimacy. Second, he assesses desire for one's partner (in contrast to what might be seen in early sexual response cycles as a desire for sexual behavior). Last, Schnarch is interested in purposefully, consciously chosen desire—something that is more than mere biological drive.

Schnarch offers one of several emerging second-generation models that will be discussed in greater detail in subsequent chapters, as the focus on interpersonal relationships and personal maturity is a contrast to the more physiology/drive models first proposed. Again, while there are several models of sexual arousal and interaction, we appreciate the interest in making models more accessible to the public. We like to see language and phases that are easier to discuss with couples, less reductionistic, and more likely to facilitate a discussion of ways to enhance intimacy with each other. These last two models are especially helpful in that way.

KEEPING IT REAL

Imagine you were meeting with a couple for premarital counseling. They are young and come across at times as a little naive about sex. They share with you that their wedding night will be their first time either of them has experienced sexual intercourse. How would you explain to this couple what they might expect during sexual intimacy? Read back over the various models of sexual response and think about what you would want to draw on to discuss this important topic with the couple. Would you draw from more than one model, or is there a specific model you like? What would you want to be sure to convey? How would you describe your tone? What do you want to have come across in how you discuss the topic? Would you think it important to talk about different types of desire? When it comes to anatomy, would your language be more medical/clinical? In describing the cycle itself, would you use language found in the Masters and Johnson model or a similar model, or would you draw on the language of the lovemaking cycle? If so, why?

The reality is that few couples are that interested in a technical discussion of the sex response cycle. If they are unclear about what to expect during sexual intimacy, then they will want greater clarity about what they are going to experience. Since men and women have different experiences throughout the sexual response cycle, it is helpful to make note of differences, as we see in the Basson model. The introduction of more accessible language—by David Schnarch and by Christopher McCluskey and Rachel McCluskey—makes some of the newer models a little easier to discuss with clients.

CLOSING REFLECTIONS

It goes without saying that our values and morals guide and direct the choices we make. If we value honesty, we are less likely to lie. If we value commitment and honor, we are more likely to pursue relationships in spite of conflict. In the same way, our values help us to judge whether or not sexual options with respect to behavior are considered morally acceptable.

However, let us set aside our values and judgments for a moment and pursue a biological reductionist model. If we consider sexuality from this perspective, what might we perceive and experience? In considering other biological drives, like hunger and the need for sleep, we might engage in behaviors because of sexual urges. As an example, some women experience an increase in sexual arousal and desire prior to menstruation, expressing that more frequently than usual, they feel "horny." In those moments, from a biological reductionist perspective, it may make sense for a woman in that physical, mental, and emotional state to sleep with a friend as a means of relieving sexual tension. A client who grew up in a conservative religious household and had a limited number of sexual partners expressed that thirteen months after terminating a twelve-year marriage, she felt "horny" one night, decided to go to a bar, got picked up, and had a one-night stand with the guy who delivered the "best line." She did not intend to pursue a relationship with him and merely slept with him because she wanted the sexual release. She experienced some feelings of guilt but decided to set those aside in lieu of her sentiment that she had acted out of her "need."

Some may say that this client's values reflected a hedonistic state as she was directed by the pursuit of pleasure. From this perspective sexual desires may not invoke moral considerations, as the thought *If it feels good, why not?* or *If it feels good, do it* may justify actions.

So much of the field of psychology is based on the assumption that people do well "to live with a sense of wholeness in one's experiential self" (APA, 2009, p. 18). Indeed, as we discussed in chapter one, this has been referred to as *organismic congruence*. It refers to achieving congruence or a "sense of wholeness" with reference to "the unfolding of developmental processes, including self-awareness and personal identity" (p. 18).

One of the risks of biological reductionism is that it supports organismic congruence to the exclusion of other considerations. Well, what are these other considerations? If we are critical of organismic congruence, what are the alternatives?

Again, as we shared in chapter one, Christianity gives priority to what has been referred to as *telic congruence*, which refers to "living consistently within one's valuative goals" (APA, 2009, p. 18) or what a person has come to value as important to him or her, giving rise to a discussion of strivings and intentions. Rather than turn to one's impulses to determine morality and sexual ethics, the Christian turns to his or her beliefs and values, which lie outside the person's desires and help that person determine how best to live. Telic congruence brings to mind a trajectory—a direction we are moving toward and the kind of person we intend to become.

Note that it is important for clinicians to have an understanding of biological bases for behavior. We want clinicians to know and be prepared to provide psychoeducation on sexual anatomy, physiology, the sexual response cycle, and so on. But we also want to critique the underlying assumptions in our field that move toward biological reductionism and attempt to derive a sexual ethic from our impulses.

C. S. Lewis put it aptly in *The Abolition of Man*:

> Telling us to obey instinct is like telling us to obey "people." People say different things: so do instincts. Our instincts are at war. . . . By the very act of listening to one rather than to others we have already prejudged the case. If we did not bring to the examination of our instincts a knowledge of their comparative dignity we could never learn it from them. And that knowledge cannot itself be instinctive: the judge cannot be one of the parties judged: or, if he is, the decision is worthless and there is no ground for placing preservation of the species above self-preservation or sexual appetite.

We want to be aware of these different worldview considerations and these different assumptions so that they can be translated in meaningful ways to the clinical setting. Just being aware of the difference between *organismic* and *telic* congruence could provide a foundation for a constructive discussion.

As we bring this chapter to a close, ask yourself, What would you encourage your client to do if she were in the same position and had not made that decision yet? What if your client were somewhat fixated on the importance of her biological experience at this moment? How do you talk to her about the underlying perspective she may hold but not be aware of? Is this something that you would discuss? Is it best to set that aside and follow her lead?

REFERENCES

American Psychological Association. (2009). *Report of the task force on appropriate therapeutic responses to sexual orientation*. American Psychological Association.

Basson, R. (2002). Female sexual dysfunctions—the new models. *The British Journal of Diabetes and Vascular Disease, 2*(4), 267-70.

Basson, R. (2007). Sexual desire/arousal disorders in women. In S. R. Leiblum (Ed.), *Principles and practice of sex therapy* (4th ed., pp. 25-53). Guilford Press.

Basson, R. (2012). Women's difficulties with low sexual desire, sexual avoidance, and sexual aversion. In S. B. Levine, C. B. Risen, & S. T. Althof (Eds.), *Handbook of clinical sexuality for mental health professionals* (2nd ed.). Routledge.

Kaplan, H. S. (1995). *Sexual desire disorders: Dysfunctional regulation of sexual motivation.* Routledge.

Masters, W. H., & Johnson, V. E. (1966). *Human sexual response.* Little, Brown.

McCluskey, C., & McCluskey, R. (2006). *When two become one: Enhancing sexual intimacy in marriage.* Revell.

Rathus, S. A., Nevid, J. S., & Fichner-Rathus, L. (2001). *Human sexuality in a world of diversity* (4th ed.). Pearson.

Schnarch, D. (1991). *Constructing the sexual crucible: An integration of sexual and marital therapy.* W. W. Norton.

Schnarch, D. (2009). *Passionate marriage: Keeping love and intimacy alive in committed relationships.* W. W. Norton.

Schnarch, D. (2011). *Intimacy & desire: Awaken the passion in your relationship.* Beaufort Books.

Sims, S., & Yeager, S. (2022). *Next level: Your guide to kicking ass, feeling great, and crushing goals through menopause and beyond.* Rodale.

Stayton, W. R. (1996). A theology of sexual pleasure. In A. Thatcher & E. Stuart (Eds.), *Christian perspectives on sexuality and gender* (pp. 332-46). Eerdmans.

FOUR

SEXUALITY IN CLINICAL PERSPECTIVE

THERE WAS NOTHING QUITE LIKE IT. The country was not prepared for it. No one had really talked about it in a public way. We are referring, of course, to the first commercial by then-Senator Bob Dole on behalf of Viagra. This was followed up a few years later by NASCAR driver Mark Martin, who endorsed Viagra on his stock car, further legitimizing sexual dysfunction and to a more Southern constituency. Today it is nothing to see several advertisements for various medications to improve erectile functioning. But back when it all started, when no one high profile had been featured in an ad, it was something to see Bob Dole discussing the reality of erectile dysfunction or ED, as he referred to it. In some ways these commercials marked a turning point in discussing sexual performance. It was as if sexual dysfunctions gained a new level of legitimacy (Leiblum & Rosen, 2000).

What Bob Dole did for the nation is what we hope you want to do in your sessions. No pressure! We want you to be able to provide clients with a sense that their sexual concerns are legitimate and worthy of professional time and attention. You want to aspire to be the Bob Dole of sex therapy!

We have no idea what led Bob Dole to participate in ED commercials. In order to facilitate constructive discussions with clients, however, it is important for you to be intentional about setting an atmosphere for learning and constructive engagement with individuals and couples. To do this, it can be helpful to reflect on your own attitudes, knowledge, experiences, and feelings associated with sexuality and your own sexual development.

Sexual attitudes, for example, are difficult to mask from clients. Clinicians will convey their attitudes through what they choose to discuss, how they discuss those topics, the questions they ask, nonverbal expressions, and so on. As Joyce Penner and Cliff Penner (2005) observe, there are helpful and unhelpful attitudes that are conveyed in our work with clients. Common helpful attitudes include that sexuality is a natural part of human experience and that it can be a pleasurable and fulfilling rather than aversive or discontenting.

PERSONAL REFLECTION

We want you to begin to reflect on your own personal attitudes, knowledge, experiences, and feelings associated with sexuality. Please take a few moments to reflect on how you were educated about sexuality and sexual behavior. You might find it helpful to journal about your experiences so you have a place to reflect and process what you learn about yourself. What did you learn in your home growing up about sexuality and sexual behavior? How was the topic addressed? How would you describe the overall atmosphere in your home when it came to discussing sex?

Think also about any more formal sex education you had, whether a church program, public school program, or other. What was its quality (wonderful or poor)? Did you have a college class in sexuality? Taken together, how would you describe your knowledge about sexuality and sexual behavior?

Reflect on your lifetime sexual experience in terms of your own sexual desire and behavior. In what specific ways do your experiences (or lack of experience) influence how you approach the topic of sexuality and sexual behavior?

How would you describe your current moral stance on sexual issues? How settled are you in your thinking on these issues? In some discussions this might range from "I have given these matters careful thought, have firm opinions that are unlikely to change, and firmly believe my views are right" to "To be honest, I am confused, bewildered, and up in the air about the matter of sexuality."

How comfortable are you with discussing sex? For any number of reasons, this might range from "The topic of sex makes me feel rather threatened and conflicted, such that talking about it even in small groups will be painful and difficult" to "I am at ease and open."

Sexual knowledge refers more to your education at the undergraduate and graduate level, as well as continuing education courses and relevant trainings on sexuality and related topics. Keep in mind too that sexual knowledge can be enhanced through good supervision and consultation on difficult cases.

Sexual experience refers to what you have personally experienced in your own sexual development and sex life. When we train students to receive certification as sex therapists, we often have them reflect on their own sex history so that they can understand how life experiences affect them today, as well as gain some insight into the challenges people face in discussing their sex history with others.

We encourage people to reflect on how sex was discussed in their homes growing up, what they were exposed to in terms of modesty or nudity in their homes, and how affection was expressed (verbally and nonverbally), as well as how they responded to changes at puberty, first dating experiences, and so on up until the present. Sexual experience also includes but is not limited to some of the challenges you may have faced. Have you ever struggled with a sexual dysfunction? Or have you ever dealt with addiction? Sexual identity concerns? It could be with desire disorder, orgasmic disorder, painful intercourse, addiction to pornography, and so on. If you have never struggled with any of these issues, that too can affect the services you provide (Penner & Penner, 2005), as sometimes our personal struggles increase our capacity to empathize with others. If you are married, we join the Penners in encouraging you to have or be working on a healthy, fulfilling sexual life together. If you are single, we encourage you to have or be working on a healthy sex life in the broadest sense of the terms from chapter one, that is, your own gender sexuality (as male or female) and erotic sexuality (insight into the longing for completion in another, which is only ultimately experienced in God), both of which are experienced to some degree in how we relate to one another as sexual beings.

It is also important to understand the feelings you have about your own sexuality and sexual expression. Feelings can range considerably from comfort to discomfort, peace to anxiety, confidence to guilt or shame, and more. Some people are remarkably comfortable discussing various facets of sex and sexual functioning. Others are notably shy and reticent to discuss anything having to do with sexual behavior. Most people fall somewhere in between. Similarly, how we present as our gendered selves reflects our level of comfort and discomfort with our gender sexuality, and as such, our actions may reflect feelings and attitudes that may be apparent to others.

The book you are reading is a resource for thinking about sexuality and sexual behavior from a Christian perspective. The fact that such a book could be written underscores the importance of reflecting on your own belief system or values pertaining to sexual behavior. We encourage you to have or be developing a working Christian theology of human sexuality.

We turn our attention now to models of training and competency that are helpful for both preparing to do work in this area and recognizing the limitations of what one does and does not know. The purpose in reviewing these models is to help students gain some familiarity with when to intervene and when to refer, based on one's level of education, training, and supervised clinical experience.

THE PLISSIT MODEL

One well-known model to be familiar with is Annon's (1974) PLISSIT model for counseling around sexuality issues. The acronym stands for

P—permission giving

LI—limited information

SS—specific suggestions

IT—intensive therapy

Permission giving is often a supportive response to an individual or couple who may feel particularly anxious about sex or have concerns that they are doing something wrong when what they are doing is rather common or certainly not outside the realm of what many other couples have experienced. For example, you might meet with a couple who is worried that they are obsessed with sex because they have sex five to six times a week. While this is higher than what most couples report, it may not be a particular concern and might be more common among younger couples with relatively higher sex drives, no children, and other considerations. Permission giving here could involve listening to the concern, clarifying any other explanation for the frequency of their sexual intimacy, and essentially giving them permission to experience what they are doing. It might involve being familiar with and educating the couple on the range of experiences other couples have and how what they are reporting appears to be within those limits and, provided there is no other important information missing in their presentation, is likely fine and something that they can enjoy.

For Annon (1974), *limited information* refers to the client's lack of information that may need to be broadened. It might, for example, include educating a couple about the sexual response cycle. A couple might be having some difficulty with arousal or orgasm, and a discussion of the sexual response cycle might provide them with sufficient information to confront myths or distortions couples often have about anatomy, physiology, sexual response, and so on.

Specific suggestions are tied to the issue that a couple may be coming to counseling to discuss. For example, some men who suffer from rapid ejaculation (or premature ejaculation) have found it helpful to dramatically increase their intercourse frequency for a month. It is a noninvasive intervention in the form of a suggestion that is specific to that concern.

Intensive therapy refers to a more traditional, ongoing sex therapy service in which the client or couple comes in for ongoing treatment of an identifiable condition or concern.

While we appreciate Annon's PLISSIT model in terms of giving students a broad overview of levels of involvement with couples and how these levels reflect differing competencies and clinical responsibilities, we are particularly appreciative of Rosenau, Sytsma, and Taylor's (2002) DEC-R model, a four-step process for helping clients deal with their sexual concerns that was developed in light of limitations in the PLISSIT model.

THE DEC-R MODEL

In the DEC-R model the clinician introduces the topic of sexuality and sexual behavior and creates a safe place for *dialogue*. The *discussion* about sexuality progresses into *education* as appropriate for the purposes of the consultation or clinical services. If needed, *coaching* can be offered to guide the person or couple through basic steps or self-help. A *referral* could then also be indicated if there is a need for more advanced professional care.

Part of what we have been discussing is what Rosenau et al. (2002) refer to as preparing yourself for dialogue. In addition to what we have been discussing (e.g., making peace with your own sexuality), keep in mind that (1) your own sexual reactions can be responsive, (2) there is value in desensitizing yourself somewhat so that you are able to deal professionally with the topic of sex in counseling, and (3) it is helpful to create a safe environment for those who seek your professional services. Let's discuss each of these.

What does it mean when they say that sex can be responsive? Sometimes we think about sexual interest or desire as initiating desire. In other words, it is a desire that begins perhaps out of biological drive (think hormones, such as testosterone) and initiates interest in another. But sexual desire can also be conceptualized as a response to having other needs met, as when a person feels cared for, respected, loved in a relationship. The ways that a person feels cared for (think here about the "love languages" and how people express and receive messages that they love and care for one another) can lead to responsive desire—a desire for the other that is expressed in response to (rather than initiating from).

As we learn about these different concepts, we want to help you as you read and learn how to address sexuality in clinical practice. As the DEC-R model suggests, you want to begin to ask, How can you desensitize yourself to the topic of sex in counseling, and what are the benefits in doing so? Many desensitization strategies involve overexposure (to the point of saturation) to various sexual stimuli; that is not what we are recommending for training. Rather, we want to have you practice talking about various topics related to human sexuality and sexual functioning. There is no substitute for taking time to practice what to say and how to say it while also maintaining good eye contact and perhaps even receiving feedback from a third party who is watching you and is capable of helping you learn from your mistakes.

In training, we often divide students into groups of three or four so that they can break to complete structured assignments. One student can interview the other while a third student observes and provides feedback on the exchange, including nonverbal messages or indicators of anxiety on the part of the student who is the clinician in the role-play. We want to reiterate that there is no substitute for logging hours practicing (and making mistakes) with words that you may not be accustomed to saying (e.g., penis, orgasm, vulva, testicles).

Finally, much of what we have covered goes into creating a safe environment. Remember our friend Bob Dole? He helped to foster a national discussion in which it was okay to talk about ED and the broader topic of sexual functioning. What can we do to facilitate and create a safe, nonthreatening environment? It can be helpful to speak clearly and respectfully about sex, to demonstrate a positive attitude toward education and learning in this area, and to convey the significance and uniqueness of a person's sexuality and their experiences with sexual expression. In this context it is also important to set boundaries around certain discussions so that you do not discuss your own sexual countertransference with clients (Rosenau et al., 2002).

In the DEC-R model, after dialogue comes education. This involves many things, including being able to discuss and apply a working theology of sexuality (including challenging the misuse of Scripture), acquiring information you do not have (via other resources, such as journal articles, textbooks, and the internet), challenging incorrect information such as myths about sex (e.g., "all men want to get lucky and score") or incorrect assumptions (e.g., "sex will create instant intimacy"), and understanding sexual response (Rosenau et al., 2002, p. 503).

Concerning this last point of sexual response, a helpful, practical way to address false expectations, incorrect assumptions, or myths about sexuality is to walk a person through one or more models of the sexual response cycle. The model itself gives you a focal point for education and allows for a kind of springboard from which you and the person can jump into a discussion of common false expectations.

As we discussed in chapter three, Masters and Johnson offer one of the most well-known models of sexual response. Theirs is a four-stage model of arousal, plateau, orgasm, and resolution. Arousal refers to the sexual excitement that is experienced; it is accompanied by increased myotonia (neuromuscular tension) and vasocongestion (increased blood flow to the genitals). Plateau refers to a time when arousal levels off and is maintained prior to orgasm. Orgasm itself refers to the muscular contractions and related pleasure experienced at the climax of sexual excitement. It involves the release of neuromuscular tension. Resolution is the return to the pre-arousal state. Unfortunately, the model itself is somewhat mechanistic and can run the risk of reducing intimacy to biological responses, which can be counterproductive to the kinds of discussions clinicians want to facilitate with couples.

Christopher McCluskey has offered an adaptation of the Masters and Johnson cycle that he refers to as the "lovemaking cycle." The four stages here are atmosphere (which includes attending to energy, time, and setting the stage for intimacy), arousal (including exploration and attention to the senses during foreplay), apex (which includes letting go and delighting in each other, orgasm), and afterglow (enjoying being with each other following apex, reflection, and feedback).

So a clinician could say to a couple, "As we go through what is sometimes called the sexual response cycle, or we can call it the lovemaking cycle, let me point out a couple of common misconceptions about sexuality. I mentioned a moment ago that the four stages of one model are atmosphere, arousal, apex, and afterglow. Well, when we discuss the first two stages, atmosphere and arousal, one common misconception is that men are always interested in sex, that they are always ready to perform and will quickly or instantly have an erection with no or only minimal stimulation. The reality is that men vary considerably, just as do women, in terms of their experience with arousal as well as how much stimulation they may need or benefit from for them to achieve and maintain an erection."

A related misconception is that women seldom think about or fantasize about sex. That too could be discussed in the context of educating a couple about the sexual response cycle. We generally talk to couples about the range of experiences among men and women—in this case around frequency of sexual thoughts or interests or fantasy—and that there is great diversity in experience, so that no one else's experience should be seen as the standard by which this couple (or person) has to measure themselves.

Couples also deal with false expectations. A common one is that they will simply have a terrific sex life without giving it much attention or putting much energy or effort into it. This expectation probably relates to how sex is portrayed in the entertainment industry. Very seldom are people exposed to stories of couples having to be intentional about their sex life; rather, sex is often portrayed as either easy (no effort or intentionality) or simply a disappointment to the couple (often tied to married couples in movies or on TV, so that the message is that sex in marriage is typically not enjoyable). The reality is that most couples have to be intentional about this part of their life.

A related expectation that might be more common with religious clients is that couples who make all of the "right" decisions before marriage (i.e., they wait to have intercourse until they marry) will not have any difficulties with their sex life. But sexual concerns can be caused by an array of issues, often multiple issues or factors that can be difficult to pinpoint, and the challenges couples face are often not the direct result of their prior behavior, nor does the decision to abstain until marriage safeguard a couple from various sexual dysfunctions. In addition, it can be helpful to educate the client that many behaviors require practice before there is a fluidity that accompanies that action. It is the same with intimacy; it requires practice.

Coaching refers to the process by which a clinician guides a couple beyond education and into a place of improved sexual intimacy. The guidance that is offered often takes the form of specific suggestions, such as self-help exercises that are often used with specific presenting concerns. These suggestions, often coupled with good bibliotherapy readings, can provide a basis for specific changes that may improve sexual intimacy for the couple. Asking a couple to read, discuss, and process chapters from *A Celebration of Sex* by Doug Rosenau or *The Gift of Sex* by Joyce and Cliff Penner may help with a particular presenting concern.

The last aspect of the DEC-R model is referral. A counselor might offer a referral to address medical or physical health concerns (or to rule out a medical condition that could be causing the symptoms). A referral can also be made due to competence; sometimes it is in the best interest of the couple if they see someone with additional skills and training in the treatment of a particular concern. Some counselors find it helpful to make a referral when the topic they are working with hits too close to home; they may consider a referral to essentially maintain their own emotional health and safety if they are themselves wounded in an area.

As Rosenau et al. (2002) discuss, referrals may be made to any number of professionals, organizations, or ministries. Sometimes referrals are made to a physician, urologist, or gynecologist. Other times a referral is made to someone who provides adjunctive support to counseling. This might be a dietitian or physical therapist. Referrals might also be made to specialists who might treat substance abuse or other issues. Community resources and groups are also a consideration, as when a referral is offered to groups like Sex Addicts Anonymous or Celebrate Recovery. A referral might also be made to a more experienced professional sex therapist or someone with greater expertise with a specific issue or presenting concern.

CHANGES IN THE FIELD

The field is always changing (Peterson, 2017; Wincze & Weisberg, 2015; cf. Leiblum, 2007; Leiblum & Rosen, 2000). It is important to keep up with these changes by reading journal articles and attending professional conferences.

Sexual pharmacology. Probably the most dramatic changes we have seen in the field are tied to sexual pharmacology. We mentioned earlier that former senator Bob Dole's very public declaration around ED validated the condition and gave people permission to talk about it. Dole implied that he was taking Viagra and that it was an effective treatment for ED. That was part of a larger, sweeping interest in sexual pharmacology that is ongoing today. Given the success of Viagra and related medications for the treatment of ED in men, there is increased interest in finding pharmacological interventions for other sexual dysfunctions.

The concern that is at times a point of discussion today is whether successes in sexual pharmacology will lead to a kind of sexual reductionism. What we mean by that is whether the field will reduce discussions of healthy sex to what medications can accomplish. Is there a risk, then, of the field of sex therapy becoming too focused on medical interventions at the expense of both intrapersonal (within the person) and interpersonal (between people) considerations?

Throughout parts two and three of this book, we will discuss how various advances in pharmacology are shaping the field when it comes to the various dysfunctions, addictions, and other clinical concerns. We will also contrast that with discussions about intrapersonal and interpersonal considerations that are still central to effective sex counseling today.

Advances in technology. Although there are other noted changes in the field—such as how we are conceptualizing pain disorders, which will be discussed in the relevant and corresponding chapters—the other major change to keep track of has to do with advances in technology.

How does the internet affect sexuality and sexual functioning? On the positive side the internet can certainly place helpful information and educational resources in the hands of the consumer or client that were not as readily available previously. This should not be underestimated. Not long ago people had to make a concerted effort to find information through professionals who were limited in terms of their practice location. Specialists were few and far between, and finding accurate information could present a considerable challenge to a person or couple who was seeking information, let alone professional services.

The concern is that inaccurate information is also readily available on the internet. The fact that information is available does not mean that the information is always accurate, nor does it follow that the information will be applied to the unique issues the person or couple is currently facing.

Another concern is the ubiquity of pornographic images and other paraphilic and paraphilic-related stimuli that are increasingly accessible. Smartphones and other devices place pornography at our fingertips in literally a click of the button. As a clinician the availability of pornography and other sexually explicit materials elicits concern regarding important psychological processes, such as the delay of self-gratification, self-control, the development of addiction, and other issues that affect health and well-being.

A related concern is that all kinds of diverse sexual interests are represented on the web. There is really no sexual variant for which a person cannot find a sense of shared identity and community. While this can be a strength for those who are struggling with shame and isolation, it can also reinforce patterns of arousal and behavior that may conflict with the person's overall beliefs and values, and make it that much more difficult to make choices that reflect those values.

DEBATES IN THE FIELD

We also see several ongoing debates in the field. Some of them are tied to how dysfunctions are conceptualized, and we see these as sharpening our focus as science advances in challenging preconceived notions. Other discussions have a similar quality but can often turn into more of a political debate. For example, while homosexuality is not a psychopathology, it continues to be a concern among some who would prefer to pursue heterosexual relationships or at least refrain from behavior they believe is immoral. Existing diagnostic nomenclature leaves little by way of diagnostic categories for these individuals.

Gender identity is another topic that has come under greater scrutiny. The debates have intensified as to whether gender dysphoria is likely to desist in children diagnosed with it and whether the preferred model of care for minors should include medical interventions.

Debates also continue around sexual addictions. Some are internal, for instance, whether the condition is more of an addiction or a compulsion. Other debates are whether there is such a thing as an addiction and whether it meets criteria as a psychopathology.

There are also voices calling for mental health professionals to move out of the area of sexuality and sexual functioning. These voices often see pathologizing sexual interests and behavior as a leftover from religious conservatism rather than scientific endeavor.

These debates also raise important questions for conventionally religious people and communities. For example, how does their understanding of scientific findings line up with their understanding of Scripture? There are many aspects of human sexuality and behavior that are not explicitly addressed in Scripture (for example, birth control and masturbation).

There may be benefits found in religiously congruent sex therapy. This is especially true for religiously conservative couples whose personal beliefs about which behaviors are permissible versus comfortable or desired may rally against those of a sex therapist who is not a religious conservative. Values in conflict may lead to a referral as attitudes and worldviews risk becoming pathologized or stigmatized as unhealthy or restricted when they may merely reflect a set of religious beliefs and values that reflect a larger worldview.

ASSESSMENT OF SEXUAL CONCERNS

Most assessments are conducted through an extensive clinical interview and sex history. We will discuss these shortly. Before we do, it can be helpful to have an overview of how a person or couple ends up in sex therapy given other issues that may be of concern.

David Barlow has a helpful map of the terrain. He discusses how the clinician considers whether there are other issues that need to be addressed prior to providing sex therapy. For example, does one or the other person have a known medical condition that should be treated first? If so, the person should be seen by the appropriate medical professional (e.g., gynecologist, urologist) and treated for that concern before entering into sex therapy.

Similarly, does one or the other person have a known psychiatric condition, such as a depressive disorder or anxiety disorder, that should be treated first? If so, the person should be seen by the appropriate mental health professional (e.g., psychologist, counselor) and treated for that concern before beginning intensive sex therapy.

Likewise, if one or the other person has a substance use problem, he or she should receive a referral to a substance abuse treatment specialist first before embarking on sex therapy.

In addition to individual medical and psychiatric concerns, it is also important to determine whether there are relational concerns that would make sex therapy particularly difficult to pursue at this time. Sometimes difficulties in sexual functioning can contribute to relationship stress, but what we are talking about is when there is considerable relational strife such that the couple does not yet have adequate resources to bring into more intensive sex therapy. This can sometimes be difficult to discern.

MEASURES AND SEX HISTORY FORMS

Assessment measures. There are a number of measures that can be used in sex therapy. The measures themselves provide a link between research and clinical practice by providing professionals with reliable and valid measures, questionnaires, scales, inventories, and so on (Fisher et al., 2011; Milhausen, Sakaluk et al., 2020). Some assessment measures are more widely used for research, while others are used in clinical practice. In some settings, various measures might be provided to each client as he or she initiates therapy, as they may be part of a broader clinical research program or otherwise reflect a common presenting issue seen at that clinical setting. For example, if a clinic serves primarily gender identity issues, it might offer all clients who present with gender dysphoria the Recalled Childhood Gender Identity/Gender Role Questionnaire (Zucker et al., 2006). In other settings, sex therapists will interview the client(s) before determining which assessment measures will glean the most relevant information for therapy.

Among the various measure of sexual attitudes and beliefs, there is the Brief Sexual Attitudes Scale (Hendrick & Hendrick, 2020), the Attitudes Toward Sexuality Scale (Fisher, 2020), and the Sexual Dysfunctional Beliefs Questionnaire (Nobre et al., 2020).

Measures of desire and interest include the Sexual Want and Get Discrepancy Measure (Blunt-Vinti et al., 2020), the Sexual Desire Questionnaire (Chadwick et al., 2020), and the Sexual Desire Inventory-2 (Spector et al., 2020).

Measures of communication include the Dyadic Sexual Communication Scale (Catania, 2020a), the Sexual Self-Disclosure Scale (Catania, 2020b), and the Partner Communication Scale (Milhausen, Sales, & diClemete, 2020). For further reading in this area, Milhausen, Sakaluk et al. (2020) and Grover and Shouan (2020) offer comprehensive listings of various sexuality-related measures.

For most clinicians much of the assessment is conducted in the clinical interview and sexual history interview; although there is certainly variability among clinicians, the various measures are not as frequently used in outpatient clinical practice (as contrasted with a clinical research setting).

Sex history forms. Sex history forms are different from sex assessment measures, scales, and inventories. They provide a structure (or semi-structure) for conducting an interview in which the clinician is collecting important information about a person's sexual history and current sexual problem history, as well as acute and chronic concerns and patterns of relating that may be relevant to case conceptualization and treatment planning.

There are many sex history forms available to the sex therapist. We have often used the Purdue Sex History (Fontaine, 1984), the Keith Hawton Sex History Guide (Hawton, 1985), and/or the Penner and Penner Sex History (Penner & Penner, 2005). The Purdue Sex History (Fontaine, 1984) is a basic sex history form that provides a structured overview of sexual interests, concerns, and so on. After covering current family structure and family of origin history, the Purdue Sex History goes into significant past relationships, current relationship, and emotional assessment. Then there are specific sex history questions.

The Keith Hawton Sex History Guide (Hawton, 1985) is not as broad and encompassing as other sex history forms, but it uniquely goes into greater detail with specific dysfunctions. For example, if a clinician suspects painful intercourse, the sex history guide offers questions to help assess the pain, such as, "Where does the pain occur (at the entrance in, or deep in, the vagina)?" (p. 107). Most sex history forms do not offer detailed questions that are specific to particular dysfunctions.

The Penner and Penner Sex History (2005) is perhaps one of the broadest and most encompassing sex history forms. It includes sections on physical history, background, sexual evaluation, and sexual assessment feedback. This last subsection, sexual assessment feedback, is particularly important for new therapists who may need help organizing the data they have gathered in a way that will be helpful to case conceptualization and feedback as given to the client.

A more recent publication by Wincze and Weisberg (2015) has a chapter dedicated to psychosocial assessment that has prompts for both sexual problem history and a sex history (see chapter 12). An additional chapter is dedicated to assessing for co-occurring conditions common to sexual disorders (see chapter 14).

PURPOSES OF ASSESSMENT

Assessment is intervention (Rosenau et al., 2007). When we say assessment is intervention, we mean that assessment helps clients by providing them with both language and story. Language refers to how they talk about sex (what actual words they use) and their comfort level with discussing sex. Assessment also helps with story; it provides them with a narrative for how they came to have the sexual concern, as well as a story for how it will be addressed.

Along these lines, Penner and Penner (2005) discuss three purposes of conducting an assessment. The first purpose is to gather information. At the most basic level, assessment provides the clinician with important information that will be critical in determining case conceptualization and treatment planning. Assessment should be far reaching in terms of gathering sufficient information to make a diagnosis, to conceptualize the case accurately, and to provide a direction for care.

The second purpose in conducting an assessment is to direct the focus of the client. This is what we referred to earlier as telling their story. A good clinical interview and sex history interview helps the client begin to consider perspectives different from those they might have come in with, which will facilitate treatment. Understanding clients' beliefs, attitudes, and worldview while evaluating their background and relational experiences is important in identifying potential barriers to healthy sexuality.

The third purpose of conducting an assessment is to develop the therapeutic relationship. We do not want to underestimate how difficult it can be for a client to honestly share his or her concerns in the area of sexuality. The assessment fosters the therapeutic relationship with the client by creating a sense of safety—the client is able to open up about a difficult matter and have that information heard and validated by a professional who is trained to help.

FOUR LEVELS OF ASSESSMENT

It has also been noted that there are various levels of assessment. Penner and Penner (2005) discuss four: general assessment of appropriateness, sexual problem history, preparation, and problem conceptualization/feedback. Let's take a look at each of these four levels of assessment.

The first level of assessment is a general assessment for the appropriateness of sex therapy. There are many reasons why a person or couple may not be an appropriate candidate for sex therapy at this time. They may have medical or psychological or relationship concerns that need to be addressed prior to providing sex therapy. A good assessment helps tease out whether sex therapy per se is indicated or whether the person or couple would benefit from other services at this time.

The second level of assessment involves taking a sexual problem history. Problems rarely appear out of nowhere or with no history or story behind them. Problems are like barnacles on a ship: they grow on you. So taking a sexual problem history entails asking relevant questions that help the counselor come to a better understanding of the nature of the sexual concern, when it began, and how it has developed into the kind of concern that would bring this person or couple in for therapy.

Third, an assessment prepares the person or couple for the work of therapy. It gives them an idea of what will be discussed, how it will be discussed, and how they will be talking to one another. By taking a sex history the clinician ends up using terms and phrases that might not be commonly discussed by the person or couple. We discuss this further later, but it is important to use correct terminology and to put the person or couple at ease in the sense that you as the clinician are comfortable addressing these issues. It also allows the clinician to model how each person will be approached around matters of sexuality and sexual behavior. There is respect shown to both human sexuality and the people in the room who are distressed about their presenting concern. Modeling respect goes a long way in helping the couple think about their concern in a more constructive manner.

The fourth level of assessment is problem conceptualization and feedback. A good sex history assessment will provide the clinician with a way to make sense of the presenting concerns. These issues can then be shared with the person or couple in a way that facilitates the work that is ahead of them. For example, if you are meeting with a couple who is dealing with a desire disorder, you could imagine being able to point out that there is a discrepancy between their levels of desire that can be discussed and resolved in therapy (rather than more finger pointing at one person as having "the problem" that is messing everything up in the marriage).

We would add to this the need for a general sex history. This takes the sexual problem history mentioned earlier and places that in the broader context of each person's own sex history. A general sex history will cover a person's earliest exposure to the topic of sex—how they were educated (or not) in the home, by their peers, and in the context of broader cultural messages they received about sex, sexuality, and sexual expression. What attitudes were conveyed in discussing sex in the client's home growing up? How was nudity and modesty addressed and modeled? Also, what was the client's experience going through puberty? What were his or her experiences with masturbation? Was the client ever exposed to pornography? Or did the client ever experience unwanted sexual touch or exposure to a highly sexualized atmosphere at home? These questions and many others are part of a general sex history. There are elements of the Purdue Sex History, the Keith Hawton Sex History Guide, and the Penner and Penner Sex History that can serve as helpful guides to a general sex history.

GENERAL COMMENTS

We want to offer a few general comments related to the clinical work in this area (for an expanded discussion, see Penner & Penner, 2005). First, acknowledge that it is often difficult to talk about sexuality and sexual behavior. It is difficult to talk about sex, especially in an honest, respectful, and vulnerable manner. It is much easier to be crass or to make jokes about it (or other behaviors) that enable a person to avoid the discomfort. You can acknowledge and respect that fact while also encouraging the person or couple to be as specific as possible. The anxiety associated with discussing sexual behavior can lead to abstractions—broad concepts and considerations that seem a little detached from the couple. You want to encourage specificity about the concerns that bring them in to see you.

Common sources of anxiety include having to use explicit sexual terminology and having an explicit discussion about sex. People do not spend their typical Tuesday talking about penises and vaginas—they tend not to use these words or terminology, and they are not adept at discussing this part of their lives.

The clinician's gender is frequently a source of anxiety. There is nothing you can do about this; you are male or female, and some male or female clients will react to your gender. You can ask how it is for them to talk about their concerns with a female or male. We do not recommend leading with that, as it can create an awareness of anxiety that might not have been there. If you sense anxiety in talking with you, you could note the anxiety using a ubiquity statement. For example, if you are a female therapist, you could say to a male client who is talking to you about a desire disorder, "Many men struggle with a desire disorder, as you have been discussing. Some men have also found it difficult at times to talk about it, particularly with a female. How is it for you to discuss it here?" This gives them permission to acknowledge anxiety if they do experience it.

Clients often struggle too with talking about taboo topics. This could include anxiety that comes from discussing immoral behavior. They might consider the behavior immoral, they might think the behavior is considered immoral by others, or they might think that you consider the behavior immoral. Some clinicians have found it helpful to share that they work from a nonjudgmental perspective. Another important disclosure is that other clients have told stories like theirs in the context of receiving sex therapy. This helps normalize this process of disclosure and increases their sense that they are not the only ones with this concern.

Anxiety could also arise from discussing secrets, such as abuse or fantasy or an affair. A husband or wife admitting to the ongoing use of pornography could be difficult. It could be hard to be honest about the use of fantasy during sex.

Anxiety can also exist around feeling like no one else struggles with what they are dealing with. A couple might not believe that others have an unconsummated marriage, for example. They may feel completely isolated and ashamed, which magnifies the anxiety they may already feel about discussing sex.

Last, an individual or a couple can feel anxiety about sharing with you their own values. They have their own beliefs and values about sexuality and sexual behavior. Sometimes discussing sex with a counselor creates anxiety about what the counselor will think about their values. Will the counselor think the person is a prude? Too conservative? Too liberal? A sex maniac? In any case, this is another common source of anxiety in sex therapy.

Before we close out this section, we would like to note that these anxieties are not just for the client; many clinicians feel anxious about talking about sexuality and sexual behavior. Our anxiety can make us complicit with an anxious client, and we could collude with them to skim over important information in an interview. Keep in mind the most common mistake of novice sex therapists: not getting sufficiently detailed information.

As we suggested, be generous in the use of ubiquity statements. These help put the client at ease: "Many people experience _____; how about you?" If you are providing services to a woman who is seeing you for anorgasmia, an example of a ubiquity statement that could facilitate disclosure would be, "Many women we work with do not experience orgasm every time they have sexual intercourse. What has been your experience?" This kind of phrasing gives the client "permission" to disclose something that might otherwise be difficult to discuss, in part because you are saying she is not the only person to report this experience.

BASIC PRINCIPLES IN ALL SEX THERAPY

Although we will offer specific suggestions for intervening with people with a range of sexual concerns, there are a few basic principles in all of sex therapy.

Responsibility. When working with couples in the treatment of sexual dysfunctions, it is important to foster a sense of mutual responsibility. Many couples enter therapy hurt and defensive. They may together or as individuals have a narrative that explains their pain and suffering. That narrative is often tied to a linear explanation—a diagnosis of a problem in their partner and the need for that person to get help from you. Mutual responsibility means helping them see how the way they relate to each other can contribute to or exacerbate an existing sexual problem.

When working with individual clients with other sexual concerns, it is also important to help foster a sense of responsibility for their work in therapy. For example, the man who enters therapy for sex addiction will need to take responsibility for his recovery. The clinician may establish a framework for recovery that specifies certain activities, such as participating in a self-help or mutual aid support group, participating in ongoing therapy, securing a sponsor and meeting with the sponsor regularly, having an accountability partner, and managing one's environment (e.g., adding software for accountability with pornography, removing items that are stimulating for that person). The invitation is made for the person struggling with sex addiction to enter into that framework for recovery, and the client is asked to take responsibility for participating in that framework.

Accurate information. Another basic principle involves providing the individual or couple with accurate information. It should be noted that in the internet age, there is ample information just a few keystrokes away from a client. So we are not talking about clients who have no access to information. The information on the internet can vary considerably in quality, so that is one consideration. In addition, the application of information to the unique circumstances an individual or couple faces is another consideration. The clinician will need to be familiar with the most recent data concerning the area they are addressing in therapy, but the clinician also needs to be able to tailor that information and apply it in clinically meaningful ways to the lived experiences of their clients.

Sex therapy also often works from the standpoint that self-knowledge is a place to begin to foster sustainable changes in sexual attitudes and behavior. Sometimes the accurate information is what the person learns from doing homework exercises in which they learn about their own body, as when a person is instructed to conduct a genital self-examination or keep a pain diary. These are personal experiences that facilitate self-understanding that can be processed in therapy and can eventually be shared with others, such as a spouse, as appropriate.

Lifestyle priorities. Often, it can be helpful to make lifestyle changes. For example, for a couple where both partners work full time, are raising three kids, and are involved in various church ministries, it may come as no surprise that they have difficulty finding the time and energy to prioritize their sex life. That may or may not cause their concern, but a couple's lifestyle may affect the success of sex therapy, as they may need to make a concerted effort to set aside time for each other and for the reestablishment of a life of greater sexual intimacy.

In other areas of sexual counseling, it may be important to make changes in lifestyle as part of a recovery plan for sex addiction (e.g., not working late shifts, incorporating self-help and mutual aid support groups into one's daily or weekly routine). Limiting exposure to problem stories about sexual identity—stories that go against the beliefs and values the client holds that characterize the direction he or she wants to go in therapy—can be important. Being with others who support an emerging counternarrative or other way of thinking about oneself and forming a sexual identity may entail changes in daily or weekly routines that may be difficult at times.

Attitude change. Another common principle in sex therapy is changing attitudes. That is, there is an element of depathologizing or destigmatizing elements of sexuality as movement toward healthier attitudes toward sexuality.

Some clinicians may find it helpful to think of helping clients have a *sex-positive* attitude, which refers primarily to giving oneself permission to be sexual and to pursue sexual pleasure. Others may find it helpful to think of attitude change as moving people from a "sick" role into a "learner" role. A sick role focuses more on the pathology, on the deficit, on what is wrong with the person. It can become discouraging to some clients (and to some therapists). A learner role is a more sex-positive, forward-thinking posture that assumes we all have things we could benefit from learning. The person or client we work with could benefit from learning more about him- or herself, or the partner, about their interactions, their capacity for intimacy, and so on.

Even in some of the more challenging areas to address—such as the paraphilic disorders—there may be benefits found in approaching clients with an understanding that they may want a better life, that they are able to set goals for themselves and their life in ways that are attainable provided other issues are addressed. They may have a diagnosable disorder, and they would do well to understand the nature of their condition and the best steps for addressing the issues that arise, but they may also gain something from identifying what they can learn as they try to build a healthier view of themselves and others, particularly around matters of intimacy and sexual expression.

Additional principles. One additional principle that is tied more to treatment of sexual dysfunctions than, say, the paraphilias or sexual addiction might include reducing performance anxiety.

Another principle has to do with increasing communication. The sex therapist can approach this generally—increase communication for the couple regardless of topic—as well as specifically. The specific area for improvement is typically in the area of sexuality. Several interventions have been designed to enhance and expand communication in this important area.

The last couple of principles for couples' sex therapy involve increasing sensual awareness and learning new skills. As a clinician, you certainly want the couple to be increasingly attentive to their own sense of sensuality apart from a goal-focused sexual encounter; you want them to enjoy and delight in each other and to increase their comfort with that.

Skill acquisition can sometimes be very specific. Sometimes one or both partners in a relationship do not know what to do or are not doing it well. Poor communication or other issues can hinder them in learning about their deficiencies and making corrections or improvements. So helping either or both learn new skills is a common part of sex therapy.

COMMONLY USED TECHNIQUES

In addition to the common principles of sex therapy, it can be helpful to highlight commonly used techniques in sexual counseling. These techniques are related to the principles we have already mentioned.

For example, psychoeducation is important and is tied to the principle of providing information. We often provide information through psychoeducation. This can take the form of didactic teaching in a session, complete with detailed diagrams or explanations of topics such as the sexual response cycle, a diagnosable disorder, and so on.

Bibliotherapy is another common intervention associated with psycho-education. Bibliotherapy entails recommending to the individual or couple a specific resource the clinician has read and has identified as helpful for the presenting concern. The client then reads that book—for example, *A Celebration of Sex* (Rosenau et al., 2007) or *Enduring Desire* (Metz & McCarthy, 2011)—and discusses and processes it with the clinician so that the information can be tailored and applied in the context of a larger treatment plan.

Another common intervention is the use of incremental homework assignments. This is particularly common in cognitive-behavioral therapy (CBT), and it often involves providing homework for the person or couple to implement, such as having them work on a communication exercise, and then evaluating their experience with it during the following session. Communication exercises, while also common in therapy, can then be provided on a graduated scale, in which more challenging topics are introduced. In sex therapy these are often referred to as sofa sessions. The couple, for instance, might sit down on their sofa and discuss their experience in counseling so far, their experience of their sexual script, their use of sexual positions, their lifestyle and roles and how those may affect sexual intimacy, and so on. A sex therapist can rank various topics based on how challenging they might be for the couple, and then assign a topic that is somewhere in the easy-to-middle range on the list as a homework assignment. During the next session the couple's experience with that assignment would then be discussed, and any difficulties would be especially important to address before moving on to the next assignment.

In addition to assigning communication exercises and sofa sessions, other common homework in treating sexual dysfunctions includes a genital self-examination, sensate focus exercises, anxiety reduction exercises, systematic desensitization, and directed masturbation.

Genital self-examination is common, particularly when treating female sexual dysfunctions (but can also be assigned when treating male dysfunctions), and it involves giving a client an image of genitalia—often as a page, image, or handout—that the client can then take home and use to identify her genitalia, locating, for example, her clitoris, labia majora, labia minora, and so on. During the process of self-examination, the client can observe and take notice how touching certain parts may feel to him or her. This information can then be included in treatment.

Assigning genital self-examination, however, is a potentially powerful exercise that should always be tied to specific goals for treatment. Is the goal to learn about oneself and one's responsiveness to stimuli? Is the goal to teach one's partner what he (or she) can do during times of sexual intimacy? Assigning an intervention like a genital self-examination can also easily be misused or misunderstood by a client, so having a more extended, intentional discussion of the intervention, its purposes, and how those purposes are tied to larger treatment goals is important. For instance, the purpose of a genital self-examination is not necessarily to experience arousal, but it could be useful in identifying what a person finds stimulating so that that information can be shared with one's partner. We discuss the use of genital self-examination more in chapter six on treatment of female orgasmic disorder (see Rosenau et al., 2007, chap. 3, for a helpful discussion of practical issues in assigning a genital self-examination).

Sensate focus exercises are often described as nondemand sensual touch exercises. This is also a powerful exercise that is used in the treatment of a number of sexual concerns. They are nondemand insofar as the goal is not to achieve orgasm or really to further the sexual response cycle as such. But they do involve sensual touch, and so there are typically three levels. The first level in sensate focus is to have the couple spend fifteen minutes or so with, say, the wife laying on her back, disrobed, and her husband touching her with different variations of pressure and in ways that are pleasing to her. He avoids touching breasts or genitals during this first level. After fifteen minutes, she would then turn over and he would continue for another fifteen minutes. They then switch positions so that she is now giving him a nondemand sensual massage. Sensate focus exercises can have them not talk but just enjoy sensual touch during this time, or they can involve communication about what is pleasing, what is uncomfortable, and so on. We prefer having the couple communicate during the exercise, but each therapist has their own preferences, as may the couple.

The second level of sensate focus includes the breasts and genitals. Each person in the couple takes a turn for about thirty minutes (fifteen minutes on each side). The third level of sensate focus includes penile-vaginal intercourse at the end of the exercise, so we will discuss some of the ways in which it is introduced and discussed in the treatment of various dysfunctions in part two.

As we discussed with genital self-examination, sensate focus can be a powerful exercise that should always be tied to specific treatment goals. What could be the purpose of sensate focus? It could be assigned to help a client learn about oneself and one's responsiveness to stimuli. It could be to enhance communication around intimacy specifically. Perhaps the couple has sufficient communication skills but is struggling with transferring those skills to times of sexual intimacy, particularly in conveying what each of them likes or does not like in terms of stimulation. The goal could be to teach one's partner what he or she can do during times of sexual intimacy. Or it could be to expand foreplay and related activities for the couple.

New therapists can too quickly assign sensate focus exercises after an initial exposure to the intervention in class or a reading. They could be misused or misunderstood by a client. So as with genital self-examination, it is important to have an extended, intentional discussion of the intervention, its purposes, and how those purposes are tied to larger treatment goals. We discuss the use of sensate focus more in chapter eight on treatment of erectile disorders (see Rosenau et al., 2007, chap. 9, for a discussion of sensate focus).

Anxiety reduction exercises are also common in the treatment of sexual dysfunctions. They might include learning deep breathing, muscle relaxation, imagery exercises, or mindfulness exercises. A goal here can be to modulate emotions, whether anxiety or even anger and hostility, for instance. As Meana (2012) notes, "These strong emotions can make clients feel helpless and out of control, and they can work to entrench the sexual difficulty" (p. 55). In the context of sex therapy, then, "helping the client and her partner modulate emotional reactivity can reduce stress and help them progress thorough treatment" (p. 55).

Mindfulness exercises have also been used in sex therapy (Meana, 2012) and with sexual identity concerns (Tan & Yarhouse, 2010). In the context of sex therapy, mindfulness techniques can "decrease distracting, negative, and anxiety-producing cognitions that prevent individuals from being fully engaged in the present moment" (Meana, 2012, p. 56). In sexual identity therapy, mindfulness exercises can help a person come to terms with the reality of their same-sex sexuality without making immediate value judgments about either their attractions or themselves as a person.

Systematic desensitization is another specific way to help clients reduce anxiety. It is based on classical conditioning. A person is first taught relaxation exercises and then establishes a hierarchy of the kinds of fears that make something difficult in their sexual script. The most common use of systematic desensitization in sex therapy is in the treatment of genito-pelvic pain/penetration disorders, particularly in cases in which a woman experiences muscular spasms in the outer third of her vagina, which make penetration impossible. We will discuss systematic desensitization in more detail in chapter seven, which deals with the treatment of sexual pain disorders among women.

Additional, common exercises include journaling and thought records. Journaling is a way for people to track their experience with different interventions and experiences throughout the course of sex therapy. Thought records function as more structured journals with a focus on identifying unhelpful thoughts with more realistic, helpful thoughts. They are also used to help clients see the relationship between their thoughts, feelings, and subsequent behaviors.

Journaling needs to be tailored to the presenting concern and the circumstances the client are facing. For example, a woman suffering from a genito-pelivc pain/penetration disorder might be instructed to keep a pain diary as a way of journaling. This use of a journal helps validate the reality of her pain and provides important information to her treatment team, which could include a sex therapist, physical therapist, pain specialist, and gynecologist. In contrast, someone in treatment for sex addiction can keep a journal to establish a baseline of problematic or targeted behaviors, as well as have a better sense for the addictive system and how they experience that system in terms of core beliefs, unhelpful thoughts, and the addictive cycle. This understanding of addiction has to be tailored to the particular client seeking treatment, and a journal or log can help facilitate application.

There are many other common interventions and techniques. But this gives the reader a sense for some of the common ones and how they might be used in the treatment of sexual disorders, atypical sexual behaviors, and other presenting concerns.

CLOSING REFLECTIONS

As we bring this chapter to a close, we want to encourage you to reflect on how you develop your identity as a Christian who is working with sexual concerns in clinical practice. For example, we want you to begin to think about how you would describe yourself today. We begin by noting that there are several ways of being a Christian in the field of sexuality and sex therapy. The following are a few descriptors that reflect variations in the broader integration discussion.

Are you becoming a clinician who works with sexual issues and who also happens to be a Christian? We are thinking here that you might view the fact that you are a Christian as largely removed and distinct from your clinical practice. Perhaps you see your personal beliefs, values, and faith commitments as personally meaningful and important, but somewhat removed from direct influence on your clinical practice. You might think that there would be little if any difference between what you or any other competent clinician would select from among the best approaches to any particular sexual concern. If that seems to fit with how you see yourself at this stage of your training, what does this mean about how you see your Christian faith in relation to your professional role and identity? How would you describe your approach to a colleague who was also a Christian? How would you describe your approach to a secular colleague or a colleague from another faith background?

Are you becoming a clinician who works with sexual issues in a more self-conscious and intentional way as a Christian? What does it mean to you to be more self-consciously Christian in practice? For example, Tan (2011) distinguishes between the use of *explicit* Christian protocols, such as God image protocols (Moriarty, 2006) or forgiveness protocols (Worthington, 2003) or the use of prayer in clinical practice, and implicit Christian protocols, which might provide an approach that provides an alternative to methods that may be a conflict for the Christian practitioner. For example, Christian sex therapists who do not incorporate erotica in the treatment of sexual dysfunctions are providing implicitly integrative practice insofar as the use of erotica is a value conflict for Christian clinical practice. Tan also recommends that Christian clinicians function as intentional integrationists. That is, he argues that Christians invite the Holy Spirit to be present in their work and to more intentionally discern what God would lead them to do in their clinical practice.

Does this way of seeing yourself affect the kinds of cases you work with? Does it influence the interventions you see yourself selecting? Also, what does it mean to be intentional? Does that mean that you are more likely to use explicitly Christian interventions in practice? Or would you see yourself as choosing not to use certain interventions in favor of other interventions that reflect less of a conflict with your beliefs and values? For example, we know some Christian sex therapists who by virtue of being intentionally Christian choose not to assign erotic books to enhance fantasy when treating a couple in which one partner has been diagnosed with a desire disorder. Do you see yourself not choosing among certain interventions because of your faith? How would you describe your approach to a colleague who was also a Christian? How would you describe your approach to a secular colleague or a colleague from another faith background?

Are you a clinician whose theory and approach are self-consciously biblical? Does that language resonate more with you? If so, why? What does it mean to you to think of a *biblical* approach rather than a *Christian* approach? Do the words carry different meanings for you? Do you see Scripture as providing the level of detail needed to provide clinical services in the various areas covered in this book? How would you compare and contrast your approach to someone else who works with sexual issues in a self-conscious and intentional way as a Christian? Is there yet another description that fits even better than any of the descriptors we have offered?

As you think about your answers to these questions, you might consider how practice setting affects your professional identity. Do you practice in a group practice affiliated with primary care in a public medical setting? Are you in a group private practice that is self-consciously Christian? Or are you in your own private practice? Do you practice in a church setting or on the mission field?

What about licensure? Are you a licensed mental health professional? What does that mean in terms of your role in providing services to the public? Or are you a coach? Or, again, do you practice on the mission field or in another setting that is not regulated by a professional mental health body?

We raise these questions not to tell you how to resolve this issue of bringing together Christian faith and theology with clinical practice in the area of sexuality but to invite you to be intentional about your professional identity and development. The steps you take early in your professional identity formation will likely lay a foundation for who you will be and how you will function in the years to come.

REFERENCES

Annon, J. S. (1974). *The behavioral treatment of sexual problems*. Kapiolani Health Services.

Blunt-Vinti, H. D., Walsh-Buhi, E. R., & Thompson, E. L. (2020). The Sexual Want and Get Discrepancy Measure. In R. R. Milhausen, J. K. Sakaluk, T. D. Fisher, C. M. Davis, & W. L. Yarber (Eds.), *Handbook of sexuality-related measures* (4th ed., pp. 277-79). Routledge.

Catania, J. A. (2020a). Dyadic Sexual Communication Scale. In R. R. Milhausen, J. K. Sakaluk, T. D. Fisher, C. M. Davis, & W. L. Yarber (Eds.), *Handbook of sexuality-related measures* (4th ed., pp. 212-14). Routledge.

Catania, J. A. (2020b). Sexual Self-Disclosure Scale. In R. R. Milhausen, J. K. Sakaluk, T. D. Fisher, C. M. Davis, & W. L. Yarber (Eds.), *Handbook of sexuality-related measures* (4th ed., pp. 218-21). Routledge.

Chadwick, S. B., Burke, S. M., Goldey, K. L., & van Anders, S. (2020). The Sexual Desire Questionnaire. In R. R. Milhausen, J. K. Sakaluk, T. D. Fisher, C. M. Davis, & W. L. Yarber (Eds.), *Handbook of sexuality-related measures* (4th ed., pp. 280-83). Routledge.

Fisher, T. D. (2020). The Attitudes Toward Sexuality Scale. In R. R. Milhausen, J. K. Sakaluk, T. D. Fisher, C. M. Davis, & W. L. Yarber (Eds.), *Handbook of sexuality-related measures* (4th ed., pp. 94-95). Routledge.

Fisher, T. D., Davis, C. M., Yarber, W. L., & Davis, S. L. (Eds.). (2011). *Handbook of sexuality-related measures* (3rd ed.). Routledge.

Fontaine, K. L. (1984). Appendix: Purdue sex history form. In T. S. Trepper & M. S. Barrett (Eds.), *Systemic treatment of incest* (pp. 252-55). Brunner/Mazel.

Grover, S., & Shouan, A. (2020). Assessment scales for sexual disorders: A review. *Journal of Psychosexual Health, 2*(2), 121-28.

Hawton, K. (1985). *Sex therapy: A practical guide*. Oxford University Press.

Hendrick, S. S., & Hendrick, C. (2020). The Brief Sexual Attitudes Scale. In R. R. Milhausen, J. K. Sakaluk, T. D. Fisher, C. M. Davis, & W. L. Yarber (Eds.), *Handbook of sexuality-related measures* (4th ed., pp. 100-102). Routledge.

Hoon, E. F., Hoon, P. W., & Wincze, J. P. (1976). An inventory for the measurement of female sexual arousability: The SAI. *Archives of Sexual Behavior, 5*(4), 291-300. https://doi.org/10.1007/BF01542081

Leiblum, S. R. (2007). Sex therapy today. In S. R. Leiblum (Ed.), *Principles and practice of sex therapy* (4th ed., pp. 3-24). Guilford.

Leiblum, S. R., & Rosen, R. C. (2000). Introduction: Sex therapy in the age of Viagra. In S. R. Leiblum & R. C. Rosen (Eds.), *Principles and practice of sex therapy* (3rd ed., pp. 1-13). Guilford.

Meana, M. (2012). *Sexual dysfunction in women*. Cambridge, MA: Hogrefe.

Metz, M. E., & McCarthy, B. W. (2011). *Enduring desire*. Routledge.

Milhausen, R. R., Sakaluk, J. K., Fisher, T. D., Davis, C. M., & Yarber, W. L. (Eds.). (2020). *Handbook of sexuality-related measures* (4th ed.). Routledge.

Milhausen, R. R., Sales, J. M., & diClemete, R. J. (2020). The Partner Communication Scale. In R. R. Milhausen, J. K. Sakaluk, T. D. Fisher, C. M. Davis, & W. L. Yarber (Eds.), *Handbook of sexuality-related measures* (4th ed., pp. 230-32). Routledge.

Moriarty, G. (2006). *Pastoral care of depression: Helping clients heal their relationship with God.* New York: Routledge.

Nobre, P. J., Tavares, I. M., & Pinto-Gouveia, J. (2020). Sexual Dysfunctional Beliefs Questionnaire. In R. R. Milhausen, J. K. Sakaluk, T. D. Fisher, C. M. Davis, & W. L. Yarber (Eds.), *Handbook of sexuality-related measures* (4th ed., pp. 111-15). Routledge.

Penner, J., & Penner, C. (2005). *A clinician's guide to sex therapy* (2nd ed.). Word.

Peterson, Z. (Ed.). (2017). *The Wiley handbook of sex therapy.* John Wiley & Sons.

Rosenau, D., Neel, D. C., & Fox, W. E. (2007). *A celebration of sex guidebook.* Xulon.

Rosenau, D., Sytsma, M., & Taylor, D. (2002). Sexuality and sex therapy: Learning and practicing the DEC-R model. In T. Clinton & G. Ohlschlager (Eds.), *Competent Christian counseling* (pp. 440-515). Waterbrook.

Spector, I. P., Carey, M. P., & Steinberg, L. (2020). The Sexual Desire Inventory-2. In R. R. Milhausen, J. K. Sakaluk, T. D. Fisher, C. M. Davis, & W. L. Yarber. (Eds.), *Handbook of sexuality-related measures* (4th ed., pp. 293-96). Routledge.

Tan, E. S. N., & Yarhouse, M. A. (2010). Facilitating congruence between religious belief and sexual identity with mindfulness. *Psychotherapy, 47*(4), 500-511. https://doi .org/10.1037/a0022081

Tan, S.-Y. (2011). *Counseling and psychotherapy: A Christian perspective.* Baker.

Wincze, J. P., & Weisberg, R. B. (2015). *Sexual dysfunction: A guide for assessment and treatment* (3rd ed.). Guilford.

Worthington, E. L., Jr. (2003). *Forgiveness and reconciling: Bridges to wholeness and hope.* InterVarsity Press.

Zucker, K. J., Mitchell, J. N., Bradley, S. J., Tkachuk, J., Cantor, J. M., & Allin, S. M. (2006, October). The Recalled Childhood Gender Identity/Gender Role Questionnaire: Psychometric properties. *Sex Roles.* https://doi.org/10.1007/s11199-006-9019-x

PART TWO

SEXUAL DISORDERS

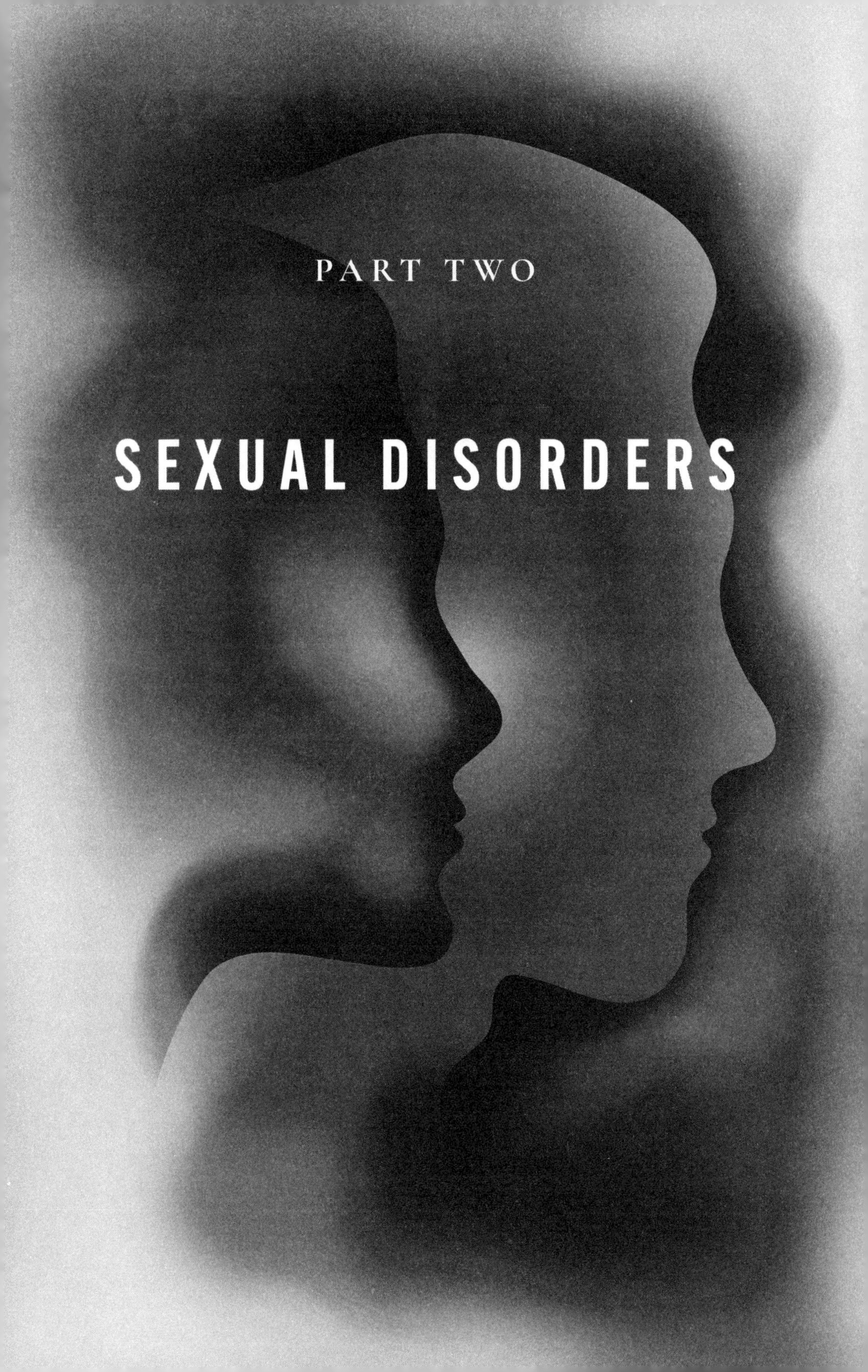

FIVE

SEXUAL INTEREST AND
AROUSAL DISORDERS

SEXUAL DESIRE. WHAT COMES TO MIND when you hear those two words? Do you think of your own experiences as they are? Does an image from a movie or a song come to mind? Do you notice a pang of emotion associated with the thoughts about sexual desire? If so, what are the feelings you have about it? The reality and the concept of sexual desire may be congruent for some, yet not so for others, particularly some women. For some individuals it may be a concept that is romanticized and is cast with expectations that reflect themes we are bombarded with, given our exposure to media.

It is notable that even the definition of sexual desire itself is complex and as such can set parameters for what is or is not understood to be a part of the experience of sexual desire. Levine (2003) describes sexual desire as an experience that falls along a spectrum, varying from aversion to passion, and which tends to evolve over the lifetime. From a clinical perspective, Levine conceptualizes sexual desire according to drive (i.e., the biological experience), motive (i.e., the personal and interpersonal factors), and wish (i.e., the values and rules comprising the cultural component). All of these components are affected by age, gender, health, and social situations.

In this model sexual desire may be conceptualized as a spectrum: aversion—disinclination—indifference—interest—need—passion (Levine, 2003, p. 280). As an influential factor our social situations may affect whether the experience of desire is likely or problematic. For example, a couple with a newborn baby may have very different levels of sexual desire compared with a childless couple. Another factor to consider is gender. Research suggests that female sexual drive may be more affected by social situations compared with male sexual drive. Other influences can stimulate sexual desire, such as wanting to be pregnant, listening to a sexually stimulating exchange between partners, or repairing a recently troubled relationship.

Sexual motivation and drive may not be consistent; for example, a person may experience sexual drive that is not directed toward his or her partner. Although an individual may behave in a way that suggests relational commitment, the thoughts of being sexually intimate with someone other than his or her partner may create feelings of guilt or secrecy that disrupts desire (Levine, 2003).

Interestingly, most of the early models of the sexual response cycle were linear and based primarily on biological drive. The models often assumed sexual desire was present and then described essentially physiological changes that occur during various stages, for example, excitement, plateau, orgasm, and resolution (Masters & Johnson, 1970).

Helen Singer Kaplan and Harold Leif independently proposed a category of persons who experienced low sexual desire. Leif's version (Inhibited Sexual Desire) and Kaplan's version (Hypoactive Sexual Desire) both opened the door to new understanding of sexual desire, as it had previously been assumed that problems in sexual functioning had a physiological basis or were due to performance anxiety (Kaplan, 1995). These new understandings ushered in an era of examining possible intrapsychic and interpersonal or relational contributions to sexual disorders.

As we mentioned in chapter three, Kaplan's understanding of three phases of the sexual response cycle (desire, excitement, and orgasm), which included desire, led to a restructuring of how sex therapists diagnosed and treated sexual disorders, as well as the organization of the *Diagnostic and Statistical Manual-III* (*DSM-3*).

Rosemary Basson (2002, 2007, 2012) proposed that sexual desire may not be a unilateral experience leading to other stages of the sexual response cycle. She observed that the sexual response cycles proposed by Masters and Johnson as well as Kaplan present a linear model proceeding from desire to arousal, followed by the plateau of sexual excitement, culminating in orgasm, and finishing with resolution. However, motivational factors, such as need for intimacy and various incentives for sexual experiences, are not accounted for in these models. Similarly, biological and psychological factors that affect a woman's level of arousability are not considered (Basson, 2012). In her model Basson reflects that psychosocial issues affect a woman's experience of sexual arousal. Within the context of long-term relationships, whereby most women report decreasing satisfaction and decreased frequency of sexual activity, a desire for emotional closeness and intimacy may lead a woman to participate in sexual intimacy. The desire for intimacy may encourage a woman to become more sexually aroused with her partner through various means, including direct stimulation, conversation, and so on. Once she is aroused, she may experience sexual desire, which motivates her to continue the sexual contact.

Although males may associate sexual arousal with the physical reaction of an erect penis, women are less likely to correlate a vaginal response with feelings of sexual arousal or desire. "In fact, women are likely to have a vaginal response to a sexual stimulus even when they dislike it or find it threatening" (Bancroft, 2010, p. 167). As such, the distinction between sexual arousal and sexual desire is less obvious for women. Prause et al. (2008) suggest that how information is processed may affect sexual desire levels. According to them sexual desire may be a cognitive aspect of sexual arousal, and it is conceptualized as a person's "predisposition to respond to sexual stimuli with subjective feelings of sexual arousal" (Prause et al., 2008, p. 935). For some women, emotional reactions do not predict levels of sexual desire, which suggests that sexual stimuli may not be seen as more negative for those with lower levels of sexual desire.

While many men may engage in sexual activity due to spontaneous sexual desire, previous research has indicated that women may engage in sexual activity without this same kind of innate sexual desire (Basson, 2001, 2007). As such, sexual desire may be preceded by sexual arousal, which is better understood with references to many reasons, motivations, and incentives a woman has for participating in sexually intimate activities (Basson, 2002). This understanding of responsive desire, then, introduces a discussion of context and emotional intimacy that has historically been overlooked in previous discussions of desire (Basson, 2012). The study of and clinical interventions surrounding interest or desire are best integrated into broader psychosocial considerations, such as relationship satisfaction and the duration of the relationship, when considering the desire a woman may experience for sexual activity.

Another way to conceptualize this is that men's and women's motivations for sex may be different. Women's motivations for sex tend to be quite diverse, for example. Among a sample of 3,587 Portuguese women, 30.7% women reported that they usually experienced desire after arousal (Carvalheira et al., 2010). Fifteen and a half percent of women reported that they participated in sexual activity only when they experienced sexual desire. Women who had been in longer-term relationships (42%) participated in sexual activity more frequently in spite of a lack of desire compared with women in shorter-term relationships (22.4%). There were more women who reported that in spite of difficulty with arousal, they engaged in sexual activity without any desire at initiation. In this study the results also suggested that women who found it difficult to become sexually aroused tended to be less satisfied with their partners as well as their own sexuality. Many women in the sample tended not to base their experience of arousal on genital sensations.

These results call into question the idea that genital lubrication be used as a definition of sexual arousal. Carvalheira et al. (2010) found that both women who experienced sexual arousal easily and those who did not reported that they would like their sexual partners to provide more physical sexual stimulation. As such, it is possible that sufficient stimulation may offset lower levels of arousal. It is important to consider evaluating partner dynamics when diagnosing sexual arousal. Their results also found that women who were in longer relationships tended to have sexual experiences without sexual desire at initiation. In addition, there was a greater tendency to participate in sexual activity to please a partner. These women also reported that they tended to initiate sexual activity less and experienced decreased sexual satisfaction as the relationship continued.

The necessity of including desire in evaluating sexual response suggests that without desire as a construct, sexual response seems "incomplete and automatic. It lacks agency, . . . does not align well with the observed and self-reported complexity of human sexual experience" (Meana, 2010, p. 104). In addition, utilizing a "male analog" to describe women's sexual experiences has resulted in the pathologizing of women's sexual desire and response (Meana, 2010). Through this lens Meana points out that (1) sexual desire is presumed to be a spontaneous urge to participate in sexual activity, (2) sexual response is presumed to be linear, beginning with desire and ending with orgasm, (3) the relational context of sexual interactions is dismissed, and (4) forces external to women's sexual desire and behavior, such as socioeconomic status and political and cultural influences, affect women's experiences.

Meana (2010) questions whether it is be possible that for some women sexual desire is its own end. "What if being desired and desiring are turn-ons for women, in and of themselves, without any necessary further action?" (p. 107). She also asks, What is being desired? "If we conceptualize desire as a goal-driven state having sex as the endpoint, we may be overlooking the rewarding nature of desire itself" (p. 108). In a study of nineteen married women, Sims and Meana (2010) found that declines in sexual desire during marriage were attributed to institutionalization of the relationship, overfamiliarity, and desexualized roles. To facilitate understanding of desire and arousal, Meana offers nine recommendations (2010, p. 117):

1. Investigate whether an empirically validated distinction can be made between desire and subjective arousal.

2. Stop making "spontaneous desire" the default explanation when we fail to identify a sexual stimulus.

3. Investigate the construct of "desire for desire."

4. Beware of the theoretical drift from the construct of responsiveness to the construct of relationality.

5. Pursue an atheoretical approach to the investigation of the phenomenological experience of sexual desire in women.

6. Make sexual desire (rather than sexual activity) the dependent variable in research on female sexual desire.

7. Investigate factors that predict action tendencies toward the fulfillment of sexual desire.

8. Engage in a balanced consideration of gender differences in sexual desire.

9. Make diagnostic criteria for [hyposexual desire disorder] as conservative as possible.

In sum, sexual desire is a complex phenomenon, particularly for women. We turn our attention now to the current conceptualizations of interest, desire, and arousal concerns.

SEXUAL INTEREST AND AROUSAL DISORDERS

Because the expression of sexual behavior itself cannot be assumed
to possess any survival value for individual members of a species, it
could be completely left out of the behavioral repertoire without
incurring a penalty. . . . Therefore, absent or low sexual interest is
not intrinsically pathological. (van Lankveld, 2008, p. 155)

Low sexual desire might also be approached as the consequence
of problematic functioning in other domains of sexuality, of the
partner relationship, or of the physical and psychological condition
of the female client or her partner. (van Lankveld, 2008, p. 175)

The ways in which disorders of interest, desire, and arousal are currently conceptualized can be seen in the diagnoses of Male Hypoactive Sexual Desire Disorder and Female Sexual Interest/Arousal Disorder (APA, 2022). The diagnostic criteria for the former references "persistently or recurrently deficient (or absent) sexual/erotic thoughts or fantasies and desire for sexual activity" that last for about six months, cause the person clinically significant distress, and are not better accounted for by another mental disorder or "severe relationships distress" (p. 498).

As for Female Sexual Interest/Arousal Disorder, the *DSM-5-TR* references three of the following criteria:

1. Absent/reduced interest in sexual activity.
2. Absent/reduced sexual/erotic thoughts or fantasies.
3. No/reduced initiation of sexual activity.
4. Absent/reduced sexual excitement/pleasure during sexual activity in almost all or all . . . sexual encounters.
5. Absent/reduced sexual interest/arousal in response to any internal or external sexual/erotic cues.
6. Absent/reduced genital or nongenital sensations during sexual activity in almost all or all . . . sexual encounters (APA, 2022, p. 489).

In both diagnoses the disorder can be lifelong (since the person became sexually active) or acquired (after a time of normal sexual functioning), as well as generalized (not limited to a specific situation or partner) or situational (limited to a specific situation or partner).

This understanding of sexual interest, arousal, and desire has received criticism. Before we turn to those criticisms, it should be noted that even obtaining prevalence estimates can be difficult. Previous studies suggest prevalence estimates of low sexual desire varying from 10.2% to 43% (Brotto, 2009); in another study about 20% of men and 33% of women (Laumann et al., 1999). It should be noted that low desire is the most frequently reported sexual disorder among lesbian couples (Cohen & Savin-Williams, 2017), which may be a reflection on gender differences in desire, as we will discuss below. Assessment is complicated, and these differences may be related to differences in methodology, operational definitions, and timing. Brotto (2009) observed that defining sexual desire is complicated by the difference between a clinical definition and a woman's subjective definition of her own desire. A behavioral definition of sexual desire does not account for interpersonal factors such as partner characteristics, which may influence low sexual desire. Additionally, measuring sexual desire is also complicated. Frequency of sexual activity, feeling sexual desire, frequency of initiation and receptivity to sex, liking sexual activity, and strength of desire for sex with a partner versus oneself (p. 5) are some attempts to quantify and qualify sexual desire.

In terms of concerns about the current conceptualization of interest, arousal, and desire concerns, Brotto (2009) contends that a proportion of women do not experience sexual fantasies in their experience of sexual desire, which would lead to the overpathologizing of women if "lack of fantasies" is a focal point. Some women may intentionally evoke fantasy to boost sexual arousal. The idea of responsive desire is that a woman may not have the spontaneous experience of sexual desire in the moment; however, given the context of the initiation of sexual intimacy, a woman may experience desire to participate because it may augment the experience of the relationship, or it may produce a sense of emotional closeness. Although it may be valid, it is difficult to test responsive desire empirically. Basing diagnostic criteria on the lack of spontaneous sexual desire may pathologize the experiences of many women for whom sexual desire is a triggered response. As such, the lack of desire for sexual activity is not sufficient to suggest a sexual desire disorder for women.

Brotto (2009) also comments that current understanding of interest, arousal, and desire concerns does not differentiate between the distress of a woman with low levels of desire or her partner's distress. She observes that the incidence of low desire without distress is higher than having low desire with distress. Factors that are known to contribute to the experience of low desire in the absence of distress include age and relational status. On the other hand, relational difficulty and distress are highly correlated. Capturing the intensity of relational influences would be helpful for the diagnosis of a desire disorder.

For some women sexual desire precedes sexual arousal. The problem with the term *hypoactive* (which is in use with the male presentation but not currently with the female presentation) is that it suggests a deficiency of activity, which may be somewhat reductionistic, as the loss of desire is equated with a lessening of sexual activity (Brotto, 2009). However, for many women the distress regarding her experience of desire is due to the discrepancy in levels of desire between her and her partner. To provide clarification regarding this experience, Brotto suggests that the terminology of *desire* be replaced with the "lack of sexual interest" (p. 14), which is the direction that *DSM*-5 has taken. This seems to address the idea that desire or interest is variable depending on the model of sexual response a woman identifies with.

Such a shift in conceptualization also recognizes that there are women who do not initially experience spontaneous sexual desire but are receptive to and willing to participate after their partner's initiation. These women may experience excitement during sexual activity but would not meet diagnostic criteria for a desire disorder.

In contrast to a focus on interest or desire, concerns about arousal among females had previously referred to "persistent or recurrent inability to attain, or maintain until completion of the sexual activity, an adequate lubrication-swelling response of sexual excitement" (APA, 2004, p. 502). The *DSM-5-TR* combines interest and arousal, and suggests that clinicians expect "different symptom profiles across women, as well as variability in how sexual interest and arousal are expressed" (APA, 2022, p. 490). In one woman this could be reflected in lack of interest in sex and the lack of erotic thoughts, while in another woman this could be reflected in the inability to experience arousal or excitement with corresponding physical signs of sexual arousal, such as vaginal lubrication.

It may be helpful to consider desire combinations among couples. For example, Feldhahn and Sytsma (2023) reported on desire combinations among married couples. It was unusual (5%) for both partners to have initiating desire; it was much more common (53%) for one spouse to have initiating desire and the other spouse have receptive desire. Nearly a third (29%) reported that they both had receptive desire. (Another 13% of couples reported that one or both spouses had "resistant" desire, which is more of an "active resistance to sex," p. 87.)

ETIOLOGY

As Maurice (2005) observes, we do not know what causes the experience of low (or no) sexual interest or desire that is lifelong and generalized. When we consider acquired and situational experiences of low sexual desire, we consider a range of possible contributing factors.

Neuroendocrine factors. Bancroft's (2010) Dual Control Model posits that sexual arousal and sexual response is an interplay between the excitatory and inhibitory physiological systems. According to this model, individuals who have low sexual inhibition may be more prone to participate in high-risk sexual behaviors (p. 169). Conversely, those who are prone to sexual inhibition or have low sexual excitation trended toward sexual dysfunction. Montgomery (2008) elaborated on this further, stating that ruling out the possibility of a medical disorder as a factor in decreased sexual desire is necessary prior to diagnosing hyposexual desire disorder or an aversion disorder. For example, hypothyroidism could cause a decrease in sexual desire.

Although the frequency and proportions are different, desire disorders and aversion disorders affect both genders. The etiology of hyposexual desire disorder may be related to its subtype: generalized or situational, lifelong or acquired. Neuroendocrine mediators of sexual desire include dopamine and prolactin. It is hypothesized that dopamine increases desire through the reward pathway, whereas prolactin is conceptualized as decreasing libido. Dopamine inhibits the release of prolactin through the pituitary gland. Montgomery also posits that desire disorders in men may be misdiagnosed as erectile dysfunction.

Physiological factors: Aging. Understanding the effects of aging on sexuality requires the examination of factors influencing sexual desire: social context of a woman's life, drive, beliefs and values, motivation, and physiological changes in men and women (Kingsberg, 2002). Sexual abstinence in some older adults may be due to the lack of a partner or health problems. Physical changes observed as women age that likely contribute to diminished sexual desire are declining estrogen levels, which affects lubrication of the vagina as a result of reduced blood flow, and loss of elasticity in the vagina, which can also contribute to discomfort. Due to aging, the clitoris may be reduced in size and may not be as engorged. Other changes may include decreased muscle tension, slowed nerve impulses, and decrease in vibratory sensation, reaction time, and touch perception (p. 433).

Physical changes observed in men as they age include gradual decreases in levels of testosterone, decreased energy, an increased length of time to achieve an erection, and a longer refractory period or the length of time between erections. As men age they also may need more direct stimulation to achieve an erection, and their erections may not be as firm as they were at a younger age. These changes vary significantly among men and may also be related to health status, any chronic conditions (e.g., cardiovascular disease, cancer, hypogonadism), and use of medications (e.g., antipsychotics, antidepressants, mood stabilizers, medications to treat cardiovascular disease), which often increases with age.

In spite of these physiological changes the subjective experience of satisfaction does not appear to change, particularly for women. Female sexuality and concerns about interest and desire cannot be reduced to a simple biological theory, such as androgen insufficiency. Low interest, desire, or arousal is considered to be the most prevalent female sexual concern. Age is a significant correlate as opposed to menopausal status with respect to declining desire. For example, a decline in drive is associated with age, as opposed to the assumption that menopause contributes to a decline in drive. Drive is the biological manifestation of desire through the process of neuroendocrine mechanisms (Kingsberg, 2002, p. 434). It is expressed through sexual thoughts, feelings, erotic attraction, pursuit of sexual activity, fantasies or dreams, and genital tingling and sensitivity. Values, beliefs, and expectations about sexual activity comprise the second component of desire. The last component of desire is motivation, which is affected by emotional and interpersonal factors. It manifests as willingness to participate in sexual behaviors with a partner.

It is important to be aware of the difference between drive and desire because treatment will differ depending on which aspect of desire has declined. A woman's self-perception, which is how she feels about her thoughts, feelings, and opinions, can affect desire. Physiological changes in partners can also affect desire, as evidenced by a decrease in frequency of sexual intimacy because a male partner may experience erectile dysfunction, which affects body image and tends to decrease desire. It is important for aging couples to adjust to the changes they are experiencing cognitively and physically (Rathus et al., 2011). A woman's aging vagina may have difficulty with intercourse as a result of atrophy, which may lead to a secondary sexual dysfunction, such as vaginismus or dyspareunia. Physical health factors, such as illness, lack of energy, or strength; side effects of medication; or having a partner who is affected by these physical factors may decrease desire. Healthcare providers may be beneficial for educating aging couples about the benefits of expanding their sexual repertoire so that sexual intimacy is not just limited to sexual intercourse, but may include manual and oral stimulation, erotic activities, and sensual touch.

Biological factors are often accompanied by psychosocial factors, given the integrated nature of our experiences as humans. It is often difficult to separate what is psychological from what is biological, as demonstrated by the experience of depression. With respect to sexual desire, the following are some biological mechanisms that may mediate the experience.

PSYCHOSOCIAL FACTORS

Living systems. In consideration of the role that sociocultural factors may play in mitigating sexual desire, this section examines some of the research elucidating those findings. Using a "living systems" conceptualization (Clement, 2002), a systematic approach may be taken when assessing low sexual desire. Three mechanisms must be considered: (1) whether the couple construes a desire discrepancy, (2) the territorial splitting of power and behavioral power, and (3) the lack of communication of individual differences in sexual profiles between partners.

In this conceptualization Clement suggests that as a system, couples reduce complexity and increase coherence as means of managing discrepancies in sexual desire. An example of reducing complexity may include communicating (i.e., using body language or other nonverbal means beyond verbal) or not communicating specific scripts, habits, or rules. Since conflict is likely to be an aversive experience, couples may inadvertently develop coherence by engaging in conflict management for the purpose of eliminating incompatible elements. As an example, over the course of time the female partner may just accept her male partner's initiation in spite of how she feels at that moment in order to not argue.

To further examine the role of desire in a couple, Clement (2002) asks, Is desire a part of sexual function? Is it an individual trait or a function of a couple's dynamics? He suggests that in some instances, low desire may be an act of "active negation" whereby as a result of individual experiences (e.g., inhibition), interactional experiences (e.g., conflict), or cultural experiences (e.g., religious or moral standards) desire may be blocked. Thus, rather than focusing on "quantity," perhaps the "quality" of the interaction and the experience of desire needs to be considered. In other words, what is the individual's subjective experience of sexual desire versus frequency of sexual intimacy?

Clement points out that the "emergent function" of sexual desire suggests several things (2002, p. 243): (1) the dynamics of desire within a couple cannot be truncated into individual differences in desire levels because these differences do not explain the nature of their sexual interactions, (2) the discrepancy between partners' desire levels may be a transaction between them, which may contribute to the consistency of the desire problem, and (3) identifying one partner as the one who has low desire and the other as one who has high desire precipitates the conflict between them. To be in touch with differences in levels of desire, couples can either communicate the difference or maintain the differences without communication through avoidance or denial.

Emotional satisfaction. Is emotional satisfaction correlated with a lack of spontaneous sexual desire? The correlation between the two is much lower than what is initially perceived. Durr (2009) studied ten heterosexual women who reported choosing to participate in sexual intimacy with their partners for reasons that were unrelated to desire. The women who participated in this study expressed difficulty discriminating between sexual desire and sexual arousal. Within this sample, some of the women experienced a decrease in sexual desire with their long-term partners; however, some of these women experienced strong sexual desire for males other than their partners.

Although the experience of sexual intimacy without desire was described to be somewhat unpleasant, the women in the study chose to engage in sexual behavior because they were inclined to satisfy their partners' needs. The experience of low sexual desire was not reported to significantly affect the relationships; however, there were other supportive behaviors that contributed to the satisfaction of the relationship. Various factors contributed to the decline in sexual desire, including mood, religious reasons, and sense of self. Stage of life also contributed to a woman's availability for sex (e.g., young motherhood versus being a mother whose children are out of the house). Durr's participants reported that sexual desire tended to decrease over time in relationships regardless of the level of happiness or unhappiness; however, negative emotions and emotional distance contributed significantly to the diminishment of desire.

The women also reported that societal scripts and roles appeared to affect their perceptions of sexuality. They felt that their individuation and a sense of separation were necessary for sexual connection. The women in the study appeared to demonstrate a situational lack of desire, suggesting that emotional closeness and eroticism may contribute to the maintenance or decline of sexual desire. For some the lack of responsive desire suggests that it would be important in treatment to address the lack of motivating factors.

In conclusion, it is essential to address the present context regarding a woman's sexual problems—interpersonal, psychological, and biological. Similarly, considering the factors that contribute to the lack of arousal will help to not make a woman feel guilty for her lack of response or desire. Coaching to broaden incentives as well as the sexual repertoire can increase pleasure for both partners. As such, sexual intimacy can be used as a means to promote emotional connection through differentiation and expression of those needs.

Men who present with hypoactive sexual desire disorder may also struggle with emotional intimacy. This may be due to emotional-sexual blocks, fear of intimacy or closeness, relationship conflicts, or trauma (Maurice, 2005; Penner & Penner, 2005). Some therapists may prefer to work on these issues in individual therapy, while others will see conjoint therapy as an opportunity to explore and address issues with intimacy or closeness, relationship conflicts, and so on. Keep in mind that men are not socialized to identify and express their emotions, which can sometimes complicate sexual intimacy and expression, contributing in some ways to a desire disorder. The clinician can process any blocks or fears about intimacy by helping the man learn to identify his present emotional state and how his emotions are affected by his partner and other life circumstances, as well as attributions and meaning making.

Relationship conflicts are also commonly reported among men presenting with a low sexual desire disorder (McCarthy & McDonald, 2009).

Of course, low desire and how that is responded to in a relationship can be the cause of conflicts, just as relationship conflicts can contribute to low sexual desire.

Depression is also associated with low sexual desire among men. The clinician should assess for negative emotions, such as depression, and consider treating the depression first to facilitate changes in energy levels and desire that may then be resolved in therapy with him and his partner as a couple.

Gender differences in sexual desire. Sexual desire, or the lack thereof, is more frequently observed in women than men. To assess factors contributing to the experience of sexual desire and differences between males and females, Carvalho and Nobre (2010) studied men's and women's responses. Among a subset of men and women who reported low sexual desire, Carvalho and Nobre found that men tended to experience increased fear and shame during sexual activity, whereas women tended to feel more emotional hurt and higher levels of symptom distress during sexual activity. In addition, upon examination of dyadic adjustment, those who had low desire reported lower levels of dyadic adjustment. Previous literature has noted that male sexual desire may not be as affected by conflict in the relationship, whereas a lack of sexual desire in females is related to relationship dissatisfaction. As such, sexual desire may be cued by different triggers, depending on the gender.

Other significant findings included that older participants reported less sexual desire compared with younger participants (Carvalho & Nobre, 2010). Women as a group reported lower levels of sexual desire compared with men. Women also reported higher levels of psychopathology, which may suggest that psychopathology is a significant factor in low sexual desire among women. Those who reported lower sexual desire also reported higher dissatisfaction, as well as feelings of disillusionment.

Of note was the high level of shame reported by men who indicated that they experienced low sexual desire, compared with the women who had similar levels of shame in both the high and low sexual desire groups (Carvalho & Nobre, 2010). These results suggest the possibility of sociocultural influences, especially those related to performance. The males in this study also reported use of sexual behavior as a mediator to negative or unpleasant psychological states. Both males and females who reported high sexual desire also experienced higher cohesion, affection, and satisfaction in their relationships.

The majority of research regarding male sexual disorders has largely focused on erectile disorder and premature ejaculation versus sexual desire disorder. For some men, hypoactive sexual desire disorder may be influenced by the experience of a sexual secret, which may include "variant arousal pattern," the preference for masturbation as sexual stimulation as opposed to intimate sexual activity with a partner; sexual trauma that has not been adequately processed; and a conflict regarding sexual orientation. As such, it may not be a lack of sexual desire but a "secret/shameful desire/arousal pattern" (McCarthy & McDonald, 2009, p. 59). It is important to destigmatize the problem in assessment. The experience of variant arousal is often mitigated by a pattern of shame, eroticism, and secrecy.

Secondary interest and arousal concerns may be a result of a reaction to sexual dysfunction. For many men the experience of hypoactive sexual desire disorder may manifest as discomfort and loss of confidence regarding arousal, intercourse, and orgasm because the anxiety regarding uncomfortable intercourse may lead to avoidance (McCarthy & McDonald, 2009). Assessment of factors contributing to inhibited sexual desire is important, whether it is psychological or medical. For males who experience a desire disorder, management of thoughts and feelings regarding performance, predictability, and autonomy is important. As such, focusing on a flexible sexual response is more adaptive than striving for perfect performance. Adapting his sexual script to include other erotic activities aside from intercourse will be more consistent with the more flexible sexual response of a female partner. Management of anxiety by adopting a relapse prevention approach can reduce the possibility of regressing to a frustration-avoidance cycle. Strategies include adopting an erotic nonintercourse scenario, the commitment to initiate sexual intimacy after a disappointing experience, and good communication with his partner to avoid the cycle of anxiety.

Although a large body of research has not supported the perceived correlation between childhood sexual abuse and a lack of sexual desire, this perception continues to exist. Rellini and Meston (2007) examined the correlation between a history of childhood sexual abuse (CSA) and thought patterns regarding sex. Although they expected that women with a history of CSA would use words that were more associated with sexual desire dysfunction, this was not the case. As such, the authors speculated that women with CSA who had problems with sexual desire did not appear to be overly preoccupied with the reexperience of trauma. Although women with CSA used more sex words when writing about a nonsexual topic compared with women who did not have a sex abuse history, the frequency of these words did not appear to be linked with difficulty in sexual desire. As such, the authors propose that the etiology and mechanisms of sexual desire difficulties may not be different between women with CSA and those without.

The gender differences noted in different degrees of sexual interest or desire may also reflect a tendency to study spontaneous desire rather than other experiences of desire, such as responsive desire (Basson, 2010). In other words, if what is studied is largely based on a linear, biologic model of innate desire that overlooks psychosocial considerations and response to incentives or motivations, context, and relationship, then we may indeed report gender differences in desire but only a truncated expression of desire and not the range of complex options and considerations in the study of sexual desire and interest.

In the study of desire combinations cited earlier (Feldhahn & Sytsma, 2023), men were more likely to report initiating desire (53.9%) than receptive desire (41.0%), while women were more likely to report receptive desire (75.5%) than initiating desire (16.2%). However, that 41% of men reported receptive desire is an important consideration so that we do not always equate one type of desire with men and another type of desire with women. There is considerable variability here to take into account. It is important to assess the couple in front of you and their experience, which brings us to assessment and clinical presentation.

ASSESSMENT AND CLINICAL PRESENTATION

"In all honesty, I just don't really care to have sex. It doesn't really do anything for me," Erica's female client stated. In spite of her declaration, the tears in her eyes belied her desire to experience what she perceived was a deeper emotional and sexual connection that she felt she *ought* to have with her husband.

That is a difficult place to be. You can hear in this client the ambivalence—the feelings that are in conflict within her. Perhaps to cope with having low desire, she makes a declaration that reveals feelings of loss just below the surface. Add to that the level of expectation about what a person should feel and does not, and you have a complicated area that is best approached with sensitivity and care.

As you consider assessment, keep in mind that the clinician needs to distinguish between lifelong and generalized low or absent desire and acquired and situational or another combination. Maurice (2005) offers this breakdown based on the various subtypes:

1. If lifelong and generalized, change is highly unlikely and the clinician should direct therapeutic efforts toward helping the person (or the couple) adapt.

2. If lifelong and situational, a biogenic explanation is unlikely and individual psychotherapy seems reasonable.

3. If acquired and generalized, the clinician must make substantial efforts toward finding the explanation(s) for the change. . . .

4. If acquired but situational, a biogenic explanation is unlikely. . . . In this circumstance, psychotherapy seems indicated but, depending on the parent etiology, could be provided individually or together with a partner (p. 197).

So a proper clinical assessment seeks to determine which subtype of low or absent sexual desire the person experiences.

Assessment of a possible desire disorder should consider the person's physical health, his or her psychological/mental health, and relational health and issues related to sexual intimacy for the individual and the couple, including the sexual context and script for sexual intimacy. We will discuss each of these areas, but it should be noted that various factors—psychological, physiological, relational, and emotional—may affect the neuroendocrine system (Nappi et al., 2010). So when considering biological processes, it should be noted that sex hormones affect neurotransmitters, which modulate sexual desire. When the dopaminergic system (sexual desire and excitement) and the norepinephrine system (arousal and orgasm) are out of sync, women may have difficulty with the initiation of the sexual response cycle. If the serotonergic system is overactive, it may lessen the experience of desire, and orgasm may be affected. Other key factors can include substances that affect the excitatory neurochemical system, such as tiredness or stress, which are situational factors, or medications such as SSRIs. A referral for a medical evaluation can help rule out illnesses (e.g., diabetes, depression) and treatments (e.g., chemotherapy, antidepressants) that may be associated with low desire.

When we consider psychological/mental health, a good clinical interview and sex history should consider whether depression is present, as well as issues of self-esteem, body image, and overall quality of life and associated concerns with stress (Basson, 2007).

Weeks, Hertlein, and Gambescia (2009) offer the following questions that may be asked during assessment:

1. How often do you have sex?
2. How often do you feel like having sex?
3. Do you believe your desire level is too low?
4. When did you first notice losing desire for sex? What was happening at that time?
5. Did you lose desire rapidly or slowly?
6. What was your level of sexual desire earlier in your relationship?
7. Any changes in your health? What medications are you taking now?
8. On a scale of 1 to 10 how much desire do you feel in general? Prior to sex? During sex?
9. How often do you think about sex or fantasize about romantic scenarios? (p. 87)

When considering relational health, the clinician can assess the quality of the relationship, the affection expressed toward each other, approaches to communication, and conflict resolution styles and skills (Weeks et al., 2009). It can also be helpful to assess whether there is a desire disorder localized in one partner or whether it is more helpful to conceptualize the concern as one of desire discrepancy. Keep in mind that higher levels of desire are rarely questioned in our cultural context; rather, we assume higher levels are normal and that lower levels are the clinical concern. In some cases, then, the difference between levels of desire is assessed and may be a more helpful clinical starting point than pathologizing any one partner in the relationship.

When the context of sexual intimacy is assessed, Basson (2007) recommends gathering information on when they are likely to be sexually intimate, how they typically initiate (e.g., who tends to do the initiating, when, how), how declining is received and interpreted. The entire sexual script, then, can be assessed in terms of behaviors, skills, and so on that may affect arousability (Basson, 2007).

Van Lankveld (2008) also proposes that the client's self-perceived sexual motivation be assessed in addition to inquiring about the frequency of erotic thoughts and fantasies, and the frequency of initiation of self-directed or partner-directed sexual acts. Specifically, it may be helpful to ask, "Can you, in time, respond to the sexual touching and stimuli and then feel some desire to continue?" This question can then lead to an evaluation of aspects of the client's sex history that elucidate the rewards or withholding of rewards that might motivate her to engage in sexual activity (e.g., lack of sexual arousal, poor lubrication, problems with orgasm, pain during sex, poor communication skills).

Use of inventories such as the following may also be helpful to gain a more well-rounded view of the client's experience. Grover and Shouan (2020) note three commonly used measures of sexual desire: the Decreased Sexual Desire Screener (DSDS) (Clayton et al., 2009), the Hurlbert Index of Sexual Desire (HISD) (Hurlbert, 1992), and the Sexual Desire Inventory (SDI) (Spector et al., 1996). The DSDS is a screening instrument used by clinicians who do not specialize in sex therapy and can be helpful in diagnosing desire disorder in adult women. The HISD is a longer, twenty-five-item measure of desire. The SDI is a self-report measure with fourteen items.

It can also be helpful to assess the way men and women process sexual activities. For example, what thoughts do they have when they are with their partner in an intimate exchange? Have the concerns about arousal and desire made it difficult to be present? Is the person distracted or experiencing stress due to other concerns that are not about sexual intimacy?

Although we have focused on low sexual desire, it should also be noted that people can report high sexual desire (or hypersexuality). If one partner is dealing with high sexual desire, the other partner may feel that they have low sexual desire in contrast. (We discuss hypersexuality in detail in chapter eleven.)

In addition to hypersexuality, we should also note a trend in discussions about *asexuality*. While low sexual desire is distressing for some people, it may not be for others. There is growing interest in the area of asexuality as more individuals are becoming vocal about their experiences of lack of attraction or the lack of sexual behaviors as being normative, and possibly an expression of sexual orientation.

Brotto et al. (2010) observed that asexuality has variable definitions, varying from the lack of attraction to others to an emphasis on behavioral definitions pertaining to the lack of sexual behaviors. Individuals who report an asexual orientation tended to focus more on their experience of romantic versus sexual experiences. In a study of self-identified asexual individuals, desire and distress were correlated, which suggests that for individuals who identify as asexual, desire may be conceptualized as a negative experience. Many asexual individuals reported sexual satisfaction in spite of low levels of sexual desire. These asexual individuals clarified that there is a difference between them and those who met diagnostic criteria for hyposexual desire disorder in that the former group did not have sexual attraction. Brotto et al. found that while several asexual individuals in their sample had engaged in sexual activity, it was the lack of sexual attraction that was predominant. For these individuals, asexuality was not an approach mediated by fear, and the lack of sexual activity was not found to be due to avoidance or disgust regarding genitals. According to these individuals, "There was a general sentiment that since one could have sex without love, why could one not also have love without sex?" (p. 614). Asexual individuals also appeared to have a lack of sexual arousal or excitability.

All individuals in the asexual sample reported a belief that asexuality was biological in nature and should be thought of as a sexual orientation.

TREATMENT

Treatment for low interest, desire, and arousal. As we turn to treatment of low interest, desire, and arousal, we recognize that the treatment approach will vary based on etiology and subtype (see Leiblum, 2010, for a more in-depth discussion of range of treatment models). Keep in mind that psychotherapy will likely be most beneficial to subtypes that reflect lifelong and situational low desire, acquired and generalized, and acquired but situational. Those who present with lifelong and generalized low or absent desire will likely benefit more from strategies to help the couple adapt to the condition (Maurice, 2005).

The general principles of treatment also vary based on theoretical orientation (Leiblum, 2010; Ullery et al., 2002). Most of the traditional models of care are based on broad cognitive-behavioral therapy models that emphasize providing psychoeducation, reducing anxiety, and enhancing sensory awareness and sexual experience. More recent models have addressed relational issues and more depth-oriented, intrapsychic concerns that may be present.

Psychoeducation in theory and practice. Psychoeducation is frequently provided early on to help the couple understand sexual desire, differences between men and women, differences among men, and differences among women. Some specific models, such as CBT, will provide education too on the treatment approach and connections between key constructs, such as cognitions, emotions, and behaviors, particularly as they are associated with the desire concern (Brotto & Woo, 2010) The clinician will typically discuss different models of sexual desire and concepts such as spontaneous desire and receptive desire (Basson, 2007).

Psychoeducation is not only theoretical but also practical. Early studies in the field have identified the necessity of having strong pelvic floor muscles for increased bodily awareness, adequate genital arousal, and orgasm. Weak and deconditioned pelvic floor muscles may not be able to accommodate vaginal friction or blood flow to produce the experience of an orgasm (Rosenbaum, 2007). Assigning Kegel exercises may be helpful here, and some clients may benefit from physical therapy for more extensive interventions that focus on increasing awareness of the pelvic floor muscles, improving the ability to discriminate between muscles and muscle relaxation, normalizing muscle tone, increasing elasticity with the vaginal opening and desensitizing painful areas, and decreasing fear of vaginal penetration.

Anxiety reduction. To reduce anxiety and performance demands, it is common to teach relaxation exercises and to identify and process performance demands. Relaxation exercises include deep breathing protocols, muscle relaxation, and mindfulness exercises. Most of these protocols can be adapted for religiously accommodative treatment. For example, with relaxation exercises, clinicians can use religious or spiritually themed imagery to reflect a better fit with a religious client. It should also be noted that some more recent theorists (e.g., Schnarch, 2010) have moved in a different direction by focusing on the "sexual crucible" and hardships one must endure to grow in maturity, and we will discuss aspects of those contributions.

Mindfulness exercises have also become increasingly popular as a next wave of more behavior-based clinical services (Brotto & Woo, 2010). "By teaching patients to be aware of their thoughts in a nonjudgmental way . . . the experience of mindfulness leads patients to understand that thoughts are just thoughts and not necessarily accurate representations of reality" (p. 156). They can be incorporated into treatment to help identify and respond to unhelpful thoughts, anxiety, and judgments that may contribute to desire concerns (see Brotto, 2018, for an extended application of mindfulness to female sexual desire concerns).

Identify and challenge unhelpful cognitions. Therapy that addresses sexual desire, interest, and arousal also considers unhelpful thoughts or negative cognitive evaluation of the sexual situation (ter Kuile et al., 2010). Identification of myths that may increase shame and guilt are also important for addressing in treatment. These may include myths about what it means for women to be sexual, women's sexual responses compared with men's, and whether there are correct or incorrect ways to become aroused (Millner, 2005).

Foster intimacy. In addition to education and addressing anxiety the clinician may also want to help the couple increase their capacity for intimacy (Schnarch, 2000, 2010), their experience of nurturance (Treadway, 2010), or sensory awareness and sexual experience. A hallmark of Schnarch's (2010, p. 52) approach—referred to as "crucible therapy," among other terms—has been to help each person in the relationship grow in their capacity for genuine intimacy. Rather than reducing anxiety, Schnarch focuses on "holding onto yourself" in the midst of intense levels of "emotion, anxiety, and conflict" (p. 58). From this approach, "effectively treating sexual desire problems involves more than making the problems go away. It involves resolving them in ways that enhance both partners' personal development" (p. 59). In other words, willingness to trust the other, the ability to share oneself with each other, and fears regarding negative evaluation are points of discussion pertinent to treatment. It may also be helpful to facilitate the client's ability to differentiate herself from her partner and the relationship, which will increase the likelihood of a healthier relationship.

Couples can also grow in nurturing each other. For Treadway (2010), for example, this might entail providing one another a comforting massage and allowing one's partner to simply experience whatever they experience, letting thoughts or worries exist but not be a point of distraction.

Improve sensory awareness. In terms of growing in sensory awareness, sensate focus exercises can be assigned in which the couple focuses on non-demand sensual touch. These exercises allow each partner to receive sensual touch and to identify what they enjoy and do not enjoy. These exercises also contribute to communication in general and around sexuality and sexual behavior in particular. In conjunction with these exercises it can be helpful to ask partners to journal their thoughts and feelings, particularly about sexual intimacy. They can identify thoughts they have throughout the day, thoughts and fantasies in anticipation of, during, and after sex.

Some practical suggestions for the couple offered by Rosenau (2002) include expressing feelings to one another, laughing together, focusing on the positives in one's partner, praying together, complimenting one's partner on his or her appearance or dress, and daydreaming about one's partner or past or future sexual encounters with one's partner. Arousal may be facilitated by fantasies, which are helpful in identifying how the client is aroused, in addition to the content that the client finds arousing (Millner, 2005).

When exploring the context of sexual intimacy it can be helpful to work with the couple on how they set up their time together. This includes making time for one another, handling childcare issues, use of transition activities (e.g., taking a bath or shower), and setting up an emotionally pleasing environment that engages all or most of the senses (e.g., use of lighting, music, lotions).

The circular model of sexual interest and desire (Basson, 2002, 2012) conceptualizes the experience of low sexual desire as a consequence of problematic functioning in another domain of the woman's life beyond sexuality, such as a difficult relationship with her partner and psychological or physical concerns in herself or her partner. As such, treatment focuses on increasing positive experiences for the woman so that she is more motivated to participate in sexual activity. These rewarding experiences can include her ability to experience orgasm, reduce pain, or increase lubrication and arousal. Treatment also focuses on helping the woman to become more attuned to her own experiences of erotic stimulation and what she needs to feel aroused. Treatment can also include practices like sensate focus, which may generate positive emotions and experiences within the nonsexual aspects of her relationship (ter Kuile et al., 2010). Masturbation training is also indicated to help increase the woman's awareness of what is pleasing to her, and to help her to become more self-focused and assertive about her needs (Brotto et al., 2010). Another function of sensate focus is to increase trust by diminishing feelings of abandonment or inhibition that may be present and thus hinder arousal (Millner, 2005).

In addition to these points of focus within a CBT model, other approaches consider more intrapsychic issues. These intrapsychic considerations include fears about dependence, intimacy, or letting go/control. Again, some therapists will prefer to address intrapsychic conflicts through more in-depth individual treatment, while others leverage the relationship to facilitate greater insight and awareness of intrapsychic concerns so that the nonsymptomatic partner gains insight into the challenges their partner is facing.

Several sex therapists have developed this interest in depth approaches to suggest different paradigms of sex therapy that are more about self-validation (e.g., Schnarch, 1991, 1997, 2000, 2010; Tiefler & Hall, 2010; Treadway, 2010). In crucible therapy, for example, there is fourfold emphasis on helping clients (1) maintain a solid and enduring sense of self, (2) regulate, manage, and sooth anxiety, (3) not react to their partner's anxiety, and (4) persevere through challenging travails to grow stronger and more mature (Schnarch, 2010, p. 52). Emphasis is placed on assessing desire during sexual intimacy rather than focusing solely on desire during initiation. Similarly, Schnarch (2000) discusses desire for one's partner rather than desire for a sexual activity. He also suggests the field move away from models based on biological drive or function and toward the choice to engage freely in desire for one's partner.

According to Schnarch (2000), "sexual desire problems become a way of seeing how relationships *function* rather than seeing them as signs of *dys*function or *dys*regulation in an individual, a relationship, a family, or society" (p. 23). Schnarch is more concerned with what it means to be in an emotionally committed relationship and how we face various trials (what he refers to as the "sexual crucible") that are a normal and natural part of intimacy and emotional commitment.

Therapy along these lines facilitates self-differentiation (or what Murray Bowen refers to as differentiation of self) wherein each partner "grows up" emotionally and is able to see boundaries between one's emotional experience and that of one's partner. Schnarch (2000) defines differentiation as involving "the ability to distinguish, develop and balance two fundamental life forces: desire for communion and contact with others and desire to become more uniquely ourselves and to direct our own destiny" (p. 26). It involves managing one's own anxieties and not being emotionally reactive to the anxieties of others, including one's partner. This will inevitably mean learning to abide discomfort in order to grow (Schnarch, 1991, 2000).

We recognize that there are various psychotherapy models and approaches to the treatment of low or absent sexual desire (see Leiblum, 2010). Many clinicians today provide therapy that incorporates elements of cognitive-behavioral, systemic, and depth-oriented models, in conjunction with an understanding of biological and related pharmacological considerations (see Pridal & LoPiccolo, 2000). Generally speaking, though there may be many roads to successful treatment, such models typically (1) address negative affect, such as anger, fear, or resentment, (2) foster insight and understanding (into individual factors, relational factors, and medical/ health considerations), and (3) have practical behavioral strategies (that increase "affectionate behaviors") (Pridal & LoPiccolo, 2000, p. 70).

Pharmacological considerations. Flibanserin is approved by the U.S. Food and Drug Administration (FDA) for the management of hypoactive sexual desire disorder in premenopausal women. Flibanserin increases dopamine and norepinephrine and decreases serotonin. Initially developed as an antidepressant, Flibanserin "is specifically indicated for patients whose diagnosis is unrelated to relationship issues, psychiatric or medical conditions, or the effects of medication or drugs" (Pierrelus et al., 2023).

Since sildenafil citrate is effective in treating erectile dysfunction in men, it was thought that it may be helpful for women diagnosed with female sexual arousal disorder. Basson conducted a study (2002) that tested this hypothesis. The results indicated that while sildenafil was tolerated, it did not tend to improve sexual response in women who were either estrogenized or estrogen-deficient. They concluded that women who may benefit most from treatment with sildenafil citrate are those experiencing a lack of vulval or vaginal engorgement, in spite of feeling sexually motivated and aroused, and who are mentally sexually excited in emotionally intimate relationships that provided adequate sexual stimulation. Other women who may also benefit are those who experience desire and mental arousal as a result of sexual activity; however, some have a neurological impairment in the genital arousal response. Thus, "the phenomenon of women not attending to their genital response, which is nevertheless occurring, or of finding it present but not pleasurable is likely to be complex and is currently not well understood" (Basson, 2002, p. 374).

Other treatments that have attempted to address female sexual arousal disorder include the use of Zestra for women (Ferguson et al., 2010), alprostadil (Liao et al., 2008), testosterone (Brotto et al., 2010) and bupropion (Wylie & Malik, 2009). Zestra for women was developed from a botanical mixture for the purpose of enhancing female sexual pleasure, increasing sensations of warmth and sensitivity when applied to the clitoris, labia, and vaginal opening. As such, it is thought to facilitate arousal. Among twenty women tested with it, sexual desire, satisfaction with sexual arousal, level of sexual arousal, genital sensation, sexual pleasure, and the ability to experience orgasm improved among those who experienced female sexual arousal disorder and those who did not (Ferguson et al., 2003). In a follow-up study (Ferguson et al., 2010) of 256 women, similar results were obtained regarding the efficacy of Zestra and placebo related to increases in arousal and desire. The study was a randomized, double-blind, placebo-controlled study.

Since studies have shown that cardiovascular risk factors are correlated with complaints of vaginal and clitoral dysfunction, it was hypothesized that female sexual arousal disorder may possibly be treated with vasodilators, which increase cardiovascular functioning by relaxing vascular smooth muscles.

Alprostadil was posited to facilitate nerve reflexes of sexual organs and to enhance brain activation in regions that are involved with sexual response or behavior. If alprostadil worked as hypothesized, it would be a pharmacological intervention for symptoms of female sexual arousal disorder (Liao et al., 2008). Results of the study with 387 subjects found that alprostadil cream increased sexual arousal rates, with 900 mg being the most effective dosage.

The authors posited that alprostadil produced an effect through local vascular dilation and also acted on chemoreceptors associated with sexual functioning, increasing nerve reflexes in sexual genitalia and enhancing the sexual response. As such, the application of alprostadil cream augmented subjective reports of sexual satisfaction compared with other vasodilators.

Androgen therapy may be effective for menopausal women deficient in estrogen. It is less effective for premenopausal women. It is important to note that the long-term risks of androgen therapy on breast cancer, metabolic syndrome, and insulin resistance are not known, and as such, referral to a knowledgeable physician would be advised (Brotto et al., 2010; cf. Braunstein et al., 2005). Bupropion has been helpful in overcoming antidepressant-induced sexual dysfunction, as it increases sexual desire in addition to increasing the frequency of sexual activity (Wylie & Malik, 2009), but further research is needed to clearly identify the most helpful pharmacological treatment options (Maurice, 2005).

PREVENTION

Prevention of desire disorders centers mostly on improving sex education for individuals and for couples, promoting healthy communication and intimacy in couples, and facilitating lifestyles that enhance emotional and sexual intimacy for couples.

Education involves having a healthy and balanced view of sexuality and sexual functioning. It includes understanding the differences among men and women in terms of desire, the multifaceted nature of desire, and the circumstances and events that may enhance or depress desire. This includes normal developmental changes in the seasons of life, as a couple may have children at different ages, different responsibilities and stressors, and identifiable life events that may affect desire, such as depression, the loss of employment, and so on.

When we look at promoting healthy communication and intimacy in couples, we recognize the potential benefit of fostering discussions that bring the couple closer together. This relational intimacy sets the stage for sexual intimacy. This is the approach taken by Metz and McCarthy (2011) in their book *Enduring Desire*, a resource that couples could read to learn more about setting realistic expectations, fostering satisfaction in one's relationship over time, cultivating a sexual style as a couple, and taking a collaborative stance. In any case, emotional drift from each other can often be reflected in diminished desire for intimacy, and keeping the couple engaged in meaningful and rewarding exchanges can often be a helpful preventative step.

Prevention can also be about cultivating a lifestyle that makes intimacy for the couple more of a priority. In the course of life together as a couple, it is not uncommon for one or both in the relationship to be caught up in the demands of their work, family, or church in ways that unbalance the kind of decisions that made intimacy a priority early on in the relationship. Couples can review how they use their time, what they commit themselves to, and how they make time for each other and opportunities for sexual intimacy. Impett and Gordon's (2010) research on approach goals in maintaining sexual desire found that women's sexual desire tends to be more closely tied to their goals in relationship compared with males. As such, attempts to treat low sexual desire in women pharmaceutically may be misguided.

CLOSING REFLECTIONS

The issue of sexual interest, desire, and arousal is complex, as suggested by the literature reviewed in this chapter. Consideration of physiological, psychological, social, and relational factors is important for the purpose of treatment. Similarly, spiritual and religious factors may provide additional information regarding the experience and conceptualization of sexual desire. In addition, the language of sexual desire is most effective if it is paired with a nonjudgmental approach, particularly because the issue of sexuality is a sensitive and vulnerable topic for many.

As we noted in chapter one, there has been a history of Christianity having a low view of sexuality and sexual expression. We discussed this briefly in the context of a medieval Christian perspective. Although current discussions have certainly improved and present a more balanced view today, we still often see tension for Christians who say no to sexual desire in attempts to wait to have sexual intercourse until marriage. With the lengthening of adolescence and the delays in marrying, we see more Christians struggling with the decision to wait, often seeming to keep desire at a distance in order not to be overwhelmed by it. We also see some Christians struggle with the transition from saying no to sexual desire to saying yes to desire on their eventual wedding night.

Although we appreciate the many insights from traditional approaches to conceptualizing and treating desire, interest, and arousal concerns—approaches that emphasize education, reducing anxiety, and enhancing sensory awareness—we are intrigued by models that turn a conventional understanding of anxiety on its head by considering growth through hardship (e.g., Schnarch, 2010). There is something in this approach that at times seems to draw on qualities within the person that sometimes go untapped in some of the CBT approaches. As Christians considering the treatment of desire disorders, it will be important to reflect on the role of anxiety in contributing to and maintaining various sexual disorders, as well as the benefits gained in learning how to regulate anxiety and persevere in meaningful ways.

For those who marry, we appreciate the concept of "creative fidelity" introduced by Lewis Smedes (1994, p. 145). Smedes points out that a married person's obligation to be faithful should not be reduced to avoiding sexual behavior that detracts from the marriage; rather, there is a positive expression of fidelity that warrants our attention. Smedes develops this idea of creative fidelity as faithfulness to *calling* (the state of marriage), *service, one's partner* (and their well-being), *our own personal growth,* and so on. On the matter of desire,

> a man or woman can be just too busy, too tired, too timid, too prudent, or too hemmed in with fear to be seriously tempted by an adulterous affair. But this same person can be a bore at home, callous to the delicate needs of his partner. He or she may be too prudish to be an adventuresome lover, but too cowardly to be in honest communication and too busy to put himself out for anything more than a routine ritual of personal commitment. He/she may be able to claim that he/she never cheated; but he/she may not be able to claim that he/she was ever really honest. He/she may never have slipped outside the marriage; but he/she may never have tried to grow along with his/her partner into a deep, personal relationship of respect and regard within marriage. His/her brand of negative fidelity may be an excuse for letting the marriage fall by neglect into dreary conformity to habit and, with that, into a dull routine of depersonalized sex. . . . Anyone who thinks that morality in marriage is fulfilled by avoiding an affair with a third party has short-circuited the personal dynamics of fidelity. (pp. 146-47)

So discussions of sexual desire, interest, and arousal should not be limited to a negative discussion about what is absent; there also should be a positive discussion about what is possible. It should include a proactive posture toward one's partner (for those who are married) in terms of "creative fidelity" toward the whole person and redemptive structure of marriage itself.

Many Christians do not marry. They too experience sexual desire, and the church has not often addressed the reality of their sexual desire, particularly as they experience it throughout the lifespan. That is a discussion that is beyond the focus of a chapter concentrating on treating sexual desire disorders in couples, but it is an important one with few resources currently committed to the topic (for exceptions, see Colón & Fields, 2009; Rosenau & Wilson, 2006).

We also think about issues that may reflect Christian biases and judgments about sexual desire. Being aware of one's own biases and thoughts, judgments, and feelings about sexual desire is necessary for effective treatment of one's clients. As an example, in a conversation one of the authors had with a colleague, that colleague was expressing how he could just "give [his] wife a signal and she would respond to his invitation for sexual intimacy immediately." This author felt a sense of indignation, although the colleague did not appear to be bragging. He seemed sincere in his resolution that this was an interaction that he and his wife enjoyed and agreed to. This author questioned whether his wife really felt that way and whether she had the freedom to express her views. Or did she collude with her husband's expectation that this was appropriate to their relationship?

To play the devil's advocate, perhaps his wife bought into this model of initiation of sexual intimacy. In that instance, should her level of sexual desire be questioned? What if it was an example of responsive desire? What if she felt that it was more important to be submissive to her husband's sexual urges because that was her role? Couples develop any number of sexual scripts that are unique to them as a couple. Perhaps expanding on those scripts and cues for sex, and ways in which those scripts and cues are conveyed, interpreted, and given meaning, is ultimately enhancing to that couple.

This exchange reminded us of relevant questions such as, What would be a Christ-centered view of sexual desire? Can it be similar for a married couple, singles, and those who are engaged? Would this view change if the issue of sexual desire was confounded by the experience of same-sex attraction? What about an individual who may struggle with atypical sexual interests? Or if the person is struggling more with gender dysphoria? Is there a right or a wrong way to experience sexual desire if the desire occurs independent of behavioral expression? What are the practical differences between desire and lust?

Although we are unable to answer each of these questions in detail, we note that the concept of stewardship of sexuality may be relevant as we reflect on sexual desire. We do not necessarily see all desires as given to us from God, as though all desires and impulses come with an inherent blessing that suggests we should act on them. Rather, we see desires as something we experience in a larger, broader context of our fallen condition. The desires may be natural to us, but they do not necessarily mean either that they are from God or that behaviors associated with the desires are intended by God to reflect what makes us more Christlike. A relevant question to ask, then, is, How do I honor God in light of the desires I do experience?

The experience of desire often involves choice with respect to the actions that follow our desires. It is erroneous to believe that we are passive and helpless with what we do as a result of what we have urges for or feel inclined to do.

Our general approach has been to encourage Christians to move toward their desires independent of a decision to act on them. By *move toward* we mean become more familiar with, understand the origins of, and reflect on the meanings associated with their desires by approaching them instead of ignoring or denying their existence. This movement *toward* creates new opportunities, not only for insight and understanding but also for stewardship, that is, learning how to manage feelings and desires in a God-honoring way. Keeping desires at arm's length seems to foster a fearful, anxious response to sexuality that is less a reflection of stewardship and more of a step toward behavioral management. We have not found such an emphasis to be ultimately helpful to Christians who are trying to make sense of their desires and who want to find ways to honor God meaningfully in their sexuality and its expression. In those instances when sexuality is tended to only with behavior management, feelings of bitterness and resentment can also contribute to the myriad of emotions that hinder the practice of being intentional with one's desires.

Tending to one's desires is a complex experience. There have been many approaches posited by various Christians that may seem somewhat restrictive for some Christian clients who want to honor God and develop a healthy understanding and appreciation of their sexual desires and sexual expression while they are single. The ability to ask questions, to explore thoughts and feelings, and to share these opinions openly and honestly without being shut down is paramount to a healthy understanding and appreciation of our given sexuality.

REFERENCES

American Psychiatric Association. (2004). *Diagnostic and statistical manual of mental disorders* (4th ed.). American Psychiatric Publishing.

American Psychiatric Association. (2022). *Diagnostic and statistical manual of mental disorders* (5th ed.-Text Revision). American Psychiatric Publishing.

Bancroft, J. (2010). Sexual desire and the brain revisited. *Sexual and Relationship Therapy, 25*(2), 166-71.

Basson, R. (2002). A model of women's sexual arousal. *Journal of Sex and Marital Therapy, 28*, 1-10.

Basson, R. (2007). Sexual desire/arousal disorders in women. In S. R. Leiblum (Ed.), *Principles and practice of sex therapy* (4th ed., pp. 25-53). Guilford.

Basson, R. (2010). Complaints of low sexual desire: How therapeutic assessment guides further interventions. In S. R. Leiblum (Ed.), *Treating sexual desire disorders: A clinical casebook* (pp. 133-48). Guilford.

Basson, R. (2012). Women's difficulties with low sexual desire, sexual avoidance, and sexual aversion. In S. B. Levine, C. B. Risen, & S. T. Althof (Eds.), *Handbook of clinical sexuality for mental health professionals* (2nd ed.). Routledge.

Braunstein, G. D., Sundwall, D. A., Katz, M., . . . Watts, M. B. (2005). Safety and efficacy of a testosterone patch for the treatment of hypoactive sexual desire disorder in surgically menopausal women: A randomized, placebo-controlled trial. *Archives of Internal Medicine 165*, 1582-89.

Brotto, L. A. (2009). The DSM diagnostic criteria for hypoactive sexual desire disorder in women. *Archives of Sexual Behavior, 39*, 221-39. https://doi.org/10.1007/s10508-009-9543-1

Brotto, L. A. (2010). The DSM diagnostic criteria for sexual aversion disorder. *Archives of Sexual Behavior, 39*, 271-77.

Brotto, L. A. (2018). *Better sex through mindfulness: How women can cultivate desire.* Greystone Books.

Brotto, L. A., Knudson, G., Inskip, J., Rhodes, K., & Erskine, Y. (2010). Asexuality: A mixed-methods approach. *Archives of Sexual Behavior, 39*, 599-618.

Brotto, L. A., & Woo, J. S. T. (2010). Cognitive-behavioral and mindfulness-based therapy for low sexual desire. In S. R. Leiblum (Ed.), *Treating sexual desire disorders: A clinical casebook* (pp. 149-64). Guilford.

Carvalheira, A. A., Brotto, L. A., & Leal, I. (2010). Women's motivations for sex: Exploring the diagnostic and statistical manual, fourth edition, text revision criteria for hypoactive sexual desire and female sexual arousal disorders. *Journal of Sex Medicine, 7*, 1454-63.

Carvalho, J., & Nobre, P. (2010). Gender issues and sexual desire: The role of emotional and relationship variables. *Journal of Sex Medicine, 7*, 2469-78.

Clayton, A., Goldfischer, E. R., Goldstein, I., Derogatis, L., Lewis-D'Agostino, D. J., & Pyke, R. (2009). Validation of the decreased sexual desire screener (DSDS): A brief diagnostic instrument for generalized acquired female hypoactive sexual desire disorder. *Journal of Sexual Medicine, 6*, 730-38.

Clayton, A., Segraves, R., Leiblum, S., Basson, R., Pyke, R., Cotton, D., . . . & Wunderilich, G. (2006). Reliability and validity of the Sexual Interest and Desire Inventory—Female (SIDI-F), a scale designed to measure severity of female hypoactive sexual desire disorder. *Journal of Sex & Marital Therapy, 32*(2), 115-35. https://doi.org/10.1080/00926230500442300

Clement, U. (2002). Sex in long-term relationships: A systemic approach to sexual desire problems. *Archives of Sexual Behavior, 31*(3), 241-46.

Cohen, K. M., & Savin-Williams, R. C. (2017). Treating sexual problems in lesbian, gay, and bisexual clients. In Z. D. Peterson (Ed.), *The Wiley handbook of sex therapy* (pp. 291-305). John Wiley and Sons.

Colón, C., & Fields, B. (2009). *Singled out: Why celibacy must be reinvented in today's church.* Brazos.

Durr, E. (2009). Lack of "responsive" sexual desire in women: Implications for clinical practice. *Sexual and Relationship Therapy, 24*(3-4), 292-306.

Feldhahn, S., & Sytsma, M. (2023). *Secrets of sex & marriage: 8 surprises that make all the difference*. Bethany House.

Ferguson, D. M., Hosmane, B., & Heiman, J. R. (2010). Randomized, placebo-controlled, double-blind, parallel design trial of the efficacy and safety of Zestra in women with mixed desire/interest/arousal/orgasm disorders. *Journal of Sex & Marital Therapy, 36*, 66-86.

Ferguson, D. M., Steidle, C. P., Singh, G. S., Alexander, J. S., Weihmiller, M. K., & Crosby, M. G. (2003). Randomized, placebo-controlled, double blind, crossover design trial of the efficacy and safety of Zestra for women in women with and without female sexual arousal disorder. *Journal of Sex & Marital Therapy, 29*, 33–44.

Grover, S., & Shouan, A. (2020). Assessment scales for sexual disorders: A review. *Journal of Psychosexual Health, 2*(2), 121-28.

Hurlbert, D. F. (1992). Motherhood and female sexuality beyond one year postpartum: A study of military wives. *Journal of Sex Therapy, 18*, 104-14.

Impett, E. A., & Gordon, A. M. (2010). Why do people sacrifice to approach rewards versus to avoid costs? Insights from attachment theory. *Personal Relationships, 17*(2), 299-315. https://doi.org/10.1111/j.1475-6811.2010.01277.x

Kafka, M. P. (2009). Hypersexual disorder: A proposed diagnosis for DSM-V. *Archives of Sexual Behavior, 39*, 377-400.

Kaplan, H. S. (1995). *Sexual desire disorders: Dysfunctional regulation of sexual motivation*. Routledge.

Kingsberg, S. A. (2002). The impact of aging on sexual function in women and their partners. *Archives of Sexual Behavior, 31*(5), 431-37.

Laumann, E. O., Paik, A., & Rosen, R. C. (1999). Sexual dysfunction in the United States: Prevalence and predictors. *Journal of the American Medical Association, 281*(6), 537-44.

Leiblum, S. R. (2010). *Treating sexual desire disorders: A clinical casebook*. Guilford.

Levine, S. B. (2003). The nature of sexual desire: A clinician's perspective. *Archives of Sexual Behavior, 32*(3), 279-85.

Liao, Q. P., Zhang, M., Geng, L., Wang, X., Song, X., Xia, P., Lu, T., . . . & Liu, V. (2008). Efficacy and safety of alprostadil cream for the treatment of female sexual arousal disorder: A double-blind, placebo-controlled study in Chinese population. *Journal of Sex Medicine, 5*, 1923-31.

Masters, W. H., & Johnson, V. E. (1970). *Human sexual inadequacy*. Bantam Books.

Maurice, W. L. (2005). Male hypoactive sexual desire disorder. In R. Balon & R. T. Segraves (Eds.), *Handbook of sexual dysfunction* (pp. 67-110). Taylor & Francis.

McCarthy, B., & McDonald, D. (2009). Assessment, treatment, and relapse prevention: Male hypoactive sexual desire. *Journal of Sex & Marital Therapy, 35*, 58-67.

Meana, M. (2010). Elucidating women's (hetero)sexual desire: Definitional challenges and content expansion. *Journal of Sex Research, 47*(2-3), 104-22.

Metz, M. E., & McCarthy, B. W. (2011). *Enduring desire: Your guide to lifelong intimacy*. Routledge.

Millner, V. S. (2005). Female sexual arousal disorder and counseling deliberations. *Family Journal, 13*(1), 95-100.

Montgomery, K. A. (2008). Sexual desire disorders. *Psychiatry, 5*(6), 50-55.

Nappi, R. E., Terreno, E., Martini, E., Albani, F., Santamaria, V., Tonani, S., & Polatti, F. (2010). Hypoactive sexual desire disorder: Can we treat it with drugs? *Sexual and Relationship Therapy, 25*(3), 264-74.

Penner, J., & Penner, C. (2005). *A clinician's guide to sex therapy* (2nd ed.). Word.

Pierrelus, C., Patel, P., & Carlson, K. (2023, November 10). *Flibanserin*. National Library of Medicine. www.ncbi.nlm.nih.gov/books/NBK589649/#:~:text=Flibanserin%2C %20initially%20developed%20as%20an,(HSDD)%20in%20premenopausal%20 women

Prause, N., Janssen, E., & Hetrick, W. P. (2008). Attention and emotional responses to sexual stimuli and their relationship to sexual desire. *Archives of Sexual Behavior, 37*, 934-49.

Pridal, C. G., & LoPiccolo, J. (2000). Multielement treatment of desire disorders: Integration of cognitive, behavioral, and systemic therapy. In S. R. Leiblum & R. C. Rosen (Eds.), *Principles and practice of sex therapy* (3rd ed., pp. 57-81). Guilford.

Rathus, S. A., Nevid, J. S., & Fichner-Rathus, L. (2011). *Human sexuality in a world of diversity* (8th ed.). Allyn & Bacon.

Rellini, A. H., & Meston, C. M. (2007). Sexual desire and linguistic analysis: A comparison of sexually-abused and non-abused women. *Archives of Sexual Behavior, 36*, 67-77.

Rosenau, D. (2002). *A celebration of sex* (Rev. ed.). Thomas Nelson.

Rosenau, D., & Wilson, M. T. (2006). *Soul virgins: Redefining single sexuality*. Baker.

Rosenbaum, T. Y. (2007). Pelvic floor involvement in male and female sexual dysfunction and the role of pelvic floor rehabilitation in treatment: A literature review. *Journal of Sex Medicine, 4*, 4-13.

Schnarch, D. (1991) *Constructing the sexual crucible: An integration of sexual and marital therapy*. Norton.

Schnarch, D. (1997). *Passionate marriage: Sex, love and intimacy in emotionally committed relationships*. Norton.

Schnarch, D. (2000). Desire problems: A systemic perspective. In S. R. Leiblum & R. C. Rosen (Eds.), *Principles and practice of sex therapy* (3rd ed., pp. 17-56). Guilford.

Schnarch, D. (2010). Using crucible therapy to treat sexual desire disorders. In S. R. Leiblum (Ed.), *Treating sexual desire disorders: A clinical casebook* (pp. 44-60). Guilford.

Sims, K. E., & Meana, M. (2010). Why do passions wane? A qualitative study of married women's attributions for declines in sexual desire. *Journal of Sex & Marital Therapy, 36*(4), 360-80. doi:10.1080/0092623X.2010.498727

Smedes, L. (1994). *Sex for Christians* (Rev. ed.). Eerdmans.

Spector, I. P., Carey, M. P., & Steinberg, L. (1996). The sexual desire inventory: Development, factor structure, and evidence of reliability. *Journal of Sex & Marital Therapy, 22*, 175-90.

ter Kuile, M. M., Both, S., & van Lankveld, J. J. D. M. (2010). Cognitive behavioral therapy for sexual dysfunctions in women. *Psychiatric Clinics of North America, 33*, 595-610.

Tiefler, L., & Hall, M. (2010). A skeptical view of desire norms and disorders promotes clinical success. In S. R. Leiblum (Ed.), *Treating sexual desire disorders: A clinical casebook* (pp. 114-32). Guilford.

Treadway, D. (2010). Dancing to their own music. In S. R. Leiblum (Ed.), *Treating sexual desire disorders: A clinical casebook* (pp. 165-80). Guilford.

Ullery, E. K., Millner, V. S., & Willingham, H. A. (2002). The emergent care and treatment of women with hypoactive sexual desire disorder. *The Family Journal: Counseling and Therapy for Couples and Families, 10*(3), 346-50.

van Lankveld, J. (2008). Problems with sexual interest and desire in women. In D. L. Rowland & L. Encrocci (Eds.), *The handbook of sexual and gender identity disorders* (pp. 154-87). Wiley.

Walters, G. D., Knight, R. A., & Langstrom, N. (2011, February 3). Is hypersexuality dimensional? Evidence for the DSM-5 from general population and clinical samples. *Archives of Sexual Behavior.* https://doi.org/10.1007/s10508-010-9719-8

Weeks, G. R., Hertlein, K. M., & Gambescia, N. (2009). The treatment of hypoactive sexual desire disorder. In K. M. Hertleim, G. R. Weeks, & N. Gambescia (Eds.), *Systemic sex therapy* (pp. 81-106). Routledge.

Winters, J., Christoff, K., & Gorzalka, B. B. (2010). Dysregulated sexuality and high sexual desire: Distinct constructs? *Archives of Sexual Behavior, 39,* 1029-43.

Wylie, K., & Malik, F. (2009). Review of drug treatment for female sexual dysfunction. *International Journal of STD & AIDS, 20,* 671-74.

SIX

FEMALE ORGASMIC DISORDER

THERE IS A STORY about a man and a woman who were seated next to each other on a flight from Chicago to Dallas. The man was reading a detective novel when the woman sneezed. She politely took a tissue from her purse, wiped her nose, and then shuddered for about ten seconds.

The man went back to reading his novel.

Several minutes later, the woman sneezed again. And again she took a tissue from her purse, wiped her nose and shuddered again for another ten seconds—this time more pronounced. Thinking she had a cold, the man was rather curious about the fact that she kept shuddering. After another several minutes, the woman sneezed once again. She took a tissue and again wiped her nose, followed by her body shuddering once again, this time still more pronounced.

The man finally turned to her and said, "I'm sorry, but I couldn't help but see that you've sneezed quite a bit here but that you shudder rather significantly. Are you okay?"

"I'm sorry if I've bothered you. I have a rare medical condition. Whenever I sneeze I have an orgasm."

The man, now rather wishing he hadn't brought it up, still had a lingering question he couldn't resist asking. "I've never heard of that condition before," he said. "Are you taking anything for it?"

The woman nodded and replied, "Pepper."

As this joke suggests, orgasms are pleasurable experiences enjoyed by most sexually active women. This chapter examines the challenges that arise when a woman has difficulty with either arousal or orgasm to the extent that it meets criteria for an arousal or orgasmic disorder.

Arousal refers to a physiological response to stimuli that, in the sexual response cycle, facilitates sexual intimacy and creates a context for orgasm.

Orgasm refers to the full-body response of pleasure at the apex of sexual intimacy; it involves the release of neuromuscular tension that has built up in the context of the sexual response cycle.

As we look at the topic of sexual arousal, some women who otherwise desire sex do not have a physiological response of arousal to sexual stimuli. Yet, because they desire emotional intimacy with their partners, they may join their partners in sexual intimacy, eventually succumbing to the excitement and pleasure of the moment.

For many women sexual arousal precedes sexual desire. Sexual activity usually requires several processes: (1) the support of a sexual response in an intact system, (2) meaningful sexual stimuli that can activate the sexual system, and (3) circumstances that support the pursuit of sexual activity (Both et al., 2010). Sexual stimuli are often meaningful because of learning—either positive or negative associations. As such, sexual stimuli may become less attractive or less positive if they are paired with unpleasant experiences, such as anxiety, disappointment, or pain during intercourse.

Unfortunately, even the latter experience escapes some women, who in spite of attempts at becoming motivated may still struggle with the absence of arousal. Other women participate in sexual intimacy without having the pleasure of an orgasm. If these experiences are reported as distressing by the woman and affect her relationship, she may have an orgasmic disorder.

It is suggested that the conflation of hypoactive sexual desire disorder and female sexual arousal disorder into sexual interest/arousal disorder is due to the fact that some women are not able to distinguish between desire and arousal (Basson, 2008). In addition, they may not accurately assess the experience of genital congestion—once conceptualized as a sign of sexual arousal—as they may experience vasocongestion due to visual stimuli that is sexual yet not erotic or sexually arousing. In spite of the initial lack of sexual desire at the initiation of sexual stimulation, a woman may experience increased arousal depending on "the type of stimulation, the context, her ability to attend, the number of distractions, and the expected outcome influence the likelihood of her becoming aroused" (pp. 73-74). Adequate intensity of stimulation may contribute to an increase in arousal, which may then trigger desire; however, there is no set temporal sequence of occurrence. Thus, according to Basson (2008), a woman's experience of sexual functioning is highly dependent on context. As such, dysfunction may reflect other factors, such as inadequate stimulation, a lack of emotional closeness and intimacy with her partner, and other problems in the sexual environment. These factors may be indicated when there is no physiological basis for sexual dysfunction.

Contrary to the position that arousal and desire can be conflated because of the difficulty distinguishing between them, Kleinplatz (2011) posits that it is the clinician's responsibility, not the client's, to "perform the differential diagnosis" (p. 4). Rather than assessing sexual desire in terms of frequency of sex or the desire for sex, she states the need to evaluate "what exactly is the nature or quality of the 'sex' patients do not desire?" (p. 4). Collapsing the categories would reflect some of the beliefs about sexual arousal and desire in women: (1) desire is not possible to define operationally, (2) desire and arousal overlap, and (3) women's sexual desire is more responsive.

Difficulty assessing the experience of arousal and the reported discrepancy between awareness of arousal between men and women may be due to methodology. Whereas men have the opportunity to gauge arousal with the erection of their penis, women have traditionally been assessed via the vagina instead of the clitoris (Kleinplatz, 2011). In addition, most people lack sexual education. As such, it becomes the responsibility of the clinician to not only educate the client but to tease out difficulties the client may experience with desire or arousal.

In evaluating the experience of low sexual desire or arousal, the emphasis is often on frequency as opposed to the quality of sex that the client does not want or desire. Kleinplatz (2011) points out that for many individuals with low sexual desire, they do not complain about missing magnificent sex. These individuals often report a decrease in frequency of sexual encounters accompanied by a decrease in the quality of sex during those experiences. However, these individuals are likely to continue to participate because of relational commitment, which then tends to diminish the experience of arousal. As such, the partner with low sexual desire may initiate sexual activity or respond to it as a means of terminating the experience sooner. To summarize the dilemma of arousal and desire, she writes,

> The nature and spectrum of both sexual and non-sexual motives for sex deserve our attention. They are inclined to be more complex in men and women than the appetitive drive currently posited by many of those worried about both high and low desire disorders. We tend to minimize men's relational needs for sex and women's desires for more intense pleasure during "sex." We ignore the meaning

of men's pain when their male or female partners report lower desire; such men can live with sexual deprivation (much as they wish it were otherwise)—but they despair of not being wanted by their beloved spouses. Instead, we tend to pay attention to men's sexual motives only when we disapprove of them in "hypersexual" men, referring to what they seek as evidence of "affect regulation." (Kleinplatz, 2011, p. 12)

The concern presented by Kleinplatz (2011) was reflected by DeRogatis et al. (2010), who studied the symptoms of women with HSDD and FSAD. Their concern was that while more women may be diagnosed with Sexual Interest/Arousal Disorder if the symptoms are collapsed together, the clinical meaningfulness of the combined diagnosis may be diminished. However, Brotto et al. (2010) challenged DeRogatis et al. in their evaluation of symptoms, stating that lack of empirical evidence to support separate diagnoses was confirmation to support the merging.

Brotto et al. (2010) posited that the criteria for Sexual Interest/Arousal Disorder appear to be valid for men as well as women.

DEFINITION

There are several distinctions made between desire/arousal disorders and orgasmic disorders. Some of the symptoms are physical, while others are not. Diagnosis of an interest/desire/arousal disorder or an orgasmic disorder cannot be made solely on the presentation of symptoms. These disorders take place within the context of a relationship, and as such, assessment and evaluation of the quality of the relationship, as well as the presence of symptoms and their manifestation, are an important consideration.

We shared in chapter five that interest/desire/arousal disorders refer to a lack or absence of desire for sexual activity or the capacity to achieve or maintain arousal (APA, 2013). The American Urological Association Foundation (AUAF) also describes the absence of fantasies and desire as a component of desire disorders, and includes scarce or absent motivations for attempting to become sexually aroused as factors to consider. Another qualitative component proposed by the AUAF in diagnosing desire disorders is that the lack of interest is "beyond a normative lessening with life cycle and relationship duration" (Brotto et al., 2010, p. 587).

The current conceptualization from *DSM-5-TR* of female orgasmic disorder references "marked delay in, marked infrequency of, or absence of orgasm" or "markedly reduced intensity of orgasmic sensations" for about six months that cause clinically significant distress (APA, 2022, p. 485). These symptoms should occur in "almost all or all" occasions, but can be distinguished in terms of being situational (limited to specific stimulation, situations, or partners) or generalized (not limited to specific stimulations, situations, or partners), as well as lifelong (since becoming sexually active) or acquired (it became a concern after a time of normal function).

Prevalence estimates from nationally representative samples suggest that 10% to 34% of women are unable to achieve orgasm, while the percentage of women who have difficulty achieving orgasm ranges from 11% to 30% (Graham, 2010; Meana, 2012). The *DSM-5-TR* notes a wide range of prevalence estimates in the literature (8-72%) for female orgasmic problems (APA, 2022) but that international data suggests about 10% of women indicate lifetime inability to experience orgasm. Difficulty achieving orgasm is not reported as often among lesbian couples than among women in heterosexual relationships. However, assessment of the sexual response cycle and whether low desire or interest is present may be an important adaptation for working with lesbian couples, as we do see higher rates of low desire reported among lesbian couples (Cohen & Savin-Williams, 2017).

About half or fewer of women who report difficulty with achieving orgasm report distress (Meana, 2012), which suggests that experiencing orgasm, while important to many women, is not necessarily the centerpiece to sexual intimacy in quite the same way it is for men, though there is likely considerable variability among men and women in this regard.

In their report on married couples, Feldhahn and Sytsma (2023) indicated that 36% of females reported *always/almost always* experiencing orgasm during sex, while 21% indicated *usually* being orgasmic, 11% *often*, 16% *occasionally*, 8% *rarely*, and 7% *never/almost never*. As the authors observed, 31% (combining *never/almost never, rarely,* and *occasionally*) "say they only occasionally *do* get there—and sometimes not at all" (p. 45). How various frequency terms translate into specific diagnoses may be difficult at times to say, but it is important for us to consider pathways of etiology, assessment, and intervention.

ETIOLOGY

As we turn to etiology, we organize our understanding of these concerns around biological factors, psychological and personality factors, and interpersonal factors. It should be kept in mind that these multiple contributing factors are likely weighted differently for different women.

Biological factors. The *DSM-5-TR* (APA, 2022) notes many genetic and physiological risk factors associated with orgasmic disorders, including a number of medical conditions and medications to treat various concerns. Medical conditions include "multiple sclerosis, pelvic nerve damage from radical hysterectomy, and spinal cord injury" (p. 487). Heart disease and kidney disease have also been associated with anorgasmia (IsHak et al., 2010). Women who experience vulvovaginal atrophy (characterized by "vaginal dryness, itching, and pain") are also at greater risk of reporting orgasm concerns (APA, 2022, p. 487).

Neurophysiological factors that affect orgasm include anatomical features, such as the clitoris and vagina, as well as the G spot (or Grafenberg spot). In addition to physical sensations of arousal exhibited by the clitoris and vagina, the brain is also an important source of sexual arousal and orgasm for women. Several studies have found women who do not have direct stimulation to the genitals still report experiences of orgasm (Heiman, 2007).

In terms of medications, some background information may be helpful. Dopamine is a key neurotransmitter in the experience of orgasm for humans. D2 and D4 postsynaptic receptors facilitate orgasm, and medications blocking these receptors inhibit orgasm (Komisaruk et al., 2006). In men the brain region that is activated during ejaculation is the ventral tegmental area. The nucleus accumbens is activated in women during orgasm. However, it is noted that dopaminergic drugs on their own do not produce an orgasm by turning on the orgasm switch. In essence, dopamine activates the reward-pleasure limbic system circuits when sensory impulses are generated by genital and other sexual stimulation.

In contrast, serotonin tends to facilitate inhibition of orgasm, which is why antidepressants and antipsychotics that increase serotonergic activity via reuptake are likely to produce anorgasmia (Komisaruk et al., 2006).

Specifically, some neuroleptics (i.e., antipsychotics that tend to produce parkinsonism) tend to affect sexual functioning, particularly those in the class of phenothiazines, such as chlorpromazine, fluphenazine, and thioridazine, resulting in a strong to intense effect on sexual disorder. In contrast, new antipsychotics, such as clozapine, olanzapine, and risperidone tend to have a low to moderate effect on sexual dysfunction. As such, antipsychotics have been used to treat paraphilias (Komisaruk et al., 2006).

Tricyclic antidepressants and selective-serotonin reuptake inhibitors (SSRIs) tend to have a strong to intense effect on sexual dysfunction by increasing serotonergic activity. Atypical antidepressants, such as bupropion, trazodone, mirtazapine, nefazodone, and reboxetine, have fewer effects on sexual functioning. Orgasmic disorder resulting from monoamine inhibitors (MAOI) is likely due to the increase in serotonergic activity, which has an inhibitory effect, compared with the elevated levels of dopamine and norepinephrine.

In addition to biological considerations in the etiology of orgasm disorders, we also want to consider psychological and personality factors.

Psychological and personality factors. Although there has not been a lot of definitive research on psychological and personality factors, "it has been suggested that stress, levels of fatigue, sexual identity, health, and other individual attributes and experience may alter sexual desire or response" (McCabe, 2009b, p. 214). Concerns about life stressors, such as unemployment, warrant further study, as does depression and anxiety, particularly as anxiety may become associated with arousal, performance, and whether the person is going to experience orgasm (McCabe, 2009b).

Penner and Penner (2005) also discuss how women who either lack knowledge about their bodies or expect themselves to be more passive during sex may struggle more with orgasm difficulties. Concerning the former, "Women who have difficulty with orgasm release may lack knowledge about their own bodies, the sexual response cycle, or effective stimulation" (p. 217). Perhaps because they "have no expectation of receiving pleasure from the sexual experience, . . . mentally they do not connect with the building of the arousal response in their bodies" (p. 217).

Regarding women who are more passive, Penner and Penner (2005) observe,

> Similarly, women may see themselves as passive receptacles of the man's aggressive sexuality, so they are totally passive during all sexual experiences. They become aroused because arousal is controlled by the parasympathetic branch of our autonomic nervous system, the passive branch. But their arousal stops at the end of the plateau phase right before the orgasmic response. It is as if they cannot make it over the hill. We believe that this is the point at which the involuntary control shifts from the passive (parasympathetic) to the active branch (sympathetic) of the nervous system. The heart rate increases, the breathing intensifies, and the involuntary thrusting starts. Overt, active sexuality has to kick in. If the woman is passive, those responses will not happen. (p. 217)

Research on personality factors suggests that "introversion, emotional instability, and not being open to new experiences were significantly associated with orgasm infrequency," as is being low on emotional intelligence (the ability to identify and manage emotional states in ways that are helpful and productive) (IsHak et al., 2010, p. 3257).

Interpersonal factors. Lack of effective communication has been observed to be a significant factor in couples who have difficulty with sexual functioning. Couples with female orgasmic disorder in one partner are more likely to have an interactional pattern of blaming and lack of receptivity compared with couples who do not report the disorder (Kelly et al., 2004, 2006). A correlation is found among women with higher rates of relationship dissatisfaction and sexual dysfunction. Women with desire disorders are reported to have poorer conflict resolution, and less attraction to and emotional closeness with their partners. Problematic communication about desires, wishes, needs, and conflicts is likely to negatively affect the woman's desire to participate in sexual activity (Brotto et al., 2010 p. 593; McCabe, 2009a).

Specifically, since direct clitoral stimulation is observed to likely maximize female sexual responsiveness, problems communicating about what a woman needs to experience with regard to pleasurable clitoral stimulation may contribute to the development and maintenance of female orgasmic disorder (Kelly et al., 2004). As such, prolonged foreplay can help to increase arousal and the likelihood of orgasm (McCabe, 2009a). Since treatment of female orgasmic disorder utilizes directed masturbation, many women with either lifelong or acquired anorgasmia may experience this condition as a result of inadequate sexual stimulation (Brotto et al., 2010).

The rates of inability to orgasm among women vary, depending on the time period and the method of assessment. The absence of orgasm in a woman's sexual relationship may not have anything to do with her experience of relationship satisfaction. Personal distress about not being able to achieve orgasm will vary between women. While men may express more concern about their genital responses (e.g., ejaculation or erection), women are more likely to discuss the subjective quality of their sexual experience (e.g., lack of arousal or pleasure). Poor physical and mental health and relationship difficulties are cited as the most consistent factors contributing to orgasmic problems in women (Graham, 2010).

In discussing sexual dysfunction, how can normal variation be expressed without pathologizing it? And how can the relational context of sexual problems also be addressed? Although inclusion of a distress criterion is necessary, it is also insufficient as a sole criterion for any sexual dysfunction. More precise criteria with respect to frequency, duration, and severity may also be helpful with the diagnosis. Graham (2010) makes a recommendation to deemphasize the physiological aspect of orgasm. Both the physiological and subjective experiences of orgasm are variable across women. Criteria that differentiate duration and severity will help to identify persistent sexual problems. Treatment may emphasize the relational context of orgasmic problems. Distinguishing between lifelong and acquired orgasmic problems is important to assessment because a woman's capacity for orgasm and her past experience is data for treatment.

Distinguishing between generalized and situational subtypes is helpful clinically; however, the situational subtype "is not misinterpreted to mean experience of orgasm with clitoral stimulation but not during vaginal inter- course" (Graham, 2010, p. 266). Women who experience orgasm with cli- toral stimulation but not during penile-vaginal intercourse do not meet criteria for orgasmic disorder.

McCabe (2009b) observes that some women may be affected by intergen- erational influences, such as problems socializing, gender or sexual identity difficulties, and negative attitudes about sex and sexual pleasure. Some in- dividuals with histories of childhood sexual abuse have cited anorgasmia; however, its contribution is not definitive.

McCabe (2009b) notes too that concerns in this area can contribute to difficulties with not only sexual touch but also nongenital touch and the intimacy associated with physical contact in general: "Discomfort with non- genital and genital touching impedes the development of intimacy, which in turn leads to a breakdown in relationship functioning and eventually to sexual dysfunction in one or both partners" (p. 216).

ASSESSMENT AND CLINICAL PRESENTATION

Maggie sat down a little far from her husband, Tim, on the couch in the thera- pist's office. It became clear in the course of the interview that the space created in where they sat reflected the distance she was feeling in the relationship. She shared that she had not been orgasmic with Tim, and that that realization has had huge symbolic importance. She had been orgasmic in a prior relationship in college. Tim was the second man she had had sex with, and she was frustrated by the lack of orgasm for her and the difficulties she said she had just "getting ready" for sex, by which she came to mean the struggles she had not experiencing sufficient lubrication during foreplay and throughout intercourse.

Maggie and Tim's presentation is a good example of how symptoms of an interest/desire/arousal disorder may coexist with symptoms of an orgasmic disorder. To determine whether there is comorbidity here or whether one or the other dysfunction is primary and perhaps the cause of the symptoms that suggest the other, a clinician needs to conduct a thorough assessment. Generally speaking, that assessment should go through the entire sexual response cycle to provide a larger context for understanding their concerns. In addition, assessment of the identified client and of the couple is essential. We will discuss assessment, then, with reference to individual and couples assessment.

Individual assessment. In their meta-analysis of studies that estimated the prevalence of problems with sexual desire, arousal, and orgasm, Brotto et al. (2010) found that low desire was 10% to 40%, depending on methodology, participants, and geographical location; however, this percentage dropped by about half when the complaint of sexual distress was also included. This drop in prevalence was also observed in studies assessing sexual arousal impairment when distress was assessed. As such, they suggest that the severity of distress be assessed in the context of arousal or desire difficulties. They also purport that "sexual satisfaction is rarely correlated with sexual frequency and is not consistently associated with sexual symptoms; thus, sexual satisfaction must be assessed clinically" (Brotto et al., 2010, p. 591).

Thoroughly assessing female orgasmic disorder requires an in-depth personal interview assessing the adequacy of sexual stimulation. The biopsychosocial interview is an opportunity for the clinician to become more familiar with the client's experience of the presenting problem, as well as any factors that may predispose her to sexual difficulties and the things that may maintain them. Relevant life-stage stressors can include biological experiences, such as infertility or childbirth, or relationship factors, such as discord, sexual partner inadequacy, extra-relationship affairs, divorce, partner loss, traumatic sexual experiences, or situational stressors such as unemployment. Being able to identify the precipitating or predisposing factors and triggers to sexual difficulties will facilitate the first stages of treatment. Important maintaining factors to consider include things that may affect sexual expression, including any medical or psychiatric concerns, medications, substance abuse, and relationship satisfaction. A separate interview that includes the partner in this clinical assessment will also be necessary (Brotto et al., 2010).

Assessment measures are sometimes used (Grover & Shouan, 2020). These include general sexual functioning measures, such as the Sexual Function Questionnaire (SFQ-28) or the Female Sexual Function Index (FSFI), as well as measures specific to orgasmic disorders, such as the Orgasm Rating Scale (ORS) (Mah & Binik, 2002) and the Female Orgasm Scale (Mcintyre-Smith & Fisher, 2011).

While some clinicians may use self-report tools to assist in their assessment, caution is advised if the measure tends to focus on quantity of sexual experiences versus quality (Brotto et al., 2010). So beyond questions about the frequency of sexual activity, ask about the sexual script and the quality of the time together in terms of personal satisfaction, quality of communication, variation, technique, and so on.

Although the clinician may be able to assess psychological, cognitive, and emotional factors that may precipitate and maintain sexual dysfunction, it is also important to refer the client to a gynecologist for a physical exam. This portion of the assessment is important because it provides an opportunity for the woman to explore and express her perceptions, attitudes, and beliefs about her genitals and her body while she is being exposed to it. The gynecologist can educate her about her anatomy and encourage her to take a positive view of herself. It would also be important for the gynecologist to assess her voluntary control of her pelvic floor muscles, whether there are any signs of vaginal atrophy, and the presence of infection or pain.

Considering the diagnosis and formulation for women's sexuality, Brotto et al. encourage the adoption of a "three windows" approach (Brotto et al., 2010, p. 601) that evaluates several perspectives: (1) the current context of the client's situation, (2) the presence of vulnerability factors, such as past history and personality factors, and (3) any health-related influences on sexual response, including mental and physical health.

Assessment of female sexual orgasmic disorder needs to be comprehensive, including the experiences of arousal in a multidimensional manner: cognitive sexual excitement, genital sensations such as throbbing, the experience of sexual satisfaction when genitals are stimulated, sexual satisfaction when breasts and other body parts are stimulated, variability in blood pressure and heart rate, and vaginal lubrication (Millner, 2005). Considerations for assessment include:

- Conducting a sexual history to identify the pattern regarding sexual dysfunction—whether it is lifelong or acquired. Times, places, and partners are important data points regarding the sexual problems.
- Inquire when the client experienced satisfactory sexual arousal.
- Inquire about experiences of sex education in the family of origin, including types of touch that were accepted, ability to make eye contact, trust of others, expression of empathy, self-image, and personal power. How did the client's family of origin communicate about sexuality?
- Assess individual factors, such as personality disorders, history of sexual abuse, and so on that may interfere with sexual functioning.
- Assess the client's sexual and emotional attraction to her partner. If the client is not attracted to her partner, assess whether this is situational or persistent.
- Assess the client's ability to communicate her sexual needs to her partner.
- What is the client's view of herself? Sexual problems may reflect poor self-image.
- What are cognitions and emotions that the client has regarding her sexual experience?
- How have the client and her partner coped thus far as a couple with this sexual difficulty? What are their sexual scripts?
- Assess the client and her partner's "body map," which identifies areas of the body acceptable to touch.

Assessment of what is lacking may also provide valuable insights to our clients' experiences. For example, Kleinplatz (2011) asserts that clinicians need to be more attentive to understanding what would make our clients excited about sex, for example, by asking what kinds of sex they imagine themselves having when they are most aroused.

Basson's (2008) strategy for assessment is the following: Evaluate the stages of the woman's sexual response cycle. Include partners and assess them together, as well as separately. Assess the woman's motivations and reasons to be sexual, in addition to the fit with context. Continue the assessment into her self-image, her past sexual experiences, and mood. The types of stimulation, as well as their effectiveness, are important pieces of information. Inquiring about her experiences of distraction will also contribute to understanding. Sexual details regarding the focus of the experience, such as timing, orgasm (the need or the experience), sexual discomfort, and partner dysfunction are also evaluated. To facilitate this process Basson uses a "quick review of assessment A-G" (p. 77): *About*— what happens, thoughts, feelings; *Both* partners' sexual response; *Context*— relationship, environment, culture, why now; *Depression*—relevant symptoms, behaviors, and cognition, as well as treatment history; *Experience*— past; *Feelings* for partner—then and generally; *General* health—medications and so on.

Couples assessment. There are significant differences in communication patterns between couples who experience sexual dysfunction in the form of an anorgasmic female partner (in a heterosexual relationship) and couples who do not have sexual dysfunction (Kelly et al., 2006). Successful sexual stimulation requires that the female partner know what she needs or wants sexually, and that information must be conveyed in a clear and nonblaming manner to a partner who is nonblaming and receptive. Anorgasmic women express more difficulty communicating comfortably regarding direct clitoral stimulation. Thus, problems with communication may be significant in the etiology and maintenance of a female orgasmic disorder. Anorgasmic women also tended to be less receptive when discussing intercourse. Men whose wives were reported to be anorgasmic also tended to be less comfortable discussing intercourse than men whose wives did not have that concern. Thus, evaluation of a couple's pattern of communication via self-report and behavioral evaluation may be important in treating female orgasmic disorder. Similarly, another study found anorgasmic women tended to report lower levels of comfort communicating than women in the control group. Reflecting the transactional nature of this dynamic, it was found that men who were partnered with anorgasmic women also reported more difficulty communicating comfortably. In addition, these men also appeared to have a less accurate view of their partner's sexual needs (Kelly et al., 2004).

Questions to consider in assessing couples may include the following (Heiman, 2007):

- How does each partner of the couple describe the problem?
- What is the affect demonstrated regarding the problem?

- How does each partner describe the level and frequency of desire, arousal, orgasm, sexual satisfaction, and genital pain?
- Are there any medical conditions that may be affecting orgasmic response?

Assessment typically takes two to three sessions, so that there is ample time spent with the identified patient who is symptomatic, as well as time spent with the couple, which provides important information about inter-actional patterns. Assessment also provides the clinician with an opportunity to frame the presenting symptoms in a more constructive manner. For example, just acknowledging that there is a need to assess whether the woman experiences adequate stimulation in their existing sexual script opens up a discussion of how they as a couple approach times of sexual intimacy and the purpose and place of intimacy in the life of the couple.

TREATMENT

When we turn our attention to treatment, we note several areas that are commonly addressed in the context of sex therapy (e.g., reducing anxiety, improving communication). For women who experience anorgasmia, the combination of sex education, strategies to reduce anxiety, directed mastur-bation, and CBT are the main tools for treatment (Brotto et al., 2010). The following principles reflect common approaches from a CBT perspective.

Education and attitude change. The CBT approach to female orgasmic disorder emphasizes a change in attitudes and thoughts that increase anxiety by increasing orgasmic ability and sexual satisfaction. Sometimes sex therapists refer to changes in attitudes as fostering a "sex positive" attitude. For example, one consideration for changing attitudes has to do with giving oneself permission to pursue sexual pleasure. Penner and Penner (1993, 2005), for instance, discuss taking "responsibility to go after sexual needs and desires" (p. 252). "It means that you give yourself permission to be sexual. You decide that you are going to actively pursue sexual feelings, expressions, and intensity. You are going to allow your body to respond and enjoy those responses" (Penner & Penner, 1993, p. 252).

Providing education around Kegel exercises and assigning them as homework can be helpful. Although Kegel exercises do not constitute evidence-based treatment for primary anorgasmia, they are believed to be useful insofar as they help a woman develop awareness of her own body, specifically her genital muscles (e.g., pubococcygeus muscles), including muscle tension and relaxation (ter Kuile et al., 2010). She can be instructed to identify the muscles she uses to stop and start the flow of urine when she urinates. She can then practice tightening the muscles, holding for a few seconds and relaxing. These can be practiced a few times each day.

Another important consideration is to teach the client to establish transition activities from her normal day and routine to the specific homework assignments that the woman (and the woman and her partner) will participate in throughout treatment. This would be about a twenty-minute activity, such as listening to soothing music, taking a bath, or using meditation.

Learning about one's body. The next step is to encourage the client to learn more about her body in general and her genitals in particular. Concerning the former, this might include time viewing herself in the mirror undressed, noting her thoughts and feelings, particularly if she were to be critical or judgmental. These thoughts and feelings can be kept in a journal and discussed in session.

Concerning the latter, a genital self-examination is often recommended. The clinician would provide the client with an appropriate image of female genitalia, often a page from a textbook with the relevant image and level of detail for identifying anatomy. The client is then instructed to take the image home and—using a handheld mirror—identify her genitalia, locating her clitoris, labia majora, labia minora, and so on. This exercise can be empowering because it gives her permission to come to a better understanding of herself as she begins to take notice of how it feels to identify and name her own genitalia. She can journal her thoughts and feelings and discuss or process her reactions in therapy.

As we suggested in chapter four, genital self-examination is a potentially powerful exercise that should be tied to specific therapeutic goals, which can often be incremental and build on each other. For instance, one goal might be to learn about oneself. Genital self-examination can also move in the direction of kinesthetic knowledge wherein the client touches herself in different ways and identifies and processes her responsiveness to various stimuli. Another possible goal would be to teach one's partner what he (or she) can do during times of sexual intimacy. Presumably, such a goal is based on improving self-understanding first, and then teaching one's partner based on what one has experienced.

Assigning an intervention like a genital self-examination can also easily be misused or misunderstood by a client, so having a more extended, intentional discussion of the intervention, its purposes, and how those purposes are tied to larger treatment goals is important. For instance, the purpose of a genital self-examination is not necessarily to experience arousal, but it could be useful in identifying what a person finds stimulating so that that information can be shared with one's partner (see Rosenau, Neel, & Fox, 2007, chap. 3, for a helpful discussion of practical issues in assigning a genital self-examination).

Kinesthetic knowledge and directed masturbation. In the treatment of orgasmic disorder in women it is common to transition at some point from genital self-examination to directed masturbation. Directed masturbation has been found to be successful as a treatment for women who experience primary orgasmic disorder. Part of the benefit may be the creation of connections between positive feelings and sexual behavior (Heiman, 2007). Various studies suggest success rates as high as 80% to 90% with directed masturbation for women who have lifelong anorgasmia (Meana, 2012). Success rates range considerably (10%-75%) in studies of women with secondary or acquired anorgasmia (Heiman, 2007).

Including and teaching one's partner based on self-knowledge. The next major principles involves having the woman take all that she has learned about herself and use that to teach her partner. This often begins with the assignment of sofa sessions and nondemand sensual touch exercises (sensate focus). Sofa sessions are intended to facilitate interpersonal communication, and as poor communication has been indicated as a factor in the experience of sexual arousal and orgasmic disorders, treatment for the disorder includes educating the client and her partner about clear, non-blaming, and receptive communication (Kelly et al., 2006). Sofa sessions entail making a list of topics for discussion and taking time to sit down together and discuss those topics (e.g., how therapy is progressing, their expectations of treatment, their sexual script, what they each prefer in terms of touch, pleasure, and intimacy).

Sensate focus involves a full-body caress, each one taking turns in giving and receiving. This is done in stages, with the first stage not including breasts and genitals, while later stages will include breast and genital stimulation and eventually intercourse. The couple can work on identifying what kinds of touch they like, as well as how they communicate preferences in a way that facilitates trust and intimacy (for an example of sensate focus, see chap. 8).

As the couple eventually moves toward breast and genital stimulation, the client can share with her partner what she has learned about her own genitalia, including what she has found arousing. For the primary anorgasmic woman, she is essentially learning to have an orgasm in the presence of her partner. The emphasis here is on her husband learning what she likes, and an exercise that has her guide her husband's hand in stimulating her can be helpful toward that end. The idea is that he is learning (based on her self-knowledge) so that they can together incorporate that understanding into their sexual script.

Although masturbation may produce an orgasm, this may not be the case when attempting sexual activity with a partner. Thus, couples treatment focuses on enhancing communication, adequate clitoral stimulation, and participating in a variety of positions during intercourse that maximize clitoral stimulation (ter Kuile et al., 2010). Many women do not experience an orgasm through penile-vaginal intercourse, so it can be helpful to the couple to incorporate genital stimulation into foreplay. They can receive education about different sexual positions that might allow access to the genitals for stimulation (e.g., female superior position). If genital stimulation occurs during intercourse, some women may prefer to stimulate themselves, while others may prefer to have their husband stimulate them.

Another technique is coital alignment, during which the male partner uses an up and down rocking motion during penetration instead of the push-pull thrust. Use of the up-down rocking motion helps to ensure that the base of the penis rubs against the clitoris, to increase clitoral stimulation (ter Kuile et al, 2010).

Differences in treatment of primary versus secondary orgasmic disorder have been noted. In treating primary orgasmic disorder, directed masturbation is a large component in addition to psychological treatment, such as encouraging positive sexual thoughts and attitudes, reducing anxiety, sensate focus exercises, and education (Meana, 2012). Treatment of secondary orgasmic disorder necessitates intervention with the couple, often includes elements of what was discussed previously, and focuses even more on relationship issues and dynamics, as well as communication and adequate clitoral stimulation (ter Kuile et al., 2010).

Additional approaches to CBT from a therapeutic perspective include psychoanalytic theory (i.e., evaluating object relations, intimate relations, ego functioning, and working through conflicts) and systems theory to understand the dynamic interactions that exist within a relationship (Heiman, 2007). It is often helpful to understand the meaning of the orgasm for the client and her partner. As such, understanding symbolic issues is a part of the process of supporting a woman who is anorgasmic and her partner. Another facet of treatment may include assessing how the clients feel about their bodies. Many anorgasmic women feel as though their body does not belong to them or that they have a diffuse sense of ownership over their bodies (Heiman, 2007).

At this time there are no approved medications used to treat female orgasmic disorder. Although testosterone has some positive effects among postmenopausal anorgasmic women, there are risks in going this route (Meana, 2012). Medications such as Viagra, Cialis, and Levitra have not thus far been shown to be effective in increasing orgasms among women, despite some positive findings in some studies (Meana, 2012). This will undoubtedly be an area for ongoing research.

Since many antipsychotics and antidepressants have adverse effects on sexual functioning, treatment may include switching to other medications that do not have this side effect. If that is not possible, reducing the medication dosage to therapeutically effective levels while absolving the deleterious effects on sexual functioning may be an option (Komisaruk et al., 2006). Other clients may plan a "drug holiday" prior to a preplanned sexual interaction.

PREVENTION

Cognitive and emotional factors are significant contributions to sexual dysfunction. When women with sexual dysfunction experience unsuccessful sexual situations, schemas related to a sense of incompetence may get triggered. For women with hypoactive sexual desire and difficulties with arousal, beliefs centered in sexual conservativism and the belief that sexual desire and pleasure are sinful have been found to be correlated. In addition, these women may also experience feelings of sadness, guilt, disillusionment, and lack of pleasure. Women with orgasmic disorders may also have maladaptive thoughts regarding body image, believing that a certain body image may be central to sexual activity. Women who have sexual desire disorders and arousal disorders are also more likely to have thoughts of failure and a lack of erotic thoughts (Nobre & Pinto-Gouveia, 2008).

Prevention of arousal and orgasmic disorders relies on understanding the role of context for women who struggle with these issues and their partners. If there are underlying unpleasant emotions, communication is likely to be inhibited, which then affects the dynamics of the relationship. Resolution may be facilitated through skills training emphasizing more accurate communication. At the same time, exposure to more effective methods of physical stimulation through directed masturbation and coital alignment is necessary to counter-condition unpleasant emotions associated with the experiences of having low arousal and anorgasmia, and to increase awareness of what feels good physically for the woman.

CLOSING REFLECTIONS

In conversation one day, a friend of ours told us about a "good, solid, Christian couple" who reported they had sex five times a week. This raised some eyebrows because this couple was reported to be in their forties with children and very busy lives. They were having sex more than the national average! While it was originally conceptualized as something to celebrate for the couple, it quickly came to light that things were not as they seemed. For one, the wife reported she had never had an orgasm in the ten-plus years she had been married, and every week in those ten years she and her husband were sexually intimate no less than five times a week. In 2,600 experiences of sexual intercourse, she had never had an orgasm. At times, she stated she felt as though it were "prostitute sex." That was disheartening to hear because it made us wonder what the messages were about sex that she and her husband believed.

This story is not uncommon in the church. Many women do not know what to do with their sexuality apart from the sociocultural messages about how women should relate to their husbands. Many women may not know what feels good to them or what would be pleasurable because they may believe that they "should not" be in touch with or express their sexual preferences. Without this knowledge it is difficult for these women to celebrate God's gift of sexual pleasure and intimacy if sex feels like a chore and something they are obligated to do. It is no wonder sexual desire and sexual arousal may be reported as low or nonexistent.

The Song of Solomon is replete with examples of desire and arousal from both a man's and a woman's perspective. The language and sentiment of the

Song of Songs are not just poetic and metaphoric; they are a realistic expression of desire and arousal of one lover for another. What would it be like if men and women were able to step outside the stereotyped patriarchal roles designated by the sociocultural messages into roles prescribed by the Song of Songs?

How beautiful your sandaled feet,
    O prince's daughter!
Your graceful legs are like jewels,
    the work of an artist's hands.
Your navel is a rounded goblet
    that never lacks blended wine.
Your waist is a mound of wheat
    encircled by lilies.
Your breasts are like two fawns,
    like twin fawns of a gazelle.
Your neck is like an ivory tower.
Your eyes are the pools of Heshbon
    by the gate of Bath Rabbim.
Your nose is like the tower of Lebanon
    looking toward Damascus.
Your head crowns you like Mount Carmel.
    Your hair is like royal tapestry;
    the king is held captive by its tresses.
How beautiful you are and how pleasing,
    my love, with your delights!
Your stature is like that of the palm,
    and your breasts like clusters of fruit.
I said, "I will climb the palm tree;
    I will take hold of its fruit."
May your breasts be like clusters of grapes on the vine,
    the fragrance of your breath like apples,
    and your mouth like the best wine.

She

May the wine go straight to my beloved,
    flowing gently over lips and teeth.
I belong to my beloved,
    and his desire is for me.
Come, my beloved, let us go to the countryside,
    let us spend the night in the villages.

Let us go early to the vineyards
    to see if the vines have budded,
if their blossoms have opened,
    and if the pomegranates are in bloom—
    there I will give you my love.
The mandrakes send out their fragrance,
    and at our door is every delicacy,
both new and old,
    that I have stored up for you, my beloved. (Song 7)

A discussion of arousal disorders and orgasmic disorders raises broad
questions about the ways that the Fall touches our lives, even the most intimate aspects of human experience. It can be difficult to sit with women
who have struggled so much to experience arousal or orgasm, experiences
that come easily to others. The clinician's own difficulties in this area (or lack
of difficulty) and the gender of the clinician can become obstacles at times.
There is also the risk that clinicians may minimize the importance of arousal
or orgasm if they are not comfortable recognizing female sexuality and en-
joyment of sexual pleasure. It is important to reflect on whether a tacit assumption about women "not really enjoying sex anyway" has entered into
the clinical work that is taking place. This idea that women are not really that
into sex is a broader sociocultural message that is often contrasted with the
image of the male who is always looking for or interested in sex. We find that
these stereotypes—particularly negative views of female sexuality and sexual
pleasure—are particularly evident in the local church. We encourage the
clinician to assess for these sociocultural messages and any related messages
from within the Christian subculture about female sexuality and sexual en-
joyment. We also encourage the clinician to focus on empathy and the validation of the experiences of women who continue to suffer from difficulties
in their experience of sexual intimacy.

One critique we would offer about the broader field of secular sex therapy
is that it too easily treats people as largely interchangeable in service of an
individual's sexual goals, in this case, orgasm. We appreciate the more holistic and relational perspective seen in Christian contributions to this discussion. We would want the Christian clinician to explore how they would
work with a woman presenting with an arousal disorder or an orgasmic
disorder—how would they address her physical, emotional, relational, and
spiritual needs? How can these needs be addressed as a couple or in service

of them as a couple rather than individual interests? We see this as an area that Christian sex therapists can develop further and make available in their work with women.

We also want to address a sensitive issue in some training contexts. The reader will note that treatment for arousal and orgasmic disorders typically includes activities that some women, particularly those who grew up in conservative families, may have apprehension about. Directed masturbation, in particular, can become a point of discussion and some ambivalence. Depending on their background, many women may not have conducted a genital self-examination or experienced self-stimulation. We invite clinicians to reflect on how you feel about this technique being a part of a treatment plan, as well as how you might respond to a client who expressed opposition to using it as an intervention.

MASTURBATION

As a Christian clinician interested in helping people navigate sexual concerns, how do you approach the subject of masturbation? It is often discussed in the context of whether it is morally appropriate and whether it is an example of either a healthy or unhealthy self-soothing activity. In work with couples there is also the question of whether and how masturbation or mutual masturbation can be incorporated into a couple's sexual script. Many married women are not orgasmic via penile-vaginal intercourse; for them, direct stimulation (by themselves or their partner) is going to be the means by which they are orgasmic.

We recognize that this is a complicated topic that deserves time and attention, as well as balanced reflection. Gerali (2003) offers one of the more helpful reflections on the topic of masturbation. He discusses it in the context of wisdom, by which he means (among other things) that it "could be sin for some and not for others" (p. 179). Reflecting carefully on Scripture, various historical considerations, and our current cultural context, Gerali wants to create an atmosphere in which Christians can search and study the Bible for principles that inform their decision making in this area.

In our experience the question of whether masturbation is right or wrong seems less salient to distressed clients than what kinds of interventions are deemed valid and reliable ways to improve orgasmic potential. In that sense we have not seen it come up as much in the treatment of sexual dysfunctions in couples. When a woman has never experienced an orgasm, for instance, the desire to experience that as a couple often supersedes the emphasis on it being right or wrong, as though it were merely a theoretical analysis. This seems especially the case when the couple is learning together what is personally and mutually stimulating so that their learned experiences can be shared toward the mutual goal of improved sexual functioning and intimacy.

As a Christian counselor you can be a resource to your clients as they ask questions or want to discuss directed masturbation further. As appropriate, you can foster in your clients a desire to grow spiritually such that they can turn to the Holy Spirit for wisdom and guidance.

In our experience, while some people respond with disapproval to the idea of directed masturbation in theory, when people present in therapy and have never experienced an orgasm with their husbands, they are quite open to nearly any interventions that might help them achieve orgasm. We are not suggesting that the ends justify the means; at the same time, we want to acknowledge that the treatment options are not merely academic. Certain techniques and interventions have been shown to be more helpful than others. When ambivalence is present, it can be discussed openly and processed in counseling. Toward that end, we can discuss directed masturbation not as an endpoint but as a transition activity to foster personal self-awareness and confidence, as well as provide information through self-knowledge that can facilitate activities to later be shared with (and enhance intimacy with) her husband. For some clients who express ambivalence about masturbation as intervention, it can be thought of as a bridge activity rather than the final stop.

It is not uncommon for women to present with concerns about arousal or orgasm in the context of the sexual response cycle. Although there are many theories about the etiology of the various concerns addressed in this chapter, there are also several strategies for assessment and intervention that have been shown to be helpful for enhancing sexual intimacy.

REFERENCES

American Psychiatric Association. (2013). *Diagnostic and statistical manual of mental disorders* (5th ed.). American Psychiatric Publishing.

American Psychiatric Association. (2022). *Diagnostic and statistical manual of mental disorders* (5th ed.-Text Revision). American Psychiatric Publishing.

Basson, R. (2008). Women's sexual desire and arousal disorders. *Primary Psychiatry, 15*(9), 72-81.

Basson, R., McInnes, R., Smith, M. D., Hodgson, G., & Koppiker, N. (2002). Efficacy and safety of sildenafil citrate in women with sexual dysfunction associated with female sexual arousal disorder. *Journal of Women's Health & Gender-Based Medicine, 11*(4), 367-77.

Both, S., Laan, E., & Schultz, W. W. (2010). Disorders in sexual desire and sexual arousal in women, a 2010 state of the art. *Journal of Psychosomatic Obstetrics & Gynecology, 31*(4), 207-18.

Brotto, L. A., Bitzer, J., Laan, E., Leiblum, S., & Luria, M. (2010). Women's sexual desire and arousal disorders. *Journal of Sex Medicine, 7*, 586-614.

Cohen, K. M., & Savin-Williams, R. C. (2017). Treating sexual problems in lesbian, gay, and bisexual clients. In Z. D. Peterson (Ed.), *The Wiley handbook of sex therapy* (pp. 291-305). John Wiley and Sons.

Davison, S. L., & Davis, S. R. (2011). Androgenic hormones and aging—the link with female sexual function. *Hormones and Behavior, 59*(5), 745-53.

DeRogatis, L. R., Laan, E., Brauer, M., Van Lunsen, R. H. W., Jannini, E., et al. (2010). Responses to the proposed DSM-V changes. *Journal of Sexual Medicine, 7*(6), 1998–2014. https://doi.org/10.1111/j.1743-6109.2010.01865.x

Donahey, K. M. (2010). Female orgasmic disorder. In S. B. Levine, C. B. Risen, & S. E. Althof (Eds.), *Handbook of clinical sexuality for mental health professionals* (2nd ed., pp. 181-92). Routledge.

Feldhahn, S., & Sytsma, M. (2023). *Secrets of sex & marriage: 8 surprises that make all the difference.* BethanyHouse.

Ferguson, D. M., Steidle, C. P., Sing, G. S., Alexander, J. S., Weihmiller, M. K., & Crosby, M. G. (2003). Randomized, placebo-controlled, double blind crossover design trial of the efficacy and safety of Zestra for Women in women with and without female sexual arousal disorder. *Journal of Sex & Marital Therapy, 29*(5), 33-44.

Gerali, S. (2003). *The Struggle.* NavPress.

Graham, C. A. (2010). The DSM diagnostic criteria for female orgasmic disorder. *Archives of Sexual Behavior, 39*, 256-70.

Grover, S., & Shouan, A. (2020). Assessment scales for sexual disorders: A review. *Journal of Psychosexual Health, 2*(2), 121-28.

Harris, J. M., Cherkas, L. F., Kato, B. S., Heiman, J. R., & Spector, T. D. (2008). Normal variations in personality are associated with coital orgasmic infrequency in hetero-sexual women: A population-based study. *Journal of Sex Medicine, 5*, 1177-83.

Heiman, J. R. (2007). Orgasmic disorders in women. In S. R. Leiblum (Ed.), *Principles and practice of sex therapy* (4th ed., pp. 90-123). Guilford.

IsHak, W. W., Bokarius, A., Jeffrey, J. K., Davis, M. C., & Bakhta, Y. (2010). Disorders of orgasm in women: A literature review of etiology and current treatments. *Journal of Sexual Medicine, 7*, 3254-68.

Kelly, M. P., Strassberg, D. S., & Turner, C. M. (2004). Communication and associated relationship issues in female anorgasmia. *Journal of Sex & Marital Therapy, 30*, 263-76.

Kelly, M. P., Strassberg, D. S., & Turner, C. M. (2006). Behavioral assessment of couples' communication in female orgasmic disorder. *Journal of Sex & Marital Therapy, 32*, 81-95.

Kleinplatz, P. J. (2011). Arousal and desire problems: Conceptual, research and clinical considerations or the more things change the more they stay the same. *Sexual and Relationship Therapy, 26*(1), 3-15.

Komisaruk, B. R., Beyer-Flores, C., & Whipple, B. (2006). *The science of orgasm*. Johns Hopkins University Press.

Liao, Q. P., Zhang, M., Geng, L., Wang, X., Song, X., Xia, P., Lu, T., . . . & Liu, V. (2008). Efficacy and safety of alprostadil cream for the treatment of female sexual arousal disorder: A double-blind, placebo-controlled study in Chinese population. *Journal of Sex Medicine, 5*, 1923-31.

Mah, K., & Binik, Y. M. (2002). Do all orgasms feel alike? Evaluating a two-dimensional model of the orgasm experience across gender and social context. *Journal of Sex Research, 39*, 104-13.

McCabe, M. P. (2009a). Anorgasmia in women. *Journal of Family Psychotherapy, 20*, 177-97.

McCabe, M. P. (2009b). Anorgasmia in women. In K. M. Hertlein, G. R. Weeks, & N. Gambescia (Eds.), *Systemic sex therapy* (pp. 212-35). Routledge.

Mcintyre-Smith, A., & Fisher, W. A. (2011). Female orgasm scale. In R. R. Milhausen, J. K. Sakaluk, T. D. Fisher, C. M. Davis, & W. L. Yarber (Eds.), *Handbook of sexuality-related measures* (3rd ed.). Routledge.

Meana, M. (2012). *Sexual dysfunction in women*. Hogrefe.

Millner, V. S. (2005). Female sexual arousal disorder and counseling deliberations. *Family Journal, 13*(1), 95-100.

Nobre, P. J., & Pinto-Gouveia, J. P. (2008). Cognitive and emotional predictors of female sexual dysfunctions: Preliminary findings. *Journal of Sex & Marital Therapy, 34*, 325-42.

Penner, J. J., & Penner, C. L. (1993). *Restoring the pleasure*. Word.

Penner, J. J., & Penner, C. L. (2005). *Counseling for sexual disorders* (2nd ed.). Word.

Rosenau, D., Neel, D. C., & Fox, W. E. (2007). *A celebration of sex guidebook*. Xulon.

Rosenbaum, T. Y. (2007). Pelvic floor involvement in male and female sexual dysfunction and the role of pelvic floor rehabilitation in treatment: A literature review. *Journal of Sex Medicine, 4*, 4-13.

ter Kuile, M. M., Both, S., & van Lankveld, J. J. D. M. (2010). Cognitive behavioral therapy for sexual dysfunctions in women. *Psychiatric Clinics of North America, 33*, 595-610.

Ullery, E. K., Millner, V. S., & Willingham, H. A. (2002). The emergent care and treatment of women with hypoactive sexual desire disorder. *The Family Journal: Counseling and Therapy for Couples and Families, 10*(3), 346-50.

Wylie, K., & Malik, F. (2009). Review of drug treatment for female sexual dysfunction. *International Journal of STD & AIDS, 20*, 671-74.

SEVEN

SEXUAL PAIN DISORDERS

WHAT ARE SOME ACTIVITIES you enjoy doing the most? Do you like to read? Go on long walks? Enjoy traveling? Or do you like taking ballroom dance lessons? How about sports—perhaps a game of golf, soccer, basketball, or another activity? Imagine for a moment doing the thing you enjoy doing the most. Now imagine experiencing pain while you are trying to do the same activity that normally brings you joy. That pain could be sharp and acute, or perhaps the pain you feel is nagging and chronic. But the pain is now there every time you engage in the activity you used to enjoy.

As you imagined some of your favorite activities, the phrase *normally brings you joy* is important. It reminds you that the things you do are not normally meant to cause you pain; quite the contrary, you normally do the things you delight in with little worry that you will feel pain throughout. (You might feel some pain after a physical activity, but that is a different matter.)

Now imagine trying to do that favorite activity while you feel pain. Maybe it is a sharp pain. Maybe you feel a dull ache or throbbing pain. Most people do not experience as much joy and delight in their favorite activities when they have to face those activities in pain. In fact, most people will avoid those activities over time.

This gives you some sense for how pain can detract from the things you enjoy doing. That can also happen with sexual intimacy. Indeed, the *DSM-5-TR* (APA, 2022, p. 493) refers to "genito-pelvic pain/penetration disorder" as a condition in which one or more of the following symptoms is present for about six months or longer:

- the inability to have vaginal penetration
- marked vulvovaginal or pelvic pain during intercourse/penetration

- significant fear or anxiety about vulvovaginal/pelvic pain or penetration
- marked tensing or tightening of pelvic floor muscles during attempted penetration

The concern could be lifelong (since the woman became sexually active) or acquired (emerging after a period of normal sexual functioning). The personal distress or impairment is clinically significant and is not attributable to another mental health disorder, and is not due to the effects of a substance, medication, or a medical condition, or severe relationship stress.

It is not clear how many women meet the criteria for genito-pelvic pain/penetration disorder. However, the *DSM-5-TR* estimates that as many as 10% to 28% of women in the United States experience recurring pain during intercourse. This is similar to international rates that range from 8% to 28% (APA, 2022, p. 495). Sexual pain disorders are not reported as often among lesbian couples as among women in heterosexual relationships. This is likely related to the emphasis on penile-vaginal intercourse for heterosexual women. Lesbian couples are also often considered more likely to be egalitarian, which may lead to different sexual habits and activities that are unlikely to contribute to pain or penetration difficulties.

One manifestation of a genito-pelvic pain/penetration disorder is not always painful but refers to vaginal tightness caused by the involuntary tightening of the pelvic floor (what had been referred to as vaginismus in *DSM-IV*). This may result in discomfort, burning, or pain, but the primary concern is with penetration or the inability to have sexual intercourse. This happens when the pubococcygeus (PC) muscle groups spasm and tighten, making insertion or penetration difficult or impossible.

Experiences of these symptoms as a penetration disorder vary among women. Some are unable to have anything inserted into their vagina at all. Other women may be able to accept a tampon and complete a gynecological exam; however, they are unable to have a penis inserted. Yet other women are able to tolerate the insertion of a penis; however, it may be painful. While the initial insertion may not create too much discomfort for some women, they are unable to proceed from arousal to orgasm because of the impending tightness and discomfort. Consequently, they experience discomfort instead of orgasm. Sometimes muscle spasms in this area contribute to muscle spasms elsewhere. Some women tolerate years of uncomfortable intercourse; however, the gradual increase in pain and discomfort interrupts their sexual experience. It is not uncommon for women to avoid sex as a result of these difficulties or for fear of failure.

Some women who suffer with genito-pelvic pain/penetration disorder may discover it the first time they attempt to have sexual intercourse. A woman's partner may not be able to achieve penetration. This would be experienced as though he bumped up against something at the opening that was blocking penetration. And this is correct: he has bumped up against the outer third of the vaginal musculature as it has contracted (or what has been referred to as vaginismus). This unique kind of genito-pelvic pain/penetration issue may be the cause of many unconsummated marriages and, as we have suggested, it is not uncommon for women with this disorder to also have difficulty with insertion of tampons or gynecological exams.

Concerns in this area may develop due to several factors, including pelvic pain as a result of a medical condition, emotional distress, the anticipation of pelvic pain, or for no reason at all. Women in all stages of life may be affected by a pain/penetration concerns; however, it is most common when there are temporary pelvic pain difficulties, such as urinary or yeast infections, menopause, surgery, or pain from birthing a child (Binik et al., 2007; Leiblum, 2000). Although the initial medical condition has been treated, the pain or problems with penetration persist. Consequently, concerns about pain/penetration may be maintained because of a conditioned response, yielding involuntary vaginal tightness when intercourse is attempted.

If concerns about pain/penetration go untreated, it tends to worsen because the PC muscle contraction increases in intensity and duration as sexual pain continues. Difficulties with pain/penetration can also inhibit the experience of orgasm because the feelings of pain may interrupt the experience of arousal.

Last, vulvodynia is the chronic pain around the opening of the vagina without any identifiable cause. Feelings of pain, burning, or irritation may cause discomfort such that sitting for a long time or having sex becomes difficult. Experiences of vulvodynia include burning, soreness, stinging, rawness, throbbing, itching, and pain during intercourse. The pain from vulvodynia may be intermittent or constant and can last for months up to years; however, the pain can also terminate for no apparent reason and without notice. The pain may be generalized to the entire vulvar area, or it can be limited to a certain area, such as the opening of the vagina.

ETIOLOGY

Both physical sources and emotional factors can cause painful intercourse. It can be difficult to discern these causal factors because unpleasant emotions often accompany physical experiences.

The pelvic floor muscles are innervated by the autonomic nervous system and sensory and motor nervous systems. The sensation of pain involves cognitive-evaluative, affective-motivational, and sensory-discriminative aspects. This multidimensional experience of pain may be due to activity from the neural network or from direct sensory output, such as in the case of injury, inflammation, or other sources of pathology (van Lankveld et al., 2010). For some individuals, pain may result from neurogenic inflammation from injury or stress. According to van Lankveld et al. (2010), "Genital pain disorder appears to be associated with *pain hypersensitivity* to both visceral and somatic stimuli. Some local hypersensitivity may result from increased innervation and/or sensitization of nociceptors in the vestibular mucosa" (p. 617). As such, provoked vestibulodynia (PVD) may develop as a result of neurogenic inflammation referred pain (i.e., peripheral tissue injury release inflammatory mediators), which leads to peripheral sensitization (i.e., neuropathic pain lowering of nociceptive thresholds), culminating in central sensitization (i.e., the systemic pain response is enhanced).

Physical factors that contribute to pain during penetration may be the result of

- *Insufficient lubrication.* Without enough foreplay, women may lack sufficient lubrication to prepare for penetration. In addition, a decrease in estrogen after menopause, after childbirth, or during breastfeeding may contribute to this. Medications, such as antidepressants, blood pressure medications, sedatives, antihistamines, and certain birth control pills may act on systems of the body that lead to dryness, making sex painful.

- *Injury, trauma, or irritation.* Accidents, pelvic surgery, episiotomy, a congenital abnormality, or female circumcision may cause pain during penetration (see Goldstein et al., 2009).

- *Inflammation, infection, or skin disorder.* Painful intercourse may be due to an infection in the genital area or a urinary tract infection. Skin problems, such as eczema, may also contribute to pain. The most common causal connections to PVD include infections, hormonal influences, psychosexual factors, and a genetic predisposition. Many women with PVD report a history of yeast infections. Chronic inflammatory conditions that frequently affect vulvar skin and mucosa include vulvar dermatoses. Genital infections including candidiasis, herpes, and bacterial vaginosis may lead to chronic pain in women who are young and highly sexually active. HPV infection can also irritate vulvar skin and mucosa (van Lankveld et al., 2010).

Pain is not always limited to initial penetration but can also be experienced during deep penetration in certain positions. Physical factors that contribute to deep pain include

- *Surgeries or medical treatments.* Treatment of issues related to the pelvic or genital area with surgery can leave scarring that may cause painful intercourse (e.g., hysterectomy). Chemotherapy and radiation for the treatment of cancer may also elicit changes that increase painful intercourse.
- *Illnesses and conditions.* Ovarian cysts, hemorrhoids, uterine fibroids, uterine prolapse, pelvic inflammatory disease, endometriosis, retroverted uterus, and cystitis can cause painful intercourse.
- *Female genital mutilation* (FGM). Female genital mutilation contributes to sexual dysfunction and loss of sexual pleasure for women. Vaginal dryness during intercourse, lack of sexual desire, and lower orgasmic frequency are just a few problems observed in circumcised women. There are four types of FGM (van Lankveld et al., 2010, pp. 619-20):

  Type I: removal of the clitoris foreskin

  Type II: removal of the clitoris with partial or total excision of the labia minora

  Type III: infibulations or pharaonic circumcision that removes the clitoris and the labia majora and minora, restricting the orificium vaginae and leaving only a small opening for urination and menstruation.

  Type IV: pricking, piercing, stretching of the clitoris or vulva, scraping of the vagina

Emotional factors may be associated with sexual activity in complicated ways and may increase sexual pain. These include

- *Stress.* Unrelated stressors may increase overall muscle tension, including pelvic floor muscles. When these are tense, they can make intercourse painful.

- *Psychological problems.* Feelings of anxiety, depression, concerns about intimacy or relational problems, and concerns with physical appearance may all contribute to pain during intercourse because of lowered levels of arousal (van Lankveld et al., 2010).

Emotional factors tend to contribute to dyspareunia because of the conditioned response of anxiety, avoidance, or fear related to physical pain. Initial experiences of pain may lead to fear that the pain will reoccur, which increases muscle tension and consequent pain. Typically, women with PVD have more difficulty with sexual arousal and lubrication during partnered activities compared with self-pleasuring and masturbation. Women with PVD tend to have more catastrophic thoughts pertaining to pain during intercourse. Women with what has been referred to as vaginismus may have increased anxiety without increases in depression; however, they also experience more difficulty with sexual desire and arousal (van Lankveld et al., 2010).

Although there may be tangible factors that contribute to the experience of painful sexual intercourse, the experience of pain is complex and involves several systems, including the sensory-discriminative, cognitive-evaluative, and affective-motivational areas. As such, this multidimensional experience may elicit pain because of "activity of neural network rather than directly by sensory input evoked by injury, inflammation, or other pathology and can even occur in the absence of an identifiable physical cause" (van Lankveld et al., 2010, p. 617). It is common for individuals who experience genital pain to also experience a hypersensitivity to pain from external stimuli.

When women present with difficulties in which penetration is difficult or impossible, the primary theory and treatment has been cognitive-behavioral insofar as it is understood to be a conditioned response associated with penetration. The cognitive dimension seen in the expectation or anticipation of pain (and associated anxiety and avoidant behaviors) upon penetration prompts contractions from the PC muscle to protect against painful intercourse. Tense PC muscles may result in sensations of pain or burning during sex and may even block penetration of the penis. However, instead of blocking the experience of pain, the tightened PC muscles cause pain.

A combination of physical and nonphysical triggers may cause the body to anticipate pain with intercourse. In reaction to the anticipated pain, the vaginal muscles automatically tighten as a protection from harm. Sex becomes painful or uncomfortable, and penetration may be difficult or even impossible with muscle tension. Further attempts at intercourse reinforce this defensive reflex response, intensifying it more. Thus begins a cycle that may be difficult to interrupt.

Nonphysical causes can include fears (e.g., fear of pain during intercourse, fear of not being healed after pelvic trauma, fear of tissue damage, fear of pregnancy, fear of a medical problem), anxiety or stress (e.g., generalized anxiety, pressure to perform, past sexual experiences that were unpleasant, negative attitude toward sex, feelings of guilt, trauma), problems with a partner (e.g., abuse, emotional distance, fear of commitment, distrust, fear of vulnerability, fear of losing control), traumatic events (e.g., past emotional, physical, or sexual abuse, witness of violence or abuse), and childhood experiences (e.g., rigid parenting, negative attitudes toward sexuality, exposure to shocking sexual experiences, poor sex education). Reissing et al. (2003) noted that in their sample, women who had difficulties with vaginal penetration (vaginismus) were twice as likely to have had experiences of sexual abuse. As with most pain patients, women with chronic sexual pain tend to have catastrophic thoughts regarding their experience of pain during intercourse and what the implications may be for this pain with respect to the impact on the relationship (van Lankveld et al., 2010).

Physical causes of difficulties with vaginal penetration can include medical conditions (e.g., urinary tract infections, yeast infections, STIs, endometriosis, genital or pelvic tumors, cysts, cancer, vulvodynia, pelvic inflammatory disease, eczema, psoriasis, vaginal prolapse), childbirth (e.g., pain from vaginal deliveries or complications with birth, C-sections), age-related changes (e.g., menopause, hormonal changes, vaginal dryness, vaginal atrophy, inadequate lubrication), temporary discomfort (e.g., related to insufficient foreplay, inadequate lubrication), pelvic trauma (e.g., pelvic surgery, difficult pelvic examinations), abuse (e.g., physical attack, physical abuse, physical assault, rape, sexual abuse or assault).

In the case of vulvodynia, possible contributing factors include injury or irritation to nerves around the vulva, past vaginal infections, skin problems or allergies, and hormonal changes. The pain and frustration from vulvodynia may inhibit sexual activity, which can then generate emotional and relational difficulties. Other complications that may contribute to vulvodynia are anxiety, depression, sleep problems, sexual dysfunction, concerns with body image, relational concerns, and life stressors.

ASSESSMENT AND CLINICAL PRESENTATION

Jaden and Olivia sat down for their first appointment. It is clear that neither knows exactly where to begin, but after the small talk subsides, Jaden finally says, "I'm not sure how to talk about it, but we have been having some difficulty and our—or her—doctor, gynecologist, really, suggested we come to see you. She can tell you more about it, but that's why we're here." As if on cue, Olivia looks up with tears in her eyes: "It is me. I have a problem that I've had now for years. But I can't have sex. It doesn't work right. We will be messing around, you know, but there is no way for us to actually have sex. I can't seem to let him in. There's something broken or something. I'm not sure. But it's been a problem for several years now. I thought it would get better, but I would say it has only gotten worse. It's just such an embarrassing thing to even talk about. We've not really told anyone."

Assessment of genito-pelvic pain/penetration disorder. It would be much easier if we could give a true-false questionnaire to our clients to assess for difficulties with sexual pain/penetration concerns; however, it is much more complicated than that. According to Lamont (2001), diagnosis of concerns associated with pain/penetration requires more than a checklist. In addition to knowledge regarding female sexual functioning (i.e., understanding sexual physiology), being comfortable discussing sexual matters and a compassionate attitude facilitates this complicated diagnosis. Asking sexually explicit questions in a manner that elicits the client's concerns about her sexual experiences in a caring manner encourages self-disclosure on a sensitive subject. It is also important to consider the interaction of physical function, relationships, and feelings.

Although the diagnosis of a genito-pelvic pain/penetration disorder is for the female partner, it is important to note that the symptoms present a problem for the couple, making this also a couple problem (Lamont, 2001). The impact of the symptoms of painful intercourse must be evaluated within the context of an assessment of the couple. As such, assessment begins by taking the history of the problem, reviewing the onset and how it has evolved into its present state. During the assessment, evaluating the couple's insight and motivation for resolving the sexual pain/penetration concerns is essential.

Assessing individual and relational factors that are both sexual and nonsexual lays the foundation for this process. Individual factors to consider during the assessment include interpersonal, sexual socialization, gender role socialization, and biological aspects (Lamont, 2001).

With respect to interpersonal factors, the following aspects require consideration: autonomy (separate functioning), competence (sense of mastery), comfort with affect (ability to experience emotions), self-esteem (feeling competent and loved), and mental status.

When assessing sexual socialization, helping the client to self-disclose information regarding familial attitudes, taboos, expectations, labels, and concerns with sexuality can provide the clinician with important perspectives regarding the client's feelings and behaviors. Specifically, identifying the client's sexual knowledge and myths, as well as her attitudes toward sensual and sexual pleasure, is imperative. During this portion of the assessment, the client may also disclose information regarding gender role socialization, that is, her sense of being female within a learned or cultural context. It will include her understanding of what appropriate behaviors are for males and females.

Finally, biological factors to be assessed include any organic disorders that may directly affect various aspects of the sexual response cycle. These include dermatological conditions that may affect the tissue of the vagina and vestibule, painful ulcers, or other biological influences, including medications used currently or previously, and previous surgical procedures.

There are rating scales specific to pain/penetration concerns that can be used (Grover & Shouan, 2020). These include the Multidimensional Vaginal Penetration Disorder Questionnaire (MVPDQ) (Molaeinezhad et al., 2014) and the Vaginal Penetration Cognition Questionnaire (VPCQ) (Klaassen & Ter Kuile, 2009). There is also a partner-version of the MVPDQ that can be administered (Molaeinezhad et al., 2014).

When assessing for sexual pain/penetration concerns, the clinician needs to acquire a detailed description of the pain and the extent to which it interferes with sexuality, relationships, and personal well-being. Some clinicians may find it helpful to use a self-report measure, such as the Brief Index of Sexual Functioning for Women (Rosen et al., 2011). The clinician should discuss with the client the location of the pain, quality of pain, intensity of pain, elicitors of pain, time course (inception and duration), and what having painful intercourse means to the client (Binik et al., 2000). These pieces of information provide important insight into the client's experience and also validate the client's pain. It is assumed that psychosexual conflicts, relationship strain, or personal distress are just as likely to be the result of as the cause of the pain. However, the experience of pain is not just subjective; it is also a physical experience. No pain case should be treated without evaluation from a good gynecologist and possibly a pain specialist or physical therapist.

Describing pain. As assessment moves into descriptions of pain, including the quality of pain, the sources of pain, and so on, it is often beneficial to have the client maintain a pain diary. You want the client to become an expert on her own experience. This is a personal, intimate, and empowering way of tracking the situations and activities that lead up to the experience of pain; thoughts and feelings before, during, and after the pain; any attempts to reduce the pain; and the effectiveness of the attempts. The act of journaling is empowering in that it creates a framework for understanding pain through personal theories, descriptions, ratings, and so on. The client is mapping her experience with pain rather than feeling helpless in response to pain.

When querying about *location* of the pain, a simple question may be, Where exactly do you feel pain (Binik et al., 2000, p. 154)? It can be helpful to use an illustration from a book of the vulva, vagina, and pelvic region to see whether the client can point to a location. If the client can identify a specific location, then we think of it as localized (or restricted or limited to a specific area). If the client has difficulty pointing to it in a diagram, it may not be localized—it may travel from one area to another.

Along these lines Binik et al. (2000) suggest it may be helpful to ask whether the pain is vulvar (by the opening) or vaginal (deeper), or some combination that resonates with the client's sense of location. This information can also be kept in the client's pain diary, and any changes in location can be noted over the next few weeks.

Another question that may give insight to the pain is, Can your gynecologist create a similar pain during an examination (Binik et al., 2000)? If the client cannot answer these questions, would she be willing to do a self-examination to aid in determining location? The purpose in doing so would be for her to identify where the pain is and to begin to get an idea of what is likely to contribute to the pain. Using the gynecological exam as an opportunity for education, it can be a therapeutic experience. Measuring pain sensitivity by palpating different areas of the vulva with a cotton swab in a random manner to prevent sensitization is helpful. A vulvalgesiometer, which measures changes in pressure-pain sensitivity, has been developed to assist in the quantification of pain (van Lankveld et al., 2010). Using a multidisciplinary approach, the authors suggest that six areas be attended to: the mucous membrane, pelvic floor, sexual and relationship function, the experience of pain, psychosocial adjustment, and the presence of female genital mutilation or sexual abuse.

For some clients, vaginal irritations (at either the opening or barrel) can cause pain with no specific, identifiable disease present. Although lubricant may be helpful and has frequently been tried (or at least recommended previously), it does not treat the cause. The pain may be due to thinning of vaginal walls related to aging. Assessing the client's diet and birth control pills may be helpful. It may also be possible that the client is reacting to her partner's seminal fluid. In that instance, it has been recommended to have the client's partner use a condom and see whether there is a difference (Penner & Penner, 2005).

Sharp pain may be the result of tears or fissures in the vagina or hymen, which can cause pain upon entry. The client could have sharp, stabbing pain associated with deep thrusting, which may suggest that she has a tipped or retroverted uterus so that the cervix of the uterus is being bumped with deep thrusts. Other causes of pain could include endometriosis, ovarian cysts, pelvic inflammatory disease, or a misplaced intrauterine device (IUD) (which can cause pain upon thrusting). The client may also have pain from childbirth trauma (i.e., sensitive scar tissue from the episiotomy, an incision between the vagina and rectum to assist the birth process) or tears in the ligaments that hold the uterus in place, in the vaginal wall, or around the opening of the vagina.

When asking about the *quality* of the pain, descriptions may include "burning," "dull," "sharp," and "shooting" (Binik et al., 2000, p. 159). The client may be able to provide her own metaphors to help the clinician understand the nature of the pain.

Understanding *pain elicitors* and *time course* requires the therapist to understand what activities, in addition to intercourse, elicit the pain and how long the pain lasts once it begins (Binik et al., 2000). Is it seconds? Minutes? Hours? Days? Does it vary from episode to episode, or is the time course more consistent? Most people have tried some type of coping activity. Is there anything that has been used or a step that she takes that relieves the pain? Is there anything that she knows increases the pain?

Asking the client about her subjective experience of *intensity* of pain during intercourse can be helpful (Binik et al., 2000). She can rate the intensity during coitus versus other times on a ten-point scale in which one equals "no pain" and ten is "the worst it has ever been." Binik et al. also have each woman rate how distressing the pain is. So, a one means it is "not at all distressing" while a ten means "the most distressing it has ever been." Again, the client can keep this information in her pain diary and track any changes throughout the course of treatment.

Inquiring about the *meaning* of the pain during intercourse can provide important information regarding her attitudes, beliefs, and concerns about sex. What is the client's personal theory of the causes or meaning of having pain during intercourse (Binik et al., 2000)? What can she point to that seems to support her beliefs? The clinician is not challenging her personal theory; if anything, there is a sense in which we are validating her experience of pain—something that may have been dismissed by other health care professionals. We are listening and providing a safe place for her to share her pain, how she has made sense of it in the past, and how she has coped.

Assessing the couple. Clinicians will have their own preferences for how to conduct assessment. When we work with couples, we tend to meet with them together, followed by individual interviews with both partners, followed by a feedback session with them as a couple. This allows us to see them as a couple and track their interaction style but also have individual sessions to hear more about each person's specific theories, concerns, emotional state, and so on. The feedback session allows us to frame the issue in a way that leads into a helpful treatment plan by virtue of how we conceptualize the presenting concern, past attempts to address it, and helpful strategies for moving forward with treatment.

When assessing the couple, there are both relationship and sexual factors to assess. The relationship factors include communication, negotiation, and support, while the sexual factors to consider include sexual function, range of behaviors, satisfaction, and experience with reproduction (Lamont, 2001). For some couples painful intercourse may be related to conflict regarding sexual boredom, sexual techniques, sexual timing, frequency of sexual intimacy, priorities in relationship, contraception, infertility treatments, or family size. Poor and difficult communication between members of the couple likely contributes to the aforementioned factors.

Remember the visualization exercise at the start of this chapter? We asked you to take a favorite activity and then imagine having acute or chronic pain when engaging in that activity. Many people who face such a situation tend to avoid the activity. The same thing can happen with sexual intimacy. The couple can avoid sexual intercourse and any other sexual activity. What the clinician can do is help the couple acknowledge that they have avoided sex, discuss whether pain may be one of several reasons for avoiding sex, and then begin to identify any unhelpful "beliefs, inhibitions, or maladaptive attitudes about pain and sex" (Bergeron et al., 2010, p. 206). We will discuss this more in the section that follows, but activities like sensate focus exercises can reintroduce pleasurable sexual activities that are free from pain.

Many couples may have made their own assessment and laid blame on one another, although typically the blame is placed on the woman. There is a tendency to view painful intercourse as a linear (cause and effect) problem that "she has" rather than to take a more expanded view of the possible causes of painful intercourse and the history of how they as a couple have responded to the challenge of painful sex, as well as how they have treated one another in the process. It is quite understandable for people to avoid painful activities, so the clinician can help either (or both) move away from blame and criticism toward a more constructive frame. A feedback session that allows you as a clinician to reflect on case conceptualization and treatment planning will allow you to foster a new way of thinking about the presenting concern and get them into a mindset for making movement forward and in a healthy direction.

TREATMENT

According to van Lankveld et al. (2010), better outcomes in treatment are related to the following:

- attributing sexual pain to psychological causes
- feeling positive toward her own genitalia
- desiring pregnancy
- increased sexual knowledge
- compliance with assigned homework in sex therapy
- increased marital satisfaction in the female partner with sexual pain

Negative outcomes in treatment are related to the following:

- problems with sexual desire pretreatment
- fears related to STIs
- exposure to negative sexual attitudes from parents
- previous operations for vaginismus
- any organic abnormality
- sexual dysfunction in either partner
- history of sexual abuse

Treatment of genito-pelvic pain/penetration disorder will be determined by the outcomes of assessment with respect to the individual, the couple, and the physical examination (i.e., pelvic exam), as well as which symptoms are particularly salient. The first step in treatment is psychoeducation regarding the experience of genito-pelvic pain or penetration concerns in addition to communication that there are steps that can be taken to help reach attainable goals for reducing and coping with pain and improving relationship intimacy.

Utilization of individual therapy may be beneficial for addressing intrapersonal concerns, fears, and other aspects that contribute to pain during intercourse. It is common to use behavioral therapy to address patterns of avoidance that maintain the cycle of pain. Insight-oriented therapy may be helpful regarding attempts to change emotions. Couples therapy can be used to address problems with communication. Specifically, behavioral techniques such as systematic desensitization may be helpful for building up to vaginal insertion of the penis; however, it may begin with use of dilators or even the client's own fingers so that she can get feedback regarding contraction and relaxation of different muscles in her vagina.

Treatment requires interaction between all the physicians and treatment providers. As such, it is a multidisciplinary approach involving consultation between the gynecologists, clinicians/sex therapists, physical therapists, or pain specialists (Bergeron et al., 2010). The goals of therapy include reducing, managing, and coping with the pain; dealing with the consequences of having pain (at an individual level and as a couple); and cultivating an enjoyable sex life (Binik et al., 2000).

The least invasive form of treatment is usually recommended as the first step (Binik et al., 2000). As such, treatment often comprises a psychosocial element, including cognitive-behavioral interventions for pain, couples

therapy, hypnosis, relaxation, biofeedback, and sex therapy, utilizing interventions such as sensate focus, Kegel exercises, and vaginal dilation. Medical
and surgical interventions include management of diet, use of medications,
topical applications, laser surgery, and vestibulectomy.

Pain management also requires a multimethod approach. Since not just
one member of the couple is affected, communication is necessary. It is
important for the female to communicate to her partner about the pain,
letting him know that she feels pain so the activity can change without necessarily hindering intimacy. It is also beneficial for the female to identify
when the pain comes and how long it lasts, where it is located, and what type
of pain is experienced in the moment. We see this as beneficial to her (for
her own self-understanding) and potentially valuable for her to share with
her partner to enhance sexual intimacy.

Instead of suffering silently with the pain, pain management also requires
that the client has confidence in her ability to take charge of her pain by
relieving it. Medication, topical applications, and so on may be ways of
alleviating pain.

It is often beneficial for couples to use this time of treatment as an opportunity to discover other pleasurable activities that promote emotional
and relational intimacy, not just physical or sexual, instead of focusing solely
on the problem of pain.

When the primary concerns associated with a genito-pelvic pain/
penetration disorder center on vaginal penetration during intercourse, some
specific goals can be a part of treatment planning. These include (1) work
through psychological conflicts that may be impeding sexual intimacy,
(2) build trust between the client and her partner to give and receive sexual
pleasure, (3) gain genital control over the PC floor muscles that spasm
to create the pain, and (4) achieve penile-vaginal penetration (Reissing
et al., 2003).

If the client is using self-dilation for treating concerns about vaginal penetration, she should be referred for an exam with a gynecologist knowledgeable about this condition. We should note that we recently treated
a young woman whose source of pain actually stemmed from a long-
unidentified cyst, and the difficulties were made worse by clumsy and insen-
sitive gynecological exams, so it may be more difficult to rebuild trust under
these circumstances. It will be important to familiarize yourself with good
local referrals to sensitive and competent gynecologists in your area.

The clinician can begin psychotherapy to deal with a woman's expectations and aversions, and to teach cognitive strategies to manage catastrophization and hypervigilance. It is possible that if the woman experienced unwanted sexual experiences as a child, the development of positive cognitive representations of herself and her sexuality may have been affected (Reissing, 2003). During this time, it is important to ban intercourse, which will require her partner's understanding and support. Therapy can provide an essential source of support not only for the client but also her partner and for them together as a couple. During this time in treatment, the therapist focuses on building an alliance with the client and her partner (if it is couples therapy), educating her about the process of treatment and various modalities, and identifying goals. A key component of treatment in this phase is relaxation therapy, which can also support an overall sense of mastery in the client as she learns to manage her anxiety and concerns through intentional relaxation of large and small muscle groups. Kegel exercises are often prescribed to maximize the client's sense of control over her vaginal area.

It may be beneficial for the client to work with a physical therapist trained in treating sexual dysfunction. The goal of gaining control over her vagina requires releasing involuntary tightness of the pelvic floor muscles, especially the PC muscles. These muscles are trained to eliminate involuntary muscle reactions that produce pain or tightness (Rosenbaum, 2007).

Although a self-directed dilation program is a possibility, it needs to not be attempted too early (Binik et al., 2007). When it is appropriate to proceed with a self-directed program of dilation, it can be done with a set of dilators. The client can work with her sex therapist and with as-needed consultation with her gynecologist on the self-directed dilation program. Implementation of a self-directed program accomplishes a couple of things: It develops and structures the client's control over her own body. In the event that she may have a partner who struggles with clumsiness, insensitivity, or lack of awareness, a self-directed program directs their interaction. It also provides an opportunity for in-vivo desensitization, that is, desensitization in the moment (Meana, 2012).

Systematic desensitization during the ban on intercourse can include use of sensate focus to teach relational change and increase each partner's awareness. Sensate focus begins with no genital contact, but sensual touch of other body parts is encouraged. This is also an opportunity for couples to increase intimacy while there is a ban on intercourse.

When the woman is able to fully dilate herself, treatment transitions to having her partner dilate the client under her direction. She can essentially teach her partner what she has been learning. When the largest dilator is easily encompassed by the client, it is time to move toward penile-vaginal penetration with dilation before, ample lubrication, and gradual entry with the woman controlling it. She would then be in the female-superior position for intercourse. In this phase, the penis is passively contained by the woman until she decides that she is ready to induce movement. Although thrusting may not cause pain, it is important for the couple to use dilation prior to intercourse for several months after successfully experiencing penetration. It is common for couples to experience setbacks in spite of successful treatment; the clinician can discuss this with them in advance and set reasonable expectations, as well as predict problems and setbacks and prepare the couple for them.

Although there are few controlled outcome studies, treatment typically entails use of insertion training and self-dilation at some point. To enhance the effects of treatment, relaxation exercises are taught in conjunction. For some women systematic desensitization using a hierarchy of situations involving imaginal vaginal insertion, from the smallest cotton swab to the largest penis, may be helpful.

However, dilation should not be done too soon, nor should it be approached mechanistically. Rather, it should be considered in the larger context of a well-thought-out treatment plan that fosters times of sexual intimacy. Key considerations in facilitating sexual intimacy include setting aside time for one another, building desire and arousal, and fostering feedback-rich communication (rather than punitive communication) (Meana, 2009).

Recent discussions among professionals have moved away from too much emphasis on penetration and the elimination of pain as a measure of successful treatment (so, less emphasis on self-dilation) and more discussion around improved sexual intimacy and functioning, broadly defined (Bergeron et al., 2010). As Bergeron et al. note, clinicians can organize their treatment around both pain reduction goals and sexual intimacy goals to make sure that both areas of concern are addressed throughout the course of treatment.

Vulvodynia. Treatment for vulvodynia, which is pain around the opening of the vagina, focuses on relieving symptoms. Although there are different options for symptom relief, no one treatment works for every woman with vulvodynia. As such, it may be a combination of treatments that works best.

Medication treatment may include use of tricyclic antidepressants or anticonvulsants for reducing chronic pain. Antihistamines can help to reduce itching. Biofeedback therapy can be helpful for reducing pain by cuing relaxation of the pelvic muscles, which tend to contract in anticipation of pain and increase chronic pain. Ointments such as lidocaine have provided temporary symptom relief prior to sexual intercourse for some women (Goldstein & Burrows, 2008); however, the numbing effects may also affect the woman's partner. Topical corticosteroids and topical antifungals do not appear to improve vulvodynia in most cases (Goldstein & Burrows, 2008). However, some women who do not experience relief from the topical treatments report benefits from intralesional injections of triamcinolone acetonide (a synthetic corticosteroid) and bupivacaine (an anesthetic or numbing agent) (Goldstein & Burrows, 2008). Pelvic floor therapy with a physical therapist has also been helpful for strengthening muscles that support the uterus, bladder, and bowels associated with vulvodynia. An additional option is surgery (i.e., vestibulectomy) to remove affected skin and tissue for women who do not respond to these other less-invasive interventions.

Interventions helpful for reducing pelvic floor tension include pelvic floor physical therapy, CBT, Kegel and relaxation exercises, vaginal electromyography (EMG) biofeedback, transcutaneous electrical nerve stimulation (TENS), and local anesthetic nerve blockade (van Lankveld et al., 2010).

PREVENTION

It may be beneficial for couples to manage sexual pain by changing the sexual routine. One suggestion is to change positions. Some women may experience pain during sexual intercourse because the penis strikes the cervix or puts pressure on the pelvic floor muscles during thrusting. This in turn may cause aching or cramping. By changing positions, such that the woman is on top of her partner during sex, the woman gains control and is able to regulate the depth of penetration so that it is comfortable.

Aside from making a physical change, it is important for the woman experiencing dyspareunia to communicate with her partner about what feels good and what does not. If she needs her partner to slow down and to take more time with foreplay to increase lubrication, that is an important need.

Some women need longer foreplay in order to feel more fully aroused prior to penetration, which can decrease the likelihood of pain.

Use of lubricants can also help reduce discomfort during sexual intercourse. Lubricants should not contain propylene glycol, which can cause irritation. Natural oils (such as olive oil) can be used. It may be included as part of foreplay, which can reduce any feelings of shame or discomfort about having to use a lubricant.

Managing vulvodynia. Goldstein, Pukall, and Goldstein (2011) offer a helpful guide to treatment based on a distinction between generalized vulvodynia (GVD) and provoked vestibulodynia (PVD). The treatment of GVD needs to be individualized, but some women have found certain treatments helpful. Topical treatments, such as anesthetic ointments and creams (e.g., lidocaine), are often a good resource. We have not found topical steroids or topical antifungals to be helpful, although they are often prescribed. Oral medications, such as tricyclic antidepressants (e.g., Elavil) and selective norepinephrine reuptake inhibitors (e.g., Effexor XR, Cymbalta), and anticonvulsants (e.g., Neurontin) may help alleviate pain. Injections of an anesthetic into the nerves believed to be causing the pain are being studied. Physical therapy and biofeedback have also been helpful to many women suffering from GVD.

Various other recommendations may be helpful, including use of all-cotton underwear (with no detergent or fabric softener), hypoallergenic soaps and creams, dye-free cotton, unscented menstrual pads or tampons, lubricants (not containing propylene glycol), and washing the vulvar area with warm water after urination (Goldstein et al., 2011).

Provoked vestibulodynia (PVD) is sometimes referred to as vestibulodynia or vulvar vestibulitis syndrome. It refers to "pain in the vulvar vestibule that occurs in response to some type of contact" (Goldstein et al., 2011, p. 79).

CLOSING REFLECTIONS

Painful intercourse is cited as one of the most common causes of unconsummated marriages, which can contribute to feelings of shame, guilt, frustration, and anger in those relationships. Helping couples to manage their emotions during this time, focusing on what they are able to do together—versus what they are not able to do just yet (i.e., intercourse)—can help to promote intimacy in an area of their lives that may feel vapid and stagnant.

Some couples may unknowingly participate in the proliferation of myths about sexual intimacy and sexual intercourse that they have been exposed to through media, friends, books, and other influences with expectations about what their sex lives "should be." This puts undue pressure on the partner with a genito-pelvic pain/penetration disorder.

Other clients make a deal with God. The basic arrangement is that if they are good they will not have any sexual difficulties. In cases where they do struggle with a sexual dysfunction, it can lead to significant obstacles in the person's relationship with God. For example, we once provided treatment to a young Christian woman and her husband, and in one of the early assessment interviews, she shared how she had been a "good girl," by which she meant she had not had premarital sex, nor had she even kissed a boy until she was engaged to be married to her husband. She was absolutely devastated to then struggle with the inability to experience vaginal penetration during intercourse, a struggle that began on their honeymoon and meant that their marriage was unconsummated some three years later (when she was coming in for treatment). There are some unique situations that religious clients face—situations that at times reflect bargaining with God.

Of course, we can all be tempted to do this, to say to ourselves (or in a silent prayer steeped in assumptions), "If I do ___, God will provide me with ___." In our experience, when applied in the domain of sexuality, sexual intimacy, and behavior, there can be tremendous frustration, anger, and resentment toward God for not living up to his end of the bargain. This clinical presentation takes time and needs to be responded to with patience and sensitivity, as do all feelings of injury. It may be an opportunity to explore and process a person's emotional experience of God (see Moriarty, 2006).

Relationship problems may also surface with these kinds of implicit faith deals or arrangements. If as a couple they did more than one had wanted to, or if one or both regrets the level of sexual activity either one or both engaged in prior to marriage, any sexual difficulties can quickly represent punishment to them. This is also an area for discussion and represents an important issue to work through together.

Consider this: treatment of a genito-pelvic pain/penetration disorder is not restricted to physical treatment of symptoms. It is also treatment of the heart for the couple who struggles with the pain—emotional, physical, and relational—associated with these symptoms. As such, encouraging grace, love, patience, kindness, faithfulness, joy, peace, goodness, and self-control before, during, and after treatment is necessary for helping the couple move beyond their pain.

REFERENCES

American Psychiatric Association. (2022). *Diagnostic and statistical manual of mental disorders* (5th ed.-Text Revision). American Psychiatric Publishing.

Bergeron, S., Meana, M., Binik, Y. M., & Khalife, S. (2010). Painful sex. In S. B. Levine, C. B. Risen, & S. E. Althof (Eds.), *Handbook of clinical sexuality for mental health professionals* (2nd ed., pp. 193-214). Taylor & Francis.

Binik, Y. M., Bergeron, S., & Khalife, S. (2000). Dyspareunia. In S. R. Leiblum & R. C. Rosen (Eds.), *Principles and practice of sex therapy* (3rd ed., pp. 154-80). Guilford.

Binik, Y. M., Bergeron, S., & Khalife, S. (2007). Dyspareunia and vaginismus: So-called sexual pain. In S. R. Leiblum (Ed.), *Principles and practice of sex therapy* (4th ed., pp. 124-56). Guilford.

Cohen, K. M., & Savin-Williams, R. C. (2017). Treating sexual problems in lesbian, gay, and bisexual clients. In Z. D. Peterson (Ed.), *The Wiley handbook of sex therapy* (pp. 291-305). John Wiley and Sons.

Goldstein, A., Pukall, C., & Goldstein, I. (Eds.). (2009). *Female sexual pain disorders*. Blackwell.

Goldstein, A., Pukall, C., & Goldstein, I. (2011). *When sex hurts: A woman's guide to banishing pain*. Da Capo.

Goldstein, A. T., & Burrows, L. (2008). Vulvodynia. *Journal of Sexual Medicine, 5,* 1-15.

Grover, S., & Shouan, A. (2020). Assessment scales for sexual disorders: A review. *Journal of Psychosexual Health, 2*(2), 121-28.

Klaassen, M., & Ter Kuile, M. M. (2009). Development and initial validation of the vaginal penetration cognition questionnaire in a sample of women with vaginismus and dyspareunia. *Journal of Sexual Medicine, 6,* 1617-27.

Lamont, J. A. (2001). Dyspareunia and vaginismus. In J. J. Sciarra, S. Dooley, R. Depp, J. R. Lurain, A. Kaunitz, A. David, & M. D. Eschenbach (Eds.), *Gynecology and obstetrics*. Lippincott, Williams & Wilkins. www.glowm.com/resources/glowm/cd/pages/v6/v6c102.html?SESSID=qsat754u3afo9ps5slsiuiofv4

Leiblum, S. R. (2000). Vaginismus: A most perplexing problem. In S. R. Leiblum & R. C. Rosen (Eds.), *Principles and practice of sex therapy* (3rd ed., pp. 181-202). Guilford.

Meana, M. (2009). Painful intercourse: Dyspareunia and vaginismus. In K. M. Hertlein, G. R. Weeks, & N. Gambescia (Eds.), *Systemic sex therapy* (pp. 237-62). Routledge.

Meana, M. (2012). *Sexual dysfunction in women*. Hogrefe.

Molaeinezhad, M., Khoei, E. M., Salehi, M., Yousefy, A., & Roudsari, R. L. (2014). Validation of the partner version of the multidimensional vaginal penetration disorder questionnaire: A tool for clinical assessment of lifelong vaginismus in a sample of Iranian population. *Journal of Education and Health Promotion, 3,* 214-17.

Molaeinezhad, M., Roudsari, R. L., Yousefy, A., Salehi, M., & Khoei, E. M. (2014). Development and validation of the multidimensional vaginal penetration disorder questionnaire for assessment of lifelong vaginismus in a sample of Iranian women. *Journal of Research in Medical Sciences, 19,* 336-48.

Moriarty, G. (2006). *Pastoral care of depression: Helping clients heal their relationship with God.* Routledge.

Penner, J., & Penner, C. (2005). *A clinician's guide to sex therapy* (2nd ed.). Word.

Reissing, E. D., Binik, Y. M., Khalife, S., Cohen, D., & Amsel, R. (2003). Etiological correlates of vaginismus: Sexual and physical abuse, sexual knowledge, sexual self-schema and relationship adjustment. *Journal of Sex & Martial Therapy, 29,* 47-59.

Rosen, R. C., Taylor, J. F., & Leiblum, S. R. (2011). Brief index of sexual functioning for women. In T. D. Fisher, C. M. Davis, W. L. Yarber, & S. L. Davis (Eds.), *Handbook of sexuality-related measures* (3rd ed., pp. 289-90). Routledge.

Rosenbaum, T. Y. (2007). Pelvic floor involvement in male and female sexual dysfunction and the role of pelvic floor rehabilitation in treatment: A literature review. *Journal of Sex Medicine, 4,* 4-13.

van Lankveld, J. J. D. M., Granot, M., Weimjar Schultz, W. C. M., Binik, Y. M., Wesselmann, U., Pukall, C. F., . . . & Achtrari, C. (2010). Women's sexual pain disorders. *Journal of Sex Medicine, 7,* 615-31.

EIGHT

ERECTILE DISORDER

IMAGINE YOU WERE A MAN who volunteered for a clinical trial of UK92480, a new substance in line as a treatment for angina. Keep in mind that angina is a heart condition that involves chest pain or discomfort that results from a lack of blood and oxygen to heart muscle. So you are not feeling great. The substance was being developed and studied through the Pfizer laboratory near Sandwich, England, a small town on the southeast coast. The thought at the time was that UK92480 blocked the phosphodiesterase type 5 enzyme (PDE5). What UK92480 was designed to do was increase blood flow to the heart muscle by blocking PDE5. Well, it may have blocked PDE5, but it did not treat angina all that well. Interestingly, some of the men in the trials reported an unusual side effect from taking UK92480: penile erections. So began the history behind the accidental discovery of what we today know as Viagra.

No one at that time could have anticipated the impact Viagra would have on society. As we shared in chapter four, not only would we begin to hear about erectile disorder (ED) from then-Senator Bob Dole, but it would change family discussions around the television for the next generation. We are talking, of course, about the proliferation of advertising for the major PDE5 inhibitors—first Viagra and now Levitra and Cialis. The so-called family hour, 8-9 p.m., is now as prime a spot as any for watching the latest ads for these miracle cures. We see men and women giving one other suggestive looks as they are ready "anytime" for sexual intimacy. This has certainly led to some interesting family discussions prompted by curious children. The discussion of the treatment of ED has never been so open and forthcoming, nor has the intervention ever been as effective as it is today.

ED refers to the inability to achieve or maintain an adequate erection for sexual activity. The *DSM-5-TR* looks at one of three symptoms being present in all or almost all occasions of sexual activity:

1. Marked difficulty in obtaining an erection during sexual activity.
2. Marked difficulty in maintaining an erection until the completion of sexual activity.
3. Marked decrease in erectile rigidity. (APA, 2022, p. 481)

In addition, ED can be lifelong (since the person became sexually active) or acquired (it occurred after a time of normal functioning). As with other sexual disorders, ED can be generalized, or not limited to specific stimulations, situations, or partners, or situational (limited to specific stimulations, situations, or partners).

ED is a fairly common concern among men, particularly as they age. In some studies, while fewer than 10% of men under the age of thirty report concerns with erectile dysfunction, this increases as men age, with about half of men over the age of sixty expressing concern about erectile dysfunction (Rosen, 2007). And, of course, men can experience ED on a continuum, from mild to moderate to severe ED.

ED is reported at higher rates among gay males than heterosexual males (Barbonetti et al., 2019). Risk factors include older age, lack of consistent partner, positive HIV status, use of SSRIs, and substance use, including alcohol (Cohen & Savin-Williams, 2017). Each of these areas would be important to assess and take into consideration in treatment planning.

In terms of diagnostic considerations, experts typically think of ED in terms of *organic* (such as vascular or hormonal causes) or *psychogenic* (suggesting a psychological rather than organic cause). A number of health concerns are correlated with erectile disorders, especially cardiovascular disease, hypertension, and diabetes. Medications frequently used to treat these health concerns may also place a man at risk for ED. Other predictors of ED include obesity, smoking, and lack of exercise.

ETIOLOGY

Most experts today agree that there are multiple factors that may contribute to ED. From a biopsychosocial perspective these include biological considerations, such as vascular, neurologic, pharmacologic, and hormonal influences; psychological issues, particularly cognitive and lifestyle considerations; and sociocultural issues, such as messages men receive about what it means to be sexual as a man.

We mentioned earlier that a number of health concerns are correlated with ED, including cardiovascular disease, hypertension, and diabetes. In fact, ED may itself be an early warning sign of cardiovascular disease, so the relationship can go in either direction (Althof & Rosen, 2010). The medications used to treat these health concerns may also contribute to sexual dysfunction.

Other medical conditions have also been associated with ED. These include prostate cancer (and its treatment), lung disease, thyroid issues, and epilepsy (Gambescia et al., 2009). A number of medications can also affect erectile functioning, including selective serotonin reuptake inhibitors (SSRIs) and other antidepressant medications, hormonal agents, antihypertensives, and anticonvulsants (Gambescia et al., 2009).

When we consider the role of psychological factors in ED, we have to look at such things as performance anxiety, various cognitive distortions, insufficient stimulation, and relationship conflicts. Of these, perhaps more attention has been given to performance anxiety. This was originally thought of as what sex therapists refer to as "spectatoring," or the act of being a spectator of one's own sexual event. Being a spectator makes it difficult to be engaged and active in the actual sexual activity. Today we think about performance anxiety this way, but we also recognize that it can reflect a worry the man has that he will be unable to have an adequate erection. This can translate into a fear of failure that extends beyond the act of spectatoring.

Distractions can also play a role in reduced sexual arousal among men and women (Rosen, 2007). Distractions reflect "alterations in perceptual and attentional processes" that may distinguish men who report ED (p. 288). For example, the distraction of obligations in work, household chores, and so on has been cited as a significant factor in decreased sexual arousal in Basson's theory (2007) of the sexual arousal cycle in women. For men these distractions can include fantasies or other sources of visual stimulation observed during the day that intrude in the midst of sexual intimacy with their partner. But distractions can be a phone call, a knock at the door, or some other minor occurrence that divides the attention.

It is also important to consider whether the man is receiving adequate stimulation. It is not uncommon for men as they age to need more physical stimulation than was needed when they were younger in order for them to achieve a sustained erection.

Of course, relationship conflicts can also factor into ED. Conflicts can have nothing to do with sexual arousal, of course. However, among aging men, it is possible that their partner may misattribute sexual nonrepon-siveness to something other than normal changes in aging (Rosen, 2007). Such a misunderstanding can contribute to relationship conflicts because it likely hinders communication about sexual intimacy and responsiveness.

In addition to biological and psychological issues, possible sociocultural messages may affect sexual functioning. An area often discussed in the literature is sociocultural messages men receive about what it means to be a man, including "traditional male attitudes toward sexuality" (Rosen, 2007, p. 287).

ASSESSMENT AND CLINICAL PRESENTATION

Antoine is a thirty-nine-year-old African American man who has been married to his wife, Donna, for nineteen years. They have two children to-gether, ages sixteen and thirteen. Antoine works as an independent consultant today, having retired from the Navy this past year. He sits down in the thera-pist's office and, having discussed the traffic congestion, the warm and humid weather, and how hard it was to find the office, finally finds the words to de-scribe his concern: "I'm having difficulty in functioning . . . I'm not sure how to describe it, and it's hard for me. As a man, I'm having a difficult time being able to function . . . to have sex the way that I used to. I'm not sure what's hap-pened. I've never really had trouble in this area. I mean, we have two children, we have a happy marriage, and we love each other. I mean, I love my wife. That's not it, at least I don't think that's it. But I'm not able to be as ready as I used to be . . . for sex, I mean. It is taking longer to 'be ready,' if you know what I mean."

Antoine and Donna are going through a difficult time in their marriage. They are struggling with symptoms of an erectile dysfunction, and Antoine is having a difficult time even talking about it, which is not an uncommon experience in sex therapy. It can be challenging for men to disclose what they often feel is a personal inadequacy.

Individual assessment. Assessment with Antoine should include a clinical interview and sex history with an additional medical history and referral for a physical examination to consider and rule out any medical risk factors, such as coronary heart disease (Rosen, 2007). As with other sexual dysfunctions, the clinician is asking about the onset, severity, and duration of the ED. When did the concerns with erection begin? On a scale of 1-10, how much of a concern were they at first? How about at present? How long has it been a concern? How would you describe any changes or fluctuation in erectile functioning during that time?

Assessment measures can also be used. These include the International Index of Erectile Function Erectile Function Domain (IIEF-EF) (Rosen et al., 1999), the Erection Hardness Scale (EHS) (Mulhall et al., 2007), the Psychological and Interpersonal Relationship Scales (PAIRS) (Swindle et al., 2004), and the Self-Esteem and Relationship (SEAR) Questionnaire (Cappelleri et al., 2004). The IIEF-EF offers a standardized categorization of ED, while the EHS is a single-item self-report measure of the hardness of the erection. The PAIRS assesses for psychological and relational aspects of ED. The SEAR questionnaire assesses sexual relationship and confidence in relation to ED (Grover & Shouan, 2020).

Metz and McCarthy (2004, pp. 52-60) offer a series of helpful summary descriptions that can be added to assessment. A clinician can review these or ask a client to read this chapter to discuss together the various potential causes of ED: physical causes, psychological issues, relational conflicts, and sexual skill deficits.

In the areas of psychological, relational, and skill deficits, it is important to identify possible domains of concern related to ED. These include variables associated with the client, the partner, the relationship, the sexual script, and the context of intimacy (Althof & Rosen, 2010).

When we consider the client during assessment, we want to be sensitive to listen for signs of performance anxiety (e.g., spectatoring, fear of failure), comorbid depression, and heightened expectations for erection or performance. In part because of cultural messages about male sexuality and functioning, some of the man's own sense of self-worth can be tied to performance. After all, male performance has been a dominant emphasis in messages about sexual behavior in contemporary society. It is communicated to men (and women) through entertainment and within one's peer group from adolescence through adulthood. These messages can have an effect on men and their own expectations for performance, as well as how their partners view them. These expectations should be assessed to see whether they have been adopted as essentially unhelpful beliefs that may exacerbate the concerns the man is discussing in therapy.

Couples assessment. As we assess partner and relationship variables, we want to consider level of interest in sex, perhaps because of the dysfunction, any illnesses, comorbid depression, medications, or changes due to menopause. It is also important to assess relationship satisfaction, as strained relationships can contribute to erectile dysfunction, just as difficulties achieving erection can contribute to relationship strain. It is important then to track relationship history with an eye for when erectile dysfunction started and how it has changed over the course of their present and past relationships.

It may also be helpful to be aware of the potential impact of "ghosts" in the bedroom. These are thoughts or experiences with past partners, thoughts about one's parents, father-in-law, mother-in-law, and possibly others. This can sometimes be teased out in discussions with each spouse about the details of their sexual script, use of fantasy, other cognitions, and so on associated with their time of sexual intimacy.

The couple's sexual script and context for intimacy should also be assessed. We would ask about this in both individual and couples assessment. The clinician can go through the entire sexual response cycle, as well as that day's context, cues for sex, initiation, foreplay, and so on. Assessment around sexual script would also include whether there are differing interests in sexual activities, past affairs or other issues of trust, and any contextual issues facing the couple, such as employment status and satisfaction, issues with children, financial concerns, and so on. We assess around these kinds of issues because significant changes in status and life pressure can affect a man's sense of self-confidence. This may or may not affect sexual functioning, but it is important to assess around it.

By suggesting any potential connection between employment status or other indicators of self-worth and performance, we also want to caution against assessing only around functioning; rather, assessment should be extended beyond "what one does" (as that can reinforce that his sexual worth is measured by performance) and about what they as a couple create together in their time of sexual intimacy. We communicate to the couple that what they create together is unique, is something that they can delight in and enjoy together as an expression of intimacy and as a time that enhances intimacy.

These messages are communicated at the time of assessment and reiterated throughout treatment. We turn our attention now to how treatment moves forward in the age of Viagra.

TREATMENT

It has been estimated that 25 to 30 million men around the world are currently taking PDE5 inhibitors (e.g., sildenafil/Viagra, vardenafil/Levitra, and tadalafil/Cialis), and that there are "an additional 50 million or more who are potential candidates for treatment" (Rosen, 2007, p. 278). It is clearly the treatment of choice among men who report difficulties with erectile dysfunction.

The PDE5 inhibitors are medications that relax the smooth muscles in the penile corpora. When this occurs, a man can more readily experience the normal response of erection when adequate stimulation is present. The PDE5 inhibitors have been shown to restore erections in most men who use them (about 75% of men) with noted differences, preferences, and side effects with the different medications (Viagra, Levitra, Cialis; Rosen, 2007). If one PDE5 inhibitor is not working, it is not uncommon to switch to another PDE5 inhibitor.

Given the widespread use of PDE5 inhibitors, what, then, is the role of sex therapy? It is generally recommended that medications such as the PDE5 inhibitors are not used alone but rather in conjunction with couples' sex therapy (Aubin et al., 2009). One of the primary reasons is that the medications do not address personal psychological issues or relationship concerns.

The general principles of psychological intervention are similar to what was proposed by Masters and Johnson (1970) in their treatment of erectile dysfunction, although many contemporary sex therapists have added various components and emphases (Rowland, 2012). The principles include providing education (particularly about lifestyle changes), addressing anxiety and distractions (including cognitive distortions and myths), and prescribing various exercises to enhance their relationship and sexual functioning.

Provide education. This includes a discussion of the sexual response cycle, information on risk factors and possible side effects of different medications, and related issues that are important for clients to understand. Another area for education has to do with lifestyle changes. As with all psychological care, a first step in treatment is to review and identify any potential lifestyle changes that are likely to lead to symptom improvement. With ED, it has been shown that lifestyle changes such as smoking cessation, weight loss, and positive changes to overall physical health have either helped delay the progressions of ED or in some cases led to remissions (Hanash, 2008). Other risk factors include excessive alcohol use and recreational drug use (Gambescia et al., 2009).

Address anxiety. When we look at anxiety reduction, it is important to establish hope—that therapy can be helpful to them—while keeping expectations modest. A first step is to lower the expectation that the man has to perform. One way to do this is to place a ban on intercourse. While this may sound extreme, it is common in sex therapy and is meant to stop the couple from continuing down a path that has not been working anyway. There is no need to further confirm that erectile dysfunction exists or deny that ED is a factor, and we want to make changes so that future sexual intimacy will be more rewarding for both of them.

Another step is to instruct the man and his partner in sensate focus exercises. Recall that sensate focus exercises refer to nondemand caressing. These exercises can help a man who is prone to spectatoring or performance demands. The practice of sensate focus exercises may also address the distractibility that is often seen in men presenting with ED; it teaches them to attend to their sensations, their partner, and the overall experience or encounter.

So what is sensate focus? The following is a standard script for sensate focus I as offered by Helen Singer Kaplan in her book *The New Sex Therapy*.

I'd like you both to get ready for bed—to take your clothes off, shower and relax. I want you [the woman] to lie on your belly. Then you [the man] caress her back as gently and sensitively as you can. Move your hands very slowly. Begin at the back of her neck, caress her ears, and work your way down to her buttocks, legs and feet. Use your hands and/or your lips. Concentrate only on how it feels to touch her body and her skin.

In the meantime, I want you [the woman] to focus your attention on the sensations you feel when he caresses you. Try not to let your mind wander. Don't think about anything else: don't worry about whether he's getting tired or whether he is enjoying it—or anything. Be "selfish," and just concentrate on your sensations; let yourself feel everything. Communicate with him. Don't talk too much or it will interfere with your responses—and his. But remember that he can't possibly know what you are feeling unless you tell him. Let him know where you want to be touched and how, and where his caresses feel especially good; let him know if his touch is too light or too heavy, or if he is going too fast. If the experience is unpleasant, tell him so. Don't talk too much or it will interfere with your sensations and his. Try to identify for yourself those areas of your body which are especially sensitive or responsive.

When you both have had enough of this, I want you [the woman] to turn over on your back, so that you [the man] can caress the front of her body. Start with her face and neck and go down to her toes. But this first time don't caress her sexual organs. Skip her nipples, her vagina and clitoris. Again, both of you are to concentrate only on what it feels like to caress and to be caressed. Stop when this becomes tedious for either of you. Now it's your [the man's] turn to receive. I want you [the woman] to do the same to him. Do either of you have any questions about this procedure? (p. 209)

Sensate focus actually has three steps. We have just looked at one way to present to a couple sensate focus I. They would do this exercise a few times a week for at least a week or more, depending on their experience with it and what problems may need to be solved (e.g., making time in their schedule, oversight of children, and so on). Later, as therapy proceeds, the couple will include nondemand sensual touch of the breasts and genitals (sensate focus II). They will do sensate focus II a few times for a week or more depending, again, on issues that arise, what problems may need to be solved, and so on. They will eventually move toward sensate focus III, which involves vaginal containment. Setbacks can occur during any of these steps and need to be addressed and worked through before proceeding.

A related step in reducing anxiety is to address cognitive distortions that impact and reflect a man's view of sexuality and sexual behavior. Common cognitive distortions identified among men who struggle with ED include the following (Althof & Rosen, 2010, p. 262):

1. All-or-nothing thinking: "I am a complete failure because my erection was not 100% rigid."

2. Overgeneralization: "If I had trouble getting an erection last night, I won't have one this morning."

3. Disqualifying the positive: "My partner says I have a good erection because she doesn't want to hurt my feelings."

4. Mind reading: "I don't need to ask, I know how she felt about last night."

5. Fortune telling: "I am sure things will go badly tonight."

6. Emotional reasoning: "Because a man feels something is true, it must be."

7. Categorical imperatives: "should," "ought tos," and "musts" dominate the man's cognitive processes.

8. Catastrophizing: "If I fail tonight my wife will leave me."

These unhelpful cognitions are often based on personally held and culturally reinforced myths about male sexuality and male-female relations. A commonly held myth, for example, is "It is the man's job to satisfy the woman." Another is "Men are always interested in, ready for, and capable of having sex." It should be noted that work with them as a couple is important in addressing these kinds of myths. The clinician wants to recognize the importance of the man achieving and maintaining an erection, while laying the foundation that an erection is not necessary to sexual satisfaction, that the woman may enjoy many facets of sexual intimacy, and that their sense of connection, commitment, and desire for one another is not measured best by the ability to have an erection.

These various cognitive distortions and myths are often addressed both in session through discussions and throughout the process of the couple completing various homework assignments. It is common practice to assign specific homework activities that can be completed weekly and reviewed the following therapy session. As noted earlier, it is common to assign sensate focus to address anxiety and performance demands.

Specific exercises. In addition to providing education and addressing anxiety and distractions, clinicians frequently assign specific exercises in the treatment of erectile disorder. For example, it is common to assign the "squeeze" technique, which refers to having the man or woman first stimulate the penis to erection and then squeeze the tip of the penis, placing pressure on the frenulum and both sides of the coronal ridge (well before the point of ejaculatory inevitability). The purpose of using the squeeze technique is to help the man grow in his confidence that he is able to achieve, lose, and regain an erection. It directly challenges the fear he may now have that he cannot achieve an erection or, if he does achieve an erection, that he will not be able to maintain it. In this unhelpful thought process, the loss of erection becomes a catastrophe. By challenging these thoughts and conclusions, the man learns that he can control when he is erect and when he is flaccid.

Another technique used in cognitive-behavioral treatment of erectile dysfunction is referred to as "quiet vagina." The man is on his back and the woman is in the female superior position. She lowers herself onto his penis, and neither does he thrust, nor does she move. Movement is added later, but the point of the exercise is to have him learn more confidence in having an

erection independent of outcome (or without focus on completing intercourse at this time).

It is also common to use guided imagery exercises throughout therapy,
particularly with men who may struggle with fear of failure. They can walk
through imagery exercises in which the man has success in achieving and
maintaining an erection, facing some of the concerns he may have about
losing an erection, evaluating cognitive distortions (e.g., catastrophic
thinking), and so on.

Another technique discussed by Penner and Penner (2005) is "paint
brushing." This refers to the man using his penis to gently move across the
vaginal entrance and clitoris to foster closeness, rather than focus on any
demands for an erection or penetration at this time.

The interventions discussed thus far presume a level of trust and understanding in the relationship. It is important that the clinician continually
assess the interpersonal relationship when providing treatment for erectile
dysfunction. Assess for any changes in the relationship or in the man's
status that could affect his sense of self-worth, such as unemployment,
conflicts at work, or other issues that could contribute to low self-esteem
(Rosen, 2007).

It is also important to note that if a couple has had difficulty not being
sexually intimate due to the man's experience with erectile dysfunction, they
may need to process the transition they are now making—either through
the introduction of a PDE5 inhibitor, sex therapy, or a combination—toward
a more intentional sex life. There can be a kind of inertia that sets in as the
man and woman avoid one another because of feelings of embarrassment
or anxiety about failure and so on (Rosen, 2007; Rosenau, 2002).

Over the course of treatment what often happens is that the man begins
to experience an erection. The clinical response to this is to generally
downplay the significance, to encourage the process, and to reduce expectations for erections.

Metz and McCarthy (2004) offer a three-phase protocol: (1) developing
relaxation and comfort, (2) enhancing your arousal and erotic flow, and
(3) enjoying confident and flexible intercourse. In the first phase the couple
takes time to talk to one another about how sex was discussed in their family
growing up, what they learned and experienced during adolescence, and the
like. They talk about their attitudes and beliefs about sex. In this first phase

the man also learns and practices deep breathing and physical relaxation exercises, as well as identifying and learning to control pelvic muscles.

In phase two of the protocol, "enhancing your arousal and erotic flow," the couple learns nondemand sensual touch (sensate focus) (Metz & McCarthy, 2004). They then learn to develop a cognitive map for sexual pleasure, in which they become increasingly aware of what each finds pleasurable. They then add to sensate focus by including genital touch (again, in a nondemand manner). These exercises eventually incorporate stimulation to erection that is then allowed to subside.

In the third phase of the protocol, "enjoying confident and flexible intercourse," the couple incorporates into sexual intercourse the various skills they have learned (Metz & McCarthy, 2004). After a time of relaxed, nondemand pleasuring, they begin intercourse without an erection and while relaxing the pelvic muscles. This may last for ten minutes or so and may or may not lead to an erection. The focus is not to act on the erection at this time; rather, the emphasis is on the experience in a relaxed manner. Exercises that follow are based on foundational skills of relaxed, nondemand pleasuring, followed by varied stimulation, sexual playfulness, and various scenarios of interest to both of them as a couple.

Taken together, psychological interventions focus on providing education, addressing and reducing anxiety, and making use of specific homework assignments. These assignments establish couple intimacy without the goal of erection or intercourse. Rather, they are given "permission" to engage in nongoal-oriented sexual intimacy with much more emphasis on the process than the outcome (Rosen, 2007).

Local therapies and surgical options. We mentioned that men welcomed the advances that led to the PDE5 inhibitors because the alternative approaches were not that appealing. In some cases, the PDE5 inhibitors are not effective, and clients may need to explore other options. These include various local therapies and surgery.

Local therapies include intracavernosal injections and use of a vacuum constriction device. Intracavernosal injection therapy involves injecting alprostadil (or mixtures such as bimix or trimix) into an area of the penis, which facilitates erection in about 5 to 20 minutes (Hanash, 2008). Although it has been shown to be effective in as many as 70% to 80% of clients (Rosen, 2007), it also has a fairly high discontinuation rate, likely due to possible side effects, such as pain and priapism (or prolonged erection).

Another local therapy is the use of intraurethral alprostadil, a semisolid pellet that is inserted into the urethra in order to achieve an erection. An erection typically occurs within fifteen minutes of insertion but in some cases has taken longer. This can also be helpful for men who do not respond to medication and has a fairly high success rate (about 65%) but also a high discontinuation rate with reports of pain, priapism, and hypotension (Rosen, 2007; see also Hanash, 2008).

A third local therapy option is to use a vacuum constriction device. This device applies "negative pressure on the flaccid penis, thus drawing venous blood into the penis, which is then retained by the application of an elastic constriction band at the base of the penis" (Rosen, 2007, p. 296). As Rosen observes, while it has also been shown to be effective in 60% to 80% of cases, use of vacuum constriction devices also suffers from a high discontinuation rate due to pain and delayed ejaculation.

Each of these cases—intracavernosal injections, intraurethral alprostadil, and vacuum constriction devices—requires education about the condition, the specific treatment approach, and practice to maximize potential benefits. Often men discontinue use because of dissatisfaction that may at times reflect misunderstanding of the proper procedure.

If a person does not respond to medication or to the various local therapies discussed, the other option is surgical intervention. This is not a common practice today, as most men are able to respond favorably to the less-invasive procedures. However, for those who do need surgery the practice involves implanting a penile prosthesis. The prosthesis can be inflatable or semirigid. The primary benefit of inflatable prostheses is that they are more concealed; however, they also carry the risk of mechanical failure (Rosen, 2007). Semirigid implants are not as easily concealed, but they have less of a risk of mechanical problems or other issues. The data on the use of surgical interventions suggests that they are typically effective and can increase a man's sense of confidence in that he knows he now will have an erection.

PREVENTION

Prevention of ED centers on sexual education and lifestyle changes. Education about the effects of various chronic health conditions, medications used to treat various health conditions, normal aging, and so on are a part of the discussion.

Lifestyle changes are also an important part of prevention. With ED it has been shown that helping a person to stop smoking, lose weight, and make overall improvements to their physical health have either slowed the progressions of ED or led to its remission (Hanash, 2008).

Another area in the prevention literature is on relapse prevention. Steps to preventing relapse in a man who has been diagnosed and successfully treated for ED include scheduling regular sensate focus (nondemand sensual pleasuring) exercises, predicting future times of not having or maintaining an erection and practicing helpful cognitive responses to such an event, and expanding the couple's sexual script to be broader and more encompassing than a more limited script that is limited to penile-vaginal intercourse (Rosen, 2007).

CLOSING REFLECTIONS

As Christians engage the growing literature on erectile dysfunction, we can welcome the greater openness and transparency that has come with more forthright discussions of ED. There has been a kind of permission given to discuss sex. Although some of this occurred in the context of the discovery of breakthrough medications, such as the PDE5 inhibitors, it is a shift nonetheless, and one that we can appreciate so long as we value human sexuality and its expression.

We would note, however, that the permission is more for discussions of male sexuality than female sexuality, and the broader culture and particularly the local church struggle more with acknowledging the reality of female sexuality, as we discuss in chapters three and six. There are some restrictions too in the discussions of male sexuality. The enthusiasm for various medications places great significant on male performance, which in some ways may underscore cultural messages about male sexuality being performance oriented, as though the man were responsible for "pleasuring the woman," if you will. These messages do not offer a full and holistic view of sexual intimacy we would like to see in the church today. Rather, we would prefer to hear a discussion of male and female sexuality that fosters a climate for sexual intimacy in the context of marriage that is lifelong and exclusive, that is not performance-driven but is mutually submissive and supportive, expressive, and creative.

As we look at our broader cultural discussions about sex, we also see that there is much less need for us to overcome repressed sexuality but rather the opposite. We are at a point where acts of a sexual nature are ubiquitous in the news media and in entertainment, where the risk is less about repression and more about the purposeful devaluing of sexuality and sexual behavior by reducing it to what someone decides to do for him- or herself and in the context of his or her own personal sexual self-actualization.

With the separation of sexuality from any sense of transcendent purpose, we are much more prone to see and experience sex from both humanistic and naturalistic perspectives. These worldviews place more emphasis on maximizing individual personal pleasure (humanism) and on a reductionistic understanding of sex (naturalism). This may contribute to the so-called hook-up culture on college campuses (Frietas, 2008, 2013), where young adults often reduce sex to simply the exchange of bodily fluids.

So it is one thing to discuss sex—which we are in favor of—and another to value human sexuality and its expression as a meaningful, purposeful aspect of what it means to be human and as something that is tied in instructive ways to transcendent purposes.

How the Christian community talks about sexuality, then, is the next step. There is a need to balance the reality of our sexuality and sexual experiences with the value and worth placed on people who reflect the image of God, and who are learning ways to enjoy and express sexual intimacy in relationship. The broader culture's openness to improving sexual functioning is an interesting start; it has led to a more overt discussion of sexual functioning and has validated in important ways that people can ask for and receive help. But we would like to see the church extend that discussion and take more of a lead on positive views of sexuality, sexual functioning, and, ultimately, sexual intimacy in the context of lifelong unions. This is part of what it means to be human, to be inherently physical and sexual. This would be a move far beyond functioning and into intimacy, a place that Christians should be able to address with some confidence.

REFERENCES

Althof, S. E., & Rosen, R. C. (2010). Combining medical and psychological interventions for the treatment of erectile dysfunction. In S. B. Levine, C. B. Risen, & S. E. Althof (Eds.), *Handbook of clinical sexuality for mental health professionals* (2nd ed., pp. 251-65). Routledge.

American Psychiatric Association. (2022). *Diagnostic and statistical manual of mental disorders* (5th ed.-Text Revision). American Psychiatric Publishing.

Aubin, S., Heiman, J. R., Berger, R. E., Murallo, A. V., & Yung-Wen, L. (2009). Comparing sildenafil alone vs. sildenafil plus brief couple sex therapy on erectile dysfunction and couples' sexual and marital quality of life: A pilot study. *Journal of Sex & Marital Therapy, 35*, 122-43.

Barbonetti, A., D'Andrea, S., Cavallo, F., Martorella, A., Francavilla, S., & Francavilla, F. (2019). Erectile dysfunction and premature ejaculation in homosexual and heterosexual men: A systematic review and meta-analysis of comparative studies. *Journal of Sexual Medicine, 16*, 624-32.

Basson, R. (2007). Sexual desire/arousal disorders in women. In S. R. Leiblum (Ed.), *Principles and practice of sex therapy* (4th ed., pp. 25-53). Guilford.

Cappelleri, J. C., Althof, S. E., Siegel, R. L., Shpilsky, A., Bell, S. S., & Duttagupta, S. (2004). Development and validation of the Self-Esteem and Relationship (SEAR) questionnaire in erectile dysfunction. *International Journal of Impotence Research, 16*, 30-38.

Cohen, K. M., & Savin-Williams, R. C. (2017). Treating sexual problems in lesbian, gay, and bisexual clients. In Z. D. Peterson (Ed.), *The Wiley handbook of sex therapy* (pp. 291-305). John Wiley and Sons.

Freitas, D. (2008). *Sex and the soul: Juggling sexuality, spirituality, romance, and religion on America's college campuses*. Oxford University Press.

Freitas, D. (2013). *The end of sex: How hookup culture is leaving a generation unhappy, sexually unfulfilled, and confused about intimacy*. Basic Books.

Gambescia, N., Sendak, S. K., & Weeks, G. R. (2009). The treatment of erectile dysfunction. In K. M. Hertlein, G. R. Weeks, & N. Gambescia (Eds.), *Systemic sex therapy* (pp. 107-30). Routledge.

Grover, S., & Shouan, A. (2020). Assessment scales for sexual disorders: A review. *Journal of Psychosexual Health, 2*(2), 121-28.

Hanash, K. A. (2008). *New frontiers in men's sexual health: Understanding erectile dysfunction and the revolutionary new treatments*. Praeger.

Kaplan, H. S. (1974). *The new sex therapy*. Routledge.

Masters, W. H., & Johnson, V. E. (1970). *Human sexual inadequacy*. Bantam Books.

Metz, M. E., & McCarthy, B. W. (2004). *Coping with erectile dysfunction*. New Harbinger.

Mulhall, J. P., Goldstein, I., Bushmakin, A. G., Cappelleri, J. C., & Hvidsten, K. (2007). Validation of the erection hardness score. *Journal of Sexual Medicine, 4*, 1626-34.

Penner, J., & Penner, C. (2005). *A clinician's guide to sex therapy* (2nd ed.). Word.

Rosen, R. C. (2007). Erectile dysfunction: Integration of medical and psychological approaches. In S. R. Leiblum (Ed.), *Principles and practice of sex therapy* (4th ed., pp. 277-312). Guilford.

Rosen, R. C., Cappelleri, J. C., Smith, M. D., Lipsky, J., & Pena, B. M. (1999). Development and evaluation of an abridged, 5-item version of the International Index of Erectile Function (IIEF-5) as a diagnostic tool for erectile dysfunction. *International Journal of Impotence Research, 11*, 319-26.

Rosenau, D. (2002). *A celebration of sex: A guide to enjoying God's gift of sexual intimacy* (Rev. ed.). Thomas Nelson.

Rowland, D. L. (2012). *Sexual dysfunction in men.* Hogrefe.

Swindle, R. W., Cameron, A. E., Lockhart, D. C., & Rosen, R. C. (2004). The psychological and interpersonal relationship scales: Assessing psychological and relationship outcomes associated with erectile dysfunction and its treatment. *Archives of Sexual Behavior, 33,* 19-30.

Wincze, J. P., & Carey, M. P. (2001). *Sexual dysfunction: Treatment manuals for practitioners.* Guilford.

NINE

PREMATURE AND DELAYED EJACULATION

IN THE OPENING SCENE from the movie *Lord of the Rings: The Fellowship of the Ring* the wizard Gandalf and Frodo the Hobbit have an exchange in which Frodo criticizes Gandalf for arriving late to the Shire for his uncle Bilbo's eleventy-first birthday party. Gandalf replies, "A wizard is never late, Frodo Baggins. Nor is he early. He arrives precisely when he means to." Let's put it this way: most men would like to be able to say the same thing. But nearly all men have struggled with arriving too early, while some deal with arriving too late.

Among the male sexual dysfunctions, neither premature nor delayed ejaculation receives nearly as much attention as other concerns. Where premature or rapid ejaculation does receive attention is in entertainment (not the Lord of the Rings), where movies and television shows might depict a young man ejaculating early, much to his embarrassment and to the chagrin of his partner.

What receives even less attention than rapid ejaculation is delayed ejaculation. In this chapter we discuss both of these sexual dysfunctions in terms of their clinical presentation, theories of etiology, assessment and treatment, and a Christian engagement of the topics.

Premature ejaculation refers to ongoing difficulties with ejaculating too quickly with little sexual stimulation. Ejaculation could occur before penetration, at the time of penetration, or shortly following penetration and thrusting. Experts usually distinguish between rapid ejaculation that is primary or lifelong, and rapid ejaculation that is secondary or acquired. Primary refers to a man struggling with this since the time he went through puberty, while secondary refers to the difficulty ensuing after the man had already experienced sufficient control over ejaculation. To meet diagnostic criteria, rapid ejaculation should not be due to a medical condition or substance use.

Premature ejaculation is one of the most common sexual concerns for men. As Polonsky (2000) observes, most men ejaculate too soon in their first experience with a partner, but most learn and experience control in subsequent times of sexual intimacy—though it may take time to learn these skills. However, those who suffer from primary premature ejaculation do not tend to report an increase in control over ejaculation with time (Waldinger, 2010). The prevalence estimates for premature ejaculation range from 20% to 30% (Althof, 2007; Polonsky, 2000), and it is reported at higher rates among heterosexual males than among gay males (Barbonetti et al., 2019).

For diagnosing premature (early) ejaculation, the *DSM-5-TR* considers whether there is a "persistent or recurrent pattern of ejaculation occurring during partnered sexual activity within approximately 1 minute following vaginal penetration and before the individual wishes it" (APA, 2022, p. 501). This would be a concern for about six months and occur on "almost all or all (approximately 75%–100%) occasions of sexual activity" (p. 502). This can be lifelong (since the person began sexual activity) or acquired (a concern after a period of normal sexual functioning). It can also be limited to specific stimulation, situations, or partners (situational), or generalized (not limited to specific stimulations, situations, or partners).

In terms of seeking treatment and the issue of comorbidity, it has been noted that most men who suffer from rapid ejaculation do not seek treatment for it, and most of those who seek treatment do not report another sexual difficulty (Waldinger, 2010). A prior diagnosis of erectile dysfunction may be associated with premature ejaculation in some men, as it is not unusual for one sexual dysfunction, with accompanying anxiety, to create other sexual dysfunctions. For example, if a man is feeling frustration and humiliation over erectile difficulty, this could affect his sexual performance in other ways.

Delayed ejaculation refers to the inability for a man to ejaculate despite sufficient stimulation. It has also been referred to as inhibited or retarded ejaculation, male orgasmic disorder, delayed or inhibited orgasm, and anejaculation, among other things (Foley, 2009). Hartmann and Waldinger (2007) refer to delayed ejaculation as "a dissociation of emission and orgasm, two processes that are normally fully integrated" (p. 244). Others (Rosenau, personal communication, June 7, 2013) consider delayed ejaculation with reference to a dissociation between arousal and orgasm. When we discuss sufficient stimulation, it should be noted that the stimulation could be penile-vaginal intercourse or self- or partner stimulation.

In terms of current diagnostic nomenclature, the *DSM-5-TR* indicates that either of two symptoms would be present in "almost all or all occasions":

- Marked delay in ejaculation.
- Marked infrequency or absence of ejaculation (APA, 2022, p. 478).

The length of time being symptomatic is again about six months, and the symptoms would cause clinically significant distress. As with premature ejaculation, delayed ejaculation can be lifelong (since the person began sexual activity) or acquired (a concern after a period of normal sexual functioning). It can also be limited to specific stimulation, situations, or partners (situational) or generalized (not limited to specific stimulations, situations, or partners).

Prevalence estimates vary widely for delayed ejaculation, ranging from as little as 1% to 2% of adult men to as many as 8% in some studies (Hartmann & Waldinger, 2007; Waldinger, 2010; Wincze & Carey, 2001). As Waldinger (2010) notes, these differences are likely due to the variety of ways that researchers ask about it or clinicians measure it. Among those who present with delayed ejaculation, the most common presentation is to be able to ejaculate through self-stimulation or partner stimulation but not through intercourse (Hartmann & Waldinger, 2007).

ETIOLOGY

There is no consensus today as to what causes either premature ejaculation or delayed ejaculation. Some of the earliest theories for the etiology of premature ejaculation considered early learning history (e.g., guilt-ridden, hurried first encounters), unresolved unconscious conflicts with women, relationship conflicts, and inability to discriminate early signals of crossing the point of ejaculatory inevitability (Polonsky, 2000; Wadinger, 2010). As Polonsky observes, some of the theories tied to premonitory signals have also considered whether some men achieve orgasm at a lower threshold of stimulation that is tied to the nervous system, but it is unclear whether the differences noted here reflect the cause of rapid ejaculation.

This last area—a neurobiological understanding—has gained some momentum in recent years and attempts to explain both premature and delayed ejaculation. The focus is on the relationship between the central nervous system and ejaculation. Animal studies suggest that diminished serotonin neurotransmission or hyper- or hyposensitivity to different serotonin receptors is associated with primary rapid ejaculation (Althof, 2007; Waldinger, 2010). DNA studies on humans support the role of diminished serotonin neurotransmission among men diagnosed with rapid ejaculation (Waldinger, 2010).

It is also possible to subjectively feel that one is ejaculating prematurely when the time is in what is considered a normal range. That range is thought to be 2 to 6 minutes (Waldinger, 2010) or 3 to 7 minutes (Metz & McCarthy, 2004). Either husband or wife may feel, for different reasons, that what is normal is too soon for them. For example, the wife may want to experience an orgasm with intercourse and need prolonged thrusting. According to Waldinger, this kind of "premature-like" ejaculatory concern may more likely be tied to relationship problems or other psychological concerns, but it is not the same thing as rapid ejaculation.

In light of this neurobiological approach, it has been suggested that there is a set point of central nervous system threshold prior to ejaculation (Waldinger, 2010). That set point varies among men. Those with a low set point are more likely to experience rapid ejaculation—with lower levels of stimulation needed to reach or surpass the threshold and cause ejaculation. Men who have more control generally have a higher set point. It is possible in this model to have a very high set point that contributes to delayed ejaculation or the difficulty some men have experiencing ejaculation at all.

As with premature ejaculation, a number of other theories have been advanced to explain delayed ejaculation. In addition to the neurobiological approach discussed previously, delayed ejaculation has been thought by some to be due to anxiety or fear (of impregnating a woman, for example), hostility or passive-aggressiveness toward women, or relationship problems. It can also be associated with performance anxiety and the spectatoring associated with erectile difficulties. Once a man struggles with climaxing, he can mentally sabotage his arousal through anxiety over whether he will climax during this time of intimacy. As men age, some struggle with delayed ejaculation from a lack of sufficient stimulation or becoming more easily distracted. Certainly psychological and relational concerns end up as the focal point of sex therapy, even if it is in conjunction with a multidisciplinary approach.

To summarize, there is no consensus today as to the etiology of either premature or delayed ejaculation. It is certainly possible that different contributing factors are weighted differently for different men. However, the neurobiological approach appears to be gaining some momentum as a model that provides a possible account for both within a more unifying theory and will certainly continue to be researched. Even the neurobiological approach, however, would likely only account for a subset of men who present with difficulties with rapid or delayed ejaculation (Althof, 2007).

ASSESSMENT AND CLINICAL PRESENTATION

Xavier presents in the initial session with a concern about his sexual functioning. He is a twenty-three-year-old Hispanic man who has been married just under one year. He does not report a significant amount of previous sexual experience, but he did have one prior relationship in his first year of college. He had been sexually active at that time, but the experiences with his girlfriend—much like his experience now with his wife—were brief, often culminating in ejaculation before penetration or just after penetration. "I'm not sure what the issue is. I have to be honest, my wife is getting angry, and I'm getting a little upset too with myself, I mean. I don't know why I can't seem to last longer, if you know what I mean. I'm a young guy. I should be able to be better at this, and now it's getting to the point where we don't really want to try—or she is at least looking at me like, 'Really? Do you want to try again?' and it's putting a wall between us."

Wayne entered therapy without looking at the therapist. He kept his eyes averted as he talked about why he needed counseling: "I'm not sure how to describe it; I'm not sure what you'll think. But when I'm with my wife in bed, I am not really getting to the point where I'm having an orgasm like I should be. Or even like she is. I don't know. It's strange to me. You'd think it would be the other way around; I mean, everyone talks about how women 'fake it,' but here I am doing the same thing. I sometimes fake it to finish up; otherwise, it's a weird thing. I don't seem to finish up the way I should."

With both premature ejaculation and delayed ejaculation, a complication that arises in assessment is that both are somewhat subjective claims. At what point does a man conclude that he is ejaculating early or late? Is that his own conclusion? Is that what his partner is saying? Is it early or late in comparison to others? Is one or are both of them wanting to extend their time of sexual intimacy, such that perhaps the "premature" dimension is more of a preference for longevity and quality of encounter rather than a sexual dysfunction? A good assessment is critical for finding answers to these and other common questions.

Grover and Shouan (2020) identify several measures that can be used to assess premature ejaculation: the Premature Ejaculation Profile (Patrick et al., 2009), Index of Premature Ejaculation (IPE) (Altof, 2016), and the Premature Ejaculation Diagnostic Tool (PEDT) (Huang et al., 2014). The PEP assesses both subjective sense of ejaculatory control and associated distress. The IPE assesses control, sexual satisfaction, and sense of subjective distress related to rapid ejaculation. The PEDT is more of a screening measure for possible rapid ejaculation (Grover & Shouan, 2020).

With premature ejaculation, in addition to a standard clinical interview, sex history, and possible assessment measure, it can be helpful to assess the entire sexual script, including duration of the excitement phase, the novelty of the situation (or partner), and sexual frequency (APA, 2022). It is also important to assess the length of time between vaginal penetration and ejaculation. Unfortunately, most men are not good at providing an accurate estimation when simply asked the question. Waldinger (2010) recommends first asking the client how long that time is. Then he asks the client to engage in a visualization exercise in which he imagines engaging in foreplay with his partner. He then imagines the moment when foreplay is over and there is vaginal penetration. As the client imagines penetration and thrusting he is to say yes when he believes (or imagines) he is ejaculating. The clinician uses a stopwatch to time how long it is between the initial visualization of penetration—when the clinician would say now—and when the client says yes (imagined ejaculation). They then discuss the time and whether there is a difference between what was stated in the interview and what is demonstrated through the visualization exercise. This assessment can also be conducted with the partner to determine an estimation of the length of time from her perspective.

Metz and McCarthy (2004) offer several excellent clusters of questions to help clients (and clinicians) determine the kind of premature ejaculation (PE) clients struggle with, including lifelong PE that could be associated with neurologic systems, psychological issues, or skill-based concerns, as well as acquired PE that could be associated with physical illness, injury, drug side effects, psychological concerns, and relationship distress (see pp. 48-54). For example, questions that might be asked to determine whether the PE is related to skill deficits include (1) "Has PE occurred in almost all situations especially with a partner?" (2) "Do you focus your sexual attention almost exclusively on your partner—her body, actions, and sexual responses?" and (3) "Are you unaware of your body's pelvic muscles and how to use them for ejaculatory control?" (Metz & McCarthy, 2004, p. 50). The authors also offer helpful assessment questions to gauge severity of PE (see pp. 54-55). These include rating the length of time PE has been a concern, identifying the percent of sexual acts in which the person experiences PE, rating the intensity of physical stimulation at ejaculation, and how troubled the client and his spouse are at the experience of PE.

When assessing delayed ejaculation, it is important to conduct a standard clinical interview and obtain a sex history. In the context of the sex history, and similar to what would be done with rapid ejaculation, the clinician can assess around the sexual response cycle to consider various situational and relationship variables that may contribute to delayed ejaculation. It is through a good clinical assessment and sex history that the clinician can also determine whether the person experiences primary/lifelong or secondary/acquired delayed ejaculation, as well as whether it is generalized (in all circumstances) or situational (limited to specific circumstances or relationships).

In the context of assessment, clinicians should keep in mind too that many men may have tried their own way of managing their symptoms. For example, men who struggle with rapid ejaculation may turn to their own methods to extend intercourse. Common strategies include use of pain or distraction (e.g., biting one's lip or the inside of one's mouth), attempts to reduce stimulation (e.g., the use of multiple condoms), and avoidance of sexual intimacy altogether (Polonsky, 2000). These are not usually helpful strategies and in some cases may do more harm than good. If the client presents with some of these methods, it is important to not trigger feelings of shame or guilt, which may hinder the assessment, as the client may be more guarded as a result of those emotions. At the same time, unhelpful and destructive strategies need to be identified and education offered so that the man can be gently but clearly redirected to more helpful strategies. The place to begin is by recognizing and essentially honoring (or validating) the strategy he is using before asking him to change it to other, more helpful strategies.

TREATMENT

Premature ejaculation. Premature ejaculation is considered by many sex therapists to be one of the most treatable sexual dysfunctions. This belief is tied to a study by Masters and Johnson (1970), who reported that none of the patients they treated for premature ejaculation still struggled with it at five-year follow-up. Although subsequent studies have called those high success rates into question, the basic model discussed by Masters and Johnson (and various adaptations of it) is still the most widely used approach today and is generally considered by many to be effective in the treatment of rapid ejaculation.

The approach rests on education, nondemand sensual touch, couples communication, and learning of premonitory signals in the context of sexual stimulation. The original approach as described by Semans (1956) introduced the stop-start method, in which the woman would manually stimulate the man's penis until just before the sensation of ejaculatory inevitability. She would stop. They wait until that sensation dissipates. Then she would resume penile stimulation. This method involved starting and stopping direct stimulation to learn control and awareness of sensations associated with ejaculatory inevitability.

The squeeze technique involves having the man or woman squeeze the tip of the penis, placing pressure on the frenulum and both sides of the coronal ridge (well before the point of ejaculatory inevitability). It would be used at different steps throughout the intervention in ways similarly to how the stop-start method was used.

The approach has remained remarkably unchanged over the years. An example of this approach can be seen in the treatment model by Robert and Antonette Zeiss (1978). The clinician begins by providing education to the couple about the stages of the sexual response cycle with special discussion of the moment of ejaculatory inevitability. The clinician then places a restriction or ban on sexual intercourse. The point in proscribing sexual intercourse is to avoid having ongoing discouraging experiences while they are simultaneously attempting to follow a corrective treatment model.

The couple is then taught two techniques: the squeeze and the stop-start technique (the stop-start technique is also referred to as the pause technique). After providing education on the difference between the squeeze and the stop-start techniques, the homework assignment is for the man to self-stimulate one time with three squeeze steps and one pause step, and once more with two of each (the squeeze and the pause). The couple would then discuss this in the subsequent meeting with the therapist and solve any concerns.

The next homework assignment is to have the man teach his partner both of these procedures. They then have three sessions that week with the woman applying the squeeze three or four times each session. Their experience with this homework can be discussed and problems can be solved at the next meeting with the therapist.

The next homework assignment is to repeat the assignment from the previous week but instead of using the squeeze technique, the couple is to use the pause technique. As they transition to intercourse, they are instructed to use both the squeeze and the pause techniques earlier, as the act of withdrawing the penis is itself stimulating at the coronal ridge of the penis and can lead to ejaculation. This homework is discussed and problems are solved in the next therapy meeting.

Next, three times during this week the couple is going to have manual stimulation of the penis and use of the squeeze twice, then containment of the penis in the vagina, which is then withdrawn for use of the squeeze technique. This is discussed in the following therapy meeting.

The next week's homework is to repeat the homework from the previous week but substitute the pause technique for the squeeze technique. The homework is then discussed and problems solved at the next meeting with the therapist. By this time there is some risk that the process may seem too mechanical or reductionistic. You want to encourage them as a couple to be present with each other throughout their homework, as their time together is an act of intimacy.

The next homework is to ad lib with the squeeze technique while extending intercourse to a minimum of eight minutes in the female superior position. This homework is processed during the next meeting with the therapist. Again, while this is a homework assignment, it is also a time of great intimacy, and you can encourage them to be present with each other, to delight in each other, while they are also following a procedure of sorts. In some ways because they are stepping into a framework for treatment, they can enjoy being together once again. They might think of the assignments as a kind of scaffolding around a structure that is being rebuilt. The scaffold provides a safe way for doing the kind of necessary reconstruction to the structure that is being cared for, in this case their time of sexual intimacy.

The last homework is to repeat the last step of achieving eight minutes of intercourse but by using the pause technique rather than the squeeze technique.

The couple can then work with the therapist on transitioning to other sexual positions and extending intercourse to match their interests. They can also solve problems related to possible relapses, which are not uncommon. It is best to prepare them for these instances so that they are able to avoid judgmental or critical thinking, which would be an added complication to this process.

It was noted earlier that there are many models and variations on this approach. In addition to the program by the Zeisses, Kaplan (1989) published a model of treatment for premature ejaculation that also utilized the stop-start method. She placed greater emphasis on keeping arousal at a lower threshold that allows for greater control on the part of the man. According to Kaplan, the man essentially learns to develop control by learning different levels of arousal and making choices to engage in behaviors that are arousing but not so arousing as to lead to premature ejaculation.

Christian sex therapist Doug Rosenau (2002) provides a similar approach for addressing premature ejaculation. He teaches men about Kegel exercises, which help to exercise the pubococcygeus muscles (PC muscles). The PC muscles are readily identified by starting and stopping the flow of urine during urination. Men learn to exercise the PC muscles with Kegel exercises in which the man contracts them during two sessions a day (and ten repetitions per session). He counts to two each time; the next week he counts to three each time and then relaxes. The man is then instructed to begin stimulation, contract his PC muscles, stop/break, and then start stimulation, each time learning more about his own arousal. Rosenau encourages including the spouse early in the process. They eventually reach a place where they practice "quiet vagina" or the practice of the man entering the woman but with no movement. They can later add to this exercise the use of slower, more shallow thrusts (i.e., referred to as shallow containment), using the stop-start technique described throughout as needed. They then add to this exercise slow and deeper thrusts with ample use of stop-start as needed.

Metz and McCarthy (2004) offer an alternative to the squeeze method for those who would benefit from learning new strategies and skills. They begin with identifying sources of relational distress and cultivating a balance between individuality and relational cohesion as a couple (or what Sells &

Yarhouse, 2011, refer to as a sense of "US" as a couple). They then focus on enhancing emotional intimacy by teaching men how important feelings are to sexual intimacy. They work with men on how to identify and express feelings. In terms of learning skills, Metz and McCarthy offer four phases: (1) comfort and relaxation, (2) pleasure toleration (increasing erotic stimulation while in a relaxed state), (3) pleasure saturation (by integrating previously learned skills into sexual intercourse), and (4) long-term satisfaction (integrating skills into other aspects of the relationship for intimacy over the length of the relationship).

The first phase, "comfort and relaxation," focuses on attending to physical sensations to relax the body, learning body image exercises, improving communication as a couple, and learning pelvic muscle control (Metz & McCarthy, 2004). Men learn to identify and relax their pelvic muscle through a number of training strategies. They eventually incorporate exercises that help them relax while aroused ("Finding Your Calm Erection," p. 118).

The second phase, "pleasure toleration," emphasizes learning ways to increase erotic stimulation while in a relaxed state (Metz & McCarthy, 2004). As a couple they learn nonerotic sensual touch in a relaxed state (sensate focus exercise without genital stimulation). They then do exercises in which they include genital exploration on one another. The next exercise in this phase of "pleasure toleration" is to have the man take steps to increase arousal during self-stimulation incorporating moments (pauses) in which he decreases (slows) both mental and physical stimulation. He can then take this knowledge and experience into a couple's exercise in which as a couple they learn and practice pausing, pacing (or slowing) themselves, focusing on one's partner, and pacing (or slowing) with a focus on one's partner. Betchen (2009) describes an exercise that is similar to pacing that he refers to as "slow-fast penile stimulation" (p. 143). In this exercise, "The man is to have his partner stroke him until he reaches a high level of sexual excitement and then to slow down rather than come to a complete stop" (p. 143).

In the third phase of the Metz and McCarthy (2004) protocol, "pleasure saturation," the couple learns to take the strategies they have been practicing and incorporate them into sexual stimulation (intercourse) without rapid ejaculation. They do relaxed pleasure sessions (sensate focus) then transition to focusing on one's own sensations. They eventually move toward more spontaneous activity, but this is after success in applying the prior skills into sexual intercourse.

In addition to these treatment exercises, Althof (2006) notes several cognitive distortions identified by Rosen and his colleagues that may exist among men who struggle with sexual dysfunctions. These cognitive distortions can be identified and processed throughout the course of counseling. They are similar to what we discussed in chapter eight for the treatment of erectile dysfunction but have been adapted for the man who presents with concerns about rapid ejaculation:

1. All-or-nothing thinking, e.g., "I am a complete failure because I come quickly"
2. Overgeneralization, e.g., "If I had trouble controlling my ejaculation last night, I won't be able to this morning"
3. Disqualifying the positive, e.g., "My partner says our lovemaking is satisfying because she does not want to hurt my feelings"
4. Mind reading, e.g., "I don't need to ask. I know how she felt about last night"
5. Fortune telling, e.g., "I am sure things will go badly tonight"
6. Emotional reasoning, e.g., "Because a man feels something is true, it must be" [or "because I feel like a failure, I must be one"]
7. Categorical imperatives, e.g., "shoulds," "ought to," and "musts" dominate the man's cognitive processes, and
8. Catastrophizing, e.g., "If I fail tonight my girlfriend will dump me." (p. 184)

The general treatment approach for rapid ejaculation appears to offer several helpful things. The man learns to delay the point of ejaculatory inevitability until he or his partner desires. The delay reflects aspects of arousal and stimulation that are under his influence. The process increases latency and enhances voluntary control. The process may also decrease spectatoring (on the part of the man) and performance anxiety.

Many clinicians today also look at possible relationship conflicts or other issues that may be unresolved within the client (Rowland, 2012). In some ways what appears to be a rather straightforward behavioral approach has been augmented by other discussions in the course of sex therapy, as psychological factors, relationship factors, family-of-origin factors, cultural factors, and other considerations may be explored throughout therapy (Betchen, 2009).

Another psychological approach that has attempted to address concerns that use of the pause and squeeze techniques is either too mechanical or otherwise interrupts the flow of sexual intimacy is referred to as functional-sexological treatment (de Carufel & Trudel, 2006). In addition to education about male and female sexual response, men learn

> to move their body differently by focusing on temporal, spatial, and energetic dimensions of their movements, to use their muscles in another way (e.g., relax the buttocks), to vary the speed of sexual activity before and during intercourse, to breathe from the diaphragm, and to use positions that require less muscular tension. (pp. 98-99)

Initial research suggests that the functional-sexological approach can also be helpful in the treatment of rapid ejaculation, with improvements noted in length of intercourse, sexual functioning, and sexual satisfaction (de Carufel & Trudel, 2006).

When the preferred psychological intervention is not effective, it is possible that the man is struggling with performance anxiety, or they may be trying to take shortcuts or otherwise fix the problem quickly by moving through the homework assignments too rapidly (Althof, 2007). By being so problem focused and by moving through the homework at too quick a pace, they end up putting their treatment at risk and may not find the exercises as helpful. This in turn may build up expectations that then contribute to maladaptive thoughts associated with feelings of failure.

Other men who do not experience success with this protocol may be taking too many risks in terms of getting too close to the line of ejaculatory inevitability. If a man crowds that threshold (of ejaculatory inevitability), he may not yet have learned when to begin either the squeeze or stop-start/pause technique and may struggle more with identifying what is certainly an important marker in the course of treatment.

As with many treatment protocols, if a man has tried this method and not found it successful, he may not be eager to put in the kind of time and energy it requires. We encourage the clinician to discuss a man's prior use of a similar treatment approach; this may help the clinician and client identify missteps along the way, including pace, how problems were processed and resolved, technique, and so on. This should be done before attempting to provide a comparable approach, so that the man understands better why an intervention did not work and can take meaningful, corrective steps.

In keeping with the neurobiological understanding of etiology discussed earlier, some men are prescribed selective serotonin reuptake inhibitors (e.g., sertraline/Zoloft, paroxetine/Paxil, fluoxetine/Prozac) to help delay ejaculation. Recall that in our previous discussion it was noted that diminished serotonin neurotransmission is thought to be associated with rapid ejaculation. The SSRIs increase serotonin by inhibiting its reuptake. Other antidepressants, such as clomipramine/Anafranil, a tricyclic antidepressant, have also been used in the treatment of rapid ejaculation.

Delayed ejaculation. Psychological treatment of delayed ejaculation focuses more on resolving internal and relational conflicts. Internal conflicts can include anxiety, fear, rigid masturbatory scripts, and other issues. Treatment could incorporate mindfulness training and focusing on experiencing pleasure. In the case of aging, addressing distractions and learning to increase arousal physically and mentally can be helpful (Rosenau et al., 2004). Relational conflicts might reflect power struggles, passive aggressiveness, and so on. Insight-oriented approaches have been used to address internal struggles, and emotion-focused approaches can facilitate self-expression. Clinicians also help men with a narrow masturbatory script to expand some of their fantasy and experiences (Foley, 2009). Sensate focus exercises that place a premium on nondemand sensual touch are often used to address relational intimacy, as are communication exercises such as sofa sessions and assertiveness training.

One myth that is discussed in the literature on delayed ejaculation is the perception that the partner is pleased with a man who does not ejaculate easily. The myth is that she is experiencing him as the ideal sex partner because he can "go longer," as though that were "the gold standard for sexual satisfaction" (Foley, 2009, p. 156). As Foley notes, this myth reflects several cultural assumptions about men and their role in sexual intimacy. The clinical reality is that the man often struggles with negative self-evaluation and shame, and the partner often reports feeling rejected.

The clinician should also be aware that various medications can contribute to delayed ejaculation (e.g., some of the SSRIs; Foley, 2009). Unfortunately, there are no medications known at this time to treat delayed ejaculation. However, it is certainly important to monitor the use of medications that contribute to the presenting concern and to work closely with the prescribing physician to navigate decisions about medication management in light of possible sexual side effects.

As we bring this discussion of treatment options to a close, we observe that advances in understanding the biological underpinnings will likely continue and may provide more options in the future. However, much of what the clinician does is to provide interventions to improve sexual functioning. The steps taken differ significantly between treating rapid ejaculation and delayed ejaculation, but both entail a comprehensive assessment and case conceptualization to be effective.

PREVENTION

Discussions about prevention center on education about risk factors associated with rapid and delayed ejaculation. It has been noted that being diagnosed with erectile dysfunction may place a man at risk for premature ejaculation. Some of the psychological theories for the etiology of premature ejaculation suggest anxiety, guilt, and relationship difficulties that could be addressed before they lead to ongoing struggles with rapid ejaculation.

Much of the education on prevention centers more on medications that have sexual side effects. The treatment of depression with SSRIs, for example, could lead to side effects that include, for some men, delayed ejaculation. As men age they are also more likely to report chronic health conditions that require medication (Foley, 2009), and with delayed ejaculation in particular, this is when we sometimes see an increase in difficulties, though adult men can report difficulties at any time throughout the lifespan.

Another area for discussion is general stress and how that affects a man's quality of life. Perhaps indirectly, stress can place a man at risk for either rapid or delayed ejaculation insofar as the demands of life may contribute to rushing through sexual intimacy on the one hand (perhaps leading to difficulties with rapid ejaculation) or not engaging with his partner and the experience of intimacy on the other (perhaps leading to difficulties with delay).

Whether poor communication and relationship difficulties are a part of the cause or a maintaining factor in either premature or delayed ejaculation, taking care of the relationship and being intentional about communication can be an important preventative measure. Being able to discuss what they both like, the time they spend with each other (in terms of their sexual script and outside that time together), and investing in nondemand sensual touch can also be helpful elements to a healthy sex life together.

CLOSING REFLECTIONS

As Christians engage the topic of rapid and delayed ejaculation, it is interesting to note a reflection by Hanash (2008) about the importance of sociocultural context. In some cultures, such as some parts of Africa, the Middle East, and the Far East, "only the man's sexual pleasure matters, so those men who ejaculate quickly most likely do not care and are not inclined to acknowledge it" (p. 185). Indeed, in a global study of 27,500 people from twenty-nine countries on sexual attitudes and behaviors, Laumann et al. (2006) reported that rates of sexual satisfaction were lower in these same regions as compared to other countries (e.g., United States, Canada, France) where men and women have more equal status. Although not a study about any one specific sexual dysfunction, it is interesting that sociocultural context may shape sexual habits that are seen in physically, sexually, and emotionally satisfying lives.

It seems to us that there is something Christian about a relationship-enhancing sexual encounter between husband and wife. We certainly acknowledge that this has not been a hallmark of Christian thinking throughout history, but it seems to reflect how Christians are engaging the topic today and in our sociocultural context. Settings in which men but not women are valued, settings that assume or explicitly teach that male pleasure but not female pleasure matters, seem at odds with a Christian vision for human sexuality and sexual expression.

On the other hand, our culture can run the risk of the other extreme: we can become fixated on how long a man lasts in terms of sexual performance. This can be a reductionistic model of male sexuality (equating sexuality with sexual performance), which seems to reflect more stereotypes and caricatures of male sexuality.

There also is a risk of pathologizing normal variations in sexual experience in order to achieve a particular end—and there is also a risk of making an idol out of optimal sexual experiences. That message can come straight from secular, hedonic entertainment and has nothing to do with a Christian vision for sexual intimacy. So there is a balance that needs to be struck between elevating the place, value, and worth of sexual encounter, and enhancing quality of life in that context. At the same time, we do not want to fuel a message that inappropriately elevates the sex act itself as though it were the final word on a person's worth, as though performance dictates value.

There continues to be a need to help Christian communities discuss and teach on human sexuality and sexual functioning, to validate the concerns of couples who may be dealing with either rapid or delayed ejaculation. The failure of the church to acknowledge and discuss sex can often be mirrored in the lives of Christian couples who themselves have a difficult time acknowledging and discussing their concerns. They may not know that there are options available to them, that there are resources that may provide them with the support and information necessary to address and resolve a concern. Room for discussions within the church community about premature ejaculation, delayed ejaculation, and other concerns can provide opportunities for correction if there are errant myths regarding what it means to be a man or masculine as these concepts are tied to sexuality. How helpful and encouraging would it be for a church to offer resources on responding to rapid or delayed ejaculation that are honest and affirming, that foster a community of both intimacy and transparency in an area that is often so difficult to discuss.

REFERENCES

Althof, S. E. (2006). Psychological approaches to the treatment of rapid ejaculation. *Journal of Men's Health and Gender, 3*(2), 180-86.

Althof, S. E. (2007). Treatment of rapid ejaculation psychotherapy, pharmacotherapy, and combined therapy. In S. R. Leiblum (Ed.), *Principles and practice of sex therapy* (4th ed., pp. 212-40). Guilford.

Althof, S. E. (2016). Patient reported outcomes in the assessment of premature ejaculation. *Translational Andrology and Urology, 5*, 470-74.

American Psychiatric Association. (2022). *Diagnostic and statistical manual of mental disorders* (5th ed. Text Revision). American Psychiatric Publishing.

Barbonetti, A., D'Andrea, S., Cavallo, F., Martorella, A., Francavilla, S., & Francavilla, F. (2019). Erectile dysfunction and premature ejaculation in homosexual and heterosexual men: A systematic review and meta-analysis of comparative studies. *Journal of Sexual Medicine, 16*, 624-32.

Betchen, S. J. (2009). Premature ejaculation: An integrative, intersystem approach for couples. In K. M. Hertlein, G. R. Weeks, & N. Gambescia (Eds.), *Systemic sex therapy* (pp. 131-52). Routledge.

de Carufel, F., & Trudel, G. (2006). Effects of a new functional-sexological treatment for premature ejaculation. *Journal of Sex & Marital Therapy, 32*, 97-114.

Foley, S. (2009). The complex etiology of delayed ejaculation: Assessment and treatment implications. In K. M. Hertlein, G. R. Weeks, & N. Gambescia (Eds.), *Systemic sex therapy* (pp. 153-78). Routledge.

Grover, S., & Shouan, A. (2020). Assessment scales for sexual disorders: A review. *Journal of Psychosexual Health, 2*(2), 121-28.

Hanash, K. A. (2008). *New frontiers in men's sexual health: Understanding erectile dysfunction and the revolutionary new treatments.* Praeger.

Hartmann, U., & Waldinger, M. D. (2007). Treatment of delayed ejaculation. In S. R. Leiblum (Ed.), *Principles and practice of sex therapy* (4th ed., pp. 241-76). Guilford.

Huang, Y.-P., Chen, B., Ping, P., Wang, H.-X., Hu, K., Zhang, T., Yang, H., Yan, J., Yang, Q., & Huang, Y.-R. (2014). The premature ejaculation diagnostic tool: Linguistic validity of the Chinese version. *Journal of Sexual Medicine, 11*, 2232-38.

Kaplan, H. S. (1989). *How to overcome premature ejaculation.* Routledge.

Laumann, E. O., Paik, A., Glasser, D., & Kang, J.-H. (2006). A cross-national study of subjective sexual well-being among older women and men: Findings from the Global Study of Sexual Attitudes and Behaviors. *Archives of Sexual Behavior, 35*(2), 145-61. doi:10.1007/s10508-005-9005-3

Metz, M. E., & McCarthy, B. W. (2004). *Coping with premature ejaculation.* New Harbinger.

Patrick, D. L., Giuliano, F., Ho, K. F., Gagnon, D. D., McNulty, P., & Rothman, M. (2009). The Premature Ejaculation Profile: Validation of self-reported outcome measures for research and practice. *BJU International, 103*, 358-64.

Polonsky, D. C. (2000). Premature ejaculation. In S. R. Leiblum & R. C. Rosen (Eds.), *Principles and practice of sex therapy* (3rd ed., pp. 368-422). Guilford.

Rosenau, D. (2002). *A celebration of sex: A guide to enjoying God's gift of sexual intimacy* (Rev. ed.). Thomas Nelson.

Rosenau, D., Childerston, J., & Childerston, C. (2004). *A celebration of sex after 50.* Thomas Nelson.

Rowland, D. L. (2012). *Sexual dysfunction in men.* Hogrefe.

Sells, J. N., & Yarhouse, M. A. (2011). *Counseling couples in conflict: A relational restoration model.* InterVarsity Press.

Semans, J. H. (1956). Premature ejaculation: A new approach. *Southern Medical Journal, 49*, 353-57.

Waldinger, M. D. (2010). Premature ejaculation and delayed ejaculation. In S. B. Levine, C. B. Risen, & S. E. Althof (Eds.), *Handbook of clinical sexuality for mental health professionals* (2nd ed., pp. 267-94). Routledge.

Wincze, J. P., & Carey, M. P. (2001). *Sexual dysfunction: Treatment manuals for practitioners.* Guilford.

Zeiss, R., & Zeiss, A. (1978). *Prolong your pleasure.* Pocket Books.

PART THREE

ADDITIONAL

CLINICAL

PRESENTATIONS

TEN

THE PARAPHILIAS AND PARAPHILIC DISORDERS

WHAT'S IN A NAME? How about this one: Richard Fridolin Joseph Freiherr Krafft von Festenberg auf Frohnberg, genannt von Ebing. That is the full name of the German neurologist and psychiatrist you may know as Richard von Krafft-Ebing, author of *Psychopathia Sexualis*. Krafft-Ebing was born in 1840 in Mannheim, studied medicine at the University of Heidelberg, and went on to become professor of psychiatry at the University of Vienna. His book *Psychopathia Sexualis* (subtitled *Eine klinisch-forensische Studie*) is translated in English as *Sexual Psychopathy: A Clinical-Forensic Study*. It was published in 1886 and became the leading reference work for psychiatric care of sexual pathologies at that time. He revised his book through twelve editions, introducing new case material and extending into far-reaching areas of sexual pathology, reviewing and popularizing terms such as *fetishism*, *sadism*, *masochism,* and *nymphomania*, as well as other concepts that lay the foundation for our understanding of contemporary paraphilias.

A paraphilia reflects a sexual deviation (a departure from the norm), an unusual or atypical sexual interest. This chapter, then, covers sexual behaviors that many in the public—not to mention clinicians and students in training—experience as distasteful or offensive. It can be a discouraging focus of treatment, and many people struggle with what it means to develop an empathic, constructive therapeutic relationship with those who contend with the paraphilias. Indeed, the paraphilias bring into the clinical setting behaviors that overlap more significantly with moral sensibilities, thus making the treatment of such behaviors a particularly challenging career path.

Diagnostically, we think of paraphilias as strong or intense atypical sexual interests. They are atypical in that they involve objects, children, or nonconsenting persons, or the suffering or humiliation of another. The *DSM-5-TR* defines a *paraphilia* as "any intense and persistent sexual interest other than sexual interest in genital stimulation or preparatory fondling with phenotypically normal, physically mature, consenting human partners" (APA, 2022, p. 779).

The DSM-5-TR distinguishes paraphilias from paraphilic disorders. The former denote sexuality outside the norm but not necessarily a mental health concern. *Paraphilic disorder* would distinguish those with a mental health issue, which appears to be reflected in whether they are distressed or impaired in some way. According to *DSM-5-TR*, "A paraphilic disorder is a paraphilia that is currently causing distress or impairment to the individual or a paraphilia whose satisfaction has entailed personal harm, or risk of harm, to others" (pp. 780). Impairment is often assessed in relation to occupational functioning or relationships. So there is sadism or exhibitionism as sexual activities that fall outside the norm of what interests most people, and these are different from sexual sadism disorder or exhibitionistic disorder, which are mental health concerns if they are impairing, personally distressing, or reflect harm or risk of harm to another.

This change reflects the ways that sexual interests and behaviors are expanding to reflect a range of diverse interests, as well as the reluctance within the mental health field to identify patterns of behavior as reflecting mental health concerns unless the person is already distressed. As most people who work with these people in this area will attest, few individuals are personally distressed by their sexual interests; so impairment in social and occupational functioning may end up being a critical distinction.

It may also be helpful to discuss the relationship between sexual addiction (discussed at length in chap. 11) and the paraphilias. Levine (2010) describes sexual addiction as a "behavioral complex, not a diagnosis" (p. 262). By this he means that sexual addiction "is based on behaviors that are obviously destructive to somebody—the person himself or herself, the spouse, lover, family, employer, or society" (p. 262). Many clients who receive treatment for sexually addictive behaviors may exhibit paraphilic behavior. As Birchard (2011) observes, sexual addictions and the paraphilias appear to be linked in several ways:

- Both behaviors are ordinarily driven by shame and commonly produce shame.
- Both were established in the family of origin.
- They are responses to narcissistic damage.
- They are a means to relieve painful affect and to manage self-regulation.
- They wax and wane with pressure and anxiety.
- They frequently bring with them harmful consequences (p. 184).

As Birchard (2011) goes on to explain, "Sexual addiction is a response to childhood trauma and to negative affect states and their replacement with eroticized intensity. A paraphilia is similarly a response to childhood trauma, a turning of trauma into eroticized triumph" (p. 184). For Birchard it is the difference between eroticized *intensity* and eroticized *triumph*, with the "triumph" being the "conversion of pain and humiliation" during childhood "into pleasure and triumph" (p. 175).

From more of a social learning perspective, the paraphilias are thought to have "been learned at some time in the past" and conditioned or reinforced (Kaplan & Krueger, 2012, p. 292). Interventions, as we shall see, focus more on essentially reducing arousal that deviates from the norm and increasing more appropriate arousal.

PARAPHILIC DISORDERS

There are many identified paraphilic disorders. The *DSM-5-TR* includes voyeuristic disorder, exhibitionistic disorder, frotteuristic disorder, sexual masochism disorder, sexual sadism disorder, pedophilic disorder, fetishistic disorder, and transvestic disorder. The argument for inclusion is that they are relatively more common than other paraphilias, and some are also "classed as criminal offenses" (APA, 2022, p. 779). The list is not, however, exhaustive, and the *DSM-5-TR* notes that "many dozens of distinct paraphilias have been identified and named" (p. 779).

Probably the most frequently researched and discussed in clinical circles and the one that receives a lot of media and public health attention is pedophilia. Other paraphilias that clinicians will likely encounter at some point include exhibitionism, voyeurism, fetishism, masochism, and sadism.

Pedophilia refers to a condition in which a person has sexual arousing fantasies or behavior that involves prepubescent children (Wylie et al., 2008). Pedophilic disorder is defined in the *DSM-5-TR* as "recurrent and intense sexually arousing fantasies, sexual urges, or behaviors involving sexual activity with a prepubescent child or children (generally age 13 or younger)" (APA, 2022, p. 792). These urges have been acted on or the urges or fantasies cause "marked distress or interpersonal difficulty" (p. 697).

Attraction to a peripubescent adolescent (at the onset of puberty) is referred to as hebephilia. Ray Blanchard and his colleagues define this as "the erotic preference for pubescent children (roughly, ages 11 or 12-14)" (p. 335). Infantophilia refers to a sexual interest in younger children, typically younger than five years old. The behavior may include exposing oneself to a child or masturbating in the presence of a child, as well as direct contact such as fondling (touching the genitals), fellatio, cunnilingus, or anal or vaginal penetration with an object or one's fingers or penis.

Not everyone who meets criteria for pedophilia has acted on those urges, nor are all child sex offenders necessarily pedophiles (Seto, 2008). However, as many as half of those who have a pedophilic sexual preference report their preference emerging before age eighteen, and data suggests that it is a fairly stable preference over the lifespan (Seto, 2008). At the same time, it is not a foregone conclusion that sexual problem behavior in childhood will translate into sexual offending behavior in adulthood. Indeed, data suggests that only a minority of children with sexual behavior problems involving peers (e.g., coercive sexual behavior such as touching another child's genitals despite resistance) go on to commit sexual offenses as adolescents, and again only a minority of adolescent sex offenders go on to commit sexual offenses as adults (Seto, 2008, p. 166).

The vast majority of people who deal with pedophilic urges are male (approximately 90% or more) (McConaghy, 1993; Seto, 2008), although it has been suggested that there is a higher incidence of female pedophiles than originally thought (Wylie et al., 2008). About 27% of those with pedophilic behavior commit incest (Hall & Hall, 2007), although some research has shown higher rates than that, and a small percentage (about 7%) report exclusive pedophilic impulses, while most have other attractions as well (Abel & Harlow, 2001). It has been estimated that "at least twice as many girls are abused as boys" (McConaghy, 1993, p. 308). Seto (2008) summarizes the literature on prevalence estimates, indicating that "sexual fantasies about children and sexual contacts with children are uncommon, and thus suggest that pedophilia appears to be rare in the male population, occurring at a frequency less than 3%" (p. 165). This is consistent with the prevalence estimate in the *DSM-5-TR*, which is cited as less than 3% of the male population (APA, 2022).

Several experts (e.g., Hall & Hall, 2007; McConaghy, 1993) distinguish between homosexual and heterosexual pedophiles, noting significant differences. For example, McConaghy asserts that homosexual pedophiles tend to have many more victims (up to the hundreds; Hall & Hall, 2007, indicated an average of 10.7 children abused and an average of 52 acts), who are typically not known to the person; offenses tend to occur only once with that victim; the person tends to not report attraction to adults of either sex; they tend to be single; and their behavior tended to begin during adolescence.

In contrast, according to McConaghy (1993) the heterosexual pedophile tends to have relatively fewer victims (Hall & Hall, 2007, report an average of 5.2 children abused and an average of 34 pedophilic acts); the victim tends to be known to the person; offenses tend to be repeated with that same victim; the person is also attracted to adult women and is typically married, with pedophilic behavior beginning in adulthood. Other professionals conceptualize pedophilia as a sexual preference and would not distinguish homosexual and heterosexual types of pedophilia in this same manner (Seto, 2008). Sexual interest in children often emerges prior to age eighteen and does not abate in the person who contends with pedophilic urges:

> It is possible that pedophiles and nonpedophiles share the same curiosity about seeing other children nude when they are children themselves, but that pedophiles remain fixed at this stage and do not develop a sexual attraction to postpubertal individuals as they reach puberty, like most other men. (p. 166)

Since this is probably the most discussed paraphilia, we would note common rationales offered by the person who experiences pedophilic urges for engaging in pedophilic behavior are that such activities offer "educational value" to the child or that (in their view) the child experiences pleasure or in some way indicated he or she was willing or interested.

Other relatively common paraphilias include exhibitionism, voyeurism, fetishism, masochism, and sadism. It is difficult to get an exact prevalence estimate for the various paraphilias, although we often have a sense for how common they are relative to other specific paraphilias based on clinical samples.

Exhibitionism "is the name given when a person gets sexual pleasure from exposing their genitals to unsuspecting strangers, sometimes masturbating at the same time" (Wylie et al., 2008, pp. 121-22). Exhibitionistic disorder is defined in the *DSM-5-TR* as "recurrent and intense sexual arousal from the exposure of one's genitals to an unsuspecting person, as manifested by fantasies, urges, or behaviors" (p. 783). These urges have been acted on "with a nonconsenting person, or the sexual urges or fantasies cause clinically significant distress or impairment" in social or occupational functioning (p. 783). It is difficult to obtain solid prevalence estimates, and it is likely significantly underreported, but it appears to be one of the more common patterns of paraphilic activity for which a person seeks treatment (McConaghy, 1993). National samples suggest that 4% to 5% of adult men and 2% of adult women have exposed themselves for sexual pleasure (Murphy & Page, 2008). The *DSM-5-TR* places the lifetime prevalence estimates at about 4.1% of males and 2.1% of females, citing a study from Sweden (APA, 2022, p. 784). Those who do expose themselves often report being shy or withdrawn socially (McConaghy, 1993). They tend to have numerous victims. The risk of being caught and the element of thrill appear to be a part of the sexual arousal. It is more common for men to expose themselves than it is for women, and when men engage in exhibitionism, their target is typically women, children, or adolescents. When women do deal with exhibitionism, it is more likely to have an attention-seeking quality rather than the thrill or risk elements seen with men. Those who expose themselves typically report beginning prior to age eighteen, and there is some reason to believe the severity decreases for some at around middle age (Murphy & Page, 2008).

Voyeurism is the act of observing an unsuspecting person who is disrobing, nude, or otherwise engaged in a sexual activity. Voyeuristic disorder is defined in the *DSM-5-TR* as "recurrent and intense sexual arousal from observing an unsuspecting person who is naked, in the process of disrobing, or engaging in sexual activities, as manifested by fantasies, urges, or behaviors" (p. 780). These urges have been acted on "with a nonconsenting person, or the sexual urges or fantasies cause clinically significant distress or impairment" in social or occupational functioning (p. 780). The element of thrill and risk of being caught appear important in sexual arousal. Onset of voyeuristic behaviors varies. In one study discussed by Lavin (2008), 50% of a sample of adolescent offenders reported an interest in voyeurism before age fifteen. The *DSM-5* places the highest lifetime prevalence estimates at 12% of males and 4% of females (APA, 2013). They tend to have a history of being shy or withdrawn socially (McConaghy, 1993). Those who exhibit themselves have often also engaged in voyeurism (APA, 2022); some people who have been voyeurs report a history of prior exhibitionism. Voyeurs tend to be men rather than women (Lavin, 2008).

Fetishism refers to sexually arousing thoughts and fantasies or behaviors that involve inanimate objects, which can vary considerably. Fetishistic disorder is defined in the *DSM-5-TR* as "recurrent and intense sexual arousal from either the use of nonliving objects or a highly specific focus on nongenital body part(s), as manifested by fantasies, urges, or behaviors" (APA, 2022, p. 786). These fantasies, urges, or behaviors cause "clinically significant distress or impairment" in functioning, and the objects "are not limited to articles of clothing used in cross-dressing" as would be evidence of Transvestic Disorder. It is a relatively rare phenomenon even among those with mental health concerns. Probably less than 1% of a clinical sample would meet criteria, and maybe 8% of those seeking services specifically for a paraphilia would present with a fetish (Darcangelo, 2008). Almost any object can become a fetish, but the more common objects are clothing, rubber, shoes or boots, parts of the body, and leather. Some fetishes reflect an activity, such as enemas or the act of cross-dressing. When an object is the fetish, the person will often masturbate while rubbing, smelling, or just holding the object. If they have a sex partner, they might ask their partner to wear the object during sexual intimacy (McConaghy, 1993). They tend to find it arousing to watch people holding or wearing the object, such as when a person scours the public library to watch women wearing a particular shoe or going barefoot. Others will stare at the fetish object, suck on it, roll in it, or cut or burn it. When asked about their history with the fetish object, it is not uncommon for the person to report strong associations and pleasure found in the object in their childhood. The emotional experience with the fetish object has been described as comparable to what a child experiences with a transitional object, such as a special blanket (McConaghy, 1993). The fetishistic behavior, then, begins typically at adolescence with the onset of puberty and the object becoming sexually arousing (McConaghy, 1993). Again, fetishes are a mostly male phenomenon.

Masochism and *sadism* refer to intense sexual impulses or behaviors to either include suffering or experience humiliation (masochism) (Hucker, 2008; Wylie et al., 2008) or harm or humiliate one's partner (sadism) (Yates et al., 2008). Sexual masochism disorder refers to "recurrent and intense sexual arousal from the act of being humiliated, beaten, bound, or otherwise made to suffer, as manifested by fantasies, urges, or behaviors" (APA, 2022, p. 788). These fantasies, urges, or behaviors cause clinically significant distress or impairment. In contrast, sexual sadism disorder refers to "recurrent and intense sexual arousal from the physical or psychological suffering of another person, as manifested by fantasies, urges, or behaviors" (APA, 2022, p. 790).

In this context, flagellation and bondage are more common activities, while piercing, hypoxyphilia (or sexual asphyxia), use of razors or knives, or electric shock are less common (Hucker, 2008). The *DSM-5-TR* (APA, 2022) notes difficulties in identifying prevalence estimates but notes that 2.2% of males and 1.3% of females in an Australian study "had been involved in BDSM [bondage and discipline, domination and submission, sadism and masochism] behavior in the past 12 months" (p. 789). In samples of sexual offenders, between 2% and 5% appear to experience sexual sadism (Yates et al., 2008).

There are other paraphilias—many more, actually. The human capacity to find or experience sexual arousal through so many avenues is actually quite remarkable, if not sobering. Additional paraphilias include sexual pleasure associated with rubbing or pressing one's penis up against others (*frotteurism*), corpses (*necrophilia*), animals (*zoophilia*), feces (*coprophilia*), vomit (*emetophilia*), and urine (*urophilia*).

ETIOLOGY

Given the wide range of what we are describing—and the remarkable capacity to experience sexual arousal via so many diverse stimuli—it is difficult to determine the cause of a given paraphilia.

Most of the studies conducted on etiology are retrospective studies of adults who deal with a paraphilia telling researchers about their childhood (Wincze, 2000). From these studies we get the impression that etiology is tied to early environmental experiences (nurture) but may also have more fundamental roots in risk factors from nature.

A number of models have been proposed over the years. Some are more of the view that paraphilias are habituated practices that reflect excitement more so than sexual arousal per se (e.g., exhibitionism, voyeurism) (Mc-Conaghy, 1993). This has suggested to some theorists more of a compulsivity model. Others extended this to consider motivational level and complications that arise if the "general arousal system of the brain is involved" (p. 332). Others have argued for an addiction model and various cognitive models.

Gene Able offered an early and influential four-stage theory on the etiology of a paraphilia (Wincze, 2000). In the first stage a child is exposed to sexual stimuli in his environment. That exposure could in theory be direct or indirect sexualized stimulation. The second stage involves cognitively rehearsing sexualized stimulation with either positive or negative consequences. The third stage is that the child acts out the behavior and actual (real) consequences are experienced. The fourth and final stage is that the behavior is repeated, varied, and ultimately shaped into any number of manifestations.

This perspective was particularly influential at a time when behavioral approaches and learning theory were more widely adopted. Today we see more interest across all experiences of psychopathology in biological antecedents that may contribute to the clinical issue under discussion.

So while we still do not know the causes of the paraphilias as a group, nor of specific paraphilias, some of the paraphilias, such as pedophilia, have been associated with differences in neuroanatomical brain structure and functioning, including differences in IQ, handedness, and memory (see, e.g., Cantor et al., 2004; Hall & Hall, 2007). Others appear from retrospective studies to be related to earlier exposure and modeling, sexual abuse (e.g., an association between adolescent and adult offenders against children and a history of childhood sexual abuse; Hall & Hall, 2007; Seto, 2008), and other relational deficits and associations to sexual stimuli.

When we look at these conditions from a biopsychosocial perspective, we can appreciate research on biological predispositions to the paraphilias, but they appear to be indirect, perhaps through temperamental and personality differences, including a neurophysiological basis for inhibition and risk-taking that become tied to sexual activities such that there is then a sexual inhibition and sexual risk-taking as part of their experience (Wincze, 2000). Differences in impulse control, self-regulation, and high sex hormones appear to also play a role in "increasing the salience and availability of sexual goals and strengthen their influence in the life of an individual" (Ward & Beech, 2008, p. 25; Dillien et al., 2023).

In their review Wylie et al. (2008) describe multiple theories for the etiology of paraphilias, including a history of childhood abuse (emotional or sexual abuse, family dysfunction, etc.), an imbalance in serotonin transmission, and neurological injury. These are all independently researched areas of consideration with varying degrees of support. Research on hormonal abnormalities has not received much support in terms of difference in levels of testosterone.

In the sexual offending literature—which overlaps but is not identical to the mental health literature on paraphilias—a similar emphasis is placed on an integrated theory of sexual offending (Ward & Beech, 2008). To summarize this perspective, sexual offenses occur

> as a consequence of a network of causal factors: biological factors (evolution, genetic variations, and neurobiology); ecological variables (social and cultural environment, personal circumstances, physical environment); and core neuropsychological systems. (Ward & Beech, 2008, p. 21)

This integrated model, then, offers a theory in which nature (brain development in particular) and nurture (social learning and circumstances) both contribute to individual vulnerabilities. Ward and Beech (2008) offer a theory that

> brain development (influenced by biological inheritance and genetics) and social learning interact to establish an individual's level of psychological functioning. This functioning may be compromised in some way by poor genetic inheritance, biological damage, or developmental adversity to make it more difficult for the individual concerned to function in an adaptive manner; this will lead to problematic psychological functioning and subsequent clinical symptomatology. (p. 25)

There are almost certainly multiple influencing variables that appear to impact the origins of any given paraphilia. These lead to multiple trajectories and unique clinical presentations. Clinicians would do well to keep in mind these integrated models/theories and diverse trajectories so that interaction between these factors is taken into consideration in assessment. A nuanced understanding of etiology translates into a more comprehensive assessment and focused case conceptualization.

ASSESSMENT AND CLINICAL PRESENTATION

Dennis is a forty-eight-year-old Caucasian male who identifies himself as a conservative Christian. As he enters into the counseling office, he reports a problem with "lust." A more detailed sex history indicates the following: (1) masturbation while looking at women in underwear at age ten, (2) masturbation to mother's and sister's underwear, (3) sneaking women's underwear in college to masturbate, (4) sexual thoughts of his own children when giving them a bath or having them sit on his lap, (5) viewing of sexually explicit movies, and (6) sexual thoughts and activities with animals (e.g., dog, goat). Dennis reports being investigated by Child Protective Services and is able to produce a letter indicating that the investigation was "unfounded." He denies phone sex, internet chat, and use of prostitutes.

Dennis reports being married for twenty-two years and is the father of four children. He indicates difficulty in their marriage and shares his problems with communication. For example, his wife would say that she experiences Dennis as emotionally "unavailable" and cites frequent emotional stonewalling and what she experiences as "threatening" stares at her. Dennis shares that he knows he has a problem with intimacy with others, and he admits that he does not enjoy penile-vaginal intercourse with his wife.

Dennis reports a family history of sexual concerns on his paternal side. (His father had had a long, incestuous relationship with Dennis's sister and inappropriate sexual contact with two of Dennis's female cousins.) He also reports a family history of alcoholism on both his paternal side (grandfather) and maternal side (uncle). Dennis also reports a history of being sexually abused by older boys when he was age seven and by his uncle at age nine.

Just reading through some of the initial information confirms in many students' minds that providing services to someone like Dennis is not for everyone. There are distortions to sexual intimacy and behavior that create real challenges for the clinician.

Let us begin with initial exchanges with someone who contends with a paraphilia. We can begin with motivations. People like Dennis often present in counseling with ambivalent feelings. There may be a part of them that recognizes that counseling is a good idea, that they need help. More likely, there is a larger part of them that is comfortable with the status quo; on their own they would not likely seek change from what is familiar to them. What is familiar has also become satisfying to them at some point, so that is a further disincentive from seeking services.

Moreover, people who contend with a paraphilia do not tend to see their behavior as causing themselves or others harm. This way of seeing themselves and their behavior feeds the part of them that is not interested in counseling.

So, ambivalence at the outset of treatment is to be expected. Ambivalence sustained over time is unlikely helpful and may result in treatment failure, so we will return to this.

Keep in mind, then, that few people dealing with a paraphilia will visit a counselor on their own; rather, they typically present to a counselor at the insistence of another. That insistence might be a legal requirement (e.g., court ordered), or it could be at the insistence of a spouse, a girlfriend, or a religious authority figure, such as a pastor or elder.

It can be helpful conceptually and in the spirit of building empathy that underneath the ambivalence and mixed motivations usually resides a self that contends with shame. When conducting an initial assessment, it will be important to convey reassurance that you work with this population and are able to provide resources for helping them.

Assessment usually involves a clinical interview and sex history. The sex history can be general but will also need to focus at times on the atypical sexual behavior. Other possible areas for assessment that involve the administration of questionnaires include social functioning (e.g., Relationship Questionnaire; Bartholomew & Horowitz, 1991), empathy (e.g., Interpersonal Reactivity Test; Davis, 1983), coping (e.g., Sex as a Coping Strategy; Cortoni & Marshall, 2001), cognitive distortions (e.g., Young's Schema Questionnaire; Young & Brown, 2001), sexual interests (e.g., Multiphasic Sex Inventory; Nichols & Molinder, 1984), substance use (e.g., Michigan Alcoholism Screening Test; Selzer, 1971), criminality (e.g., Measures of Criminal Attitudes and Associates; Mills & Kroner, 1999), and general mental health concerns (e.g., Minnesota Multiphasic Personality Inventory; Hathaway et al., 1990) (Marshall et al., 2011). Assessment information may also be obtained from a spouse or partner and family members.

An additional consideration during assessment is one of the first clinical issues: reducing dangerousness (Wincze, 2000). This can be thought of two ways. First, reduce risk to potential victims if applicable. Keep in mind whether there are any children at risk, for example. It may be important to shore up boundaries and isolate the client from situations that place others at risk. There may be specific obligations associated with the state where you are licensed that will dictate the steps taken here, so be familiar with your reporting laws and statutes of limitations where you provide services. The use of pharmacological agents to reduce sex drive may also be a consideration, and we will discuss this in the next section.

Second, reduce risk to the client. The person may be dealing with a co-morbid depression or suicidal ideation or intent, depending on the behavior in question and how it has come to light that the person contends with this paraphilia. This is probably the most overlooked consideration for new clinicians working with this population. They tend to center on the potential risk to others, such as children, but they may overlook the risk to the person who contends with the paraphilia. Be sure to assess for risk for self-harm.

TREATMENT

Clinical interventions for those presenting with a paraphilic disorder are multifaceted. They often involve individual psychological interventions, such as cognitive-behavioral therapy, group therapy, and psychopharmacology. The most cutting-edge models today look more at self-regulation rather than relapse prevention.

The psychological interventions have often followed a cognitive-behavioral therapy approach (Wylie et al., 2008). An initial step in a CBT approach is to have the person keep a log or journal of their thoughts, emotions, and behaviors. The use of a journal can provide initial baseline information on current thoughts, emotions, and behaviors, so there is an added assessment benefit to keeping a log. Journaling also can help interrupt current thought patterns (Wincze, 2000).

Another early step is to remove sexually stimulating materials and limit access to stimuli. This would include removing videos, magazines, or objects that are sexually stimulating. Limiting access to the internet, use of smartphones, and so on is also an important consideration. As you discuss this step with the person, keep in mind that there may be emotions behind any attempt to limit access to these items. This can be thought of as resistance, but we have found it more helpful to conceptualize emotion as a fearful part of the person that has now become activated and is concerned about what is being given up: a pattern of behavior that has essentially been a reliable friend or partner to them for many years. The paraphilia has filled a void, and any attempt to treat it will likely cause concern that can be discussed in counseling.

CBT approaches will identify and challenge unhelpful thoughts that have in the past facilitated atypical sexual behavior. This is done first through documenting through the client's journal the thoughts that he or she has in the circumstances that lead up to acting-out behavior. These thoughts usually reflect a lack of empathy for those who may be victims of their behavior. In some cases the client does not recognize a victim either because no one else is involved (in the case of a fur fetish), while other times those who are involved may not know it or may be viewed as cooperative (in the cases of voyeurism or in the distorted belief that a child is "learning" something of "educational value" in pedophilic acts).

Unhelpful, distorted thoughts can be challenged in therapy, and alternative thoughts can be explored. More helpful thoughts might come from an understanding of how the client's own history has distorted the client's view of him- or herself or others. Insight into core beliefs about the client and others, about the world around him or her, and the importance of sexuality are worth understanding. To understand the experience of others, CBT approaches often do some kind of victim empathy training. This might involve reading accounts of people who at one time were victimized by atypical sexual behaviors.

Orgasmic reconditioning (or masturbatory retraining) involves changing deviant fantasies to appropriate sexual fantasies at the time when orgasm is imminent (McConaghy, 1993).

Alternative behavioral completion refers to the use of imaginal desensitization to establish a hierarchy of anxiety-producing sexual experiences and then desensitizing the client to these scenarios as played out in his imagination. This approach is coupled with imagery exercises of engaging in appropriate behavioral alternatives in the fantasy script (Maletzky, 2002; McConaghy, 1993).

Aversion therapy has taken many forms and is somewhat controversial today. Based on classical conditioning models, aversion therapy may involve electric shock, unpleasant smells, or covert sensitization (visualized deviant behavior followed by visualized aversive consequences for engaging in the behavior).

Group therapy is common for sex offenders. It is believed that the group format allows patients to receive accountability and to learn and practice some social skills. Group therapy is typically offered alongside individual behavior therapy and pharmacological interventions as indicated.

So CBT approaches, while common, are based primarily on maintenance of gains and relapse prevention. They focus on addressing comorbid concerns, such as depression, anxiety, and so on. They can also be used in conjunction with group therapy and medications to lower sexual drive (anti-androgens such as medroxyprogesterone acetate and cyproterone acetate; Wylie et al., 2008). Selective serotonin reuptake inhibitors (SSRIs) have also been used because they increase the activity of serotonin, which has been associated with "decreased libido, ejaculatory problems and anorgasmia" (p. 123). Such medications can be helpful in reducing sexual desire and arousal, but they need to be maintained, as discontinuation of medications is associated with relapse (Wincze, 2000).

Self-regulation approaches. More recent models are based on self-regulation. They take a positive view of the possibilities for the person struggling with atypical sexual interests. These models come primarily from working with sex offenders (Marshall et al., 2011; Marshall & Marshall, 2017) and are thought of as the heir apparent to CBT models concerned more with relapse prevention (Laws & O'Donohue, 2008).

For example, the Good Lives Model draws on what is useful in general clinical practice and from positive psychology. It does this by working from the assumption that part of the offender wants a good life—not unlike those who do not struggle in this area (Willis et al., 2017). The Good Lives Model works then with the person to identify the kind of life they want to lead and to identify the steps that need to be taken to achieve those goals.

In applying positive psychology to this population, James Haaven discusses the "old me" and "new me" by exploring what allowed or enabled the person to commit an offense and the actual choices that they are responsible for (old me) and the plans they have for their future that are associated with their strengths (new me) (Marshall et al., 2011; Marshall & Marshall, 2017).

Motivational interviewing is also often used in work with those who are receiving treatment for a paraphilia. This kind of interviewing sets a collaborative tone between the clinician and the client by evoking insight into next steps for treatment based on a realistic appraisal of the events and circumstances surrounding them. It is not psychoeducational, in which the clinician provides a summary of what we know or do not know about a topic. Rather, it creates what are referred to as "invitations to responsibility" (p. 23) to guide the client into narratives that reflect their responsibilities for their behavior (past, present, and future).

In addition to this emphasis on self-regulation and positive psychology, the current model treatment programs identify and target criminogenic factors or "deficits in functioning" that have been shown to predict offending behaviors (Marshall et al., 2011, p. 10). This can be conceptualized in a broader risk-need-responsivity model in which risk of relapse is considered, but also in terms of needs that may precipitate acting-out behavior, and the person's capacity to respond to interventions (see Olver, 2017). Some of the deficits in functioning that are often targeted, then, include attitudes, beliefs, issues with self-regulation, relationship deficits, and sexual issues.

Attitudes and beliefs. Attitudes and beliefs are far reaching. They can include beliefs such as the thought that they are at low risk to reoffend, as well as adversarial sexual beliefs, such as antisocial characteristics and attitudes (Marshall et al., 2011; Marshall & Marshall, 2017). Additional beliefs and emotional issues include child abuse–supportive beliefs, such as the belief that their own abuse of a child had educational value or was a reflection of genuine mutual affection. A related emotional issue would be identifying (emotionally) with children.

Issues with self-regulation. Issues with self-regulation can be complex and far reaching. They include poor behavioral regulation, difficulties with coping and problem solving, and difficulties with regulating emotions (Marshall et al., 2011; Marshall & Marshall, 2017). In the integrated model of etiology discussed earlier (Ward & Beech, 2008), there are actually two neuropsychological systems involved in different deficits of self-regulation: problems with self-regulation that are tied to one's motivational/emotional system may lead to problems of mood, while concerns tied to action selection/control system may present as impulsivity. In both cases, clinicians will be working with clients on negative affect and impulsivity when addressing self-regulation in the course of therapy.

Relationship deficits. Relationship problems include difficulty with establishing and maintaining intimacy with others and can also include emotional loneliness and deficits in relationship skills (Marshall et al., 2011; Marshall & Marshall, 2017). Indeed, Ward and Beech's (2008) integrated model includes a discussion of the motivational/emotional system—limbic, cortical, and brainstem brain structures—that may reflect deficits in a limited or constricted range of goals, failure to identify one's own emotional state, and lack of skills in creating and maintaining interpersonal relationships.

Sexual issues. Sexual issues can range from deficits in knowledge about sexuality and sexual functioning to atypical, paraphilic sexual interests and attitudes that reflect sexual entitlement ("I have a right to this sexual behavior") and preoccupation with sex (persistent thoughts or fantasies about sex) (Marshall et al., 2011; Marshall & Marshall, 2017).

The idea is that addressing and developing behaviors and attitudes will address the factors and deficits in functioning that seem to put people at risk for reoffending.

Additional self-regulation strategies. Current models address more than these deficits in functioning. They also address self-esteem and work to reduce shame. Building a sense of self-worth is one way to address personal shame. For example, in the Rockwood Program emphasis is placed on identifying positive features about the person dealing with a paraphilia. They essentially distinguish between the person and the behavior. Positive features might include loyalty or a good work ethic. Self-esteem is worked on from that standpoint, while also attending to coping and mood management and empathy.

Coping and mood management involve learning problem-solving skills and assertiveness. Appropriate use of humor can also be a part of treatment. Empathy is an important part of self-regulation strategies. Like most empathy-training approaches, the client learns to identify emotions in others through perspective taking and role playing. The clinician would then also discuss various possible consequences for the victim of a paraphilic behavior.

Finally, self-management is another strategy in current approaches to treatment. This goes back to the "Good Lives" goals mentioned earlier (Willis et al., 2017). The clinician and client work on identifying specific goals that reflect a good life, the life the person would like to live, much like anyone else. The clinician then works with the client on specific steps to attain those goals.

An avoidance plan is then also developed. In some ways this may seem reminiscent of a classic relapse prevention plan, but the assumptions and practices are different. Relapse prevention plans typically involve generating an extensive list of situations and behaviors that place a person at risk for relapse. Strength-based models tend to identify a limited number of common-sense strategies based on the nature of the paraphilia. For example, not being alone with a child would be a part of a plan for self-management and avoidance for someone struggling with pedophilic impulses. At the same time, the clinician is working with the person to identify and develop an "approach plan" for pursuing goals for improving their lives (Marshall et al., 2011, p. 158; Marshall & Marshall, 2017).

PREVENTION

There has been very little done in the area of preventing the paraphilias and paraphilia-related disorders. One suggestion has been to pursue education and to tailor it to areas of particular susceptibility. For example, McConaghy (1993) suggests that in light of the propensity for men to be sexually aroused by female children, efforts should be made to educate men (through school and media programs already in place) of this propensity and to teach skills for avoiding circumstances or coping with unwanted sexual attractions. McConaghy sees this as especially important since many first offenses against children occur "in response to an unexpected opportunity in which they experience this arousal, of which they were previously unaware they were capable" (p. 362). This is essentially education with the aim to help potential offenders control deviant sexual arousal. This may be applied to a number of atypical sexual behaviors, and proper education may remove stigma that can keep people from learning skills that might aid in prevention.

Relapse prevention is a hallmark of behavioral interventions for the paraphilias, and it involves identifying and avoiding high-risk situations, as well as preparing specific coping behaviors and tendencies to rationalize behaviors that place them at further risk of reoffending.

CBT approaches also often have a relapse prevention plan associated with them. The plan is essentially an adaptation of Marlatt's approach to addiction. Relapse prevention plans target high-risk exposure to stimuli that lead to relapse, as well as the circumstances that make such exposure likely. Relapse prevention also entails identifying other ways of responding— healthy and adaptive alternatives to the preferred but unhealthy sexual behavior. Relapse prevention also typically involves a support system, which is understood as relationships with others, including a sponsor or accountability partner, who can be called during difficult times of heightened risk for relapse. Relapse prevention typically addresses the "abstinence-violation effect" seen in substance abuse counseling, that is, the tendency to binge once a person has had a drink. Also referred to as the "What the hell" phenomenon, it is the tendency to say to oneself, *Well, I've already blown it, I might as well enjoy* _____ *because I have to admit that I crossed the line anyway.* Such thinking can lead to many more hours of sexual behavior that is again highly reinforcing, thus undermining many of the gains made in treatment so far.

Current self-regulation and strength-based approaches do not tend to frame their interventions as "relapse prevention," but they do include an avoidance plan, as noted previously. Avoidance plans reflect a limited number of common-sense suggestions and strategies based on the nature of the concern. More common in these models is an "approach plan" that reflects some of the basic principles of identifying and pursuing goals in the Good Lives Model (Marshall et al., 2011, p. 158; Willis et al., 2017).

CLOSING REFLECTIONS

As Christians approach the study of the paraphilias, we would reiterate the inherent challenges of studying behaviors that are often so off-putting to students in training. Many find it difficult to empathize with the kinds of clinical concerns reflected here.

At the same time, a number of questions arise for the Christian. For example, we noted that most of these concerns are atypical, which could mean uncommon or not frequently engaged in by others or not engaged in by many others. What are the inherent tensions in defining deviant behavior based on statistical infrequency? In other words, what are we saying when we compare to what most people do? As we look at the direction the mental health field is moving—toward distinguishing pathological sexual behaviors from nonpathological based primarily on subjective distress and functioning—we see a failure to find adequate conceptual models for sexual paraphilias. The lack of conceptual consensus has left the field with little to offer other than the obvious recognition that such behaviors do not reflect the norms that others adhere to. With the mental health field unable to find language for moral categories or sexual ethics, we are left with descriptions of what most people do or do not do, and what may be distressing to oneself personally. One danger in such a conceptual vacuum is that what people do within a cultural context is likely to change. What if more people engage in a pattern of behavior? Does that make it typical and therefore not a mental health concern? This brings us to interesting developments on sexual liberation from a sociocultural perspective.

An ongoing discussion in the field is the sociocultural context we live in and how a culture may pathologize a behavior that is currently atypical. For example, Seto (2008) notes that age-of-consent laws are established by a society (and in the United States it varies from state to state) and are culturally relative. Some have reasoned that such cultural relativity has historically led to the demonization of certain sexual minorities, such as gay, lesbian, and bisexual persons. Laws and O'Donohue (2008) note that the most recent group to articulate a position of sexual liberation (as a movement) are those who identify as pedophilic in their sexual preference. Persons and groups (e.g., North American Man/Boy Love Association, the Rene Guyon Society) can point to influential sex researchers (e.g., Alfred Kinsey, John Money) who have themselves supported their cause (Laws & O'Donohue, 2008).

Strategies for persuading the public to reexamine its views of pedophilia include using descriptive language (e.g., "adult-child sex" rather than "child sexual abuse"), suggesting that children are capable of consenting to sex with adults, questioning claims of harm to children, and removing pedophilia from diagnostic manuals (Laws & O'Donohue, 2008).

Some Christians will likely see this promotion as one more extension of a "sexual liberation movement" that reflects a slippery slope that has no set endpoint. Others will see it as further evidence of the corruptibility of the modern mental health establishment. They may have never trusted psychiatry or psychology, and this development provides further support for their conclusion.

WORKING WITH PEOPLE WHO PRESENT WITH ATYPICAL SEXUAL BEHAVIOR

What challenges would you face empathizing with a client who was "giving up" an atypical behavior—something that is perhaps distasteful to think about but one that has been a powerful source of pleasure? In this chapter we have discussed a range of paraphilias, including exhibitionism, fetishism (e.g., foot, fur), pedophilia, and other possible presenting concerns. These are not often the easiest topics to think about, let alone organize your thoughts into a coherent assessment, case conceptualization, and treatment plan. Perhaps working through some of your own reactions to the topics discussed in this chapter will provide a place for personal insight and reflection that will further your capacity to work more effectively with this population.

Here are a couple of questions to get you thinking:

- How do you think you will respond to someone who discloses engaging in atypical sexual behavior?
- What questions do you have about your own ability to empathize and build a therapeutic relationship with someone who needs to address atypical sexual behavior in treatment?

A Christian perspective on all human experience is that sin plays a role. To discuss sin, we do not need to limit ourselves to overt behaviors; we can also discuss our fallen condition, the fallen structures of society, and the effects of sin on the clients we work with. So when we look at the topic of the paraphilias, we can ask, In what ways does sin play a role in the presentation of a paraphilic interest and behavior? If our sin functions as a kind of comorbid condition in relation to atypical sexual behavior, then at what point does the Christian address the sin in addition to other comorbid factors (e.g., depression, anxiety, marital stress)?

When it comes to clinical considerations, what can Christianity contribute to a believing client's motivational levels? We noted previously that a person's motivational level is a serious issue and a consideration to be gauged during assessment; it plays a role in successful treatment. The challenge when bringing Christianity into the discussion of motivations is that often the person needs to work through his or her emotional experience of God before tapping into the divine as a resource for ongoing care. If the client (and the well-meaning Christian clinician) do so prematurely, the client may find him- or herself experiencing Christian resources in unhealthy ways that further exacerbate the sense of shame. We encourage the use of Christian resources in treatment of those who are Christian and consent to the use of religiously accommodative treatment plans, but we want to encourage a clinical process in which concerns such as God image (a person's emotional experience of God) are addressed so that the person can truly utilize Christian resources, such as prayer, reading and study of Scripture, and corporate worship, in ways that facilitate rather than undermine goals for treatment.

REFERENCES

Abel, G. G., & Harlow, N. (2001). The Abel and Harlow child molestation prevention study. Excerpted from *The stop child molestation book*. Xlibris. www.childmolestation prevention.org/_files/ugd/4b2901_d91e1a1c004d4e68b7d2b45157971961.pdf

American Psychiatric Association. (2013). *Diagnostic and statistical manual of mental disorders* (5th ed.). American Psychiatric Publishing.

American Psychiatric Association. (2022). *Diagnostic and statistical manual of mental disorders* (5th ed.-Text Revision). American Psychiatric Publishing.

Bartholomew, K., & Horowitz, L. (1991). Attachment styles among young adults: A test of a four-category model. *Journal of Personality and Social Psychology, 61,* 226-44.

Birchard, T. (2011). Sexual addiction and the paraphilias. *Sexual Addiction & Compulsion, 18,* 157-87.

Blanchard, R., Lykins, A. D., Wherrett, D., Kuban, M. E., Cantor, J. M., Blak, T., Dickey, R., & Klassen, P. E. (2009). Pedophilia, hebephilia and the *DSM-V. Archives of Sexual Behavior, 38,* 335-50. https://doi.org/10.1007/s10508-008-9399-9

Cantor, J. M., Blanchard, R., Christensen, B. K., Dickey, R., Klassen, P. E., Beckstead, A. L., . . . & Kuban, M. E. (2004). Intelligence, memory, and handedness in pedophilia. *Neuropsychology, 18*(1), 3-14.

Cortoni, F. A., & Marshall, W. L. (2001). Sex as a coping strategy and its relationship to juvenile sexual history and intimacy in sexual offenders. *Sexual Abuse, 13,* 27-43.

Darcangelo, S. (2008). Fetishism: Psychopathology and theory. In D. R. Laws & W. T. O'Donohue (Eds.), *Sexual deviance: Theory, assessment, and treatment* (2nd ed., pp. 108-18). Guilford.

Davis, M. H. (1983). Measuring individual differences in empathy: Evidence for a multi-dimensional approach. *Journal of Personality and Social Psychology, 44,* 113-26.

Dillien, T., Brazil, I. A., Sabbe, B., & Goethals, K. (2023). Unraveling the neuropsychological underpinnings of self-regulation problems in individuals convicted of sexual offenses against children: A look into reinforcement learning. *Sexual Offending: Theory, Research, and Prevention, 18,* article e7503. https://doi.org/10.5964/sotrap.7503

Hall, R. C. W., & Hall, R. C. W. (2007). A profile of pedophilia: Definition, characteristics of offenders, recidivism, treatment outcomes, and forensic issues. *Mayo Clinic Proceedings, 82*(4), 457-71.

Hathaway, S., McKinley, J., & Butcher, J. (1990). Minnesota Multiphasic Personality Inventory. University of Minnesota Press.

Hucker, S. J. (2008). Sexual masochism: Psychopathology and theory. In D. R. Laws & W. T. O'Donohue (Eds.), *Sexual deviance: Theory, assessment, and treatment* (2nd ed., pp. 250-63). Guilford.

Kaplan, M. S., & Krueger, R. B. (2012). Cognitive-behavioral treatment of the paraphilias. *Israel Journal of Psychiatry and Related Sciences, 49*(4), 291-96.

Lavin, M. (2008). Voyeurism: Psychopathology and theory. In D. R. Laws & W. T. O'Donohue (Eds.), *Sexual deviance: Theory, assessment, and treatment* (2nd ed., pp. 305-19). Guilford.

Laws, D. R., & O'Donohue, W. T. (2008). Introduction. In D. R. Laws & W. T. O'Donohue (Eds.), *Sexual deviance: Theory, assessment, and treatment* (2nd ed., pp. 1-20). Guilford.

Levine, S. B. (2010). What is sexual addiction? *Journal of Sex & Marital Therapy, 36*, 261-75.

Maletzky, B. M. (2002). The paraphilias: Research and treatment. In P. E. Nathan & J. M. Gorman (Eds.), *A guide to treatments that work* (pp. 525-58). Oxford University Press.

Marshall, W. L., & Marshall, L. E. (2017). The treatment of adult male sex offenders. In A. R. Beech, T. Ward (Eds.), & D. P. Boer (General Ed.), *The Wiley handbook on the theories, assessment, and treatment of sexual offending* (pp. 1227-45). John Wiley & Sons.

Marshall, W. L., Marshall, L. E., Serran, G. A., & O'Brien, M. D. (2011). *Rehabilitating sexual offenders: A strength-based approach*. American Psychological Association.

McConaghy, N. (1993). *Sexual behavior: Problems and management*. Plenum.

Mills, J. F., & Kroner, D. G. (1999). *Measures of Criminal Attitudes and Associates: User guide*. Bath Institution.

Murphy, W. D., & Page, I. J. (2008). Exhibitionism: Psychopathology and theory. In D. R. Laws & W. T. O'Donohue (Eds.), *Sexual deviance: Theory, assessment, and treatment* (2nd ed., pp. 61-75). Guilford.

Nichols, H. R., & Molinder, I. (1984). *Multiphasic Sex Inventory*. Authors.

Olver, M. E. (2017). The Risk-Need-Responsivity Model: Applications of sex offender treatment. In A. R. Beech, T. Ward (Eds.), & D. P. Boer (General Ed.), *The Wiley handbook on the theories, assessment, and treatment of sexual offending* (pp. 1313-30). John Wiley & Sons.

Selzer, M. L. (1971). The Michigan Alcoholism Screening Test (MAST): The quest for a new diagnostic instrument. *American Journal of Psychiatry, 127*, 1653-58.

Seto, M. C. (2008). Pedophilia: Psychopathology and theory. In D. R. Laws & W. T. O'Donohue (Eds.), *Sexual deviance: Theory, assessment, and treatment* (2nd ed., pp. 164-82). Guilford.

Ward, T., & Beech, A. R. (2008). An integrated theory of sexual offending. In D. R. Laws & W. T. O'Donohue (Eds.), *Sexual deviance: Theory, assessment, and treatment* (2nd ed., pp. 21-36). Guilford.

Willis, G. M., Prescott, D. M., & Tates, P. S. (2017). Application of an integrated Good Lives approach to sexually offending treatment. In A. R. Beech, T. Ward (Eds.), & D. P. Boer (General Ed.), *The Wiley handbook on the theories, assessment, and treatment of sexual offending* (pp. 1355-68). John Wiley & Sons.

Wincze, J. P. (2000). Assessment and treatment of atypical sexual behavior. In S. R. Leiblum & R. C. Rosen (Eds.), *Principles and practice of sex therapy* (3rd ed., pp. 449-70). Guilford.

Wylie, K. R., Ng, E. M. L., Chambers, L., Ward-Davies, L., & Hickey, F. (2008). Sexual disorders, paraphilias, and gender dysphoria. *International Journal of Sexual Health, 20*(1-2), 109-32.

Yates, P. M., Hucker, S. J., & Kingston, D. A. (2008). Sexual sadism: Psychopathology and theory. In D. R. Laws & W. T. O'Donohue (Eds.), *Sexual deviance: Theory, assessment, and treatment* (2nd ed., pp. 213-30). Guilford.

Young, J. E., & Brown, G. (2001). *Young Schema Questionnaire: Special edition*. Schema Therapy Institute.

ELEVEN

NON-NORMATIVE AND ALTERNATIVE SEXUALITIES

WHEN *FIFTY SHADES OF GREY* was published in 2011, no one antici-pated that it would become the best-selling book it became, or that it would later be made into a record-breaking movie that would sell $94.4 million in tickets over Valentine's Day weekend in 2015. *Fifty Shades*, which is based on Twilight fan-fiction, was originally an on-demand book that was being shared and discussed word-of-mouth by a small but enthusiastic readership. Anne Messitte, who was at that time the publisher of the Vintage line under Random House, read it and realized its potential. She, along with Valerie Hoskin and E. L. James, would be instrumental in relaunching the book as a paperback publication.[1] Indeed, the book and movie captured many peo-ple's imagination and reflected a growing interest in and fantasies about non-normative sexual experience. Many viewed it as capturing something vaguely reminiscent that harked back to the sexual revolution in the 1970s and brought sexual exploration and play to a crescendo. Others viewed it as part of a larger cultural shift that has undermined norms around sexuality and gender: "The narrative of explicit and humiliating behavior is helping to reset the mainstream baseline for acceptable sexual behavior, a shift that has been under way for years" (Goodale, 2015).

In spite of its success as a book series and a movie, *Fifty Shades of Grey* has also been criticized by members of the kink and BDSM community (BDSM refers to bondage and discipline, domination and submission, sadism, and masochism) for the misinformation portrayed about the

---

[1]Penguin Press, "Fifty Shades of Grey, the viral myth, and the truth about how things get popular," Medium, February 23, 2017, https://medium.com/@penguinpress/ever-wonder-how-fifty -shades-of-grey-became-such-a-phenomenon-6aab6657b819.

practice of BDSM: "For example, the lack of aftercare, a period of affection given to the submissive after a session to avoid any actual psychological damage, is noted by several members" (Chen, 2021). The worry from members of the kink community is that the practices shared in *Fifty Shades of Grey* might "lead beginners unwittingly into corrupt relationships." Other criticisms include the themes of abuse of power and sexual abuse of females by males that are couched as BDSM, which is harmful to the kink and BDSM community because it misrepresents values and practices that safeguard the participants physically, sexually, emotionally, and psychologically, as well as to curious individuals who assume that BDSM is what is portrayed in *Fifty Shades of Grey* without adequate research, consultation, mentorship, and education.

As we enter into the topic of non-normative and alternative forms of relationship and behaviors, we can already see the value in nuancing the conversation. We can see in response to popular media portrayal the curiosity and enthusiasm of those who are outside these practices, and the perspective of those who are practitioners within these communities of alternative and non-normative sexualities. In reading through this chapter, we ask that readers try to understand how these practices function for people who are participating so that you are in a better position to understand them, their relationships, and ways in which you as a sex therapist may be helpful.

There are many directions we could take this chapter, but we will focus on consensual non-monogamy, BDSM, and kink. Consensual non-monogamy (CNM) is a broad term that refers to a wide range of practices. Sheff (2014) described different types of non-monogamy. These include polygamy (marriage between more than two people), open relationships (for example, a long-term marriage between two people that brings in a third or more people for the purpose of sexual experiences), swinging (committed couples "swapping" partners), polyamory (having multiple sexual, emotional, or romantic relationships at once, which for some may be practiced hierarchically with primary or secondary partners, or non-hierarchically).

BDSM is considered an umbrella term for a wide range of possible activities and identities.[2] Bondage refers to placing limits on a partner's movement. This might occur, for example, with a scarf, tie, or handcuffs. Discipline refers to various ways one partner can control another partner.

---

[2]Adapted from www.webmd.com/sex/what-is-bdsm-sex.

Dominance refers to the authority one partner exercises over the other. Submission refers to the deference or obedience one person shows to another. Sadism refers to pleasure one partner feels by inflicting harm on their partner, while masochism refers to pleasure one partner feels when they experience pain or humiliation. Taken together, BDSM can reflect varied activities and interests.

While there are some clients who may participate in BDSM with practices that induce pleasurable sensations of pain, for others, the interactions with those in the community may have other functions and purposes. As an example, one individual was a "Financial Dom," and those who were submissives to her practice would send her varying sums of money for the purpose of learning how to be disciplined in their spending. Another individual who was a submissive had a partner who was dominant, and he would place a finger on her hand, thigh, arm, or other extremities so that she could learn to tolerate the discomfort of physical touch. As such, in working with clients who participate in BDSM, it is helpful to assess what the function of participation is for that person. It may not be a re-enactment of trauma. It may not be due to past learning of corporal punishment. It may not be due to a desire to inflict pain on others.

Merriam-Webster dictionary defines *kink* as a twist or curl, a short bend in something.[3] Kink in sexuality is, then, a bending of sexual practices or the involvement in non-traditional practices and fantasies. These practices and fantasies can include role-plays, atypical stimulation, such as bondage or spanking, or the use of objects or body parts, such as feet, for the purposes of enhancing sexual pleasure (Nichols & Fedor, 2017).

According to Nichols and Fedor (2017), the kink community, or kinksters, use the frame of "safe, sane, and consensual" in their description of their activities. *Safe* refers to being aware of and practicing behavior within the bounds of safe practice. *Sane* refers to distinguishing between a sexual fantasy and reality, and *consensual* refers to mutual consent.

A scoping review conducted by Brown et al. (2020) reported on a nationally representative sample in which nearly 70% (68.8%) had at least one kind of BDSM fantasy or practice. Fantasy and behavior should be distinguished, however, and while many people report BDSM fantasies, "only 7.6% identified as BDSM practitioners" (p. 783). Another study in the

---

[3] See www.merriam-webster.com/dictionary/kink.

scoping review looked at behaviors, such as fetishes, voyeurism, exhibitionism, threesomes, sadomasochism, group sex, and swinging, and indicated that 20% of the sample reported practicing one such behavior (and 18% reported engaging in two more more) (Brown et al., 2020). Nine percent indicated sadomasochistic behaviors, while 13% reported fetish activities. These rates are much higher than a nationally representative study from Australia that indicated that 1.8% of sexually active people (2.2% of men, 1.3% of women) said they had been involved in BDSM in the previous year (Richters et al., 2008), which may be on the low end of the broader literature.

Among those who identify as part of the BDSM community, common activities include flogging, pinching, whipping, and caning, as well as verbal or physical humiliation, sensory deprivation, submission activities, and breath play. Common role-play activities include master/slave, fear play, occupation, and animal play (Brown et al., 2020).

Brown et al. (2020) suggested that some interest in BDSM/kink may be better conceptualized as "a broadening of individuals' sexual repertoire rather than being truly 'paraphilic'" (p. 783). For others, their involvement in BDSM/kink may be more substantial, and this continuum has been described as "light" (5%), medium (40%), heavy (31%), and edge (or the "most extreme"; 15%) (Brown et al., 2020, p. 805).

When we look at how common CNM is, we can again distinguish fantasies from practices. As Scoats and Campbell (2022) observed, "sexual fantasies about threesomes and group sex are extremely common and often one of the most typical fantasies people report" (p. 2). However, it is estimated that "approximately 3-7% of the North American population are currently engaged in consensual non-monogamous arrangements" (Scoats & Campbell, 2022, p. 2). More men than women demonstrate interest in and practice CNM, and more sexual minorities than heterosexuals both show interest in and engage in CNM; "open relationships are particularly common gay male populations" (p. 3).

ETIOLOGY

Consensual non-monogamy. CNM is conceptualized in theory against the backdrop of societal preferential treatment of monogamy. Proponents of CNM will often refer to couple-centrism, monocentrism, monogamism, or mononormativity to describe the societal expectation to pursue and value monogamy (what is referred to as compulsory monogamy in terms of valuing it as a culture) (Gupta et al., 2023; Vaughan, 2022).

In their scoping review of CNM, Gupta et al. (2023) reported that while some studies showed no demographic characteristics associated with CNM, other studies "found that people who are White, younger, sexual minorities, men, nonbinary, transgender, and those who have more liberal political and religious views are more likely to engage in CNM and polyamory than their counterparts" (pp. 11-12). Other characteristics include personality variables: "people who had more active imaginations, a preference for variety and change, and a proclivity to engage in new experiences (i.e., high in openness) reported a greater desire to engage in CNM than those who were very organized, and neat, careful, and self-disciplined" (p. 12).

Perceived obstacles to CNM were "disapproval from one's partner, partner unwillingness, not knowing how to execute this fantasy, being afraid, and social disapproval" (Gupta et al., 2023, p. 12).

Gupta et al. (2023) looked at the path into CNM. The path is characterized by motivations for entering CNM relationships, identifying as being in or having a CNM identity, and navigating the relationship between a CNM identity and "other social identities (e.g., being queer, kinky, disabled)" (p. 14).

When we are working with CNM couples, it is important to keep in mind that the openness of each partner's awareness of other partners is what distinguishes CNM from infidelity. Those in CNM may experience threesomes or sex with multiple participants; however, people who participate in group sex may not be participating in CNM relationships in these experiences (Scoats & Campbell, 2022). The quality of relationships within a CNM relationship is variable, as it is possible for partners within a CNM to have different relationships with other partners within the group or "polycule," as some participants in polyamorous relationships refer to their relationships.

In their literature review, Scoats and Campbell (2022) found one difference between monogamous and CNM relationships, which is the approach to sexual and romantic jealousy. For those in CNM relationships, jealousy may not be perceived as a threat in the same way it might be in monogamous relationships, and jealousy may be seen as manageable and possibly even pleasurable for some partners when envisioning their partners having sexual experiences with others.

The stigmas around CNM are important to keep in mind when working with clients who participate in these relationships. In their reflections on possible stigma, Scoats and Campbell (2022) observe: "In Western cultures, even as same-sex marriage becomes more common, multi-person marriage is still (usually) illegal and monogamy is afforded superior status both culturally and legally" (p. 2). These stigmas about CNMs include beliefs that these relationships are not natural, will be destroyed by jealousy, are inferior to monogamy, that they just "don't work" as well, are oppressive for women, are driven by a desire for more sex, and are riskier for STIs. In addition, CNM relationships often experience discrimination, such as in the context of parenting and families or the pursuit of healthcare.

Bondage and Discipline, Domination and Submission, Sadism, and Masochism. Many people view BDSM as more behavior (what I do) than orientation (who I am), but there are people who do think of themselves in terms of identity. For example, a woman who identifies as a dominatrix has practiced dominance behaviorally, and she develops an identity associated with the practice. Indeed, Nichols and Fedor (2017, p. 426) liken the identity development process of someone in BDSM to that of early-stage models of identity development and synthesis among gay males and lesbians.

Along these lines, Kalafatis-Russell (2021) conducted a scoping review of BDSM behavior and noted the differences in conceptualizations of kink and BDSM as behavioral ("doing Kink") or identity ("being kinky"). The literature appears to distinguish BDSM as behavior, orientation, and identity. It is behavior insofar as it is activity, which is often identified in assessment. BDSM is orientation insofar as it is reflected in sexual fantasy and exploration. BDSM is identity in terms of one's community and role identification.

Kink. Similar to what has been proposed in conceptualizing BDSM, kink is thought of by some to describe behaviors a person elects to engage in, while for others kink has functioned as an expression of identity (Nichols & Fedor, 2017). Nichols and Fedor observe that coming out as interested in kink may be easier for sexual and gender minority populations who already have a non-normative sexual or gender identity than for those who are straight and develop an interest in or identify with kink behavior.

Pathology-related models of BDSM and kink assume abnormal traits among those who practice such behaviors. In their scoping review of the research in this area, Brown et al. (2020) found relatively little support for such a model. Those interested in BDSM/kink were not more prone to distress or mental instability, nor were those interested in BDSM different from controls on hostile sexism, acceptance of sexual aggression, victim blaming, risk-taking behaviors, sexual guilt, and other possible indicators of a pathology-based model.

Pathology-based understandings of BDSM and kink also assume that childhood sexual abuse (CSA) or another trauma may place a young person at greater risk of developing such interests. In their scoping review of the literature, Brown et al. (2020) reported comparable rates of PTSD among those who practiced BDSM and those who did not, with the exception that those who scored higher on submissiveness did tend to score higher on PTSD symptoms. Similarly, those engaged in BDSM did not have higher rates of personality disorders or symptoms of dissociative identity disorder. A study cited in the scoping review also found no evidence that those who practice BDSM and those who do not report different rates of sexual coercion as a child.

In terms of CSA, those who practice BDSM were more likely to report CSA than what is reported in the general population. However, as the authors observed, most (90.4%) of those who practice BDSM did not report CSA, at least in the studies they were reviewing (Brown et al., 2020). Other studies did not show that childhood trauma predicted "either dominance or submissive sexual behaviors" among those who identified as practicing kink (p. 802).

ASSESSMENT AND CLINICAL PRESENTATION

Those who are drawn to non-normative and alternative sexualities such as CNM and BDSM/kink can be understood along a continuum (Nichols & Fedor, 2017). There are those who are not drawn to these behaviors, which is most people (depending in part which behaviors are being assessed). There are those who are curious about specific activities and may want to incorporate some elements into their sexual script. The continuum moves to those who are incorporating some elements of CNM and/or BDSM/kink into their activities, such as various sex toys or enacted fantasies. Then there are those who identify as being in a CNM relationship or as a part of the BDSM/kinky community and who may be quite active with others who are part of that community.

Non-monogamy. Lauren and Peter presented to couples therapy because Peter had recently expressed that in spite of his love for Lauren and his feelings of satisfaction within their sexual relationship, he felt as though he wanted to explore more of his sexuality with males. He had recently come to an awareness of his bisexuality and didn't want to risk losing his relationship with Lauren by cheating on her and having sexual experiences with men. He stated he would feel better about these sexual experiences with men if he had her consent and agreement. Peter also proposed that if Lauren was willing, he would like to open up their relationship so they could both have sexual experiences with other people besides each other.

In meeting with a couple like Lauren and Peter, it is important for the clinician to be aware of the different types of CNM relationships and the nuances that differentiate them. In this example, Peter presents Lauren with the idea of opening up their marriage to have sexual relationships with others and makes it clear that he is not interested in cheating on her in spite of his desire to have sexual experiences with men. It is within his values to be open and transparent about his commitment to her, as well as his bisexuality.

As a clinician working with Lauren and Peter, it would be helpful to identify the "rules of engagement" for what opening their marriage would look like. This would be an important part of assessment and exploration. It would also be worthwhile to take this opportunity to facilitate any feelings of grief, anger, anxiety, fear, or resentment Lauren might experience with this request. The possibility of polyamory may also be important to explore as well, in the event that Peter and/or Lauren meets someone they would be interested in pursuing an emotional and romantic relationship with in addition to a sexual one.

BDSM and kink. *Jackie came to couples therapy with her husband, James. Jackie had been doing some reading of erotic literature and expressed a curiosity and interest in incorporating more BDSM activities into their sexual script. James was not interested. Moreover, James expressed concern that such activities would take them as a couple toward behaviors that were morally impermissible. Both Jackie and James identified as Christians. Jackie did not see the exploration of non-normative sexuality as a question of "right" or "wrong," as though it would or could be sinful. She saw it as a variation that could be explored within the context of a marriage.*

It has been suggested that two types of kink clients may come in to see a sex therapist. The first kind is asking for help with a sexual issue, and kink is revealed as part of their experience or identity (Nichols & Fedor, 2017). As

Nichols and Fedor observe, these people will likely seek out a sex therapist from within the kink community, ideally someone who is quite familiar with kink and will not be as reactive to such a disclosure.

The second type of kink client will often see a sex therapist who does not specialize in kink and who may have a reaction to it. This client might seek therapy because they have only recently gotten into kink and may be married to a spouse who is not as drawn to such practices (Nichols & Fedor, 2017).

Assessment of BDSM or kink involvement often takes the form of a sexual interest interview in which clinicians ask about interest or involvement in specific behaviors, such as bondage, spanking, humiliation, and so on.

TREATMENT

Consensual non-monogamy. Treatment would depend on the client's pre-senting concerns and whether or not the desire to be in a non-monogamous relationship is consistent with their values regarding their relationship(s). Generally, helping clients who desire non-monogamy to figure out what the "rules of engagement" are for them and their partners is part of the process for these relationships to be healthy and sustainable (see Orion, 2018).

In their review of the literature, Herbitter et al. (2021) found that many participants in studies of non-monogamy had therapists who assumed they were monogamous. In that study, participants in CNM relationships found that the most unhelpful practices by therapists included belief that CNM was the result of another problem, lacking information and willingness to learn about CNM, judgment toward CNM, indication that it was wrong, and pressuring the client to end the relationship. By questioning a client's morality or trustworthiness, the therapeutic alliance may be significantly affected.

It may also be helpful to recognize that in CNM, different partners may meet different needs, such as emotional, physical, erotic, and so on (Vilkin & Sprott, 2021). This may not be a concept familiar to most clinicians, but it is seen in the literature on CNM. Assessing for the ways in which partners may have different needs, then, can be an important consideration in working with clients in CNM relationships.

In the overlap between people who were in CNM relationships and iden-tified with kink, different levels of sexual desire is another common area of concern (more than 1 in 5; Vilkin & Sprott, 2021). Recall that we described this as "desire discrepancy" in chapter five, and this can be present in CNM relationships as well and can be extended to varied or discrepant interest in kink, which can be discussed and explored in therapy. In some cases, a person who has interest in kink may explore CNM if their partner is not as interested in kinky behavior or has a different kink they are interested in (Vilkin & Sprott, 2021).

Issues specific to CNM may arise when a person who is pursuing a CNM relationship develops stronger feelings that are not shared by the other person who wishes to maintain an open relationship. It is unclear how frequently this occurs, but in a report on CNM, the following case of a straight, cisgender male illustrates the challenges that can arise:

> Yeah, everything meshed really good for a long time. Just ended up not working out cuz she's poly, and . . . I kinda thought the idea at first was cool, and I also thought you know hey it would be cool I can be in love with this girl and I can mess around with other girls, and she can mess around with other guys and we can do our own thing and still be happy. And it all sounded good but it didn't work out that way. I didn't really care if she messed around with girls, I just wasn't really cool with her messing around with guys after I got to the point where I was in love with her. (Vilkin & Sprott, 2021, p. 1531)

Even in cases in which there is greater reciprocity in the level of feelings one has for the other(s) in CNM relationships, there can be instances of jealousy or insecurity that a person may benefit from exploring. For proponents of CNM, this is often assumed to be the result of exclusivity being a cultural or societal "marker" of relationship health:

> Within CNM relationships, experiences of jealousy are thought to stem partly from strong societal value on sexual and romantic exclusivity as markers of relationship strength, although feeling jealous may also be associated with individual factors. (Vilkin & Sprott, 2021, p. 1523)

With this understanding of jealousy, a clinician could explore perceived contributions to jealousy and catalytic events, and then teach skills for managing jealousy. Acceptance of feelings and subsequent self-soothing strategies have been useful according to some clinicians (see Orion, 2018), and clients often reflect varying degrees of compersion, which generally refers to delight one takes in others' joy or satisfaction, and when applied to CNM relationships refers to positive emotions one experiences when their partner is experiencing romantic or sexual satisfaction.

A related issue is just how much time each person gets in a CNM relationship. Clients may use terms such as *primaries, secondaries,* and similar designations to convey a polyhierarchy. Where a person is in that hierarchy and how much time they have with different partners can be an opportunity to improve communication, process expectations, and possibly address jealousy if that were to be expressed (Orion, 2018).

If a client(s) comes to therapy with any of the more common sexual disorders, the general approach to assessment and treatment is quite similar to what is illustrated in those chapters. We would want to avoid assuming that being in a CNM relationship is the cause of a desire disorder (discussed above), orgasmic disorder, or premature ejaculation, for instance. Rather, it would be more helpful to gain an understanding of their relationship and to also gain an understanding of the symptoms and how they came about and are maintained, just as we do with couples in a conventional marriage relationship. It may be helpful to be open to involving as many people as possible in treatment, but this should be agreed on by all parties, and some people in a CNM relationship may be more relevant than others to a specific presenting concern, so this should be discussed so that treatment can proceed.

BDSM and kink. BDSM and kink are currently conceptualized as essentially less common but simply variations in sexual interests and activities. With the distinction in *DSM-5* between paraphilias and paraphilic disorders, any atypical interest would be within the realm of possibility for sexual behavior and not rise to the level of a mental health concern provided it is not distressing to the person and that there is not a victim or potential victim.

We agree with Nichols and Fedor (2017) in their observation that "the average sex therapist is less likely to see clients who are comfortable with their BDSM sexuality and more likely to see people who have BDSM/fetish sexual preferences but who are closeted and isolated" (p. 428).

Nichols and Fedor (2017) discuss several myths about BDSM. These include that BDSM is abusive. While we agree that the intention within the BDSM and kink communities is to be "safe, sane, and consensual," we have often seen different levels of interest in couples in which one partner in particular is drawn to BDSM or kink behavior. So it ends up being more of a question of whether there is mutual interest in these activities and how to negotiate those interests in the context of a couple's sexual script.

If only one person in a relationship is interested in non-normative and alternative relationships or practices, this can become challenging for a therapist, especially if exploration of relationships or behavior leads to the dissolution of a current relationship: "Some clients, when affirmed, decide to act upon their impulses and leave their committed relationships, a potential outcome that should be explained to the client at the outset of treatment" (Nichols & Fedor, 2017, p. 429). Similarly, "If clients decide to act on their desires in a secret way, the therapist faces the ethical dilemma of being in some ways complicit in adultery" (p. 429).

Vilkin and Sprott (2021) also identify visibility and stigma management as areas of concern for people who practice CNM and/or BDSM/kink. By definition, non-normative and alternative relationship forms and practices go against societal expectations for relationships and behaviors. Clients may feel that their relationship or practices are devalued by others, and a common perception is that such relationships or practices are "less than" what is valued in monogamous relationships and conventional sexual activities. CNM relationship structures and BDSM/kink interests can be difficult to explain to one's partner (in the case of BDSM/kink interests), family, extended family, religious faith communities, health care and mental health care providers, and others (Vilkin & Sprott, 2021).

In a review of research pertaining to mental health providers working with CNM and BDSM relationships, Herbitter et al. (2021) encourage clinicians to be aware of the nuances regarding abuse and violation of relationship commitments in BDSM and CNM relationships through education about community terms, practices, and norms, without seeking this information from the client. Additionally, "Clinicians should be careful not to pathologize sexually diverse behaviors and identities; however they must also not avoid addressing them when relevant or go so far as to ignore problems that might arise" (Herbitter et al., 2021, p. 19).

In light of the readership of this book, which largely consists of Christian mental health care providers, it is important for us to reflect on our values and to pay attention to moments when there is a transaction between our values and the practices of our clients, especially if we lack understanding about CNM and BDSM relationships. Perhaps for many Christians, this will not be a population we choose to work with because the nature of the relationships or practices feel value discordant to us. For others, we may be in professional roles in which we are expected to work with a wide array of clients, some of whom are in CNM relationships or practice BDSM/kink.

PREVENTION

Neither non-monogamy nor BDSM/kink is currently conceptualized as experiences that are prevented in the mental health literature. There have been anecdotal accounts and case discussions of clinicians assisting clients who have an interest in BDSM/kink but wish not to act on those impulses.

It was noted above that Nichols and Fedor (2017) described several myths about BDSM, one of which is that people who are into BDSM/kink were abused as children. Their position is that "there no evidence of greater incidence of child abuse among the BDSM population in comparison with those who engage in vanilla sexual behaviors" (pp. 422-23). "Vanilla," in this context, refers to more traditional sexual activities, such as penile-vaginal sex, oral sex, and so on.

CLOSING REFLECTION

As we noted above, the shift in *DSM-5-TR* away from viewing paraphilic behaviors as mental health concerns in and of themselves, and the decision to distinguish such behaviors from paraphilic disorders, really opened the door to mainstreaming such activities. Proponents of such a move likely see the maneuver as reflecting cultural trends within society rather than being a catalyst for such trends. There may be some truth to both perspectives.

Books and movies like *Fifty Shades of Grey* reflect a growing interest in non-normative and alternative sexual behaviors. The mainstreaming of BDSM/kink made it more accessible to the average person. Such popular and trending portrayals, however, often include misinformation that may actually be detrimental to those drawn to such practices given the portrayals of certain aspects of BDSM/kink, as we noted above.

In the mainstream mental health field, such behaviors are viewed as variations in behaviors and activities that can and should be supported. Some proponents also speak to the strengths visible in these communities. For example, Nichols and Fedor (2017) identified several strengths they have seen among participants who engage in BDSM/kink: communication/negotiation, objectivity and non-judgmentalism, sexual variety, planning (versus spontaneity), technical skill, healing, and spirituality. These strengths are framed as ways those who are not interested in CNM and BDSM/kink can learn from those who do have such interests.

For Christian sex therapists, we have shared throughout this book that we want to improve communication in general and about sex in particular.

Because non-normative practices often require planning and intentionality, the communication may indeed be something that is widely practiced. The openness in sexuality may be seen by some as a welcome alternative to more narrow scripts that can at times be a part of the problem. For example, when we see a narrow sexual script among couples who present with erectile disorder, sex therapists want to expand that script so that a rigid erection is not a "make or break" expectation for sexual intimacy. The emphasis on planning (versus spontaneity) is also something sex therapists value in working with couples with sexual disorders. While spontaneity can be fun, it is often used by one or more partners in a marriage as a measure of their intimacy—whether they are really "in love" or doing it "right"—which is often a barrier to creating regular rhythms of intimacy and connection. The technical skill element that is often a point of pride in the BDSM community (in the area of flogging, for instance, that it is done correctly in terms of demonstrating technical proficiency; Nichols & Fedor, 2017) is something that sex therapists in general want to see improvement in. That is, we want couples to develop their technique, which may be in nondemand sensual touch or enacted exercises such as the squeeze technique or some other element of intervention.

The emphasis on healing and safety is a more recent development in which case studies have been shared of people working through trauma through BDSM practices (Nichols & Fedor, 2017). We see claims of healing of past trauma, a claim that is in need of future study, as the few case studies that are present may be insufficient to displace other, more traditional means of healing from prior trauma. The emphasis on safety, however, is important, and Christian sex therapists want the sexual intimacy that their couples cultivate to be characterized by physical, emotional, and spiritual safety for both partners. Those in the BDSM/kink community often speak of such practices as a pathway to the spiritual. The Christian views sexual intimacy as reflecting transcendent reality for a range of reasons, so we can appreciate the ways in which such practices are framed around spirituality while taking issue with whether such practices reflect God's intention for sexual intimacy.

We will likely see more interest in various relationship forms found in CNM and some of the behaviors associated with BDSM/kink. The Christian community no longer has the weight of the mainstream mental health associations suggesting such behaviors are indicators of mental health concerns. Of course, Christians do not have to have the weight of the mainstream mental health communities to raise their own questions and concerns about non-normative forms of relationships or sexual behaviors. These will increasingly present opportunities for Christians to reflect on their beliefs and values and communicate those to others who disagree.

REFERENCES

Brown, A., Barker, E. D., & Rahman, Q. (2020). A systematic scoping review of the prevalence, etiological, psychological, and interpersonal factors associated with BDSM. *The Journal of Sex Research, 57*(6), 781-811. https://doi.org/10.1080/00224499.2019.1665619

Chen, M. (2021). *Fifty Shades: BDSM community backlash.* Unsuitable. https://sites.duke.edu/unsuitable/fifty-shades-bdsm-community-backlash/#:~:text=The%20two%20protagonists%2C%20Ana%20Steel,used%20as%20an%20instruction%20manual

Goodale, G. (2015, February). How "Fifty Shades of Grey" is contributing to shifts in norms on sexuality. *The Christian Science Monitor.*

Gupta, S., Tarantino, M., & Sanner, C. (2023). A scoping review of research on polyamory and consensual non-monogamy: Implications for a more inclusive family science. *Journal of Family Theory and Review,* 1-40. https://doi.org/10.1111/jftr.12546

Herbitter, C., Vaughan, M. D., & Pantalone, D. W. (2021). Mental health provider bias and clinical competence in addressing asexuality, consensual non-monogamy, and BDSM: A narrative review. *Sexual and Relationship Therapy.* https://doi.org/10.1080/14681994.2021.1969547

Kalafatis-Russell, A. R. (2021). *Doing Kink vs. being kinky: A systematic scoping review of the literature on BDSM behavior, orientation, and identity* [Master's thesis, University of North Florida]. University of North Florida Digital Archive. https://digitalcommons.unf.edu/etd/1108

Nichols, M., & Fedor, J. P. (2017). Treating sexual problems in clients who practice "kink." In Z. D. Peterson (Ed.), *The Wiley handbook of sex therapy* (pp. 420-34). John Wiley and Sons.

Orion, R. (2018). *A therapist's guide to consensual non-monogamy: Polyamory, swinging, and open marriage.* Taylor & Francis.

Richters, J., de Visser, R. O., Rissel, C. E., Grulich, A. E., & Smith, M. A. (2008). Demographic and psychosocial features of participants in bondage and discipline, "sadomasochism" or dominance and submission (BDSM): Data from a national survey. *Journal of Sexual Medicine, 5*(7), 1660-68. https://doi.org/10.1111/j.1743-6109.2008.00795.x

Scoats, R., & Campbell, C. (2022). What do we know about consensual non-monogamy? *Current Opinion in Psychology, 48,* 1-5. https://doi.org/10.1016/j.copsych.2022.101468

Sheff, E. A. (2014, July 22). 7 Different Kinds of Non-Monogamy. *Psychology Today.* www.psychologytoday.com/us/blog/the-polyamorists-next-door/201407/7-different-kinds-non-monogamy

Vaughan, M. D. (2022). Introduction: Toward CNM-affirming, anti-oppressive, clinical practice. In M. D. Vaughan & T. R. Burnes (Eds.), *The handbook of consensual non-monogamy affirming mental health practice* (pp. 1-14). Rowman & Littlefield.

Vilkin, E., & Sprott, R. (2021). Consensual non-monogamy among kink-identified adults: Characteristics, relationship experiences, and unique motivations for polyamory and open relationships. *Archives of Sexual Behavior, 50*, 1521-36. https://doi.org/10.1007/s10508-021-02004-w

TWELVE

SEXUAL ADDICTION

THE LONGEST-RUNNING PLAY IN Spain is *Don Juan Tenorio*. It has become something of a staple in various Spanish theaters, playing annually for more than a century. It is an interpretation of the myth of Don Juan written by José Zorilla in 1844. It is not the first play written about the Don Juan legend; no, that award would likely go to *The Trickster of Seville and the Stone Guest* by Tirso de Molina, published almost two hundred years prior to *Don Juan Tenorio*. In all of these accounts—and there are many—we see the story of a rogue who delights in seducing women and is eventually dragged to hell by the ghost of a father of one young woman in particular. How is that for an annual tradition?

Don Juanism is one of the earliest nonprofessional terms for what today many professionals think of as sexual addiction. (It is unclear whether Don Juan would have resonated with the concept of addiction; he did at times describe himself as Satan or at least a devil.) Sometimes the person steeped in what some professionals today think of as addiction feels so torn by the desire to continue in a pattern of behavior that it's like a splitting of the person's will.

The diagnostic manual at one time included sexual deviations as personality disorders (*DSM-II*, APA, 1968) but did not cover addictions or hypersexuality. We saw later developments toward paraphilic disorders as recognizable pathologies (as "Psychosexual Disorders" in *DSM-III*, APA, 1980, p. 283), but there still was not sexual addiction as such. Most clinicians who provide services to people who report addictive patterns consider them problems that are not otherwise specified within the existing DSM nosology.

In 1983 Quadland used the phrase "sexual compulsivity" to describe what we are referring to here. The compulsive nature of sexual behavior is that it relieves or reduces anxiety to act out. Some professionals are more comfortable in conceptualizing these concerns as compulsivity insofar as they are primarily about anxiety reduction rather than heightened sex interest or desire as such. Those who are in favor of this view, for example Coleman (1987), see the issues as reflecting more obsessive-compulsive features in which the person engages in repetitive behaviors to reduce negative emotional affect (e.g., anxiety, shame; Kafka, 2010).

There exist today a few schools of thought about the nature of what we refer to here as "sexual addiction." Martin Kafka (2000) conceptualizes the sexual addictions as paraphilia-related disorders, indicating that they have a paraphilic quality to them, but they are not themselves paraphilias. Kafka defines paraphilic-related disorders as "intensely sexually arousing fantasies, urges, and sexual activities that are culturally sanctioned aspects of normative sexual arousal and behavior" (p. 471). Conceptualizing these concerns as an addiction is also common. It may be that for some this is a kind of "driven" sexuality that also reduces anxiety or aids in coping and therefore is reinforcing in that manner.

Kafka has written extensively on the idea of hypersexuality and has been most instrumental in its consideration in DSM revisions. He argues that what we refer to as sexual addiction reflects a dysregulation of sexual appetite, sometimes making a comparison between those who have struggled with dysregulation of appetite for food (Kafka, 2010). As such, he focuses on regulating serotonin (as well as dopamine and norepinephrine), among other interventions.

Patrick Carnes (2001, 2005) has been another influential voice in the field of sex addiction research and practice. He has for years argued that sexual behavior can be addictive in ways that are similar to what we see with various substances. We will discuss his model in greater detail later, but for now we note that Carnes identifies core beliefs as particularly central to the addictive system because they give rise to unhelpful or impaired thoughts that can lead to a cycle of addiction characterized by preoccupations or obsessions, rituals, acting-out behavior, and negative consequent emotions.

None of these terms, however, has been in the DSM. The language of "hypersexuality disorder" and "sexual addiction" has to date been rejected by committees in part because of the view that there is insufficient evidence that these patterns of sexual behavior are comparable to addiction to substances.

Yet many clinicians provide services to those who present with concerns that are often conceptualized as a sexual addiction, compulsive sexuality, or hypersexuality. What are some of the more common presentations in which sexual addiction may be seen? They include pornography, compulsive masturbation, promiscuity, massage parlors, prostitutes, affairs (or compulsive relationships), and internet-based sexual behavior such as cybersex or sexual chat rooms. It is difficult to get firm estimates of the prevalence of these behaviors. Carnes estimates about 3% to 8% of the population are truly addicted to pornography. About half of a clinical sample (those coming into a sex clinic) will have an addiction to pornography (Kafka, 2010). Compulsive masturbation has been reported by about 70% of a clinical sample (Kafka, 2010). Promiscuity—or what is sometimes referred to as "protracted" promiscuity—is reported by about half of a clinical sample. Telephone sex and cybersex has been reported by about 25% and 20% of clinical samples respectively (Kafka, 2010).

Several professionals (Ferree, 2010; Ferree et al., 2012; McDaniel & Valenti-Anderson, 2012) have also offered that there are important gender differences in the presentation of sex and love addiction. Women are much less likely than men to even identify themselves as having a sexual addiction. They tend to struggle with a greater diversity of possible presentations, so there may be issues with unhealthy relationships, a need for affirmation, and poor boundaries, as well as more of a codependent presentation or even a victim role (McDaniel & Valenti-Anderson, 2012, p. 41).

Some women struggle with the classic addiction to pornography, just as many men do. Ferree (2010) notes that between a fourth and a third of visitors to pornography websites are women and that women present with a range of issues in this area. Other women are relationship or love addicts insofar as they are drawn to a relationship that may or may not be particularly healthy for them. According to Ferree (2010), this is a woman "who repeatedly is involved in affairs or multiple relationships, whether she's married or single. These relationships are sometimes serial (happening in rapid sequence, one right after the other), or sometimes they are even simultaneous" (pp. 57-58).

Still others are romance addicts. What draws them is that early stage of romantic feelings that are lost over time as they settle into a longer-term, more enduring relationship. The woman might pursue those same feelings in a new romance or she might find herself drawn to romance novels and movies with themes that generate romantic fantasy in which she can then get lost (this person might be thought of as a fantasy addict).

Ferree (2010; cf. Carnes et al., 2007) also discusses the experience some women have as sexual anorexics. This term refers to a person who develops a profound fear of intimacy in romantic relationships. So a woman (or a man, for that matter) might starve themselves of genuine intimacy in their marriage while acting out with someone outside the relationship. There are other versions or expressions of female sex addiction, and the interested reader can review Ferree's (2010, 2012) work, among others (e.g., Campling & Vermeire, 2012; McDaniel & Valenti-Anderson, 2012).

ETIOLOGY

As we are seeing multiple presentations of sexual addiction, it may come as no surprise that it is difficult to pinpoint the cause of sexual addiction. The principle of equifinality is important here: there are multiple pathways to an endpoint. As we have seen, there are also multiple endpoints in terms of what sexual addiction may look like in a man or woman. The following is a summary of Samenow's (2010, pp. 70-75) review.

Biological antecedents. One area that has received a lot of attention is a biological basis for addiction. There is certainly an effect on the brain of participating in ongoing, addictive behaviors. We see these changes in the pleasure center of the brain, not unlike what would be seen with substance use over time (Struthers, 2009).

But what about biology contributing to the cause of sexual addiction? The main areas of research into biological antecedents are molecular, genetic, physical illness, and substances (Samenow, 2010). As Samenow observes, the research on molecular foundations to addiction come from research on other addictive problems, animal studies, persons with brain damage, neuroimaging studies, and people's responses to pharmacological therapies.

A popular model that was extended to sexual addiction by Stein and colleagues (2006; 2009) is the ABC model of impulse control. According to Stein, the amygdala (A) contributes to emotional/affective dysregulation, while behavioral (B) reinforcement is seen in the nucleus accumbens and ventral striatal circuits. Cognitive (C) control is diminished in the prefrontal cortex (Samenow, 2010). As Samenow observes, "The comparison to hypersexual disorder is the observed phenomenon of a high rate of affective disorders triggered by stress, preoccupation and reward from engaging in sexual behavior, and continued behavior despite negative consequences" (p. 71).

The "monoamine hypothesis" associated with the paraphilias has been extended to sexual addiction (Samenow, 2010; cf. Kafka, 2010). This model looks at how the various monoamine transmitters—serotonin, norepinephrine, and dopamine—interplay with sex hormones and affect sexual interests and behavior, at least in various animal models.

Genetic studies, such as family, adoption, and twin studies, have not at this point been conducted (Samenow, 2010). Some have suggested that sex addiction can run in families, although environment and modeling is then introduced and may influence behavior (Kafka, 2010).

Studies of physical illness have shown that sexual addiction is present among some people who have a traumatic brain injury (TBI), thalamic strokes, bipolar disorder, Alzheimer's disease, and Kleine-Levine syndrome (Samenow, 2010). None of these studies really speaks to etiology as much as provides hypotheses for further study regarding regions of the brain that may influence subsequent sexual behavior.

Psychopharmacological studies have also provided some evidence for biological foundations to addiction (Kafka, 2010). For example, substances that increase dopamine in the brain can increase sexual behavior, while serotonin reuptake inhibitors can lower sex drive (Samenow, 2010).

To summarize the foregoing, although there is no dominant line of research that has offered conclusive evidence for a biological basis for sexual addiction, there are studies suggesting a possible indirect route to sexual acting-out behavior that reflects temperamental and personality differences that place a particular person at risk for symptoms of sexual addiction.

Psychological theories. Psychological models typically point to prior physical or sexual abuse, attachment concerns, early exposure to inappropriate sexual stimuli (e.g., pornography), early sexual debut, and overly restrictive attitudes toward sexual expression and intimacy (Kafka, 2000; Marcus, 2010).

Although most people who have experienced childhood physical or sexual abuse do not report dealing with hypersexuality or sexual addiction, it has been observed that a relatively high percentage of people who deal with addiction say that they have physical or sexual abuse as a part of their history (Carnes, 2005). According to Carnes, "addiction in its various forms becomes a solution to the anxiety and stress of the trauma" (p. 1). It is unclear the precise relationship between early trauma and sexual addiction, although some professionals have attempted to account for it. Some people experience alarm from unresolved trauma; others pursue pleasure in the face of violence or danger. Still others experience shame, unhealthy attachments, or a numb/blocking response to trauma (Carnes, 2005). For clinical purposes it is most helpful to keep the association in mind and to ask about physical and sexual trauma in any clinical interview and sex history.

Recent developments in attachment theory, in this case, affective neuroscience, have been interesting to follow. Affective neuroscience brings together psychological theory with neurology and related fields. Attachment theory posits that sexual addiction is an "intimacy disorder rooted in impaired early attachment experiences" (Adams & Robinson, 2001, p. 23). Childhood attachment issues, such as "the chronic emotional disconnection" that often characterizes the childhood and family relationships among sex addicts, contributes to hypersexuality (Katehakis, 2009, p. 2). It has been proposed that avoidant attachment can lead to later sexual events that lack emotion or affection, such as use of pornography (Samenow, 2010). Similarly, preoccupied attachment has been thought to lead to an emotional neediness that may translate into multiple partners.

Another psychological theory is referred to as the dual-control model. It acknowledges some kind of neurobiological dimension to sexual addiction, but the main assertion is that "negative mood states such as depression and anxiety can be associated with promiscuity and masturbation" (Samenow, 2010, p. 73). This response to dysphoria among those struggling with hypersexuality is actually quite the opposite from those who do not deal with sexual addiction, who would experience a decrease in desire when depressed or anxious.

Cognitive-behavioral theory is a widely used approach to treatment that posits that core beliefs about oneself, the world, sex, and so on are foundational for the sex addict. When the foundation is cracked by means of distorted core beliefs, such as "No one would love me if they knew about my sexual desires," this can lead to irrational thoughts that facilitate acting-out behavior. For example, minimization ("What I deal with is nothing compared to what I know my coworkers do") and rationalizations ("If my wife won't meet my needs, I'll get my needs met other places") are common. There is also, of course, a classical conditioning element to the addictive behavior, as it is considered highly reinforcing due to stimulating the pleasure centers of the brain.

Sociocultural considerations. There are a number of sociocultural factors that have been discussed in the etiology of sexual addiction. There is relatively little well-designed research to support any one theory, but they include one's family of origin (upbringing), education about sexuality and sexual behavior, access to the internet and the ubiquity of pornography sites, fundamentalist religious beliefs, and socioeconomic issues, such as poverty and unemployment (Samenow, 2010). Let's discuss a couple of these in the space that follows.

With respect to family of origin and upbringing, the main areas of interest have been the quality of parent-child relationships, parental neglect, and the general sexualization of children at a younger age (Samewnow, 2010; Ferree, 2012, also discusses these issues; see chap. 2).

In terms of religious beliefs the main focus has been on fundamentalist beliefs. The nature of these beliefs can translate into a negative view of sex that does not help the person come to terms with his own sexuality and sexual interests. Left unacknowledged, these feelings can come out "sideways" through a number of behaviors and interests that may reflect a distortion or unhealthy pattern.

No one is suggesting that the internet directly causes sexual addition. However, in terms of sociocultural influence, the ease of access to explicit material via the internet creates an entry point for many people who might not have had nearly the exposure previously. The access also makes it that much more difficult for treatment and maintenance, which will need to be discussed in terms of environment management.

Spiritual considerations. There are spiritual considerations in discussions of addiction. Cornelius Plantinga Jr. (1995) addresses the overlap between sin and addiction: "Addictions often include sin—or, putting matters the other way around, . . . some sin displays the addictive syndrome" (p. 144). The following is a list he provides that reflects the overlap between sin and addiction:

1. Repetition of pleasurable and therefore habit-forming behavior, plus escalating tolerance and desire

2. Unpleasant aftereffects of such behavior, including withdrawal symptoms and self-reproach

3. Vows to moderate or quit, followed by relapses and attendant feelings of guilt, shame, and general distress

4. Attempts to ease this distress with new rounds of the addictive behavior (or with the first rounds of a companion addiction)

5. Deterioration of work and relationships, with accompanying cognitive disturbances, including denial, delusions, and self-deceptions . . .

6. Gradually increasing preoccupation, then obsession, with the addictor

7. Compulsivity in addictive behavior: evidence that one's will has become at least partly split, enfeebled, and enslaved

8. A tendency to draw others into the web of addiction, people who support and enable the primary addiction (p. 145)

The main point in reviewing this list is that the Christian recognizes sin as a condition of inner conflict and turmoil. So too with addiction.

When we turn our attention to sexual addiction, Christians recognize that addictive patterns of sexual behavior are possible because of our fallen state, and they involve sinful behavior, whether that behavior is immoral per se or simply fails to reach the purpose and potential of godly sexual intimacy (Laaser, 2004).

Summary. Taken together, there is no one model for the etiology of sexual addiction. A biopsychosocial perspective would certainly consider biological antecedents that are not fully understood at this time, along with possible attachment and related considerations. The addictive behaviors themselves are highly reinforcing, which is consistent with cognitive-behavioral theory and neurobiological understanding of the brain. The sociocultural context in which sexual addiction occurs may also play a role and should at least be assessed in terms of case conceptualization and treatment planning.

ASSESSMENT AND CLINICAL PRESENTATION

Jon (42) is a Caucasian male who presented in therapy with a history of dysthymic disorder with PTSD features, substance use dependence (in remission), and sexual addiction. He had previously been married four years and reports that problems in his marriage began in the third year. He stated he was "unable to function" with his spouse. He said he struggled with sex addiction to pornography, compulsively masturbating (reporting an average of twice a day for over a year) and feeling "compelled" to act out. He stated that he experienced impotence "against" his wife to express anger toward her. He also stated that she knew when he masturbated and would insist on sex during those times, since he would be unable to function.

Jon shared that he grew up in a blended family with an older stepsister and a younger brother. He reports believing he was sexually abused in a nursery. Jon also reports a history of fighting with peers. Under the age of fifteen, he reports a tendency toward isolation and violence. During his teen years (15-23), he isolated himself, was violent, fought peers, and engaged in fantasy, the use of pornography, and self-destructive behavior (alcohol and drugs).

Jon received sex education through his drug dealer, who also served as his moral compass through his late teen years. His drug dealer gave him two pieces of advice: "A woman does not need to have a lot of money, just more money than you," and "Don't fall in love."

As we turn our attention to assessment, we are going to want to keep people like Jon in mind.

A comprehensive review of sex addiction measures by Hook et al. (2010) identifies several instruments ranging from self-report rating scales (e.g., Sexual Addiction Scale of the Disorders Screening Inventory; Carter & Ruiz, 1996), self-report checklists (e.g., the Sexual Addiction Screening Test; Carnes, 1989), and clinician rating scales. There are also self-report measures of the consequences of sexual activity, such as the Compulsive Sexual Behavior Consequences Scale (Muench et al., 2007). The Hypersexuality Behavior Inventory (Reid et al., 2011) is a standard in the field. The comprehensive Sexual Dependency Inventory, an inventory restricted to Certified Sex Addiction Therapists (CSATS), is considered the diagnostic gold standard.

In addition, Grover and Shouan (2020) identify several measures of pornography use, such as the Cyber-Pornography Use Inventory (CPUI) (Grubbs et al., 2010), the Pornography Consumption Inventory (CPI) (Reid et al., 2011), and the Problematic Pornography Use Scale (PPUS) (Kor et al., 2014). The CPUI focuses on online pornography use and any associated guilt. The CPI identifies motivations tied to pornography use, such as curiosity, emotional avoidance, and excitement seeking. The PPUS addresses several domains, including excessive use, control difficulties, and functional problems.

The benefit to self-report rating scales is that they are usually easy to use and quick to administer, and provide some sense of how the person being treated sees him- or herself. Of course, people may not be as forthcoming in what they share about themselves in a self-report measure, so that is also a consideration.

There are benefits to clinician rating scales too (Hook et al., 2010). Because the clinician administers these, and the rating scales tend to focus on more objective symptom presentation, they may be overall more objective and may reduce the risk of a client not being as forthcoming. As a clinician you can also explain any confusing items or wording. The downside is that clinician interviews and rating scales are more time-intensive than self-administered rating scales and checklists.

In addition to the self-report and clinician rating scales tied directly to sex addiction or pornography use, attachment assessment tools might also be utilized. Common tools include the Adult Attachment Inventory (George et al., 1996; for a review of various measures of adult attachment, see Shaver et al., 2000).

Whether or not you use a specific self-report rating scale or clinician rating scale, it can be helpful to go through a standard clinical interview and then a sex history. In the context of conducting a sex history, it can be helpful to complete a general sex history and then a sexual problem history (the history of this specific sexual concern or addictive pattern).

Kafka (2007) offers the following assessment questions that home in on behavior that might rise to the level of an addiction. This aspect of the assessment may provide evidence of out-of-control behavior:

- Have you ever had recurrent trouble controlling your sexual behavior?

- Has your sexual behavior ever caused you persistent personal distress or caused significant consequences to you such as loss of a relationship, legal problems, job-related problems, or medical problems, including a sexually transmitted disease or unwanted pregnancy?

- Have you ever had repetitive sexual activities that you felt needed to be kept secret or that you felt very ashamed of?

- Have you ever been troubled by feeling that you spend too much time engaging in sexual fantasy, masturbation, or other sexual behavior?

- Have you ever felt that you have a high sex drive? For example, have you ever been sexual seven or more times/week during at least a 6-month period since adolescence? When was that? Did it last longer than 6 months? (Kafka, 2007, p. 452)

The purpose of these questions is to determine the extent of the sexual behavior. Many clinicians follow Carnes in conceptualizing an addiction cycle in which a person has in mind and in past experience a predictable sequence of events (a ritual) that leads up to his acting-out behavior. A good assessment begins to identify that sequence, as it often helps the clinician understand the client's unique obsessions with specific behaviors and the extent of his preoccupation. Of course, coming to an understanding of obsessions and preoccupations provides the clinician with access to the client's thought processes.

Keep in mind too that the person struggling with a sexual addiction is typically entering therapy following some kind of crisis. He may have been caught by his spouse or children in some sexual behavior, such as masturbating to pornography, or he may have had difficulty at work and is being sent by his employer. He also may have had some run-in with the police that led to the referral.

Assessment also involves gaining an understanding of this person's addictive system. This language is from Carnes (2001), who offers a widely used model for understanding the experience of the person who contends with an addiction. The addictive system begins with the person's core belief system. These core beliefs usually run deep and are often tied to family messages or the sum of beliefs and assumptions about the person's value and worth, his needs and experiences, his relationships, and most significantly, his understanding of the place, value, and role of sex in his life. We typically find that the person who struggles with an addiction has a low sense of his own self-worth. This person often experiences shame—a sense that there is something fundamentally wrong with him, and if others really knew him, including his struggle with addiction, he would not be loved or accepted (Carnes, 2001; cf. Lasser, 2004; McDaniel & Valenti-Anderson, 2012). Over time, sex becomes a faithful friend. It is always there for him. To the person struggling in this area, sex does not make demands on his time. It does not criticize him. In the final analysis, sex becomes his most important need, and sex makes the emotional isolation something he can now live with (Carnes, 2001).

> Generally, addicts do not perceive themselves as worthwhile persons. Nor do they believe that other people would care for them or meet their needs if everything was known about them, including the addiction. Finally, they believe that sex is their most important need. Sex is what makes isolation bearable. If you do not trust

people, one thing that is true about sex—and alcohol, food, gambling, and risk—is that it always does what it promises—for the moment. Thus, as in our definition of addiction, the relationship is with sex—and not people. (Carnes, 2001, p. 16)

These core beliefs then give rise to a myriad of thoughts and ways of processing information and experiences. Carnes refers to the unhelpful thoughts as impaired thinking. Examples of impaired thinking include denial, rationalizations, sincere delusions, suspicion/paranoia, and the blame dynamic. These unhelpful thoughts mediate the relationship between core beliefs and the addictive cycle itself. The addictive *system* refers to this whole experience with addiction, broadly understood. It includes the core beliefs and impaired thinking that are closer to the emotional roots. The addictive *cycle* is the specific experience of acting out that is tied to preoccupation with sex and the rituals that intensify preoccupation and lead up to what has become the addiction.

The unhelpful thoughts set the stage for the addiction to really take hold. It can be helpful to understand the addictive cycle in terms of initial preoccupation with sex. Carnes describes this as a trance-like state or mood in which the person's mind is really preoccupied with thoughts of sex. This time of preoccupation fosters a search for sexual stimulation that can feel obsessive.

The person who is contending with an addiction typically has his or her own routines around acting out. These routines are referred to by Carnes as rituals. Rituals intensify the person's preoccupation with sex. Rituals add to the excitement and arousal.

The sexual behavior, then, is the next part of the addictive cycle. It is the actual act, whether it is masturbation to pornography or meeting with a prostitute. The thinking in the field is that the person who has truly developed a sex addiction is unable to control his behavior at this point, which is a description of the "powerlessness" that is part of addiction. This is an important consideration for when we discuss treatment.

Sexual acting out typically leads to confirmation in the person's mind that his behavior is out of control or unmanageable, which can lead to negative affect, such as depression or despair.

Assessment, then, is intended to help the clinician identify these specific rituals and the broader catalytic events and environments that facilitate sexual acting-out behavior.

Assessment can also begin to identify any rationalizations that justify acting-out behavior. For example, a husband might blame his wife for not providing him with a sufficient number of sexual encounters each week, so in his mind his behavior is a way to meet his needs that his wife is not meeting. These questions can also get at the impact of the person's behavior on other relationships that are meaningful to them.

It can also be helpful to know that many sex addicts do not see their behavior as harmful to their partner, particularly if their behavior is masturbation and use of pornography. They are much more likely to minimize the acts. Yet research has shown that over 40% of those surveyed have shared that their partner's use of pornography makes them feel insecure and less attractive. Nearly one-third of those surveyed shared that their partner's use of pornography made them feel more like a sexual object—even though their partner's focus was on various illicit images (Bridges & Bergner, 2003).

Laaser (2004) asks three spiritual questions of the sex addict that may be helpful during assessment. In light of the ambivalence sex addicts may feel in approaching treatment, Laaser asks, Do you want to get well? He points to the Christian understanding that we can be "double-minded" (Jas 1:8). A second question that may be helpful is, What are you thirsty for? Laaser is getting at the idea that the sexual behaviors that have taken on an addictive quality do not satisfy the person; they leave the person wanting more. Persons contending with sex addiction may want God's forgiveness and grace in their life, but they may not believe they deserve it; they may be steeped in shame. This question can allow the person to reflect on what is possible. Last, Laaser (2004) asks, Are you willing to die to yourself? Contrasting selfishness with selflessness, Laaser asks sex addicts to consider what they are willing to die for. In contrast to sinful self-centeredness, people who struggle with sexual addiction consider whether they are "willing to die to something or for someone" (p. 125).

CAN GOD BECOME PART OF THE ADDICTIVE SYSTEM?

When working with religious clients, it is also important to consider how religion can become a part of the addictive cycle. Penner and Penner (2005) note that for the person who contends with an addiction, God can become part of the addictive system. Along with society or their own parents, God also makes them feel guilt or shame. Of course, this is not an accurate, helpful, or healthy view of God. But within the context of their addictive system, religious addicts can experience God as the God of the "big stick," who is ready to punish them for their wrongdoings. Scripture, which is a source of comfort to many Christians, becomes another source of scrutiny and internal conflicts. The Holy Spirit, the great Comforter to many Christians, is experienced as another source of condemnation. Many Christian clinicians make the mistake of simply turning to prayer or Scripture in working with religious sex addicts in an attempt to capitalize on faith-based resources in clinical work.

However, as Penner and Penner (2005) observe, counseling with highly religious clients often entails reworking their emotional experience of God. This could be done through various God image exercises and related interventions (see Moriarty, 2006). The idea here is that as a clinician you want to work through the clients' emotional experience of God so that God can become a resource to them rather than a source of condemnation. Keep in mind that the voice of God in 1 Corinthians 14:3 is characterized by edification (building a person up), exhortation (warning a person, challenging that person, stirring that person up), and comfort (encouragement, peace). But some people's background may make it difficult to hear the voice of God as anything like edification, exhortation, or comfort, and so it may fit into their addictive system until sufficient work is done to address it. In what ways can you imagine otherwise helpful religious resources as playing a role in supporting an addictive system? How could a person's emotional experience of God either threaten or undermine recovery?

In the context of assessment, Laaser (2004) and Carnes (2010) take an inventory of a sex addict's fantasies. Rather than have a client distance himself from fantasies, Laaser asks the client to understand the fantasy better—to understand what it represents. To do this, the client does not cut himself off from his fantasies (they will return); rather, he draws it closer initially—he learns what the fantasy represents (e.g., when the features or personality of a person in a fantasy "represents the person who most profoundly abandoned the addict," p. 158).

Before we close this section on assessment, we should note that assessment should also consider depression and a number of other co-occurring disorders ranging from substance abuse to post-traumatic stress disorder (PTSD). As we have seen in our discussion about core beliefs and addicts' sense of self-worth, they are at risk for a co-occurring depressive disorder that may need to also be treated at this time. Interestingly, one study (Yoder et al., 2005) reported that the main predictor of loneliness in their sample was time spent viewing internet pornography.

TREATMENT

Treatment of sexual addictions is typically multifaceted and comprehensive. In terms of key facets, it may involve counseling (individual, couple, or family), support groups, accountability partners, sponsors, and physicians or psychiatrists.

As the counselor you end up assisting in the oversight and coordination of care of these various facets of treatment. In individual counseling the clinician will typically work with the client on several things, including environment management, processing negative emotions, developing insight, emotional regulation, and the development of social skills, along with providing psychoeducation about the cycle of addiction. Although treatment may reflect one pure theoretical model, we offer a multi-theoretical approach based on our biopsychosocial understanding of etiology.

The counselor should conduct a thorough assessment that includes a comprehensive general sex history and a specific problem sex history. Keep in mind that a general sex history will include information on the person's sexual problem history, but places that in the context of that person's own sex history. It should cover a person's sexual development: how he was educated about sex in the home growing up, in his peer group, at school, and in the larger context of messages he heard growing up about sexuality and sexual behavior.

The therapist is learning about attitudes that were conveyed (by parents, siblings, teachers, religious leaders, and so on) about sex growing up. It will be helpful to know how nudity was addressed in the home and whether modesty was modeled. It is important to ask about the person's experience with puberty, masturbation, and exposure to erotic stimuli/pornography, among other topics. All of these questions are part of a general sex history.

A sexual problem history again refers to the issues the person is in the office to address. When did these behaviors become a concern? How did they develop? How long have they been a concern? What steps has the client taken to address the problem behaviors? How helpful have these interventions been thus far?

A good general sex history and problem sex history provides the kind of knowledge that can aid in case conceptualization and treatment planning. Particularly helpful is information that may help the client manage his environment better.

Toward this end, keep in mind that access to pornography and other related sexual stimuli is much easier today than even twenty years ago. It is important to consider ease of access to the internet, the use of software for blocking sites or content, and the use of software for helping to hold a person accountable for page views. The counselor can work with the client on those various options, as well as consider whether other forms of pornography or problematic sexual stimuli are readily available at the client's home or place of employment.

Sometimes environment management may entail resymbolizing rooms that have been host to pornography or other acts that have undermined the client's goals for counseling. One man we worked with, at the request of his spouse, moved his office to another room in the house. His office is where much of his acting out occurred in terms of internet pornography and chat rooms. The move allowed him to resymbolize both rooms, to pray over them, and to commit them to their proper purposes.

It is important not to underestimate the impact of such steps on the emotional state of the client. Keep in mind that he is removing items or access to material that has brought him comfort in the past, has been a reliable source of support, and so on. The counselor, then, is processing emotions, such as regret, guilt, loss, anger, confusion, and depression. The counselor is also helping the client identify other ways to meet emotional needs. These are healthy, adaptive reconnecting activities that are consistent with the client's goals for recovery. Examples include exercise, talking with a friend, prayer, worship, and reading.

The counselor also helps the client begin the process of journaling. Journaling can be a free-flowing reflection on one's day, emotional state, exposure to various stimuli, and so forth, or it can be a more structured intervention. We generally prefer a more structured use of journaling, which we discuss later.

The act of writing down anything can be difficult for some people, but we have found that it provides a baseline for treatment, as well as evidence of gains made over the course of time. This can be helpful later if there are any setbacks or relapses. Clients can journal about situations they face, their immediate thoughts in that moment, their feelings and emotional state, and how they responded. We often have clients do their journaling in the evening as a way to reflect on the day. Clients can then bring their journal into a session to review and identify unhelpful thoughts and how they lead to negative emotions, and how these unhelpful thoughts and negative emotions can lead to behaviors that place them at risk for sexual acting out. With more structured journaling, clients can then write down other ways they could think about the circumstances and events in their life, as well as more helpful thoughts and alternative behaviors they could engage in that are more consistent with their goals for counseling and recovery.

An additional benefit to journaling is that the act of writing things down can interrupt the normal thought process, which for sexual addicts is unhelpful at this time. The normal thought process tends to reflect rationalization, minimization, and so on. Journaling provides clients with valuable data about the way they process events and may rely on irrational ways of thinking to justify behavior that conflicts with their counseling goals.

Psychoeducation is also an important part of a comprehensive model of treatment. The counselor can educate the client on the addictive system by providing explanations and readings that can be incorporated into treatment (bibliotherapy). It is important that the client become an expert on his own addiction. This means really coming to an understanding of how impaired, unhelpful thoughts are generated from core beliefs that are unique to that client's history, as well as how these unhelpful thoughts feed into preoccupation and rituals that intensify the desire for sexual acting out.

For example, one man we treated only acted out with people he met through chat rooms. He would use his laptop to set these liaisons up while traveling for business. His ritual involved wrapping up his business meeting, going to his hotel, calling his wife and children and essentially "putting them to bed" over the phone, and then powering up his laptop to finalize a meeting with women for a sexual encounter. He would never set up a sexual encounter using any other means—no other computer, not the phone, and so on. He has a specific routine, a ritual that intensified the sexual experience.

As was indicated in the discussion about assessment, treatment often involves addressing shame and self-esteem, as well as teaching prosocial skills by identify relational deficits or other concerns, such as the capacity for emotional and sexual intimacy. In light of the growing interest in attachment theory, it can be helpful to identify the client's attachment style or to otherwise keep in mind that early experiences of neglect, trauma, or witnessing violence can impair attachment. Sexual addicts with more dismissive-avoidant and fearful-avoidant attachment styles have disavowed their feelings (distanced themselves from their own feelings) and how to express them to others (Katehakis, 2009, p. 17). The clinician will help these clients identify their feelings and learn how to communicate them to others. In contrast, the sex addict who has more of an anxious-preoccupied attachment style may need assistance regulating his emotional state through healthy self-soothing behaviors consistent with his goals for counseling (Katehakis, 2009).

Katehakis (2009, pp. 19-22) offers a helpful review of the steps that lead to affect regulation, which can be summarized as follows:

1. Observe physical symptoms of anxiety.
2. Track and identify to the client how symptoms of anxiety function as defenses against negative emotions.
3. Identify specific, bodily functions (e.g., tightness of the chest, dry mouth).
4. Monitor and track emotions/affect.
5. Attend to the clinician's prosody (i.e., volume, rhythm, tempo of speech).
6. Facilitate insight into such things as transference and counter-transference, shame, and so on.

As we mentioned earlier, shame is such a difficult part of the sexual addict's emotional state that it is important to find ways to reduce shame. This involves understanding the roots of shame and their place in the addictive system, distinguishing between shame and guilt, identifying defenses that may protect from negative or painful feelings, using specific shame-reducing interventions throughout treatment, and addressing core beliefs or foundational beliefs that support shame (Adams & Robinson, 2001, p. 25).

Strategies for reducing shame include establishing and maintaining a good therapeutic relationship, psychoeducation about shame and its place in the addictive cycle, being able to face feelings (e.g., inadequacy, loneliness, anger), finding ways to cope with and regulate negative feelings, and learning to respond responsibly to guilt (e.g., make amends for wrongs done to others) (Adams & Robinson, 2001, pp. 28-30).

Clients also often benefit from involvement in a self-help or mutual-aid support group (e.g., Sex Addicts Anonymous, Sexaholics Anonymous, Sexual Compulsives Anonymous, Sex and Love Addicts Anonymous), including various faith-based self-help groups (e.g., Celebrate Recovery). Any one support group or local ministry can vary in quality. Clients can visit and consider whether there is consistent attendance by members, a sense of order and structure to the presentations on the steps or approaches to recovery, regular rotation of responsibilities, and so on (Carnes, 2010).

A client can attend two to three meetings per week for the first several weeks or longer, keeping in mind that recovering alcohol abusers often aim for "90 meetings in 90 days" at Alcoholics Anonymous to really get traction in their recovery from alcohol. An emphasis in groups like this is often surrender of themselves to God—that they are unable to make changes without surrendering to God (or a higher power, in the language of twelve-step groups). Self-help groups also often help participants define celibacy (abstinence) for a season as they work on recovery. This is a season where the person does not engage in sexual activity for several weeks or longer. Sexual behaviors included in an abstinence period are masturbation, intercourse with one's spouse, viewing pornography, identifying and avoiding circumstances that might lead to acting out, and so on. The client learns that he can make it without sex. He will survive. He can find other, healthy ways to meet his emotional needs. In the recovery group or support group setting, the client also has access to a sponsor and others who can help encourage recovery and hold him accountable to recovery goals.

One common tool often used in mutual aid support groups like Sex Addicts Anonymous is a template with three circles. Each circle represents a different kind of behavior. The outer circle (or outer circle behavior) represents behaviors that are normal, activities that are a good and healthy part of a person's routine. One client we worked with wrote in "greeter at church, going to movies, exercise, playing guitar, lifting weights." The next circle (middle circle behavior) are those behaviors that lead to acting out. For our client it was things like cruising bookstores, fantasies of paying for a prostitute, true-crime books or TV shows, and viewing personal ads. The inner circle (or inner circle behavior) is the behaviors that reflect a relapse, such as for this person masturbation to pornography and going to child porn sites.

One goal in these discussions is to help the client come to terms with this as a likely lifelong process, much as someone who has struggled with addiction to alcohol is taught to see his or her recovery as lifelong. On the face of it this can be discouraging. However, what we do is simply discuss how everyone has a signature struggle in life (Mangis, 2008). It is usually a cluster of different things we would like to have different in our lives, but it could be a struggle with lust and self-centeredness, or it could be a struggle with anger and pride. Some are more prone to envy; others are more susceptible to greed. In the area of mental health concerns, some people are more susceptible to depressions, while others are more vulnerable to anxiety or to an eating disorder. The person you are working with who struggles with an addiction is unlikely to now struggle with a completely different issue; no, he or she is likely to have this addiction be a part of life, even if that means being more consciously aware of it and his or her environment, so that the person reduces the risk of going down the same path again.

Self-help groups often vary in quality based on who is presently in attendance, how they relate to one another, and where people are in the various steps to recovery. However, a healthy mutual-aid support group can be a helpful adjunct to ongoing counseling.

Clients working on an addiction also need accountability. We frequently refer to having an accountability partner. This is someone who has established the kind of relationship with the client such that they are able to ask the tough questions and scrutinize decisions that place them at risk for relapse. It is generally recommended that this not be the man's spouse. That person has her own work to do in processing her emotional reaction to what may have been infidelity or otherwise disturbing patterns of behavior and feelings of disloyalty. Having the spouse function as an accountability partner also keeps their relationship imbalanced, as the spouse is now overseeing the addict's progress, which may be partial at times. The spouse also will want to rebuild the capacity to trust her partner, which is not as readily present when the spouse is monitoring behavior. Trust is likely best fostered when the spouse is able to grow in her capacity to trust her husband is working a framework for treatment and recovery.

Religious clients may also express interest in a men's support or accountability group through their place of worship. These groups can vary in quality too, but they can be a helpful adjunct to counseling. A men's support group can also be a good source for finding an accountability partner and someone to call when the client feels particularly vulnerable to acting out.

Another aspect in the framework for recovery is consultation with a physician or psychiatrist. This might include medication management that could address symptoms of depression, suicidality, impulse control, and other issues.

In chapter two we mentioned that technology can be leveraged to assist people who are addressing sexual addiction or pornography. There are a number of website filters and related resources to help with accountability and environment management (see www.xxxchurch.com), as well as smartphone apps (e.g., Private Integrity) that are designed to help clients monitor their vulnerable times and develop exercises and other strategies for fostering a healthier sexuality.

Clients can also work with their counselor to develop a relapse prevention plan. This may involve helping the client scrutinize his environment, purging it of stimuli that would be too tempting or provide too strong a reminder of what he is trying to curtail.

PREVENTION

There has been relatively little development on primary prevention of sexual addiction. Broad suggestions would include proper sexual education, correcting myths about gender, reducing sexualization in media and entertainment, and curtailing the pornography industry or at least limiting access to pornography sites. However, most of the work on prevention has been in the area of relapse prevention among those already identified as dealing with a sexual addiction.

The original relapse prevention model for alcohol (Marlatt, 1982) was based on cognitive-behavioral theory and has been adapted for other addictive behaviors, including sexual addiction. It involves identifying high-risk situations that essentially threaten a person's own commitment to abstinence. The clinician can work with the person struggling with sexual addiction to identify situations that might be unmanageable or create imbalance in one's lifestyle, and decisions that might seem irrelevant but lead to risk for relapse. If this does not happen, sexual addicts can begin to experience ambivalence as they begin to anticipate the pleasure they have associated with the sexual acting-out behavior. Anticipated pleasures and a potential lapse here can diminish a person's sense of self-efficacy, which can lead to a full-blown relapse. Education about the abstinence-violation effect is important because many people who experience a lapse may rationalize a full-blown relapse due to the need to admit the first lapse at all.

Contrasting efforts at relapse prevention reflect a self-regulation model (Ward & Hudson, 1998). The approach has several phases and begins with a life event that is evaluated and may lead to thoughts and feelings (phase 1). This may be followed by a desire to engage in the addictive behavior that is the result of feeling negative emotions and wanting to feel better (phase 2). The person then plans to participate in the sexual behavior (phase 3). A strategy for engaging in the behavior is selected, such as one of several avoidant strategies (e.g., avoidant-passive strategy, in which the person feels he cannot keep from acting on it) (phase 4).

Then comes involvement in high-risk situations (phase 5), which is choosing to be in places (or engage in activities) that put the person at great risk for acting out, followed by a lapse, which is a direct precursor to relapse (phase 6). This is followed by the addictive behavior (phase 7) and post-addictive evaluation of behavior (e.g., guilt, shame) (phase 8). The final phase reflects attitudes toward future addictive behavior, for example, recommit to abstinence and reevaluation of established goals (Ward & Hudson, 1998).

CLOSING REFLECTIONS

Earlier in the chapter we introduced you to Jon, a person we had seen in counseling for sex addiction. Following up on that story, Jon shared that his struggles with sexual addiction led him into Sexual Addicts Anonymous and into therapy, where he learned more about his struggles. He completed one year of sobriety from sex and masturbation, and has initiated a dating relationship. He gained insight into his own condition and eventually learned to manage behavior that set him up to relapse, including true-crime TV, cruising bookstores, fantasy, and the like. He then explored anger in his family of origin, his rain-checking behavior (not really closing the door to a possible activity/behavior that would put him at risk), and the theme of abandonment (essentially emotional abandonment by his mother). Over time he was able to meet a woman whom he dated and eventually married. He worked on cognitive distortions that emerged and anxiety regarding performance. The relationship provided additional opportunities to revisit themes and consolidate gains in the here-and-now.

Jon is a Christian. He wanted the resources from his faith to inform his work in recovery and therapy. We want to discuss some of those considerations in this section. As we do, let's first acknowledge that Christians in some ways have a unique vantage point into the world of sexual addiction. We understand that we were—all of us—once enslaved to sin (Rom 6:20). Our condition reflects our fallen state; it is out of this condition (wired to sin) that we act, respond, and think in ways that do not meet God's standards of holiness. We often see in ourselves a splitting of the will; part of us wants to do things that reflect God's intention for ourselves and our relationships, while another part wants to fulfill self-gratifying interests. Plantinga (1995) notes that in both sin and addiction we are enslaved by our basic state;

what we do is an extension of that condition. Behavioral changes—changes made at the level of what we do—are often ineffective over time. We often cannot sustain behavioral change because it is fundamentally symptomatic of a core condition that remains unchanged.

So Christians have a unique vantage point for empathy toward any pattern of addiction, as we know too well how sin can be habit forming, lead to shame and self-reproach, and fuel statements to cease our activities, followed by subsequent failures and turning to more sin as a way of managing negative affect, such as guilt and shame. Not all sin reflects this kind of addictive syndrome, but the Christian recognizes in his or her own struggle with besetting sin some of the qualities and characteristics seen in addiction.

When we see addiction in clinical practice, we recognize that while struggles may be inevitable, we still hold people responsible for their behavior. Although responsibility may be diminished, it is not obscured. As we discussed in a previous work,

> a Christian account of addiction takes seriously the question of whether people
> are responsible for their choices. Christians assume that persons are—at some
> point in the history of their decision-making—capable of apprehending principles
> regarding what they ought to do and not do. We also assume that persons can
> exert their will in a desired direction and have some success in doing so, even in
> the face of negative conditions. (Yarhouse et al., 2005, pp. 199-200)

A question often raised in discussions of sexual addiction has to do with the role of sin in the etiology and maintenance of sexual addiction. If it does play a role, at what point does the Christian clinician address the sin in addition to other comorbid factors, such as depression and anxiety?

Perhaps one benefit to understanding the parallel between sin and addiction is that it might help a new clinician empathize with the obstacles faced by the sex addict. After all, what obstacles have each of us faced in our own struggle with "signature sins" (Mangis, 2008)? These refer to the cluster of sinful tendencies that are unique to each person based on his or her history, formative relationships, current circumstances, and so on. Even when two people struggle with lust as a part of the cluster of sin, they will struggle with lust differently due to any number of factors. The complexity here should keep any clinician humble as he or she approaches those who are trying to give up patterns of addiction. It is worth reflecting on the challenges you as a clinician might face in having empathy for a client who is giving up an addictive pattern that has been a powerful source of pleasure and met numerous emotional needs, however unhealthy that relationship may have been.

Beyond the similarities between sin and addiction—similarities that might help the Christian clinician empathize with a client struggling with sexual addiction—is there anything that Christianity can contribute to a believing client's motivational levels? We recognize that when entering treatment, motivation is often mixed; people feel ambivalent about receiving care because their own will is split. This is tricky. Religious clients who struggle with sexual addiction often have a distorted emotional experience of God. A person's emotional experience of God is referred to as that person's God image (Moriarty, 2006). It is often contrasted in the clinical literature with a person's understanding of God ("head knowledge" or God concept). Indeed, a person's God concept reflects what they think God is like: God is good, kind, loving, gracious. The challenge for many people—including the sex addict—is that while they may *think* these things, they do not *feel* them. They do not *feel* loved by God or that God likes them. They may *know* that God is forgiving, but they may not *feel* forgiven by God.

When working with Christians like Jon, it is certainly understandable that a Christian clinician would want to draw on faith-based resources, such as prayer and reading Scripture. However, careful consideration should be given to the timing of the use of these resources, as well as whether the person struggling with sexual addiction may need help identifying and bridging the gap that may exist between their God concept (what they think about God) and their God image (their emotional experience of God).

Recall that the longest-running play in Spain is *Don Juan Tenorio*. There are many interpretations of the mythical Don Juan. The seduction of women portrayed in these interpretations reflects an ever-expanding reality: addiction has the potential to seduce all who linger too close. And make no mistake, sexual addiction is a jealous lover. Today sexual addiction itself delights in our destruction. It promises so much by way of fulfillment and then demands so much more. It can take a person's most important relationships and trade on the promise of more. In the play, when the rogue is eventually dragged to hell by the ghost of a father of one of the young women who was seduced, we catch a glimpse of what the person faces who stands against addiction and the resources needed of a redemptive community to assist in his or her recovery.

REFERENCES

Adams, K. M., & Robinson, D. W. (2001). Shame reduction, affect regulation, and sexual boundary development: Essential building blocks of sexual addiction treatment. *Sexual Addiction & Compulsivity, 8*, 23-44.

American Psychiatric Association. (1968). *Diagnostic and statistical manual of mental disorders* (2nd ed.). American Psychiatric Publishing.

American Psychiatric Association. (1980). *Diagnostic and statistical manual of mental disorders* (3rd ed.). American Psychiatric Publishing.

American Psychiatric Association. (2013). *Diagnostic and statistical manual of mental disorders* (5th ed.). American Psychiatric Publishing.

Bridges, A. J., & Bergner, R. M. (2003). Romantic partners' use of pornography: Its significance for women. *Journal of Sex & Marital Therapy, 29*(1), 1-15.

Campling, S., & Vermeire, J. (2012). Special populations and treatment issues. In M. C. Ferree (Ed.), *Making advances: A comprehensive guide for treating female sex and love addicts* (pp. 215-54). Society for the Advancement of Sexual Health.

Carnes, P. (1989). *Contrary to love: Helping the sexual addict*. CompCare.

Carnes, P. (2001). *Out of the shadows* (3rd ed.). Hazelden.

Carnes, P. (2005). *The making of a sex addict*. Retrieved from https://cdn.ymaws.com /iitap.com/resource/resmgr/arie_files/m1_article_the-making-of-a-s.pdf

Carnes, P. (2010). *Facing the shadow: Starting sexual and relationship recovery* (2nd ed.). Gentle Path.

Carnes, P., Delmonico, D. L., & Griffin, E. (2007). *In the shadows of the net: Breaking free of compulsive online sexual behavior* (2nd ed.). Hazelden.

Carter, D. R., & Ruiz, N. J. (1996). Discriminant validity and reliability studies on the Sexual Addiction Scale of the Disorders Screening Inventory. *Sexual Addiction and Compulsivity, 3*, 332-40.

Coleman, E. (1987). Sexual compulsivity: Definition, etiology, and treatment considerations. *Journal of Chemical Dependency Treatment, 1*, 189-204.

Ferree, M. C. (2010). *No stones: Women redeemed from sexual addiction*. InterVarsity Press.

Ferree, M. C. (Ed.). (2012). *Making advances: A comprehensive guide for treating female sex and love addicts*. Society for the Advancement of Sexual Health.

Ferree, M. C., Hudson, L., Katehakis, A., McDaniel, K., & Valenti-Anderson, A. (2012). Etiology of female sex and love addiction: A biopsychosocial perspective. In M. C. Ferree (Ed.), *Making advances: A comprehensive guide for treating female sex and love addicts* (pp. 44-66). Society for the Advancement of Sexual Health.

George, C., Kaplan, N., & Main, M. (1996). *The Adult Attachment Interview*. University of California Press.

Grover, S., & Shouan, A. (2020). Assessment scales for sexual disorders: A review. *Journal of Psychosexual Health, 2*(2), 121-28.

Grubbs, J. B., Sessoms, J., Wheeler, D. M., & Volk, F. (2010). The cyber-pornography use inventory: The development of a new assessment instrument. *Sexual Addiction & Compulsivity, 17*, 106-26.

Hook, J. N., Hook, J. P., Davis, D. E., Worthington, E. L., & Penberthy, J. K. (2010). Measuring sexual addiction and compulsivity: A critical review of instruments. *Journal of Sex & Marital Therapy, 36,* 227-60.

Kafka, M. P. (1991). Successful antidepressant treatment of nonparaphilic sexual addictions and paraphilias in males. *Journal of Clinical Psychiatry, 52,* 60-65.

Kafka, M. P. (2000). The paraphilia-related disorders: Nonparaphilic hypersexuality and sexual compulsivity/addiction. In S. R. Leiblum & R. C. Rosen (Eds.), *Principles and practice of sex therapy* (3rd ed., pp. 471-504). Guilford.

Kafka, M. P. (2007). Paraphilia-related disorders: The evaluation and treatment of nonparaphilic hypersexuality. In S. R. Leiblum (Ed.), *Principles and practice of sex therapy* (4th ed., pp. 442-76). Guilford.

Kafka, M. P. (2010). Hypersexual disorder: A proposed diagnosis for DSM-V. *Archives of Sexual Behavior, 39,* 377-400.

Katehakis, A. (2009). Affective neuroscience and the treatment of sexual addiction. *Sexual Addiction & Compulsivity, 16,* 1-31.

Kor, A., Zilcha-Mano, S., Fogel, Y. A., Mikulincer, M., Reid, R. C., & Potenza, M. N. (2014). Psychometric development of the Problematic Pornography Use Scale. *Addictive Behaviors, 39,* 861-68.

Laaser, M. (2004). *Healing the wounds of sexual addiction* (Expanded ed.). Zondervan.

Mangis, M. (2008). *Signature sins: Taming our wayward hearts.* InterVarsity Press.

Marcus, I. D. (2010). Men who are not in control of their sexual behavior. In S. B. Levine, C. B. Risen, & S. E. Althof (Eds.), *Handbook of clinical sexuality for mental health professionals* (2nd ed., pp. 383-99). Routledge.

Marlatt, G. A. (1982). Relapse prevention: A self-control program for the treatment of addictive behaviors. In R. B. Stuart (Ed.), *Adherence, compliance, and generalization in behavioral medicine* (pp. 329-78). Brunner/Mazel.

McDaniel, K., & Valenti-Anderson, A. (2012). Definition and understanding of female sex and love addiction. In M. C. Ferree (Ed.), *Making advances: A comprehensive guide for treating female sex and love addicts* (pp. 27-43). Society for the Advancement of Sexual Health.

Moriarty, G. (2006). *Pastoral care of depression: Helping clients heal their relationship with God.* Routledge.

Muench, F., Morgentstern, J., Hollander, E., Irwin, T., O'Leary, A., Parsons, J. T., . . . & Lai, B. (2007). The consequences of compulsive sexual behavior: The preliminary reliability and validity of the Compulsive Sexual Behavior Consequences Scale. *Sexual Addiction and Compulsivity, 14,* 207-20.

Penner, J., & Penner, C. (2005). *A clinician's guide to sex therapy* (2nd ed.). Word.

Plantinga, C., Jr. (1995). *Not the way it's supposed to be.* Eerdmans.

Reid, R. C., Garos, S., & Carpenter, B. N. (2011). Reliability, validity, and psychometric development of the Hypersexual Behavior Inventory in an outpatient sample of men. *Journal of Sexual Addiction & Compulsivity, 18*(1), 30-51.

Reid, R. C., Li, D. S., Gilliland, R., Stein, J. A., & Fong, T. (2011). Reliability, validity, and psychometric development of the pornography consumption inventory in a sample of hypersexual men. *Journal of Sex & Marital Therapy, 37,* 359-85.

Samenow, C. P. (2010). A biopsychosocial model of hypersexual disorder/sexual addiction. *Sexual Addiction & Compulsivity, 17,* 69-81.

Shaver, P. R., Belsky, J., & Brennan, K. A. (2000). Comparing measures of adult attachment: An examination of interview and self-report methods. *Personal Relationships, 7,* 25-43.

Stein, D. J. (2009). Classifying hypersexual disorders: Compulsive, impulsive, and addictive models. *Psychiatric Clinics of North America, 31*(4), 587-91. doi:10.1016/j .psc.2008.06.007

Stein, D. J., Chamberlain, S. R., & Fineberg, N. (2006). An A-B-C model of habit disorders: Hair-pulling, skin-picking, and other stereotypic conditions. *CNS Spectrums, 11,* 824-27.

Struthers, W. (2009). *Wired for intimacy: How pornography hijacks the male brain.* InterVarsity Press.

Ward, T., & Hudson, S. M. (1998). A model of the relapse process in sexual offenders. *Journal of Interpersonal Violence, 13*(6), 700-725.

Yarhouse, M. A., Butman, R. E., & McRay, B. W. (2005). *Modern psychopathologies: A comprehensive Christian appraisal.* InterVarsity Press.

Yoder, V. C., Virden, T. B., & Amin, K. (2005). Internet pornography and loneliness: An association? *Sexual Addiction & Compulsivity, 12,* 19-44.

THIRTEEN

SEXUAL IDENTITY CONFLICTS AND MIXED ORIENTATION COUPLES

CYNTHIA NIXON, THE ACTRESS who played Miranda in the television series and movie *Sex and the City*, caused a stir in the gay and lesbian community when she shared in an interview with the *New York Times* that she chose her sexual orientation. "For me, it is a choice. I understand that for many people it's not, but for me it's a choice, and you don't get to define my gayness for me" (Witchel, 2012, p. MM24). She went on to comment on the idea that she was discovering who she was all along, "I also feel like people think I was walking around in a cloud and didn't realize I was gay, which I find really offensive" (p. MM24).

Critics from within the mainstream lesbian, gay, bisexual and transgender, queer, and other (LGBTQ+) community felt that Nixon was sending the wrong message; the idea that orientation is volitional would be used by opponents in the larger culture wars. Further, the claim of a self-chosen sexuality would be used by those who want to treat innocent and vulnerable gay youth. Some insisted that she recant; others wanted to educate Nixon about language and terminology. They insisted she was bisexual, and that while her own sexuality includes a capacity for response arousal to both the same and opposite sex, that capacity is not available to many other sexual minorities.

There is a potential benefit to clarifying terminology. This chapter focuses on sexual identity questions and conflicts. *Sexual identity* refers to the act of labeling oneself with reference to one's sexual preferences. Common sexual identity labels in contemporary Western culture are gay, lesbian, and bisexual. Straight is also a sexual identity label. Emerging sexual identities among younger, sexually diverse persons include androsexual, semi-sexual, panromantic asexual, demisexual, and sapiosexual. "Gay" often functions as an umbrella identity for all of these non-straight sexual identities. About 7.6% of adults adopt a gay, lesbian, bisexual, transgender, queer, or other identity (1.4% gay, 1.2% lesbian, 4.4% bisexual; Jones, 2024; see also Egan et al., 2008), with significant generational differences: 20.9% of Gen Z identify as LGB compared to 8.8% of Millennials, 3.9% of Gen X, and 2.2% of Baby Boomers (Jones, 2024).

Sexual identity is related to sexual attractions. Indeed, as we have suggested, much of what contributes to sexual identity labels is found in one's attractions. *Sexual attractions* refer to feelings of sexual or emotional interest in another. The attraction or interest in another reflects sexual desire. It has been estimated that as many as 11% of adults experience at least some same-sex attraction (Gates, 2011; Laumann et al., 2000).

When we discuss *sexual orientation,* also a topic of this chapter, we are referring to what is often thought to be a more enduring pattern of attraction to another based on one's sexual desire. There are many debates in our culture about sexual orientation—particularly about the cause of sexual orientation and whether it is an immutable (unchanging) characteristic. Orientation is often discussed in our cultural context as heterosexual (sexual desire as attraction to the opposite sex), homosexual (to the same sex), and bisexual (to both sexes). The prevalence estimates for adult homosexual orientation are about 2% to 3% (e.g., Egan, Edelman, & Sherrill, 2008; Laumann et al., 2000).

Having clarified the basic terminology, it is no surprise that Cynthia Nixon ran into some trouble with her statement. There are a number of terms and concepts to consider when we talk about attractions, orientation, and identity. Answers to questions about causes and change depend significantly on which terms we are referring to.

Although homosexuality (the experience of having a homosexual orientation) is no longer considered a mental illness by the major mental health organizations, conflicts about same-sex attraction, orientation, and identity continue to lead many people to seek professional treatment and religiously affiliated ministries. Broadly speaking, then, we will refer to these as "sexual identity concerns." We note that many people who experience same-sex attraction do not experience their attractions as a concern; rather, the issues they face may have more to do with how others respond to them whether or not they enter into same-sex relationships or adopt a gay identity. In any case, we will specify when we discuss attraction, orientation, or identity. This chapter reviews etiology, treatment, and prevention, and it provides an understanding of a Christian perspective on findings related to biological, sociocultural, and clinical issues.

ETIOLOGY

What causes the sexual identity concerns that might lead someone to seek counseling? Part of the question has to do with what causes sexual attraction, orientation, or even identity; that alone is a challenging research question. But what causes attraction, orientation, or identity to be a concern to the person seeking services? That is a different question, one we will return to in our discussion of clinical presentations. And, of course, for many people the experience of same-sex attraction, orientation, or identity does not lead to clinical questions or concerns.

As we turn to the cause of same-sex attraction and orientation, it is difficult to escape how politicized these discussions have become. Given the controversies surrounding homosexuality, both sides in what is often referred to as a larger culture war surrounding sexual orientation have been invested in their own story/narrative surrounding causation. Those on the one side write a narrative around nature, around biology and what seems natural to the person. A gay or lesbian sexual identity label is, then, a reflection of one's underlying sexual orientation, which is much like eye color or hair color.

Those on the other side of the so-called culture war develop a narrative around nurture and volition, suggesting that same-sex sexuality can be tied to key environmental factors. They presume that if the environment is the key, then choices become more central. This story often implicates faulty parent-child relationships, gender insecurity, or unwanted sexual experiences in childhood. Emphasis is placed on choosing homosexuality, leaving the question open as to what in that is volitional.

Neither of these stories or narratives about causation is completely accurate; the truth lies somewhere in between. What we see as accurate from the first story/narrative about causation is that there have been numerous studies conducted to support the role of biology (nature) in same-sex sexuality. Indeed, as we have discussed in greater detail elsewhere (Jones & Yarhouse, 2000; Yarhouse, 2010), the biological hypothesis for the origins of homosexuality has been forcefully advanced for more than two decades now.

Studies have been published on a number of supposed connections, including research on twin studies (e.g., Långström et al., 2008), fraternal birth order and handedness (e.g., Blanchard, 2008; Blanchard et al., 2006; Blanchard & Lippa, 2007; Bogaert et al., 2007), and animal models (in which homosexual behavior is either observed in nature or the result of genetic, hormonal, or other manipulations) (e.g., Demir & Dickson, 2005). Some of the most recent research has considered genetic scanning (e.g., Ganna et al., 2019; Mustanski et al., 2005) and brain symmetry and neural connections (e.g., Savic & Lindström, 2008).

The relationship between biology (nature) and sexual orientation is not one that follows the narrative being advanced. It is not just like eye color or hair color. It is not just like race. Rather, while there is no exact parallel, it appears to be more like a predisposition or a push in the direction of same-sex attraction and orientation for some people. That predisposition is likely weighted more heavily for some people than for others. But the push is not determinative; it is neither decisive nor conclusive. Other factors appear to have to be in play, and not only are those other factors hard to identify, but they are likely weighted differently for different people.

So environment/nurture also appears to play some role in the origins of sexual orientation, and that is part of what the other side has right. Unfortunately, they have focused almost exclusively on parent-child relationships and childhood sexual abuse, but the findings here do not consistently support either theory. Studies that do appear to support environmental influences point to a wide range of considerations, but the studies themselves were not designed to adequately identify the specific environmental variables.

Even the question of choice has been brought up by some. But the choice appears to be primarily around identity and behavior rather than initial feelings of sexual attraction and what we are referring to as orientation. The formation of identity—the decision to adopt one sexual identity label over another—may also reflect for some people choices made early on that foster a more salient sense of personal identity, consolidating into someone quite compelling.

Taken together, we do not know the causes of same-sex attractions or homosexual orientation (nor do we know the causes of attraction to the opposite sex, as such). Most experts today seem to believe that sexual orientation is the result of many possible contributing factors, both from nature (broadly understood) and from nurture (also broadly understood). These factors are likely weighted differently for different people.

The American Psychological Association may have it right when the organization recently summarized the research:

> There is no consensus among scientists about the exact reasons that an individual develops a heterosexual, bisexual, gay, or lesbian orientation. Although much research has examined the possible genetic, hormonal, developmental, social, and cultural influences on sexual orientation, no findings emerged that permit scientists to conclude that sexual orientation is determined by any particular factor or factors. Many think that nature and nurture both play complex roles; most people experience little or no sense of choice about their sexual orientation.

The one point we would raise about this quote from the APA is that it too conflates orientation and identity, and these can be meaningful distinctions in clinical practice, as we will develop in the sections that follow. So the vast majority of people who experience same-sex attractions did not choose to experience same-sex attraction or to have a homosexual orientation; they find themselves with attractions toward the same sex. However, they have choices in front of them, choices about behavior and identity, and it is often these choices that bring people in to see a mental health professional.

ASSESSMENT AND CLINICAL PRESENTATION

The clinical presentation surrounding sexual orientation and sexual identity issues is quite diverse and far reaching. The following are just a few examples:

Ava was a twenty-four-year-old woman who came to therapy after a devastating breakup with her girlfriend of three years. They had played together on a local college sports team, and their relationship seemed strong. Ava was often in tears as she talked about what she missed and what it would mean to move forward. She described herself as a Christian, and she shared that she felt that the relationship was not right but had difficulty setting boundaries or breaking things off.

Alexander was a twenty-six-year-old man who came to therapy because of a string of sexual encounters with men, which had him concerned. He also identified himself as a Christian. He reported feeling same-sex attraction from his teen years on. But he was in the habit of searching online for opportunities for local sexual encounters. These encounters were with college-age men who were athletic and attractive, and the time with them seemed to validate Alexander's sense of self-worth.

Kev is an eighteen-year-old man who is coming to counseling at the request of his parents. They are all Christians, and Kev's parents are reacting critically to Kev's recent disclosure of a gay identity. He is not interested in exploring other options at this time, but he has felt some tension between his religious identity as a Christian and his sexual identity as a gay man.

Evan is a forty-five-year-old man who has been married to a woman for over twenty years. They have two children. He has experienced same-sex attraction since his adolescence. He kept it hidden and thought that marriage to the woman he loved would help keep his attractions in check. Evan's attractions even seemed to diminish somewhat the first four to five years of marriage. But then they seemed to come back with a vengeance, and he has been struggling off and on ever since.

As these examples suggest, it is important to conduct a thorough assessment in part out of regard for the range of issues that might be present. Different people will present with different concerns related to sexual identity. It is important to determine the nature of the concerns faced by the client.

As we have suggested, a homosexual orientation in and of itself is no longer considered to reflect psychopathology by the major mental health organizations. However, the experience of same-sex attractions, conflicts with family, one's religious community, and other issues can frequently lead a person to seek professional services. A good clinical interview and perhaps a sex history can provide useful information. We tend to also add questions on milestone events in sexual identity development, religious identity development, and quality of life (Yarhouse, 2019).

Those who study sexual identity development often point to milestone events in sexual identity formation as a gay or lesbian person. Milestone events are important to assess. In their review of studies of developmental milestones, Savin-Williams and Diamond (2000) noted that first awareness of attraction to the same-sex occurs around ages 9 to 11, while first same-sex activity occurs at an average age of 13 to 16. First labeling as gay, lesbian, or bisexual occurred on average at ages 14 to 16. Disclosure to others typically occurred after that—at an average age of 16 to 17. Most participants (86%-95%) across the various studies reviewed engaged in same-sex behavior—it was a normative aspect of identity formation (see also Savin-Williams & Cohen, 2004).

These are considered important milestones, then, in sexual identity development among sexual minorities: first attraction to the same sex, first same-sex behavior to orgasm, first labeling of self (as gay, lesbian, or bisexual, for instance), and first disclosure to others. An assessment, then, can ask about these milestone events and the experiences the person had with each.

It is important to note, however, that not all sexual minorities experience each of these milestone events. This appears to be particularly true when research focuses on Christian samples of sexual minorities. For example, in the first study (Yarhouse et al., 2009) of sexual minorities at Christian college campuses, researchers reported that while the average ages of experiencing these milestone events were comparable, very few actually reported the developmental milestones (only 36% reported engaging in same-sex behavior; only 14% labeled themselves as gay, lesbian, or bisexual; only 20% had an ongoing same-sex relationship). These findings were recently replicated by the same research team (Stratton et al., 2011). In the follow-up study, differences were reported in identity labeling and in attitudes toward same-sex behavior based on whether the person scored high on intrinsic religiosity (valuing religion for its own sake), as well as the reported degree of attraction to the same and opposite sex. Those with relatively less same-sex attraction and relatively more attraction to the opposite sex reported more conservative/traditional Christian sexual values.

There are also noted differences between male and female experiences of same-sex attraction that appear to influence sexual identity labels. Among male sexual minorities, about two-thirds will identify as gay while about one-third will identify as bisexual. The reverse is the case among females, where about two-thirds of female sexual minorities will identify as bisexual and only one-third as lesbian (Egan et al., 2008). These findings are consistent with the view that females may be more likely to experience greater sexual fluidity than males, a finding also demonstrated in the longitudinal research of Diamond (2006), who followed eighty-nine sexual minority women over more than ten years, and it was common for the women to report attraction and sexual behavior with both men and women (even among those who identified as lesbian) and to change their sexual identity label to reflect their current interests.

So we would highlight the diversity seen among those who experience same-sex sexuality. There appear to be important differences among sexual minorities who come from religious faith backgrounds and who take their faith as important in shaping decisions about behavior and identity labels. There also appear to be important differences among male and female experiences of same-sex sexuality. All of these differences can be taken into consideration during assessment and treatment.

TREATMENT

The only question that rivals the controversies surrounding the causes of sexual orientation is the proper care. The disagreements can be traced back to when homosexuality was considered a mental illness, but given that the major mental health organizations do not classify it as such, there has been considerable criticism against anyone who attempts to change a person's sexual orientation—the practice of reorientation or conversion therapy.[1]

Reorientation therapy had as its goal the change of sexual orientation from homosexual to heterosexual. Reparative therapy was a specific form of reorientation therapy that placed emphasis on repairing a normal drive that the adherent believed had been misdirected and taken the form of homosexuality in the life of the individual with a homosexual orientation.

There is a disagreement about whether orientation can change, and some of that disagreement may be due to whether we are discussing categorical changes or meaningful shifts along a continuum. The latter seems possible for some people, although it is difficult to say exactly how frequently that occurs, whether it reflects natural fluidity or whether such movement can be facilitated through involvement in professional services or ministry. Categorical change is much less likely, if it occurs at all, but even these statements should be qualified because there is a need for better research on attempted change, particularly through involvement in professional therapy.

An American Psychological Association (APA) task force background document titled *Appropriate Therapeutic Responses to Sexual Orientation* discouraged psychologists from "promising or promoting" change of sexual orientation. The report concluded that there is "insufficient evidence" to support the efficacy of change efforts (APA, 2009).

Christians must be honest about the efficacy of change methods. In the Jones and Yarhouse (2011) follow-up study of attempted change, most of the changes reported occurred early in the process, which may suggest more of a change in identity (no longer using the word *gay* but describing oneself as *same-sex attracted*) and behavior (ceasing a pattern of behavior that the client

---

[1]This section is adapted from Mark A. Yarhouse, Jill L. Kays, & Stanton L. Jones, The sexual minority client, in R. Sanders (Ed.), *Christian counseling ethics*, 2nd ed., 2013, InterVarsity Press.

had previously engaged in). The existing data on efficacy of change methods suggests that most people do not find a "cure" in reorientation programs. The broader literature suggests that many people coming out of change efforts continue to experience same-sex attractions and may struggle with self-hatred and guilt. To present treatment less realistically or to assume overly optimistic projections of outcome of current treatment procedures is to engage in ethically questionable practice.

Emerging client-affirmative approaches. The APA task force report provided a rationale for *client-affirmative* (not gay-affirmative) approaches that are more identity-focused and client-centered. A longstanding concern has been the emphasis on gay-affirmative therapy or gay-integrative therapy as the only acceptable form of counseling with sexual minority clients, including those who may be in conflict over their sexuality for religious reasons. Fortunately, more recent developments seem to favor more client-centered approaches.

> We define an affirmative approach as supportive of clients' identity development without a priori treatment goals for how clients identify or express their sexual orientations. Thus, a multiculturally competent affirmative approach aspires to understand the diverse personal and cultural influences on clients and enables clients to determine (a) the ultimate goals for their identity process; (b) the behavioral expression of their sexual orientation; (c) their public and private social roles; (d) their gender roles, identities, and expression; (e) the sex and gender of their partner; and (f) the forms of their relationships. (APA, 2009, p. 14)

This definition of client-affirmative care allows for a variety of values, beliefs, and possible outcomes to be included in one's exploration of one's sexual identity and orientation, while still encouraging a realistic consideration given to the reality of one's sexual attractions and the possibility of change. For the client who is in conflict over his or her identity, the APA (2009) encourages therapy to contain the following components: (1) acceptance and support that includes "unconditional positive regard and empathy for the client," "openness to the client's perspective as a means to understanding their concerns," and encouraging the client's development of a positive self-concept; (2) comprehensive assessment of the client's unique history and various social and cultural contexts, as well as the possible impact of stigma on the client's life; (3) teaching them active coping strategies, including behavioral, cognitive, and emotional, to help them reduce the distress they experience; (4) encouraging and building up of multiple sources of social support; and (5) identity exploration and development (APA, 2009, p. 86). Identity exploration is described as

> an active process of exploring and assessing one's identity and establishing a com-
> mitment to an integrated identity that addresses identity conflicts without an a
> priori treatment goal for how clients identify or live out their sexual orientation.
> The process may include a developmental process that includes periods of crisis,
> mourning, reevaluation, identity deconstruction, and growth. (APA, 2009, p. 86)

This process of accepting and affirming clients' unique experiences and allowing them to work through an exploration of their sexual identity in order to achieve congruence and a positive self-concept without a previously established goal or outcome is where the multicultural and affirmative concepts are primarily demonstrated. This emphasis represents a shift in mainstream approaches to working with sexual minorities, specifically with those who are in conflict over their sexual identity. It reflects a movement toward the center of the spectrum between gay-affirmative and reorientation therapy, and challenges both sides to follow them in the process. This direction encourages clinicians to be sensitive to sexual minorities from multiple backgrounds and values, including religious individuals who may experience conflict over their same-sex attractions. The task force (APA, 2009) gave some examples of therapies that fit their client-centered model, including sexual identity therapy (Throckmorton & Yarhouse, 2006; Yarhouse, 2008).

Sexual identity therapy. Sexual identity therapy (SIT) is a client-centered, identity-focused approach to the concerns raised by conventionally religious sexual minorities (Yarhouse, 2008, 2019). SIT focuses less on sexual orientation and more on sexual identity and congruence, so that clients are able to live and identify themselves in keeping with their beliefs and values.

In their discussion of a framework for providing SIT, Throckmorton and Yarhouse (2006) discuss the four stages of *assessment, advanced informed consent, psychotherapy,* and *sexual identity synthesis.*

Assessment includes an extended discussion of the concerns the person is bringing to counseling. If the person is distressed by his or her experience of same-sex attraction or behavior, this too is assessed. It is important to consider intrinsic and extrinsic motivation for seeking services. When working with minors, it is imperative that counselors obtain assent for treatment from the minor as well as consent from the parent or guardian.

Advanced informed consent involves several steps, given the controversies in this area (Yarhouse, 2019). For example, it can be shared that homosexuality is not viewed as a mental illness by the major mental health organizations. Advanced informed consent also includes a discussion of the causes of homosexuality and the limits of the research in this area, as well as professional interventions that are available (and that there are currently no well-designed outcome studies of reorientation therapies, gay-affirmative therapies, or sexual identity therapy) and paraprofessional or ministry alternatives to professional therapy.

The *therapy* stage of the SIT framework involves helping clients reach congruence so that they live and identify themselves in ways that are consistent with their beliefs and values regardless of whether they experience shifts in attractions or orientation. From a narrative perspective, therapy involves identifying the problem stories that have been written about people who experience same-sex attraction (Yarhouse, 2019). These problem stories can come from both religious faith communities (that call these people an "abomination") and from the mainstream LGBTQ+ community (that tells them to celebrate themselves as part of an emerging culture). Conventionally religious clients navigating sexual identity and faith often find themselves in conflict with both of these program stories. Therapy can help clients create a counter-narrative that helps them move toward a place of personal congruence, so that they live and identify themselves in ways that reflect their beliefs and values.

One way to do this (see Yarhouse, 2008, for an extended discussion) is to distinguish between attractions, orientation, and identity so that a person can use more descriptive language (e.g., "I am a person who is navigating same-sex sexuality") rather than an identity label (e.g., "I am gay"). Clients can also look at the relative weight that they give to their sexual attractions over other aspects of themselves as a person, such as their gender identity, biological sex, behaviors, beliefs, and values. In this approach the counselor joins the client on an attributional search for sexual identity that has as its endpoint this experience of congruence, which is the final stage of the SIT framework, *sexual identity synthesis*.

Undoubtedly, there will still be clients and clinicians alike who prefer an approach to religious and sexual identity conflicts that focuses on sexual orientation change. We anticipate that such models will be increasingly viewed as on the periphery of mental health care (or as in conflict with mainstream understandings of mental health care). Those who provide such services may strengthen their case by conducting well-designed studies that demonstrate the effectiveness of such approaches. Of course, there is a need for well-designed outcome research in all of the areas we have been discussing.

WHAT ARE CHRISTIANS EXPECTED TO CHANGE?

In the debates about sexual orientation change, some ministries present the issue as if Christians should expect to experience meaningful change of orientation through their relationship with Christ. The argument is that Christians have a responsibility to attempt to change because maintaining a position of not trying is problematic for the believer.

Others argue that chastity may be the only change possible for some, but these clients should not call themselves "gay" and never anchor identity in sexuality—either as part of their core sense of self or as adjective.

Still others say it is morally permissible to recenter identity on Christ but still refer to oneself as "gay" because the use of *gay* is simply as an adjective, a more readily accessible way of conveying to others that one has same-sex attractions.

Of course, these are not the only three options. Some believe that gay and lesbian persons are "born that way" and that any attempt to change is inherently harmful to that person. They may also disagree with a traditional sexual ethic that limits genital sexual activity to heterosexual marriage.

What do you think? For those who believe that they should do something in response to their same-sex attractions, what are Christians obligated to pursue in the area of change? How about in the area of identity? What may be gained and what may be lost in forming identity around the word *gay*? What do you say to the Christian who uses the word *gay* as an adjective rather than identity?

PREVENTION

The idea of preventing homosexuality has also been controversial. Gender nonconformity refers to showing interest in the stereotypic games, interests, and dress of the opposite sex. Adult homosexuals looking back on their childhood frequently report gender nonconformity (Bailey & Pillard, 1995). Indeed, gender nonconformity is frequently observed or recalled in two areas: among children who are gender dysphoric and among adults who report a homosexual orientation. As we discuss in chapter fourteen, it is unlikely that gender dysphoria can be prevented, which is what we would conclude about a homosexual orientation.

We also think it is important to help parents who wish to focus on prevention reflect on what they are doing and why. It may be more helpful to focus on principles for good parenting and not prevention. There is a point when parents can also work through feelings they have toward a child who may be gender atypical in some ways or who may later experience same-sex attraction. It will be important as a child is growing up that parents express unconditional love and support to their child.

Prevention can be extended to discussions of preventing co-occurring issues often reported by those who experience same-sex attraction, orientation, or gay or lesbian identity. Some of these concerns are mental and physical health concerns, such as elevated rates of depressive disorders, anxiety disorders, substance use disorders, nicotine dependence, suicidal ideation and intent, sexual transmitted diseases such as HIV/AIDS, and other concerns (Cochran et al., 2003; Cochran & Mays, 2007; de Graaf et al., 2006; Lewis et al., 2003).

Perhaps the area that has received the most attention recently has been reducing bullying and harassment in one's peer group, particularly for elementary, middle, and high school students. Clinicians need to be aware of the risk and work with families and local school systems to reduce bullying. Some of the more effective antibullying approaches tend to target the theater of bullying (or those who see it occur) that exists by empowering those who are witness to harassment.

SINGLE SEXUALITY AND THE SEXUAL MINORITY

In her Christian integration book *Sexuality and Holy Longing*, Lisa Graham McMinn includes the topic of homosexuality in her chapter on single sexuality. Christians who are single may be single for any number of reasons. Some in their older teens or twenties are heterosexual but are not currently married; others are heterosexual and much older, perhaps in their fifties or sixties, and they never did marry. Still others were once married, but now they are single due to divorce or the death of their spouse. Christian sexual minorities often do not marry because they do not believe they should enter into a same-sex relationship, nor do they choose to be in a mixed sexual orientation marriage (in which they marry someone who is heterosexual).

How is the single state as experienced by a sexual minority similar to or different from other experiences of singleness? For example, in terms of one practical difference, single heterosexuals can date and explore physical contact (hugs, kisses) with someone of the opposite sex without concern that it will be viewed as immoral behavior. The same option for exploration is not available to the sexual minority in the church. This is a significant difference that may not be fully appreciated by those who discuss celibacy and singleness for sexual minorities. Another notable concern is that at times, Christians with SSA in the church are given the message that attempts to have their needs met emotionally or physically (e.g., touch) need to be met with caution because they may "fall" or find themselves participating in immoral behavior. One ministry leader once commented that people with SSA should not live together for fear of "falling" into a sinful sexual relationship. While this may be sound advice for some individuals, the message that could be sent to the person with SSA in the church is that he or she is hypersexual and that his or her sexuality and attractions are to be feared.

In terms of similarities we can point to the need for the larger body of Christ to provide support for singles. Much of our local church programming is oriented toward married couples and families. Programs for singles are often geared toward getting them married, as though being single in some way makes a person "incomplete" or "less than" in ways we may not want to convey. What about the question of whether the body of Christ provides singles (straight and gay alike) with enough emotional and spiritual support to make celibacy a viable possibility? Is it a legitimate question to ask, Who shoulders the burden of this glaring failure, and what does that mean in very practical terms in the local church today?

MIXED ORIENTATION COUPLES

Some people who report a conflict between their sexual identity and faith may enter into a mixed orientation relationship. A mixed orientation couple is a couple in which one spouse identifies as straight, while the other spouse identifies as a sexual minority. A sexual minority refers to a person who experiences same-sex attraction regardless of whether they adopt a sexual identity label such as gay, lesbian, or bisexual.

There is limited research on the experiences of mixed orientation couples. However, what research exists suggests that many of these couples really struggle and a fairly high percentage of couples separate or divorce. Of those that stay together, it will be important to consider how to foster resilience by understanding first their unique challenges (Kays & Yarhouse, 2010). Common challenges identified in the literature have to do with disclosure, or when and how it was shared that one spouse is a sexual minority. Sharing prior to engagement and marriage is a much better predictor of relationship quality and satisfaction than disclosure after marriage. Navigating the meaning of one's sexual orientation and identity is also important for both the sexual minority and the straight spouse. Limited social support can also be a concern for these unique couples, as it can be difficult to know who to trust with this aspect of their relationship.

Yarhouse and Kays (2010) describe the PARE model for working with mixed orientation couples. In this model, clinicians begin by providing (P) sexual identity therapy, as described earlier in this chapter. This allows the sexual minority spouse to explore the relationship between their same-sex sexuality and faith and move toward a place of congruence, so that they live and form an identity that reflects their beliefs and values. The second step is to address (A) interpersonal trauma that is often experienced by the straight spouse, especially in instances in which disclosure takes place after they are married (rather than when they are dating). The next step is to foster resilience (R) through counseling, followed by enhancing (E) sexual intimacy through sex therapy.

In order to foster resilience, we encourage clinicians to also work with mixed orientation couples on identifying and building on the strengths found in mixed orientation couples. In one study, Kays, Yarhouse, and Ripley (2014) identified the resilient factors of commitment to each other, partner-focused forgiveness, and a covenantal view of marriage. Commitment to the marriage itself was a strong predictor of relationship quality and satisfaction. Partner-focused forgiveness was also a strong predictor of relationship quality and satisfaction. Given what can be experienced as a kind of interpersonal trauma to realize that one's spouse is navigating same-sex attractions or specific hurts related to that, partner-focused forgiveness and just ongoing trait forgiveness is an important part of these marriages. Finally, having more of a covenantal view of marriage and one's vows in contrast to a contractual view of one's vows has been shown to be important for relationship quality and satisfaction in mixed orientation marriages.

Adaptations of common sex therapy interventions can also be made to mixed orientation couples (see chap. 29 of Rosenau's [2002] book, *A Celebration of Sex*, 2nd ed.). It is not uncommon for spouses to be distracted by what they think the other spouse may be thinking or wanting. It can be helpful to slow them down and encourage them to create something that is unique to them as a couple. The sexual script that they develop will be theirs alone, and we can help them process insecurities or anxieties they may have. There may be desire discrepancy present, and this should be normalized. They can look at daily rhythms that can foster a sense of cohesion as a couple and more connection and emotional engagement outside the bedroom to strengthen intimacy inside the bedroom. Mindfulness exercises may help both partners be more fully present when they are together (Yarhouse & Kays, 2010).

CLOSING REFLECTIONS

The two primary questions we are asked about homosexuality in Christian settings are, What causes sexual orientation? and Can it be changed? We hope that this chapter helps to answer these two questions. We want to take some time to reflect on some of the assumptions that frequently underlie these two questions.

Part of the issue is that the debate about etiology has factored into the church's moral debates about homosexuality, about whether to bless same-sex unions or ordain same-sex attracted pastors/ministers who are sexually active. Those who argue for change away from the Christian sexual ethic claim that because homosexuality is the result of nature, then same-sex behavior is simply a natural expression of who that person is. They assume that if same-sex sexuality is not chosen, then it must reflect God's created good for sexuality and sexual expression. Does God make some people— maybe 6% to 7% of the population—attracted to the same sex or with a homosexual orientation?

We would note first that the reality of a person's same-sex attraction or orientation does not speak to whether it is from God. Many things exist in nature that are not necessarily from God if we mean that God sees them as what he wants for that person or for complete genital sexual expression. There is really a broader question here about a theology of sexual identity, one that includes questions about theodicy.

> It is a question of how to make sense of experiences that may result from the fall. Just as we do not view the existence of predispositions toward depression or anxiety as God making a person depressed or anxious, we want to be cautious about jumping to the conclusion that the existence of an experience or condition reflects God's intention for that person. Even non-pathological concerns, such as variations in normal human temperament or personality, can be understood with reference to God's intentions for persons. People may be predisposed

to neuroticism (or emotional instability) but still have to think beyond "God made me this way" to "How does God want me to grow in Christ-likeness such that I display the fruit of the Spirit in my life and my relationships?" (Yarhouse, 2022, p. 14)

In addition to the question of causation, we are also often asked by Christians whether sexual orientation can change. More accurately, we meet Christians who assume that people can change if they try hard enough or have enough faith in the healing power of Jesus Christ. There are assumptions here that also need to be examined. Since we do not see change of orientation as a likely outcome for people in therapy or ministry, we have to look more closely at what it means to live with enduring realities, such as same-sex sexuality. We do not see learning to live with besetting conditions as a failure of the Christian. Nor do we see this as a failure of God. People deal with many issues in which they may have asked God for miraculous intervention. Although sometimes God intervenes miraculously, most of the time God answers those kinds of prayers in ways we may not expect, such as providing the patient endurance that comes from saying no to one thing (for some people this might be same-sex behavior) in order to say yes to other experiences or qualities God is developing in the person. What we have found is that it is more helpful to explore what it looks like to trust God (as a good and loving Father) with one's sexuality.

Some Christians, choosing to refrain from same-sex behavior, will also choose not to identify as gay or lesbian (Chambers, 2009); they do not believe that adopting a gay identity is in their best interest as a follower of Christ. Other Christians, who may also refrain from same-sex behavior, may adopt a gay identity as shorthand for the reality they experience every day: they feel attractions toward the same sex (Hill, 2010).

So some people essentially deconstruct a gay identity. This approach is discussed in a work that introduces the idea of a "gay script" (Yarhouse, 2010, p. 48).

A script reflects cultural expectations for behavior and relationships. We have scripts for many activities, such as when to marry, when married couples should have children, how to walk up a flight of stairs, how to listen to a class lecture, and so on. We are rarely aware of them; they are just a part of our cultural experience. There is also a "gay script," a way of making sense out of one's experiences of same-sex attraction:

- Same-sex attractions signal a naturally occurring or "intended by God" distinction between homosexuality, heterosexuality, and bisexuality.
- Same-sex attractions are the way you know who you "really are" as a person (emphasis on *discovery*).
- Same-sex attractions are at the core of who you are as a person.
- Same-sex behavior is an extension of that core.
- Self-actualization (behavior that matches who you "really are") of your sexual identity is crucial for your fulfillment (Yarhouse, 2010, p. 49).

A series of studies also revealed that there may be many other alternative scripts that people develop and follow. One in particular is referred to as an "in Christ" script because the person's identity in Christ is so personally meaningful. That script reads as follows:

- Same-sex attraction does *not* signal a categorical distinction among types of persons, but is one of many human experiences that are "not the way it's supposed to be."
- Same-sex attractions may be part of your experience, but they are not the defining element of your identity.
- You can choose to integrate your experiences of attraction to the same sex into a gay identity.
- On the other hand, you can choose to center your identity around other aspects of your experience, including your biological sex, gender identity, and so on.
- The most compelling aspect of personhood for the Christian is one's identity in Christ, a central and defining aspect of what it means to be a follower of Jesus (p. 51).

To extend the critique that began with the deconstruction of gay identity, Christian anthropologist Jenell Williams Paris (2011) discusses how both "gay" and "straight" are problematic for the Christian. As sexual identity labels, they both reflect relatively recent developments in history. As she puts it,

> Sexual identity is a Western, nineteenth-century formulation of what it means to be human. It's grounded in a belief that the direction of one's sexual desire is identity-constituting, earning each individual a label (gay, lesbian, straight, etc.) and social role. (p. 41)

Paris challenges Christians to deconstruct both "gay" and "straight" identity labels, if you will. Neither of these labels are adequate for believers. While our attractions and behavior matter, they ought not be forming and framing our identity.

> When homosexuality is seen as a disease to be cured, homosexuals seem like a distinct kind of (sick) people. However, when the focus is on care instead of cure, sexuality can be acknowledged for what it really is: a valuable part of human life in which we embody conflicted desires, and through which we receive grace. (p. 109)

Sexual identity concerns will certainly continue to be a point of controversy among mental health professionals. Christian psychologists and counselors are in a unique position to provide competent services to clients who are navigating this terrain, and they are also uniquely positioned to be a resource to the local Christian community in terms of clarifying what we do and do not know about sexual attraction, orientation, and identity. How the church navigates this issue within the body of Christ and as a witness to a broader culture will speak volumes about what Christians believe and why, as well as how to integrate Christian faith and science in the applied dimension of clinical services.

REFERENCES

American Psychological Association. (2008). *Answers to your questions for a better understanding of sexual orientation and homosexuality*. American Psychological Association. Retrieved from www.apa.org/topics/lgbtq/orientation.pdf

American Psychological Association. (2009). *Appropriate therapeutic responses to sexual orientation*. American Psychological Association.

Bailey, J. M., & Pillard, R. C. (1995). Genetics of human sexual orientation. *Annual Review of Sex Research, 6*, 126-50.

Blanchard, R. (2008). Review of theory and handedness, birth order, and homosexuality in men. *Laterality, 13*, 51-70.

Blanchard, R., Cantor, J. M., Bogaert, A. F., Breedloe, S. M., & Ellis, L. (2006). Interaction of fraternal birth order and handedness in the development of male homosexuality. *Hormones and Behavior, 49*, 405-14.

Blanchard, R., & Lippa, R. A. (2007). Birth order, sibling sex ratio, handedness, and sexual orientation of male and female participants in a BBC Internet Research Project. *Archives of Sexual Behavior, 36*, 163-76.

Bogaert, A. F., Blanchard, R., & Crosthwait, L. E. (2007). Interaction of birth order, handedness, and sexual orientation in the Kinsey Interview Data. *Behavioral Neuroscience, 5*, 845-53.

Chambers, A. (2009). *Leaving homosexuality: A practical guide for men and women looking for a way out.* Harvest House.

Cochran, S. D., & Mays, V. M. (2007). Physical health complaints among lesbians, gay men, and bisexual and homosexually experienced heterosexual individuals: Results from the California Quality of Life Survey. *American Journal of Public Health, 97,* 2048-55.

Cochran, S. D., Sullivan, J. G., & Mays, V. M. (2003). Prevalence of mental disorders, psychological distress, and mental health services use among lesbian, gay, and bisexual adults in the United States. *Journal of Consulting and Clinical Psychology 71,* 53-61.

de Graaf, R., Sandfort, T. G. M., & ten Have, M. (2006). Suicidality and sexual orientation: Differences between men and women in a general population-based sample from the Netherlands. *Archives of Sexual Behavior, 35,* 253-62.

Demir, E., & Dickson, B. J. (2005). Fruitless splicing specifies male courtship behavior in Drosophila. *Cell, 121,* 320-26.

Diamond, L. M. (2006). *Sexual fluidity: Understanding women's love and desire.* Harvard University Press.

Egan, P. J., Edelman, M. S., & Sherrill, K. (2008). *Findings from the Hunter College poll of lesbians, gays, and bisexuals: New discoveries about identity, political attitudes, and civic engagement.* City University of New York.

Ganna, A., Verweij, K. J. H., Nivard, M. G., Maier, R., Wedow, R., Busch, A. S., Abdellaoui, A., Guo, S., Sathirapongsasuti, J. F.; 23andMe Research Team; Lichtenstein, P., Lundström, S., Långström, N., Auton, A., Harris, K. M., Beecham, G. W., Martin, E. R., Sanders, A. R., Perry, J. R. B., Neale, B. M., & Zietsch, B. P. (2019). Large-scale GWAS reveals insights into the genetic architecture of same-sex sexual behavior. *Science, 365*(6456). https://doi.org/10.1126/science.aat7693

Gates, G. J. (2011, April). *How many people are lesbian, gay, bisexual, and transgender?* The Williams Institute, UCLA School of Law.

Hill, W. (2010). *Washed and waiting: Reflections on Christian faithfulness and homosexuality.* Zondervan.

Jones, J. M. (2024, March 13). LGBTQ+ identification in U.S. now at 7.6%. Gallup News. https://news.gallup.com/poll/611864/lgbtq-identification.aspx#:~:text=Line%20graph.,collected%20in%202018%20and%202019

Jones, S. L., & Yarhouse, M. A. (2000). *Homosexuality: The use of scientific research in the church's moral debate.* IVP Academic.

Jones, S. L., & Yarhouse, M. A. (2007). *Ex-gays? A longitudinal study of religiously mediated change in sexual orientation.* InterVarsity Press.

Jones, S. L., & Yarhouse, M. A. (2011). A longitudinal study of attempted religiously-mediated sexual orientation change. *The Journal of Sex and Marital Therapy, 37,* 404-27.

Kays, J. L., & Yarhouse, M. A. (2010). Resilient factors in mixed orientation couples: Current state of the research. *American Journal of Family Therapy, 38,* 334-43. https://doi.org/10.1080/01926187.2010.493464

Kays, J. L., Yarhouse, M. A., & Ripley, J. (2014). Relationship factors and quality among mixed-orientation couples. *Journal of Sex & Marital Therapy, 40*(6), 512-28. https://doi.org/10.1080/0092623X.2013.788107

Långström, N., Rahman, Q., Carlström, E., & Lichtenstein, P. (2008). Genetic and environmental effects on same-sex sexual behavior: A population study of twins in Sweden. *Archives of Sexual Behavior, 39*(1), 75-80.

Laumann, E. O., Gagnon, J. H., Michael, R. T., & Michaels, S. (2000). *The social organization of sexuality: Sexual practices in the United States.* University of Chicago Press.

Lewis, R. J., Derlega, V. J., Griffin, J. L., & Krowinski, A. C. (2003). Stressors for gay men and lesbians: Life stress, gay-related stress, stigma consciousness, and depressive symptoms. *Journal of Social and Clinical Psychology, 22*, 716-29.

McMinn, L. G. (2004). *Sexuality and holy longing: Embracing intimacy in a broken world.* Jossey-Bass.

Mustanski, B. S., Dupree, M. G., Nievergelt, C. M., Bocklandt, S., Schork, N. J., & Hamer, D. H. (2005). A genomewide scan of male sexual orientation. *Human Genetics, 116*(4), 272-78.

Rosenau, D. (2002). *A celebration of sex: A guide to enjoying God's gift of sexual intimacy* (2nd ed.). Thomas Nelson.

Savic, I., & Lindström, P. (2008, July 8). PET and MRI show differences in cerebral asymmetry and functional connectivity between homo- and heterosexual subjects. *Proceedings of the National Academy of Sciences of the United States of America, 105*(27), 9403-8.

Savin-Williams, R. C., & Cohen, K. M. (2004). Homoerotic development during childhood and adolescence. *Child and Adolescent Psychiatric Clinics of North America, 13*(3), 529-50.

Savin-Williams, R. C., & Diamond, L. M. (2000). Sexual identity trajectories among sexual-minority youths: Gender comparisons. *Archives of Sexual Behavior, 29*(6), 607-27.

Stratton, S., Dean, J., Yarhouse, M. A., & Lastoria, M. (2011). Sexual minorities in faith-based higher education: A national survey of attitudes, milestones, identity, and religiosity. *Journal of Psychology and Theology, 41*, 3-23.

Throckmorton, W., & Yarhouse, M. A. (2006). The Sexual Identity Therapy Framework. Available online at www.sitframework.com

Williams Paris, J. W. (2011). *The end of sexual identity: Why sex is too important to define who we are.* InterVarsity Press.

Witchel, A. (2012, January 22). Life after "sex." *New York Times*, p. MM24.

Yarhouse, M. A. (1998). When clients seek treatment for same-sex attraction: Ethical issues in the "right to choose" debate. *Psychotherapy, 35*, 248-59.

Yarhouse, M. A. (2008). Narrative sexual identity therapy. *American Journal of Family Therapy, 36*, 1-15.

Yarhouse, M. A. (2010). *Homosexuality and the Christian: A guide for parents, pastors, and friends.* Bethany House.

Yarhouse, M. A. (2019). *Sexual identity and faith: Helping clients achieve congruence.* The Templeton Foundation.

Yarhouse, M. A. (2022). *How should we think about homosexuality?* Lexham.

Yarhouse, M. A., & Kays, J. (2010). The PARE model: A framework for working with mixed orientation couples. *Journal of Psychology and Christianity, 29*(1), 77-81.

Yarhouse, M. A., Kays, J., & Jones, S. L. (2013). The sexual minority client. In R. K. Sanders (Ed.), *Christian counseling ethics* (2nd ed.). InterVarsity Press.

Yarhouse, M. A., Stratton, S. P., Dean, J. B., & Brooke, H. L. (2009). Listening to sexual minorities on Christian college campuses. *Journal of Psychology and Theology, 37*(2), 96-113.

FOURTEEN

GENDER DYSPHORIA AND MIXED GENDER IDENTITY COUPLES

GEORGE JORGENSEN SR. AND HIS WIFE, Florence, were Danish Americans who married in 1922. George Sr. had previously served in the Coast Guard and later worked for his father's construction company and also as a carpenter. On May 30, 1926, George Sr. and Florence gave birth to a son, George William Jorgensen. George Jr. would be christened in the Danish Lutheran Church a few weeks later.

George Jr. grew up in New York City and would eventually graduate from Christopher Columbus High School in the Bronx. Compared to his peers, he was considered somewhat frail and interpersonally shy and introverted. He tended to steer clear of the more physical activities, sports, and various confrontations common among boys. He studied photography at Mohawk College in Utica and served briefly in the military when he was drafted in 1945. He later attended a medical- and dental-assistance school in Manhattan.

He often felt that he had some kind of sexual and emotional disorder. He would frequently steal away to the local medical library at the New York Academy of Medicine to try to understand his condition. In part because of his attraction to men, George Jr. often feared he was homosexual. He began to experiment with the female hormone estradiol, and it was sometime during these years that he heard about the possibility of treatment that was being conducted in Sweden that seemed to extend his own experiments with estradiol into a satisfactory resolution. He traveled overseas, sought out, and eventually found an endocrinologist, Dr. Christian Hamburger, who would help him undergo hormonal replacement therapy. Over the course of time, George Jr. had his testicles and penis removed, and later had vaginal plastic surgery (vaginoplasty). In honor of Dr. Christian Hamburger, George Jr. would eventually take the name Christine Jorgensen in 1952. The course his life had taken would make a significant splash in the United States in the 1950s. The *New York Daily News* banner headline read: "Ex-GI Becomes Blonde Beauty: Operations Transform Bronx Youth." Christine had become the most well-known case of gender confirmation surgery at that time (Jorgensen, 1967).

The gender identity concerns represented by Christine Jorgensen were controversial at that time—the 1950s. But they are still controversial today, despite cultural shifts toward more varied sexual and gender identity labels and communities that are only a click away on the internet. There have certainly been increased attempts to understand and respond to this often bewildering experience.

Diagnostically, someone with an enduring, significant cross-gender identification is thought to experience gender dysphoria. The *DSM-5-TR* references gender dysphoria in children, adolescents, or adults as a "marked incongruence between one's experienced or expressed gender and one's assigned gender" (APA, 2022, p. 511). To meet the diagnostic criteria, gender dysphoria has to be experienced for at least six months. When gender dysphoria is seen in children, six of eight symptoms would be present, and these include things such as a strong desire or insistence that he or she is the other sex, cross-dressing preferences, or the simulation of wearing clothing of the other sex. Other possible symptoms are related to "a strong dislike of one's sexual anatomy," and friendships and interest in gender-stereotypical games of the other sex (p. 512).

In adolescents and adults, at least two of six symptom presentations would be evident, including such experiences as a "strong desire to be rid of one's primary and/or secondary sex characteristics because of a marked incongruence with one's experienced/expressed gender," "a strong desire to be of the other gender" and "a strong desire to be treated as the other gender," and "a strong conviction that one has the typical feelings and reactions of the other gender" (APA, 2022, p. 513). Adolescents and adults tend to more clearly articulate their experience with gender dysphoria. They may request a social transition, with a change of name and pronouns or, as they get older, a medical transition, which could include hormonal treatment or surgery.

The understanding of gender dysphoria in *DSM-5-TR* is in keeping with those theorists (e.g., Carroll, 2000) who view gender dysphoria or gender incongruence more broadly, seeing it as an umbrella term that includes more people than just those who either meet these criteria or desire a gender change. We certainly agree that gender dysphoria can exist without necessarily the desire for hormonal treatment or surgery. We also agree that the transgender community is much broader than those who have the diagnosis of gender dysphoria.

The transgender community is often defined broadly to include many varied and cultural expressions of gender dysphoria or incongruence, including transsexuals, third sex, two spirits, drag queens/kings, transvestites, and cross-dressers (Carroll, 2007). *Transgender*, then, is a term "for the various ways gender identity can be experienced beyond male or female classification" (p. 479). Some of these expressions reflect cultural understandings, as is the case with Native American tribal people and those who are identified as "two spirit" in essence. Other expressions, such as transvestism, are not considered by some theorists to be the same kind of gender identity concern because the person is interested in cross-dressing but not particularly interested in transitioning to the opposite sex (McConaghy, 1993).

When it comes to prevalence estimates, some professionals have estimated that about 1 in 11,000 adult men and 1 in 30,000 adult women may meet the formal criteria for gender dysphoria, which are figures based on those seeking services from a specialty clinic in the Netherlands (Zucker & Bradley, 2005). The *DSM-5-TR* (APA, 2022) notes that prevalence estimates of less than 1/1,000 (<0.1%) appear to reflect clinical samples but are far less than what we see with survey research with the general, non-clinical population. For example, the 2023 Gallup Poll reported that 0.9% of adults in the United States identify as transgender, with significant differences across generations: 2.8% of Gen Z, 1.1% of Millennials, 0.5% of Gen X, and 0.2% of Baby Boomers (Jones, 2024). In other words, prevalence estimates are higher among children, adolescents, and adults who identify as transgender (some of whom may experience gender dysphoria along a continuum but may or may not meet criteria for the formal diagnosis as such and are not going to a specialty clinic). The fact that it appears to be more common in childhood than in adolescence or adulthood suggests it may be more difficult to obtain accurate prevalence estimates from studies of adults seeking specialized treatment.

ETIOLOGY

The cause of what we are referring to as gender dysphoria, or sometimes gender incongruence, is unclear. Carroll (2000) explains how part of the challenge resides in the diversity found in the transgender community: "Part of the difficulty is that etiological theories have to account for such diverse phenomena as cross-dressing, androphilic and autogynephilic male-to-female gender dysphoria, drag queens, and gynephilic female-to-male gender dysphoria" (p. 378).

Early theorists developed the view of imprinting (Money, 1986), that is, that there is a window early on in development when a child learns sex identity. This was essentially a behavioral theory that was extended to suggest that what was learned included "sex identity, sex-linked behaviors identified as masculine or feminine, the sex to which one wished to belong, and the sex of persons to whom one was attracted" (McConaghy, 1993, p. 163).

As theorists in the field moved beyond behaviorism and learning theory, they began to consider whether and how biology might play a role in the etiology of gender dysphoria. Some of the studies were prompted by research on intersex/hermaphrodite conditions. Investigations initially considered hormonal differences among adults, but the research has not supported this theory.

Today, researchers tend to study some of the same areas that are studied when considering the etiology of sexual orientation. This includes research on prenatal hormonal exposure, genetic inheritance, animal models, and neuroanatomical brain structures, among other areas. Differences have been reported in some areas (e.g., neuroanatomical regions of the brain, handedness) but not in other areas (e.g., genetic inheritance, postnatal hormone levels). Some of the differences reported could also be explained by treatment (when using hormonal interventions) and may not in all cases represent differences between transgender and nontransgender persons (Carroll, 2000, 2007).

In addition to these areas that reflect nature, there have also been investigations into nurture. Some models are based on learning theory in which gender identity is thought to follow "from gender role behavior, which . . . is shaped by external contingencies" (Carroll, 2007, p. 483). The thought is that because "gender categories and behavior in children" are socialized from birth, "cross-gender behavior and identity must be reinforced and gender congruent behavior must be punished" (p. 379). Similarly, Zucker and

Bradley (1995) suggest that children with gender dysphoria are often brought up in homes where cross-gender behavior is tolerated and where a nonresponsive parent was typical. In some instances parents may have encouraged the behaviors rather than discouraged them. Other theorists have suggested similar concerns, and research continues to be conducted on such factors in etiology (and maintenance) as expressed emotion (including criticism and overinvolvement) in mothers of boys who are gender dysphoric (e.g., Owen-Anderson et al., 2010).

The etiology of gender identity concerns continues to remain a question. Given the range of experiences under the umbrella "transgender," it is likely that there are multiple influencing factors from both nature and nurture that interact in ways we do not yet understand.

ASSESSMENT AND CLINICAL PRESENTATION

The mother of a six-year-old Caucasian boy calls for services. She reports concern about his mannerisms and voice inflection—that it is more effeminate—and that she fears he will be teased in school. She has already had family members and people at the park comment on his mannerisms.

The mother and father report that their son's cross-dressing started at age three through use of a towel or blanket as long hair or a dress and that he would play dress-up as a female at his friend's house. They noticed female gestures and mannerisms at age five (e.g., hand on hip, wrist). They indicate his play group is primarily females.

His parents confirm that their son stated that he wished God had made him a girl. They report consistent identification with his mother, stating that he wanted to be like her, and little identification with his father or older brother.

When assessing children who present with gender dysphoria, it is important to keep in mind that they often become isolated from their peers, which can lead to problems with self-esteem. In some instances school aversion and increased risk of dropping out of school is also present and should be assessed (Carroll, 2000). Children who present with gender dysphoria may also present with a co-occurring anxiety disorder or depressive disorder (Carroll, 2000).

As children get older and enter adolescence, they often respond negatively to changes at puberty and report strain with their parents and peer groups (Di Ceglie et al., 2002). Teens are also at a greater risk for depression, thoughts of self-harm, and attempted self-harm (Carroll, 2000).

Onset of cross-gender interests and activities among children with early-onset gender dysphoria is usually between ages two and four years, but few families bring a child in for a consultation at that age. Rather, children are more frequently referred for an assessment or consultation at about the age they start kindergarten or first grade, probably because what may be understood within the family may soon become a source of ridicule among one's peer group. With more time passing, there also may now be more of a concern that what they thought was a phase has not passed (Carroll, 2000).

An area of controversy in the field is whether a significant percentage of children with strong gender identity concerns will continue to have symptoms that meet criteria for a formal diagnosis in later adolescence or adulthood. This is referred to as the "desistance versus persistence" debate, which we will discuss below.

Developmental trajectories. Although there is relatively little research on gender dysphoria as compared to many other sexual concerns, there has been some preliminary research (Steensma et al., 2010) on possible developmental trajectories among those who persist (in their experience of gender dysphoria) and those who desist (or who do not continue to experience gender incongruence).

When these two groups are compared, it is interesting to note that there are apparent differences in underlying motives in cross-identification, as well as differences in responses to changes at puberty. In considering motives for cross-identification, one persister shared the following: "In childhood (and still), I had the feeling that I was born as a boy. I did not 'want' to be a girl. To myself I 'was' a boy, I felt insulted if people treated me as a girl. Of course I 'knew' I was a girl, but still, in my view I was not" (Steensma et al., 2010, p. 6). In contrast to this, a desister shared this: "I knew very well that I was a girl, but one who wished to be a boy. In childhood I liked the boys better, the girls were always niggling [petty, nagging]. I was tough and wanted to be as tough as the boys" (p. 6).

When the researchers looked at the different responses to puberty, they noted the strong reaction against these changes among those who persisted with their gender incongruence. One persister shared the following: "It was terrible, I constantly wanted to know whether I was already in puberty or not. . . . I really did not want to have breasts, I felt like, if they would grow, I would remove them myself. I absolutely did not want them!" (Steensma et al., 2010, p. 8).

Again, in contrast, a desister shared this: "Before puberty, I disliked the thought of getting breasts. I did not want them to grow. But when they actually started to grow, I was glad they did. I really loved looking like a girl, so I was glad my body became more feminine" (Steensma et al., 2010, p. 12).

Keep in mind that both groups engaged in some cross-identification at a young age, about six or seven years old. However, Steensma et al. (2010) reported that for those who desisted—whose gender dysphoria abated over time—that change occurred at ten to thirteen, whereas the gender dysphoria seemed to increase for those who were called persisters.

The persisters would go on to disclose and make a plan for some kind of transition at the ages of ten to thirteen, while those who desisted tended to identify with their birth sex at age thirteen and older.

The idea of "desisters" and "persisters" has been controversial and challenged by those who believe that these are essentially "apples" and "oranges" (Ehresnsaft, 2018, p. 47) and that we have not properly distinguished truly transgender youth from those who may show some signs of gender atypicality (and may identify later as gay, for instance). More recent research (e.g., Olson et al., 2022) seems to support a different way (from "persister" and "desister") of conceptualizing youth and supports normalizing exploration of gender identity.

These debates inform assessment. If you tend to support the distinction between persisters and desisters, you might assess for some of the differences that have been reported. Other methods of assessment include interviews with parents or interview of the child (or observation of the child, depending on his or her age, typically for children ages three to eight years old). The parent interview covers experiences they recall of their child engaging in cross-dressing behavior, cross-sex mannerisms, voice inflection and gestures, play with peer group, and so on.

The observation can be of the child's interest in sex-typed play activities. Observations are typically of the child alone in the room, although some clinicians have assessed with parents in the room or the clinician in the room. The Gender Identity Questionnaire (Johnson et al., 2004) can be administered to parents. Clinicians can also conduct an assessment in the home setting or school setting.

Gender dysphoria in adolescence and adulthood. When we consider gender dysphoria in adolescence and adulthood, there are again some controversies about how to conceptualize various presentations.

One development was the field's decision to move away from Blanchard's typology of gender dysphoria (toward the subtypes of early and late onset). For a brief review, Blanchard suggested three common presentations: (1) female-to-male gender dysphoria, (2) male-to-female gender dysphoria (androphilic type), and (3) male-to-female gender dysphoria (autogynephilic type) (Blanchard, 1990a).

According to this typology, those who are biologically female at birth but feel that they are male in their gender identity (female-to-male or FtM, or referred to more recently as transmen) typically have long identified as masculine and did not want to be dressed in female attire. They frequently spoke of wanting to be a boy (or that they were a boy), and they had a negative response to the changes their bodies went through at puberty (Carroll, 2007).

Clients who are biologically male at birth but feel that they are female in their gender identity (referred to as male-to-female or MtF or, more recently, as transwomen) have two common presentations: androphilic type and autogynephilic type. A person who presents as androphilic is more of the direct parallel to the previously discussed transmen. The androphilic person was viewed as more effeminate from a young age (Carroll, 2007). The act of cross-dressing is not sexually arousing (in contrast to the autogynephilic type), but a way of managing dysphoria.

The person presenting as MtF (transwoman) autogynephilic type, according to Blanchard's typology, is sometimes referred to as expressing the heterosexual or transvestic form because in some descriptions it appears as a kind of fetish. According to Blanchard (1990a), this person's early history is not unlike that of others who present with transvestism in that most are interested in gender-typical male activities as boys; most experience some arousal when cross-dressing.

Blanchard described other clinical presentations of gender dysphoria, such as the bisexual gender dysphoric type (with a history of sexual arousal to the same and opposite sex) and the asexual/analloerotic type (with no or little arousal pattern) (Blanchard, 1990a). As noted above, the field has moved away from this conceptualization, although some professionals will still reference it.

The main controversy in work with adolescents in particular has to do with the reported rise in late-onset cases, especially among natal females. This has led to questions about whether this is a new and different pathway to gender dysphoria. Some have argued that this gender ratio flip (more natal females than males, whereas most cases had been more early-onset cases of natal males more so than females) represents a kind of "social contagion" not unlike what has been documented in the eating disorder literature. It is fairly well established that eating disorders are more culture bound, that is, they exist in a culture that has ubiquitous messaging about what is attractive, standards of beauty, and ideal weight, shape, and size. These messages can be communicated or passed along within peer groups in such a way that can lead to or maintain eating disorders. What some people have charged is that this social contagion best describes what we are seeing in the rise of late-onset cases of gender dysphoria.

Others have dismissed these claims. They favor more of a model of self-acceptance or self-knowledge in which transgender young people were there but did not have the social acceptance to name that reality and come out and identify as having a different gender identity.

We have approached this debate by recognizing that there is likely something true about both of these claims, but that another model may be needed to really account for the recent changes we are seeing. The approach we have taken follows Ian Hacking (1995) and his "looping effect." A looping effect accounts for changes in how people think about themselves (individually and as a group) in response to how they are classified. Since we classify people in mental health categories, an important consideration is, how do people change their self-perception as transgender in light of the shift away from professionals seeing such people has having a gender identity disorder (in *DSM-IV*) to today seeing them as having gender dysphoria or distress associated with gender incongruence? A looping effect has five elements: the category itself, in this case gender dysphoria; the people who are navigating the way they are categorized and the language available to them as they navigate gender identity questions; the institutions that arise in society to care for people navigating gender identity questions—and we have seen a significant rise in gender identity clinics in recent years; the conjectural knowledge or set of assumptions about transgender and other diverse gender experiences that are passed along and shared in digital and social media, among peers, on talk shows, in school, and so on; and the experts who determine what counts as true knowledge about the topic of diverse gender identities and weigh in to settle some of the debates we have described in this chapter (Hacking, 1995; for a more extended account of the looping effect as it applies to emerging gender identities, see Yarhouse & Sadusky, 2020).

Standards of care. The widely recognized standards for care in the case of gender dysphoria are the Standards of Care of the World Professional Association for Transgender Health (WPATH; formerly referred to in the literature as the Harry Benjamin International Gender Dysphoria Standards of Care) (Coleman et al., 2022). They are updated and currently available at www.wpath.org. Guidelines for hormonal treatment are published by the Endocrine Society.

Current standards of care de-emphasize diagnosis in favor of a more positive view of gender diversity. It is a "move from a narrow focus on psychological requirements for 'diagnosing transgenderism' and medical treatments for alleviation of gender dysphoria to gender-affirming care for the whole person" (Coleman et al., 2022, p. 58). The emphasis throughout the standards is to work collaboratively with clients in a holistic fashion to identify what is best for them.

Recommendations for health professionals who provide care to adolescents include a comprehensive biopsychosocial assessment and work with families, schools, and other institutions to provide support, health education, and so on.

Recommendations for mental health professionals who provide care to adults include assessing for readiness for medical interventions (in cases in which the "gender incongruence is marked and sustained"; p. 532), ruling out other issues that may appear to be gender dysphoria but are not, assessing and treating any co-occurring concerns, and so on.

The evaluations of adolescents and adults are sometimes referred to as "readiness evaluations" when an adolescent or adult is considering hormonal treatment or gender confirmation surgery. A readiness evaluation is an evaluation of the readiness to proceed with one or the other step. The idea of being evaluated has been criticized as "gatekeeping" by mental health professionals and not sufficiently trans affirmative to some. The most recent Standards of Care attempt to walk a fine line between conducting comprehensive assessments and functioning as gatekeepers.

We are beginning to discuss implications for treatment by introducing the Standards of Care. We turn our attention now to the controversies surrounding treatment. There are age-related questions and concerns, as well as questions about treatment and prevention, along with innovations in the use of hormone blockers that are gathering interest and criticism.

TREATMENT

Care for children. There have historically been three broad approaches to working with children with gender dysphoria. The first approach has been to attempt to align gender identity with biological markers in an attempt to address gender incongruence. Today this is considered Gender Identity Change Effort (GICE), the equivalent of sexual orientation change efforts and widely discouraged as unhelpful and potentially ethically problematic (SAMHSA, 2023). A second approach with children has been "wait and see" to essentially work with parents to be supportive and problem-solve difficult circumstances until a child reaches adulthood and can be referred to an adult gender clinic. The "wait and see" approach has been criticized more recently as insufficiently supportive of transgender young people who need more support and care than that model provides. The third approach is gender affirmative insofar as there is support for social transition and possibly even medical options (puberty suppression).

Puberty suppression. More recent and controversial with older children and adolescents is the practice of puberty suppression or the use of hormone blockers (gonadotropin-releasing hormone analogs) to delay puberty. Children between the ages of ten and thirteen are prevented from entering puberty by injecting hormone blockers that keep the gonads from making estrogen or testosterone. This in turn prevents the expected changes at puberty, such as girls developing breasts, starting their menstrual cycles, and so on; boys will not grow body and facial hair, nor will their voices deepen, for example. The idea is to then allow over time the child to enter into adolescence and for the teen (at around age sixteen) to eventually decide whether to develop a gender identity in accord with his or her birth sex or with his or her preferred/psychological/phenomenal sex. If they pursue their phenomenal sex, their preferred gender, they can begin to take hormones of the opposite sex.

Proponents note that while this does not change a person's sex, it does provide a smoother transition to the other gender insofar as the physical changes and appearance reflect such a transition. This is sometimes referred to as appearance congruence, and these steps are understood to help decrease gender dysphoria.

As we note below, a number of European countries have recently placed restrictions on access to medical interventions. Criticisms of puberty suppression range from concerns about the effects on bone-mass development, to brain development, to the concern mentioned previously about comorbid mental health issues not being resolved (Kreukels & Cohen-Kettenis, 2011). Critics also express the preference that adolescents complete psychosexual development. Proponents of puberty suppression have pointed to the lack of consensus on what that is and how such advice is a response to the clinical dilemma of gender incongruence (Kreukels & Cohen-Kettenis, 2011). They have also admitted that more research is needed on possible effects on brain development, but that each of these concerns must also be weighted against risks associated with delaying intervention.

Care for adolescents. When considering care for adolescents, it should be noted that there is much less published research available to inform clinical decision making. This has led to a number of European nations (for example, Norway, Sweden, the United Kingdom) limiting access to medical interventions for minors in recent years (Davis, 2023). As a general principle there is interest in exploring a range of alternatives, such as making a social transition, to the more invasive procedures, such as medical transition (e.g., hormonal replacement therapy and gender confirmation surgery—with important exceptions noted later). Therapy can explore the gender dysphoria itself, questions regarding sexual orientation, and any comorbid mental health concerns, such as anxiety or depression (Zucker, 2001). Exploration of the gender dysphoria includes an ongoing reflection of the meaning of the client's desire for gender confirmation surgery and whether there are other viable "lifestyle adaptations" available (p. 2085). It has also been important to explore whether the dysphoria is a negative response to homosexuality or same-sex sexuality rather than an actual desire to change one's sex. This is thought to be more often the case among those who express a strong desire for sex change closer to puberty (Zucker, 2004). In this case, it can be explored whether a homosexual adaptation is possible, although this may not seem like a viable option for some for whom entering into same-sex relationships is also a concern.

The more recent trend in late-onset cases among natal females in adolescence has raised the question of slowing down to determine how the adolescent came to experience gender dysphoria and whether there are any untreated co-occurring concerns, such as depression or anxiety.

In keeping with these concerns, a colleague (Edwards-Leeper, 2022) has used the analogy of traffic lights: blinking green (proceed with caution), yellow light (consider slowing down), and red light (stop for the time being). Blinking green would be warranted when there is a childhood history of gender dysphoria, minimal or no mental health concerns, previous social transition has been helpful, parents are supportive and experienced the previous social transition as helpful, and so on. Yellow light would refer to the presence of untreated or significant mental health concerns, sudden-onset gender dysphoria (post puberty), concerns that there may be an attempt to escape from gender norms, questions about possible online and/or social influence, supportive but cautious parents, and so on. Red light would be severe mental health concerns, untreated trauma, clear confusion about gender identity, inability to provide informed consent, and so on.

Outcomes for adults. When we look at outcomes for adult experiences of gender dysphoria, Carroll (2000) notes four typical outcomes: (1) unresolved outcomes, (2) accepting one's biological sex and gender role, (3) engaging in cross-gender behavior intermittently, or (4) adopting a cross-gender role through gender confirmatory steps.

Unresolved outcomes simply reflect that there is a high attrition rate—estimated at up to half of clients who seek services—and this may be due to either personal ambivalence or frustration with what some have felt was a long and involved process (reflected in the Harry Benjamin Standards of Care) (Carroll, 2000, 2007).

Others come to accept their biological sex and gender role. They may feel gender dysphoric, but they live as their birth sex and adopt a lifestyle that reflects that (Carroll, 2000).

The third outcome is to engage in cross-gender behaviors intermittently (Carroll, 2000). For a natal male, this might mean growing his hair out longer, wearing makeup occasionally, and presenting as a woman either on the weekends or by wearing female undergarments during the day to manage the dysphoria. The extent to which a person presents as a woman typically reflects the degree of dysphoria and how successfully such cross-dressing behaviors reduce the felt tension within.

The last outcome is reflected in those who adopt the gender role of the opposite sex. Most socially transition full time using their preferred name, pronouns, and attire. A minority of these individuals will proceed through hormonal therapy and gender confirmation surgery. In the U.S. Transgender Survey, 44% of adults reported using hormone therapy, and 25% reported some gender confirmation surgery (James et al., 2016). The Kaiser Family Foundation Poll in 2023 (Kirzenger et al., 2023) reported even lower percentages of medical interventions among adults, with 32% indicating using either hormone therapy or blockers and 16% reporting using any gender confirmation surgeries. It is not always clear why a person might not use medical interventions, but it could include lack of insurance coverage, costs, side effects, quality of surgeries, or other reasons.

About three-fourths or more of those who complete gender confirmation surgery report satisfaction with their new identity, and only about 8% report poor outcomes (Carroll, 2000; Gijs & Brewaeys, 2007; Kuiper & Cohen-Kettenis, 1988). A more extended review from the Netherlands (from 1972–2015) reported that among those who had had a gonadectomy, there was a very low rate of regret (0.6% transwomen and 0.3% transmen) (Wiepjes, Nota, de Blok, et al., 2018). What we have seen in the past is that transmen report adjusting better, on average, than transwomen, although again there is great variability, and this may be changing. Older persons pursuing medical transition do not report having as favorable outcomes as younger persons (Carroll, 2007). If we were to consider Blanchard's typology noted above, more autogynephilic transsexual presentations end up regretting their medical transition than have androphilic transsexuals, and this may be an important consideration as we think through who benefits from which kinds of interventions in this area.

There are, then, a number of surgical options, although the most common for the biological male who is transitioning is vaginoplasty or the creation of a neovagina (with a penectomy or the removal of the penis and orchiectomy or the removal of the testes). Male hair can also be removed, and corrective surgery can be performed on the larynx. Surgery to enhance the breasts (breast augmentation) can also be performed.

For the biological female, the breasts, uterus, and ovaries can be removed. Some patients will also request phalloplasty or the creation of a neophallus. If the patient has an enlarged clitoris (sometimes as a result of taking male hormones), it may be cut loose in a way so it can be experienced more like a penis (metoidioplasty).

WHAT IS THE FOCUS OF CHANGE—THE MIND OR THE BODY?

Perhaps the most challenging question for the Christian in this area is, Do you treat to change the person's psychological sense of identity to match the body or change the body to match the identity? What do we do with our existing knowledge of how helpful treatment approaches are in either direction?

Lewis Smedes (1994) offers the following:

> Clearly, what nature and God intended to be one sex turns out to be experienced as the other sex; so it is an abnormality. But we can be sure that no one would consciously choose to enter this agonizing experience. . . . But is the decision to exchange male for female genitals a moral issue? It is certainly an extremely crucial decision. Removing healthy genitals and replacing them with the genitals of the other sex does not seem to have the same purely medical consequences as amputating a gangrenous arm or leg. We are sensitive about mutilating sexual organs because we sense their closeness to what we are as sexual persons. . . . Is it worse to use surgery to match a person's external sexuality with his inner sexuality or to live as a male soul within a female body? (p. 46)

As you reflect on your answer to the question of whether to change the identity to match the body or change the body to match the identity, can you support your decision with a reasoned argument? In other words, *why* treat to change the identity to match the body? Or if you concluded the other direction, *why* treat to change the body to match the identity? As Christians reflect on this question, it can also be helpful to consider in what ways a response is informed by science, personal narrative, or faith/theology (theological anthropology). What weight do you give to these various sources of authority as we consider the best answer to this challenging question? How important is it to you if the person is personally distressed or in another way impaired by their dysphoria?

As one might imagine, better outcomes and rates of satisfaction among those who go through gender confirmation surgery are related to positive surgical outcomes, as well as consistent use of hormones (Carroll, 2007).

Although there is professional support for hormonal treatment and gender confirmation surgery, this direction for responding to gender dysphoria is not without its critics. For example, McHugh (1992) wrote a strong criticism of the practice of gender confirmation surgery, pointing out that just because we can do such surgeries does not mean we ought to do such surgeries:

> The skills of our plastic surgeons, particularly on the genito-urinary system, are impressive. They were obtained, however, not to treat the gender identity problem, but to repair congenital defects, injuries, and the effects of destructive diseases such as cancer in this region of the body. (p. 502)

Indeed, McHugh (1992) goes on to suggest that psychiatry has essentially catered to individual preferences and cultural pressure—"fashions of the seventies that invaded the clinic" (p. 503); he likens sex reassignment surgery to liposuction for anorexics:

> It is not obvious how this patient's feeling that he is a woman trapped in a man's body differs from the feeling of a patient with anorexia nervosa that she is obese despite her emaciated, cachetic state. We don't do liposuction on anorexics. Why amputate the genitals of these poor men? Surely, the fault is in the mind, not the member.

In the final analysis, the argument from critics of gender confirmation surgery regarding treatment for gender identity concerns is that more effort should be placed on prevention and management of gender dysphoria: "We have to learn how to manage this condition as a mental disorder when we fail to prevent it" (McHugh, 1992, p. 503).

PREVENTION

Given that the field has moved in a more trans-affirming direction, the concept of prevention is controversial. Recall that the *DSM* has historically noted that most cases of gender identity disorder in childhood do resolve by the time the child reaches adolescence or adulthood. That many desist in their experience of gender dysphoria has been noted in several studies (e.g., Steensma et al., 2010).

The controversy for prevention, then, would center on whether the resolution occurs naturally, if you will, or whether therapy can be provided to facilitate a reduction in gender dysphoria. The most vocal critics of such practices demean it (and the professionals who provide it) as GICE, a version of conversion therapy, likening it to attempts to change sexual orientation. Outspoken critics of conversion or reorientation therapy often liken it to bleaching an African American's skin in response to his or her own self-hatred and racial stigma.

If a clinician does believe that desistance is a real possibility, the studies that support desistance suggest about a 75% rate of desistance. In that sense, there really is not need to focus on prevention as such; gender dysphoria may very well abate on its own if no intervention takes place. The benefit of this approach—what we have referred to as a kind of gender patience—is that it also protects children from efforts to manipulate a gender outcome, which could be harmful (see Yarhouse & Sadusky, 2022).

In one approach to navigating gender identity and religion with conventionally religious families, Yarhouse and Sadusky (2022) focus more on identifying the fears parents have and reducing fear-based ways of parenting. This identifying and processing fears reflects a parent scaffolding approach in which a child is loved and cared for rather than focusing on prevention of a specific gender identity.

WORKING WITH MIXED GENDER IDENTITY COUPLES

In our previous chapter, we introduced the concept of mixed orientation couples, that is, couples in which one partner is straight and the other partner is a sexual minority. Likewise, we are seeing an increase in relationships in which one spouse is cisgender, that is, their gender identity corresponds to their biological markers, such as chromosomes, gonads, and genitalia, while the other spouse identifies as transgender or nonbinary. We might think of these as mixed gender identity couples (sometimes thought of as *couples in transition*).

Daryl and Denise have been married for eight years. They come in for therapy because about five months ago Daryl shared that he experiences himself as a woman. He reports that his discordant gender identity has been present from a young age (he recounts some episodic cross-dressing as a child), but he thought it largely resolved in late adolescence. He stated he married Denise in good faith. However, today he is experiencing increasing gender dysphoria. He is beginning to cross-dress almost daily (by wearing female undergarments), and he is wondering about making more of an outward social transition at home and at work. Denise says she loves Daryl but has been shocked and stunned by his disclosure of a cross-gender identity. She says she had no idea and doesn't know what to do with what he is saying today. She says, "I didn't marry a woman. I'm not a lesbian. I don't know what Daryl is expecting me to do. This is beyond me."

With mixed gender identity couples, we are most frequently seeing couples like Daryl and Denise who have been married for several years but at some point one of the spouses is indicating that they experience gender dysphoria or otherwise have a different gender identity than what their spouse has known. They may have only recently experienced gender dysphoria for the first time, or they may have experienced it earlier in life, and in the ebb and flow of severity they are now feeling it in ways that are increasingly distressing.

There is a literature on disclosure and aftereffects among mixed orientation couples that can be applied to marriages in which one spouse experiences a cross- or other gender identity. This was introduced above in the chapter on sexual identity conflicts and mixed orientation couples. Disclosure itself should be explored by assessing the experience of both spouses. Understanding the experience of gender dysphoria and what it means to the spouses is important. Disclosure is tied to the emotional response of the spouse who is learning this information. Common responses include confusion, shock, disbelief, and more. The experience is sometimes conceptualized as interpersonal trauma and should be processed with the spouse thoroughly. Teaching good coping skills can be especially helpful at this time. This initial emotional response eventually gives way to coming to terms with what the spouse is saying. This "coming to terms" may take many months or even longer, but it is important to provide care to both spouses so that they are in a better position to make decisions about the future of their relationship. Much of what is decided may be related to the severity of the gender dysphoria, what the spouse who experiences gender dysphoria decides to do in terms of managing their dysphoria, and so on. Yarhouse and Sadusky (2022, p. 164) discuss this as "finding your plateau," by which they liken societal expectations to medically transition as a "mountain top" experience that is not pursued by most adults with gender dysphoria, and that most adults plateau somewhere along the way through various strategies to manage their gender dysphoria, whether through hairstyle, clothing, name and pronouns, and so on.

If the couple decides to stay together and work on their marriage, many questions will arise about how to best obtain social support from family and friends, how to navigate their faith community, discussions with faith leaders, sharing with their children (approaches to this vary based on the ages of their children), and eventually questions about sexual intimacy. If they pursue sex therapy, it is often in the area of lower desire or interest due to the changes that may occur if the one spouse makes a partial or full social or even medical transition.

It is important when working with these couples to avoid determining in your mind as a sex therapist that there are two kinds of spouses: those who support their spouse's gender identity as they now experience it and those who do not (Lev & Sennott, 2012). Rather, it has been suggested that any given spouse may be both kinds of spouses (or another kind of spouse) on different days or weeks, and that providing them the therapeutic space that is needed to process their own journey will be tremendously beneficial.

There is significant variability in what a spouse with gender dysphoria may do to manage their experience, and this variability informs treatment approaches. Some may make a complete social and medical transition, which, while less common, would create challenges and opportunities that a spouse who made a partial transition in hairstyle and clothing would not have to the same degree. Lev and Sennott (2012) recommend clinicians help the couple move from a performance-based understanding of sexual intimacy to more of a meaning-making and experiential approach that expands the erotic possibilities. Helping them create a combination of familiar and new ways of intimacy can be helpful, and many shared experiences outside sexual intimacy can help create and maintain an experience of cohesion and connection as a couple.

CLOSING REFLECTIONS

Gender identity concerns remain one of the most difficult to fully understand. We know so little about the etiology and best course of care. Most people seem intuitively to prefer a resolution in the mind (or psychological resolution) so that the person resolves whatever gender dysphoria is experienced to reach congruence with their natal sex. However, there are really no large-scale studies of psychosocial interventions and even less optimism for such a resolution once a person has reached adulthood. Perhaps as a result the field has moved in the direction of support for those who wish to pursue hormonal treatment and gender confirmation surgery.

How ought the Christian respond? We do not see one uniquely Christian response to the complexities presented by gender identity concerns; however, we want to discuss some ways that Christians might engage the topic.

It has been suggested that there are separate dimensions of sexuality, such as the physical anatomy, hormones/endocrine system, social role, sexuality, and gender identity (Carroll, 2007). Is one or more of these considered more important or weighted more in our discussions about gender dysphoria? We find that those who struggle the most to understand the strong psychological sense of being the opposite sex often give more weight to the physical body than to other facets of sexuality and gender.

For the Christian this is likely due to the belief "that sex is fundamentally dichotomous," which some then extend into the assumption that "gender identity should also be dichotomous; there is an essential female and male mind and spirit that complement and complete one another" (Looy & Bouma, 2005, p. 166).

As Christians engage questions of sex and gender identity, we can recognize that discussions of sex refer to the biological components of chromosomes, gonads, sexual anatomy, and secondary sex characteristics. Discussions of gender refer to psychological and cultural components, such as gender identity (as a man or woman or a different gender identity from that; how masculine or feminine a person feels), sexual orientation (toward the same or opposite sex or both), and gender role (adoptions of cultural scripts for maleness or femaleness) (Jones, 2018). We agree with Jones that given so many different aspects of sex and gender, "it is perhaps remarkable that so many align consistently on all seven factors, thus experiencing the full, uncomplicated measure of being a woman or a man." Yet people do experience deviations from each one of these areas as reflected in any number of experiences and/or conditions. As Jones observes, "Resolution of . . . discord may take many forms, and require us as humble stewards to make complex choices."

While gender is more fluid than sex, when we have cases in which a person experiences gender dysphoria, what is the best way to proceed? Although the body of Christ should resist any rigid stereotypes of gender that might be unbearably restrictive, we also want to note a cultural shift that may contribute to greater uncertainty around sex and gender (Jones, 2018). Toward that end, we can see the value in locating attempts to manage gender dysphoria along a continuum, from least invasive to most invasive. Therapy can then focus on helping the person manage their gender dysphoria in the "least invasive" way possible (Yarhouse, 2015, p. 124), where hormonal replacement therapy and gender confirmation surgeries would be on the most invasive end. Given the complexities associated with these issues and the potential for many and varied presentations, pastoral sensitivity should be a priority.

Another consideration has to do with whether we are providing the best care to those who have more of an autogynephilic presentation. They appear to be at greater risk for regretting the decision to pursue medical transition. Should there be a more complete assessment and nuanced decision tree around pursuing the most invasive treatment given the greater risk that gender dysphoria may not be driving the request for surgery? The argument has been made by Lawrence (2013) in the other direction, that is, that perhaps a more nuanced assessment would allow for gender confirmation surgery for those autogynephilic men who have a more sustained cross-gender identity (which previously was assessed as a full-time presentation as female), thus giving greater weight to autogynephilic motivations.

As we close this chapter, we want to point out that there have been relatively few studies published of transgender Christians. In one study (Yarhouse & Carr, 2012), it was not uncommon for transwomen to experience conflicts between gender identity and religious identity in terms of personal faith, God, and the local church. Interestingly, some transgender Christians shared that their gender dysphoria led to a *strengthening* of their personal faith; others reported a *past struggle* with their faith, and still others left the organized religion they grew up with. For some the challenges they faced brought them closer to God, but others reported a strained relationship with God because of their gender dysphoria. What is particularly common was past conflict with the local church community or the persons and leaders who represent these organizations.

It is unclear to us at this time that one resolution is ultimately satisfying. It has historically been such a rare condition that we have had little good research from which to draw strong conclusions, and we have both known people who felt gender incongruence so strongly that they believed nothing less than their sanity and their life was at stake. They desperately sought a resolution. This is not an argument that they then should pursue the most invasive procedures, but we also acknowledge that we understand and empathize with that decision, as painful as it often is. With the recent increase in cases of gender dysphoria, we will undoubtedly see more people in need of proper care. Rather than reject the person facing such conflicts, the Christian community would do well to recognize the conflict and try to work with the person to find the least invasive ways to manage the dysphoria. Perhaps future programs of research will provide greater insight and clarity into an area that seems particularly difficult to navigate at this time.

REFERENCES

American Psychiatric Association. (2013). *Diagnostic and statistical manual of mental disorders* (5th ed.). American Psychiatric Publishing.

American Psychiatric Association. (2022). *Diagnostic and statistical manual of mental disorders* (5th ed.-Text Revision). American Psychiatric Publishing.

Blanchard, R. (1990a). Gender identity disorders in adult men. In R. Blanchard & B. V. Steiner (Eds.), *Clinical management of gender identity disorders in children and adults* (pp. 49-75). American Psychiatric Publishing.

Blanchard, R. (1990b). Gender identity disorders in adult women. In R. Blanchard & B. V. Steiner (Eds.), *Clinical management of gender identity disorders in children and adults* (pp. 77-91). American Psychiatric Publishing.

Carroll, R. A. (2000). Assessment and treatment of gender dysphoria. In S. R. Leiblum & R. C. Rosen (Eds.), *Principles and practice of sex therapy* (3rd ed., pp. 368-422). Guilford.

Carroll, R. A. (2007). Gender dysphoria and transgender experiences. In S. R. Leiblum (Ed.), *Principles and practice of sex therapy* (4th ed., pp. 477-508). Guilford.

Coleman, E., Radix, A. E., Bouman, W. P., Brown, G. R., . . . & West, M. A. (2022). Standards of Care for the Health of Transgender and Gender Diverse People (Version 8). *International Journal of Transgender Health, 23*(supl), S1-S259. https://doi.org/10.108 0/26895269.2022.2100644

Davis, E., Jr. (2023, July 12). European countries restrict trans health care for minors. *U.S. News & World Report.* www.usnews.com/news/best-countries/articles/2023-07-12/ why-european-countries-are-rethinking-gender-affirming-care-for-minors

deVries, A. L. C., Steensma, T. D., Doreleijers, T. A. H., & Cohen-Kettenis, P. T. (2011). Puberty suppression in adolescents with gender identity disorder: A prospective follow-up study. *Journal for Sexual Medicine, 8*, 2276-83. https://doi.org/10.1111 /j.1743-6109.2010.01943.x.

Di Ceglie, D., Freedman, D., McPherson, S., & Richardson, P. (2002). Children and adolescents referred to a specialist gender identity development service: Clinical features and demographic characteristics. *International Journal of Transgenderism, 6*(1), 1.

Edwards-Leeper, L. (2022). Working with transgender youth. Clinical training conducted at the Sexual & Gender Identity Institute, Wheaton College. November 29, 2022.

Ehrensaft, D. (2018). Exploring gender expansive expressions versus asserting a gender identity. In C. Keo-Meier & D. Ehrensaft (Eds.), *The gender affirmative model: An interdisciplinary approach to supporting transgender and gender expansive children* (pp. 37-53). American Psychological Association. https://doi.org/10.1037 /0000095-003

Gijs, L., & Brewaeys, A. (2007). Surgical treatment of gender dysphoria in adults and adolescents: Recent developments, effectiveness, and challenges. *Annual Review of Sex Research, 18*, 178-224.

Hacking, I. (1995). The looping effects of human kinds. In D. Sperber, D. Premack, & A. Premack (Eds.), *Causal cognition: An interdisciplinary approach* (pp. 351-83). Oxford University Press.

James, S. E., Herman, J. L., Rankin, S., Keisling, M., Mottet, L., & Anafi, M. (2016). *The Report of the 2015 U.S. Transgender Survey*. National Center for Transgender Equality.

Johnson, L. L., Bradley, S. J., Birkenfeld-Adams, A. S., Radzins Kuksis, M. A., Maing, D. M., Mitchell, J. N., & Zucker, K. J. (2004). A parent-report gender identity questionnaire for children. *Archives of Sexual Behavior, 33*, 105-16.

Jones, J. M. (2024, March 13). LGBTQ+ identification in U.S. now at 7.6%. Gallup News. https://news.gallup.com/poll/611864/lgbtq-identification.aspx#:~:text=Line%20graph.,collected%20in%202018%20and%202019

Jones, S. L. (2018). "Is Sex or Gender a Choice?" In *Holman Worldview Study Bible* (pp. 17-19). Nashville, TN: Holman Bible.

Jorgensen, C. (1967). *Christine Jorgensen: A personal autobiography*. Cleis.

Kirzenger, A., Kearney, A., Montero, A., Sparks, G., Dawson, L., & Brodie, M. (2023, March 24). *KFF/The Washington Post Trans Survey*. Available at www.kff.org/report-section/kff-the-washington-post-trans-survey-trans-in-america/

Kreukels, B. P. C., & Cohen-Kettenis, P. T. (2011). Puberty suppression in gender identity disorders: The Amsterdam experience. *Nature, 7*, 466-72.

Kuiper, B., & Cohen-Kettenis, P. (1988). Sex reassignment surgery: A study of 141 Dutch transsexuals. *Archives of Sexual Behavior, 17*(5), 439-57.

Lawrence, A. A. (2013). *Men trapped in men's bodies: Narratives of autogynephilic transsexualism*. Springer.

Lev, A. I., & Sennott, S. (2012). Transsexual desire in differently gendered bodies. In J. J. Bigner & J. L. Wetchler (Eds.), *Handbook of LGBT-affirmative couple and family therapy* (pp. 113-30). Routledge.

Looy, H., & Bouma, H., III. (2005). The nature of gender: Gender identity in persons who are intersexed or transgendered. *Journal of Psychology and Theology, 33*, 166-68.

McConaghy, N. (1993). *Sexual behavior: Problems and management*. Plenum.

McHugh, P. R. (1992). Psychiatric misadventures. *American Scholar, 61*(4), 497.

Meyer-Bahlburg, H. F. L. (2002). Gender identity disorder in young boys: A parent- and peer-based treatment protocol. *Clinical Child Psychology and Psychiatry, 7*(3), 360-76.

Money, J. (1986). *Lovemaps: Clinical concepts of sexual/erotic health and pathology, paraphilia, and gender transposition in childhood, adolescence, and maturity*. Irvington.

Olson, K. R., Durwood, L., Horton, R., Gallagher, N. M., & Devor, A. (2022). Gender identity 5 years after social transition. *Pediatrics, 150*(2): e202: e2021056082. https://doi.org/10.1542/peds.2021-056082

Owen-Anderson, A. F. H., Bradley, S. J., & Zucker, K. J. (2010). Expressed emotion in mothers of boys with gender identity disorder. *Journal of Sex & Marital Therapy, 36*, 327-45.

Smedes, L. (1994). *Sex for Christians* (Rev. ed.). Eerdmans.

Spiegel, A. (2008, May 8). Parents consider treatment to delay son's puberty: New therapy would buy time to resolve gender crisis. NPR. Retrieved from www.npr.org/templates/story/story.php?storyId=90273278

Steensma, T. D., Biemond, R., deBoer, F., & Cohen-Kettenis, P. T. (2010). Desisting and persisting gender dysphoria after childhood: A qualitative study. *Clinical Child Psychology and Psychiatry, 16*(4), 1-18. https://doi.org/10.1177/1359104510378303

Substance Abuse and Mental Health Services Administration (SAMHSA) (2023). *Moving beyond change efforts: Evidence and action to support and affirm LGBTQI+ youth.* Center for Substance Abuse Prevention. Substance Abuse and Mental Health Services Administration.

Wiepjes, C. M., Nota, N. M., de Blok, C. J. M., Klaver, M., de Vries, A. L. C., Wensing-Kruger, S. A., de Jongh, R. T., Bouman, M.-B., Steensma, T. D., Cohen-Kettenis, P., Gooren, L. J. G., Kreukels, B. P. C., & den Heijer, M. (2018). The Amsterdam cohort of gender dysphoria study (1972–2015): Trends in prevalence, treatment, and regrets. *Journal of Sexual Medicine, 15*(4), 582-590. doi:10.1016/j.jsxm.2018.01.016

Yarhouse, M. A. (2015). *Understanding gender dysphoria: Navigating transgender issues in a changing culture.* IVP Academic.

Yarhouse, M. A., & Carr, T. L. (2012). MTF transgender Christians' experiences: A qualitative study. *Journal of LGBT Issues in Counseling, 6*(1), 18-33.

Yarhouse, M. A., & Sadusky, J. A. (2020). *Emerging gender identities: Understanding the diverse experiences of today's youth.* Brazos.

Yarhouse, M. A., & Sadusky, J. A. (2022). *Gender identity & faith: Clinical postures, tools, and case studies for client-centered care.* InterVarsity Press.

Zucker, K. J. (2001). Gender identity disorders in children and adolescents. In G. O. Gabbard (Ed.), *Treatments of psychiatric disorders* (pp. 2069-94). American Psychiatric Press.

Zucker, K. J. (2004). Gender identity development and issues. *Child Adolescent Psychiatric Clinics of North America, 13,* 551-68.

Zucker, K. J., & Bradley, S. J. (1995). *Gender identity disorder and psychosexual problems in children and adolescents.* Guilford.

Zucker, K. J., & Bradley, S. J. (2005). Gender identity and psychosexual disorders. *Focus, 3*(4), 598-17.

PART FOUR

FUTURE DIRECTIONS

FIFTEEN

CHRISTIANITY AND SEX THERAPY

IN 1944 GREGORY PINCUS COFOUNDED a private laboratory in Shrewsbury, Massachusetts, called the Worcester Foundation for Experimental Biology. At a dinner party he was introduced to Margaret Sanger, who, at the age of seventy-two, was working hard to find someone to develop an oral contraceptive. Pincus was open to the possibility, particularly through the use of hormones, but he was going to need money to fund any kind of line of research. Sanger could do that. She first got Planned Parenthood and, later, other organizations to invest in a program of research that would eventually lead to the development of "the pill." The first human trials would occur in 1955, and the Food and Drug Administration would approve the use of Enovid to treat severe menstrual disorders so long as there was a warning label attached that it could prevent ovulation.[1] By the 1970s the pill was the preferred method of birth control in the United States.

These developments may seem like a footnote in history, but for those who study sexuality and provide sex therapy it is difficult to underestimate what the advances in birth control have meant. Of course, these developments were controversial at the time. Some organizations accused Planned Parenthood of "black genocide" because the pill was provided in low-income neighborhoods. In 1968, Pope Paul VI wrote in *Humanae Vitae* that the Catholic Church stood in opposition to any form of artificial birth control.[2]

Yet this cultural milestone and scientific advance is one of many that have dramatically challenged and changed the sociocultural landscape surrounding sexuality and thus our experience of sexuality and sexual behavior in contemporary Western culture. The prevailing norm was that sex was

---

[1]See www.pbs.org/wgbh/amex/pill/timeline.
[2]See www.pbs.org/wgbh/amex/pill/timeline.

fundamentally procreative in intent and so sex reserved for marriage was a widely supported expectation. That is not to say there was no sex outside marriage or prior to marriage, of course, but there was a broader cultural expectation that supported sex in marriage for multiple reasons and benefits, not the least of which was the creation of new life and the social and economic consequences of having a child outside marriage. The pill challenged this view.

The changes too would ultimately be quite dramatic. There was a ripple effect—not tied to any one event but likely to a convergence of events and discoveries—that is still felt today. The sexual revolution of the late 1960s and 1970s, including the Stonewall Riots in 1969 (which is viewed by many as the start of the modern gay rights movement), has contributed in one way or another to how we today view sexuality and sexual expression in our culture. Indeed, some mainstream LGBTQ+ scholars have argued that a sexual minority narrative and the development of a modern gay label and community—which now includes gay, lesbian, bisexual, transgender, queer, questioning, and others—would not have been possible without safely and effectively separating sex from procreation (Herdt, 1996), as well as attributing impulses and attractions to one's sense of self and the potential for self-actualization, among other historical developments.

Today we are witness to dramatic discoveries in science and technology. It may be challenging to recall our culture prior to the advent of the internet, but today we have access not only to important information to inform and enhance our understanding and experience of sex but also to a proliferation of pornography sites and an industry that makes remarkable profits and drives an estimated 30% or more of the traffic on the web (Defalco, 2012).

It is difficult to predict how future social changes and scientific discovery will shape the real-world experiences related to sexuality and sexual behavior in the years to come. We want to close out this book by reflecting on the challenges and opportunities that face Christians who are interested in the study of human sexuality and practice of sex therapy, and what Christians can expect moving forward.

CHALLENGES TO AN EVER-CHANGING FIELD

Challenges of biological reductionism. It is difficult to overestimate the effect of research on biological foundations of mental health issues over the past decade. This research has touched so much of the study of psychopathology, and the study of sexuality, sexual behavior, and sex therapy has certainly also been affected. Advances in the medical fields and in psychopharmacology, neuropsychology, and cognitive science have dramatically shaped psychology and counseling, and by extension sexuality and sex therapy. These are likely to continue with increased interest in pharmacological resources and "medical management" for various sexual dysfunctions, as well as medical treatment of the paraphilias and related concerns.

Breakthroughs in certain areas—say, in the accidental discovery of PDE5 inhibitors—have led to more confidence in the biological hypotheses about the origins of various sexual issues, as well as possible medical remedies. Rather than turn to intrapsychic, systemic, relational, or psychological explanations, we anticipate a continued emphasis or weight given to *bio* in the biopsychosocial model, as it will continue to receive primary funding for research to address related clinical concerns. Research will undoubtedly focus on neuroanatomy, genetics, the endocrine system, and other related areas.

The primary concern raised in these discussions is that there is the potential for reductionism when we focus narrowly on biology and physiology. Pharmacological reductionism also promotes individualism because the medical model emphasizes one person's diagnosis and treatment, in this case with pharmacological services.

The use of pharmacology is appealing to many clients too who often prefer the perceived benefits of medication to the extent it is able to deliver on its promises. Psychologists, counselors, and other mental health professionals will need to conduct well-designed research that looks at what such approaches contribute, as well as whether and how pharmacology is enhanced through therapy, particularly sex therapy and related clinical interventions.

Challenges to current conceptualizations. It is anticipated that the widely used *Diagnostic and Statistical Manual of Mental Disorders* will continue to go through controversial revisions. In a previous discussion of the *DSM*, we noted several issues:

> The current categorical system of the *DSM* series, which represents the best that the field of psychopathology has yet offered to classify and interpret the wide range of human function and dysfunction, is far from perfect. Comorbidity, heterogeneity, inconsistencies, exclusions and poorly defined boundaries are but a few of the challenges faced by the authors of the *DSMs*. (Yarhouse et al., 2005, p. 433)

These criticisms are also true when we think about the sexual dysfunctions and other sexual concerns discussed throughout this book (see Yarhouse et al., 2005, pp. 420-32, for a review).

Further, the *DSM* has long abandoned any effort to account for the etiology of various mental disorders; rather, it has attempted to be largely atheoretical, which corresponds well with the rise of medical models and biological reductionism. Unfortunately, by its attempting to be atheoretical, while also placing greater emphasis on biological understandings, theorists, researchers, and clinicians may not reflect on ways that biological explanatory frameworks affect their understanding of mental health concerns and sexual dysfunctions and other sexual concerns.

We would note too that there is increased interest in distinguishing between diversity of sexual expression and mental health concerns by focusing on subjective distress or impairment in functioning. There are some voices who want to normalize what has been considered aberrant behavior (e.g., pedophilia) by not pathologizing it unless it is personally distressing or otherwise an impairment to the person in some important domain of functioning. Some are suggesting that this principle should be applied across the board to various sexual interests, and that development has essentially occurred with the publication of *DSM-5* (APA, 2013). As we noted previously, "Greater clarity is still needed in the form of universally recognized and reliable identifiable boundaries between normal and abnormal psychological functioning" (Yarhouse et al., 2005, p. 423). The lack of clarity is likely tied to disunity around a coherent framework for understanding what it means to be human, to be sexual, and so on. Lack of cultural consensus will likely continue to undermine efforts to speak positively about what is healthy sexuality and sexual expression.

Limited training opportunities. An additional challenge is that with less emphasis on psychological explanations for sexual concerns, we anticipate fewer opportunities for graduate and postgraduate training in sexuality and sex therapy. Although we see professional organizations that offer certification in sex education and therapy, we do not anticipate growth in internship and residency programs that specialize in sexual issues, at least not ones that are steeped in psychological explanatory frameworks.

Training will likely be multidisciplinary with an emphasis on primary care and related health issues associated with sexual concerns. Although there are a limited number of internship sites and postdoctoral training sites for those interested in training, most students interested in training will likely seek out professional organizations for certification. The two major secular organizations are the American Association of Sex Educators, Counselors, and Therapists (ASSECT) and the Society for Sex Therapy and Research (SSTAR). An emerging secular organization is the International Association of Psychosexual Therapists (IAPST). An alternative for training from a Christian perspective is through the Institute for Sexual Wholeness with certification through the American Board of Christian Sex Therapists (ABCST) and the Christian Association of Sex Educators (CASE).

Although some regulatory boards in specific states require courses in human sexuality, many do not, and most clinicians who work with these populations will need more than even a required (or, in most cases, an elective) course in human sexuality or sex therapy.

We also anticipate two additional and related challenges for Christians who are interested in the study and practice of sex therapy. These are balancing role integration and navigating personal and professional value conflicts.

Value conflicts. We acknowledge the potential for value conflicts in some areas of human sexuality and sex therapy. Christians often face the challenge of following well-conducted research and being accepted and valued contributors and participants in the broader fields of psychology and counseling, while simultaneously practicing in ways that are congruent with their Christian faith.

What has received the most attention in recent years are the potential value conflicts when Christian mental health professionals work with gay and lesbian clients who are seeking services for same-sex relationships. We anticipate that these challenges and potential for conflict will increase as Christians identify multiple ways to practice in a broader and diverse cultural setting, while at the same time the gay community challenges Christians who may wish to limit their practice offerings to clients where the Christian clinician does not feel as much personal value conflict.

Other conflicts are also possible, of course. Some Christian mental health professionals may struggle with whether to work with couples who are cohabiting, with a woman who is giving serious consideration to an abortion, with a person interested in sex reassignment surgery, or even with an individual who is single but interested in the use of sex therapy in his or her current relationship. But while these value conflicts are real, they do not represent a symbolic tension that exists in cultural discussions about licensed mental health professionals and the place of personal values in professional services being offered. At this point, that tension seems to exist primarily around gay, lesbian, and bisexual concerns, with gender identity and transgender considerations likely to follow.

What is the Christian's role in these areas? What does a Christian bring to research and clinical practice in human sexuality? What we do not want to see are Christians relegated to a private practice with only other Christians. We think it is important that Christians are involved in the mental health field at every level, from service delivery to ongoing research, from regulating bodies to professional governance in mental health associations and beyond. How Christians ought to respond is a difficult question to answer. We are impressed by the range of responses from Christians in the fields of counseling and psychology. Some provide all kinds of professional service much the same as any qualified, secular clinician would provide comparable services. Others feel strongly that if they cross a line in providing services, they are not truly being Christian as a counselor or psychologist. And, of course, we see most Christians somewhere in between these two positions.

OPPORTUNITIES FOR CHRISTIANS IN THE AREA AND STUDY OF HUMAN SEXUALITY

We see Christianity as bringing with it a unique worldview, a truly holistic understanding of human sexuality, motivation for the study and practice of sex therapy, relevant techniques that can enhance sexuality and sexual behavior, and humility for future research and clinical endeavors.

Worldview considerations. As we have been suggesting throughout this book, a Christian worldview contrasts in important ways with the assumptions of naturalism, humanism, and pluralism (see Hathaway & Yarhouse, 2021, chap. 3 on worldview integration). It is important that Christians in the field and students in training recognize the different worldviews and how they are reflected in various assumptions about sexuality and sexual behavior. These are often subtle assumptions that are not even argued for or defended explicitly. Rather, they reflect the professional climate in which we all conduct research and provide clinical services. The dominant worldviews and related values do not typically have to justify the lens through which they see their subject matter, for example, human sexuality and sexual behavior. They can simply make statements about what is healthy and adaptive and what promotes well-being without reference to the interests a Christian worldview would hold, such as transcendent reality, theological ethics, and specific Christian virtues.

As we suggested in chapter one, Christian history also reflects difficulties in maintaining a balanced, biblical view of sexuality. There has been a tendency to view sex in a negative light, as though it were not part of what it means to be human, to be physical and sexual beings broadly defined.

Christianity provides a holistic view of sexuality. By this we mean that sexuality is not elevated to a status of self-actualization, nor is it reduced to the exchange of body fluids. Rather, sexuality is seen broadly; we discussed it as reflected in our gender sexuality, erotic sexuality (longing for completion in another), and genital sexuality (behavioral expression) (Jones, 1999). Christianity also reminds us that our sexuality is tied in important ways to transcendent reality. The context of sexual expression, that is, a committed, monogamous relationship between a husband and wife, is meant to reflect something of the relationship between Christ and the body of Christ. Yet as Christians engage a diverse culture around matters of sexuality, we will need to do so with grace and love, particularly for those whose experience with Christianity or the people who represent Christ has been anything but Christlike.

As the Christian community articulates its vision for sexuality and sexual expression, it should keep in mind that that vision, while often discussed in terms of ethics and morality, must recognize the influence of social, cultural, and economic realities (Garland, 1999), being sensitive to the ways in which various forces interact around sexuality and sexual behavior.

Christian communities are likely unable to make dramatic changes in how the broader society views sexuality and sexual behavior, but the church can find ways to engage the culture and meet people where they are, as when churches provide space for Sex Addicts Anonymous groups to meet or offer ministries to enhance relationships among men that foster accountability and transparency.

CONVICTED CIVILITY

Richard Mouw (1992) has written about the need for "convicted civility" among Christians today, a phrase first proposed by Martin Marty. We have far too many Christians who are one or the other: they are either strong on expressing their convictions but cannot treat others with civility and respect, or they are remarkably civil but do not express well their meaningful values. Mouw's point is this: we need Christians who are both.

Perhaps no topics will stretch the Christian community further in our capacity to demonstrate "convicted civility" than those centered on sexuality and sexual behavior. In a sociocultural context that pulls people to enter into a broader culture war, there will be an increased need for clarity of Christian thought on matters of sexual morality (i.e., convictions) that are conveyed to others, particularly moral and epistemic strangers in an increasingly diverse culture, in a respectful manner (i.e., civility).

What do you think of the concept of "convicted civility"? If you were to adopt this phrase as a helpful brand or way of relating to others on matters of sexual morality, how would you assess yourself so far? In what areas do you hold convictions? How have those convictions been formed? Are there areas for you that are settled? Which topics are difficult for you to hold firm convictions about?

In the area of civility, how much experience do you have sharing your convictions? What challenges have you faced in remaining civil in a social setting that may lend itself to the culture wars?

Motivation for the study and practice of sex therapy. Because Christianity holds a high view of sexuality and sexual expression, a Christian worldview provides motivation for the study and practice of sex therapy. Christians are not to be prudish about sex; rather, they recognize it as a good aspect of creation, something that is part of our intended physicality, part of what it means to be human.

We have argued throughout this book that our sexuality is best understood broadly to include our gender sexuality, erotic sexuality, and genital sexuality (Jones, 1999). So discussions about a Christian view of sexuality can branch out quickly into an informed and far-reaching discussion that touches on so much of human experience.

When Christians provide sex therapy, they have an opportunity to enhance an area where there has been a deficit or deficiency of some kind (e.g., sexual dysfunction) or a distortion or related clinical concern (e.g., a paraphilia). By facilitating growth and healing in areas related to sexuality, we do good work that is ultimately redemptive in nature.

A constructive framework for this redemptive work might be found in the language of stewardship. We introduced this concept in chapter one. It is a biblical concept (e.g., Mt 25:21; 1 Cor 6:19-20; Lk 16:1-13) that can be extended in helpful, pastoral ways to the life of the Christian sorting out sexual matters in his or her own life. As we consider our sexuality and the impulses we may feel, Christians can consider what it means to steward what they experience. These impulses are not necessarily from God just because they occur in nature or are felt to be natural. Rather, because we recognize that all of creation is fallen, we look outside our own desires and impulses to determine how to live in light of what we feel, a point C. S. Lewis made in his classic work *The Abolition of Man*. Stewardship is for those who are single and those who are married; it is relevant to those who experience attraction to the opposite sex and those who experience attraction to the same sex. As a principle for engaging one's sexuality, stewardship levels the field of differences that may exist among Christians and suggests we find ways to honor God with our sexuality and its expression.

Relevant training and clinical interventions. In the applied and clinical integration literature, a distinction can be made between explicit and implicit integration—a point we introduced in chapter four. *Explicit* integration refers to

> a more overt approach that directly and systematically deals with spiritual or religious issues in therapy, and uses spiritual resources like prayer, Scripture or sacred texts, referrals to church or other religious groups or lay counselors, and other religious practices. (Tan, 1996, p. 368)

According to Tan (1996), explicit integration harnesses the religious and spiritual interests of the therapist and the client to bring psychological theory and religious or spiritual guidance into meaningful clinical practice.

Implicit integration refers to ways in which a therapist integrates his or her religious faith in clinical practice but not in an overt manner. Tan (1996) suggests that implicit integration refers to

> a more covert approach that does not initiate the discussion of religious or spiritual issues and does not openly, directly, or systematically use spiritual resources like prayer and Scripture or other sacred texts, in therapy. (p. 368)

It might involve praying quietly for a client but not praying out loud with clients (Tan, 1996). It might also entail choosing among treatment strategies by selecting one over another because it is a better fit with the values held by the clinician. For example, many Christian clinicians have found that using sexual identity therapy (Yarhouse, 2019; see also Throckmorton & Yarhouse, 2006) as a client-centered, client-affirming therapy that has been recognized by mainstream mental health professionals (e.g., APA, 2009) has provided a helpful alternative to gay-affirmative models that at times reflect a value conflict for either the religious clinician or the religious client.

We already mentioned that one of the challenges facing the field is the lack of funding for training and education in the area of sexuality and sex therapy. This is particularly true when we consider training opportunities from a Christian worldview.

Christian mental health professionals have also developed training in sex addiction as well as trauma services. Organizations such as the Christian Sex Addiction Specialists International (C-SASI)[3] and the American Association of Christian Counselors[4] provide training in this important area of need, as do many individual practitioners and their network of colleagues. In terms of trauma services, Wheaton College's Humanitarian Disaster Institute[5] and Regent University's Certificate in Trauma Studies[6] are encouraging examples. These are important developments, and we hope to see these grounded in original research, good training models, and reliable service delivery.

The Sexual & Gender Identity Institute[7] provides trainings in sexual identity therapy (SIT) for working with sexual identity issues in clinical practice, and gender identity and religious therapy (GRIT) for addressing gender identity in clinical practice.

These organizations are promising, but many are also smaller and have had varying degrees of success establishing themselves as widely recognized or influential resources for the training of competent clinicians and educators.

In the context of developing educational programs and training sites, we have to keep in mind that being a Christian is not a substitute for professional competence. Competence is determined by education, training, and supervised clinical experience. Scholarly, informed training and research that has a Christian worldview as a value-added component can be a tremendous enhancement to what is offered in the field today, but there are

---

[3]Further information about C-SASI is available at www.c-sasi.org.

[4]AACC provides certification through the International Board of Christian Counselors as Sex Addiction Specialists at various levels (lay counselor, pastoral counselor, professional counselor, supervisor, and trainer). The Christian Association for Psychological Studies (www.caps.net) holds national and regional conferences that also provide continuing education and training in areas of sexuality and sex therapy.

[5]See www.wheaton.edu/HDI.

[6]See www.regent.edu/program/certificate-of-graduate-studies-in-trauma-counseling.

[7]See www.wheaton.edu/sgi.

no shortcuts. It will involve work that lays a foundation for competent clinical practice, accurate information for education, and well-designed and well-executed research.

Role integration. When we think of potential value conflicts in the field, we see potential benefits in what has been referred to as role-related integration (Hathaway, 2010; Hathaway & Yarhouse, 2021). Hathaway discusses the concept of role integration: the idea that one way in which Christians address integration of their faith and the mental health fields is in the roles that they may play. For example, a Christian psychologist might represent a division on the council of representatives, the main governing body of the American Psychological Association. Likewise, a Christian who is a licensed counselor might serve on the state board of counseling in the state where he or she practices. As Hathaway puts it,

> as a result of this commitment, integration becomes not just a theoretical or even a technical issue—it becomes a sociopolitical issue. Integration raises ancient themes concerning the proper role for Christians to adopt when working in civic-service positions. (p. 227)

Role integration has to do with what it means to fulfill societally granted and privileged roles while doing so self-consciously as a Christian (Hathaway & Yarhouse, 2021). This is not a new tension. It is hinted at in Scripture with the conversion to faith of Roman soldiers, for instance, and it is documented throughout history as Christians have served in various roles in society.

Unique issues arise while serving in these various roles as a Christian. The role involves providing for the common good, making decisions that benefit the broader community of mental health professionals and, of course, the public. These concerns are far reaching and not limited exclusively to Christian considerations, although there is often important overlap.

Role integration is not limited to the experiences of Christians who move into governance of the mental health profession. In fact, all Christians who are licensed mental health professionals face issues related to role integration insofar as they are licensed by their state to provide clinical services. The license places them in a fiduciary relationship of public trust (Hathaway & Yarhouse, 2021). There are obligations to honor the commitments a counselor makes to his or her professional role and what the public comes to expect when they meet with a mental health professional (or when they hear a workshop by a psychologist or learn about findings from research or assessments).

There is a need for ongoing reflection and discussion of what it means to serve with integrity in these public roles. There is a need to model and mentor others in how to serve the common good through professional mental health roles and associations, while also honoring first commitments to Christ. We discussed earlier in this chapter what we see as potential points of conflict that may make role integration increasingly challenging for licensed mental health professionals as well as those who have the opportunity to be in administrative levels of mental health governance and policy development.

CONCLUSION

As we bring this book to a close, we may not know for years to come what important developments are currently taking place in the field. We do not know what historical events and scientific discoveries will converge to contribute to remarkable changes, as we now see historically in the development of more reliable, effective contraception in the twentieth century. In the twenty-first century we are far beyond separating sex from procreation. We are now in a sociocultural context in which we have the freedom and language to discuss and explore sexual and gender self-actualization in many and varied forms with significant differences in opinion about what constitutes self-actualization. We have every sex act and identity available to us via the internet and as close to us as the smartphone in our pocket. This presents a horizon that the culture and the church faces in the West. For some it is an exciting time of exploration and sexual discovery. For others it is a time of great anxiety and concern. We are increasingly a culture of moral strangers—we do not fully understand (and are not fully understood by) others in terms of foundational beliefs, values, and worldview assumptions. For the body of Christ in general and the Christian mental health professional in particular, that status of being moral strangers creates remarkable points of tension to be sure. For the Christian trained in human sexuality and sex therapy, it is a unique time to know and practice what it means to bring together Christ and culture. It is a time to be a resource to the church and to the broader culture, to find language and categories for engaging the culture in an ongoing dialogue about the nature and purpose of sexuality and sexual expression.

REFERENCES

American Psychiatric Association. (2013). *Diagnostic and statistical manual of mental disorders* (5th ed.). American Psychiatric Publishing.

Defalco, B. (2012, April 10). Web faves XXX-posed. *New York Post.* www.nypost.com/p/news/local/web_faves_xxx_posed_iSIpORYEU12051XanYoz7M

Garland, D. (1999). *Family ministry: A comprehensive guide.* InterVarsity Press.

Hathaway, W. L. (2010). Faithful skepticism/curious faith. In G. Moriarty (Ed.), *Integrating faith and psychology* (pp. 209-29). InterVarsity Press.

Hathaway, W. L., & Yarhouse, M. A. (2021). *The integration of psychology & Christianity: A domain-based approach.* InterVarsity Press.

Herdt, G. (1996). Developmental discontinuities and sexual orientation across cultures. In D. P. McWhirter, S. A. Sanders, & J. M. Reinisch (Eds.), *Homosexuality/heterosexuality: Concepts of sexual orientation* (pp. 208-36). Oxford University Press.

Jones, S. L. (1999). Sexuality. In D. G. Benner & P. C. Hill (Eds.), *Baker encyclopedia of psychology & counseling.* Baker.

Mouw, R. (1992). *Uncommon decency: Christian civility in an uncivil world.* InterVarsity Press.

Smedes, L. (1994). *Sex for Christians* (Rev. ed.). Eerdmans.

Tan, S. (1996). Religion in clinical practice: Implicit and explicit integration. In E. P. Shafranske (Ed.), *Religion and the clinical practice of psychology* (pp. 365-87). American Psychological Association.

Yarhouse, M. A. (2019). *Sexual identity and faith: Helping clients achieve congruence.* The Templeton Foundation.

Yarhouse, M. A., Butman, R. E., & McRay, B. E. (2005). *Modern psychopathologies.* InterVarsity Press.

INDEX

An Association for Christian Psychologists,
Therapists, Counselors and Academicians

CAPS is a vibrant Christian organization with a rich tradition. Founded in 1956 by a small group of Christian mental health professionals, chaplains and pastors, CAPS has grown to more than 2,100 members in the U.S., Canada and more than 25 other countries.

CAPS encourages in-depth consideration of therapeutic, research, theoretical and theological issues. The association is a forum for creative new ideas. In fact, their publications and conferences are the birthplace for many of the formative concepts in our field today.

CAPS members represent a variety of denominations, professional groups and theoretical orientations; yet all are united in their commitment to Christ and to professional excellence.

CAPS is a non-profit, member-supported organization. It is led by a fully functioning board of directors, and the membership has a voice in the direction of CAPS.

CAPS is more than a professional association. It is a fellowship, and in addition to national and international activities, the organization strongly encourages regional, local and area activities which provide networking and fellowship opportunities as well as professional enrichment.

To learn more about CAPS, visit www.caps.net.

CAPS BOOKS
from IVP Academic

The joint publishing venture between IVP Academic and CAPS aims to promote the understanding of the relationship between Christianity and the behavioral sciences at both the clinical/counseling and the theoretical/research levels. These books will be of particular value for students and practitioners, teachers and researchers.

For more information about CAPS Books, visit InterVarsity Press's website at www.ivpress.com/christian-association-for-psychological-studies-books-set.